New-Dialect Formation in Canada

Studies in Language Companion Series (SLCS)

This series has been established as a companion series to the periodical *Studies in Language.*

Volume 97

New-Dialect Formation in Canada: Evidence from the English
modal auxiliaries
by Stefan Dollinger

New-Dialect Formation in Canada

Evidence from the English modal auxiliaries

Stefan Dollinger
University of British Columbia

John Benjamins Publishing Company

Amsterdam / Philadelphia

The paper used in this publication meets the minimum requirements of
American National Standard for Information Sciences – Permanence of
Paper for Printed Library Materials, ANSI z39.48-1984.

Library of Congress Cataloging-in-Publication Data

Dollinger, Stefan.
  New-dialect formation in Canada : evidence from the English modal auxiliaries / Stefan
        Dollinger.
     p. cm. (Studies in Language Companion Series, ISSN 0165-7763 ; v. 97)
  Includes bibliographical references and index.
  1. English language--Canada--History. 2. English language--Dialects--Canada. 3.
        English language--Variation--Canada. 4. Canadianisms. I. Title.
  PE3208.8.D655   2008
  427'.971--dc22   2007044469
  ISBN 978 90 272 3108 6 (Hb; alk. paper)

John Benjamins Publishing Co. · P.O. Box 36224 · 1020 ME Amsterdam · The Netherlands
John Benjamins North America · P.O. Box 27519 · Philadelphia PA 19118-0519 · USA

for kris

Table of Contents

List of Maps

List of Figures

List of Tables

About this book

New-dialect formation in Canada:
Evidence from the English modal auxiliaries
Stefan Dollinger

The present volume investigates the development of eleven modal auxiliaries in early Ontario English in relation to major British and American varieties. The main focus of the study is the time frame from 1776 to 1850, which serves as a test case for new-dialect formation theory (Trudgill 2004). Beyond the Late Modern English focus, the variables' developments are traced from the mid-19th century to the present day in order to reveal long-term trends.

An analysis of early Ontario English, as the socially and historically dominant variety of Canadian English, offers a first historical account of the early stages of the variety that was to become Standard Canadian English. Based on a socio-historical, variationist approach that is grounded on language-internal data from three corpora, the study explicitly includes insights from the external language history. The data come from the *Corpus of Early Ontario English, pre-Confederation section*, the first machine-readable corpus of historical Canadian English, while *ARCHER-1* and *A Corpus of Late 18th-Century Prose* provide contemporary benchmarks for cross-dialectal comparisons. The findings are based on the genres of newspapers, diaries, and letters, of which the latter offer a particularly intriguing window into the Canadian vernacular of the past. By extending the diachronic scope, the study complements in important ways available apparent-time scenarios of Canadian English, which reach back to the 1920s (e.g. Chambers 1995a, Tagliamonte 2006).

The study's theoretical underpinning, new-dialect formation, was originally developed with phonological data, making this one of the first attempts to test the theory systematically in the area of morphosyntax. While the data suggest that new-dialect formation offers an adequate account for dialect-mixing scenarios in colonial settings, it proposes three modifications and extensions in the area of morphosyntax. These adaptations pertain to a layering of the new-dialect formation into a (slower) rural and a (faster paced) urban layer, the exclusion of very slowly proceeding, long-term changes (drift) from the three-stage model of new-dialect formation and the extension of the first stage of the new-dialect formation process with one process.

The evidential base for the findings are syntactic, semantic and functional analyses of more than 4,350 modal tokens of CAN/MAY, COULD/MIGHT,

SHALL/WILL, SHOULD/WOULD, MUST, OUGHT TO and HAVE TO in a total of 19 contexts. The aggregate data allow a comprehensive characterization of the Late Modern English modal auxiliary complex in Ontario and, backed up by post-Late Modern English developments, assessments of theoretical phenomena beyond the new-dialect formation scenario. These include the notions of colonial lag, the founder principle and the focussing process of newly-formed colonial varieties.

The study provides an empirical assessment of four major types of influence on early Canadian English in form of a ranking: drift (parallel development) is the most prevalent factor operating on the modal auxiliaries in early Ontario, followed by early American English influence, with Canadian independent developments in third place, and BrE import features as the fourth most dominant factor.

As a prerequisite to the empirical, corpus-based part of the study, the different input varieties contributing to the dialect mixing scenario are assessed in detail and matched with available corpus material. The findings are used to review the classic contributions by M. Bloomfield (1948) and Scargill (1957) on the origin of Canadian English, who both argue from the external history. The two accounts are compared with the linguistic data, and a synthesis between both views is offered.

Acknowledgements

This study is a revised and extended version of the University of Vienna Ph.D. thesis *New-dialect formation in early Canada: the modal auxiliaries in Ontario, 1776-1850*, which was defended in April 2006 at the Department of English. During the work on this project, I have accumulated a number of favours and debts from friends and colleagues. Above all, I am grateful to **Herbert Schendl**, my *Doktorvater* and friend, for his support in all matters relating to this project. *þæs ofereode, þisses swa mæg* has never been his attitude. Special thanks must go to **Jack Chambers**, both for his encouragement in the early stages of this project and his readiness to act as my external examiner. *Unplugged's* 'hidden gem' sessions: the best jazz was free! A big thank you to **Laurel J. Brinton**, who was instrumental in the transition of the project from Vienna to Vancouver. It has been a privilege working with her ever since.

Werner Abraham's interest in the topic and his thoughtful methods of lobbying behind the scenes are most appreciated. One day we will attend the same conference. I wish to thank **Maurizio Gotti** for both his feedback on an earlier version of this book and his kind offer of support. **Kees Vaes** and **Patricia Leplae's** highly effective e-mail consulting and **Izabela Moldovan**'s proof-reading skills were always much appreciated.

Thanks also go to **Christiane Dalton-Puffer** and **Barbara Seidlhofer** for what must have been honey-tongued letters of recommendation. CLIL and VOICE rock! I am grateful to **Janice McAlpine** and **Margery Fee** for sharing their Canadiana materials with me at different stages. More power to the SLU.

This project was generously supported by the following institutions: *Österreichische Akademie der Wissenschaften* (Austrian Academy), DOC grant 21701; *Österreichische Forschungsgemeinschaft* (Austrian Research Society); several *University of Vienna* units: *Research Service and International Relations, Office of the Dean at the Faculty of Arts* (*Philologisch-Kulturwissenschaftliche Fakultät)*, the *Hans Pinsker Fund* at the Department of English; and the *Social Sciences and Research Council of Canada*, Postdoctoral Fellowship, 756-2007-0145.

Finally, I would like to thank my parents for who they are. My mother, **Eleonore Dollinger**, who wish I was working some place closer, and my father, **Josef Dollinger**, Sen., (1927-2003), who would have been so happy to see this book in print. Without their kind-heartedness, this book would never have been written.

Abbreviations

*	unattested form
**	grammatically incorrect form
/ /	phonemic transcription
[ ]	phonetic transcription
< >	graphemes
AAVE	African-American Vernacular English
AmE	American English
AmE-1	American English, period 1
AusE	Australian English
BrE	British English
BrE-1, BrE2+3	British English, period 1, period 2+3
BNA	British North America
BNC	British National Corpus
CanE	Canadian English
CanEs	Canadian Englishes
CanE-1, 2, 3, 2+3	Canadian English, periods 1, 2, 3, 2+3
CLA	Canadian Linguistic Association
CanOx	*Canadian Oxford Dictionary*
CL18P	*Corpus of Late Eighteenth-Century Prose*
CONTE	Corpus of Early Ontario English (periods 1-5)
CONTE-pC	*Corpus of Early Ontario English,* pre-Confederation section (periods 1-3)
d1, d2, d3	diary genre, periods 1, 2, 3
DAI	Dissertation Abstracts International
DCHP-1, (-2)	*Dictionary of Canadianisms on Historical Principles* (1st ed., 2nd ed.)
DNE	*Dictionary of Newfoundland English*
DPEIE	*Dictionary of Prince Edward Island English*
DTC	Dialect Topography of Canada
EModE	Early Modern English
l1, l2, l3	letter genre, periods 1, 2, 3
L1	first language
L2	second language
LC	lower class
LModE	Late Modern English
MC	middle class
ME	Middle English
n	absolute frequency
n1, n2, n3	newspapers genre, periods 1, 2, 3
NE	Newfoundland English
NW-BrE	Northwestern England British English
NZE	New Zealand English
OE	Old English
OntE	Ontario English
PDE(s)	Present Day English(es)
PEI	Prince Edward Island
SCE	Survey of Canadian English

ABBREVIATIONS

SIN	Scottish, Irish and Northern English
SLU	Strathy Language Unit, Queen's University, Kingston, Ont.
SVEN	Survey of Vancouver English
UBC	University of British Columbia
UC	upper class
UVic	University of Victoria, B.C.

1 INTRODUCTION

Canadians have become used to hearing and identifying various dialects
of British English (including Scottish and Irish), Australian English,
American English, and other 'Englishes', but seldom give much thought
to their own 'Canadian English'.

(Ruth McConnell in *Our own voice:*
Canadian English and how it is studied, 1978 [1979]: 2)

When aiming to discover details about the history of Canadian English, one is
bound to find out rather sooner than later that not much material is available.
This holds especially true for descriptions and findings based on linguistic data
rather than on the settlement history of the country.

This sad fact is perhaps best illustrated by juxtaposing two of the few contributions to diachronic Canadian English (CanE). On the one hand, an early
paper by Matthew Scargill (1956) is typical of some of the linguistic work on
historical Canadian English: while entitled 'Eighteenth century English in
Nova Scotia', the paper is a mere five-paragraph miscellany that hardly deserves its grandiose title. On the other hand, with the topic thus left neglected
by specialists, writers without linguistic background or training have attempted
to fill the gap: Orkin's (1970) *Speaking Canadian English*, a 276-page monograph on the variety, including its origins, is the most prominent example (see
also, e.g. Thay 2004, Thain 2003, Casselman 1995, Mazerolle 1993, Orkin
1971). While these writers generally have to be applauded for serving a need
the language specialists have largely neglected, it is self-evident that their writings cannot (and were never meant to) replace scholarly treatments of the subject matter. Orkin's book, for example, provides a very narrow view of the
variety as it almost exclusively focusses on vocabulary. With the exception of
an early text book (McConnell 1978), however, Orkin (1970) remains the only
introductory monograph on CanE, and diachronic studies are mostly confined
to miscellanies such as Scargill (1956).

The present study aims to fill this gap to some extent with a systematic
study of one area, the modal auxiliaries, and attempts to provide diachronic
information on one central area of grammar as used in early Ontario. It aims to
supply CanE with a diachronic depth that has hitherto been missing in most

studies and will contextualize the findings against changes that were to follow in a range of varieties of English.

What is probably best known about the linguistic situation in Canada is that it is an officially bilingual country and that Canadians speak English and French (and, of course, many more languages without official status; see, for instance, Chambers 1998a: 264-268). What is less known, perhaps, is a rift between English and French Canada in terms of language awareness, which finds its expression in everyday life: while French Canadians usually think of themselves as speakers of *Canadian* French, or at least as speaking *français québécois*, the language of the majority of Canadians is still usually considered to be just plain 'English'. If asked what kind of English, possibly only a few Anglophones would give 'Canadian English' as an answer, while many would be somewhat puzzled. H. A. Gleason put this sorry state of language awareness poignantly and identified a culprit some 25 years ago:

> Perhaps because of preoccupation with such largely political and social problems [as evidenced by the plethora on treatises on what it means to be Canadian, SD], Canadians seem to direct much less attention than one might expect to the language itself – at least on the English side. (Gleason 1982: 1)

While considerable accomplishments have been made since this statement was written, for example major revisions of Canadian reference works such as the *Gage Canadian Dictionary* in 1983 and 1997 (Avis *et al.* 1983, de Wolf *et al.* 1997), and entirely new publications, such as a usage guide which can be called a descriptive grammar of Canadian English (Fee and McAlpine [1]1997, [2]2007), the *ITP Nelson Canadian Dictionary* (Friend *et al.* 1997), and the highly successful *Canadian Oxford Dictionary* (Barber [1]1998, [2]2004), language awareness remains, judging by anecdotal experience, relatively low.

By working with older stages of CanE, it will be shown that for more than one and a half centuries CanE has developed its own, at times subtle, linguistic characteristics and that little language awareness is not a consequence of missing linguistic idiosyncrasies.

In stark contrast to the Canadian scenario, the linguistic situation south of the US-Canadian border has been very different for both historical and social reasons. American patriots like Noah Webster and Henry (H. L.) Mencken managed to ensure that America, i.e. the United States, is perceived as a country with its 'own' variety of English. Like in so many other cases, Canadians have taken a subtler approach. In Canadian English, the lack of an undisputed standard, in the sense of unequivocally accepted codified variants, has until recently not been an issue and it still is, in comparison to other countries, not of great concern when different spelling variants or pronunciations are used; on the contrary, perhaps, such variation is almost celebrated. There are a number of reasons for this state of affairs, such as a Canadian aversion towards *prescribed* linguistic standards as proposed by Chambers (1986: 3), or a certain unwillingness of Canadian educational institutions to address the issue of language standards in earlier times. While the former scenario is an expression of a highly salient cultural feature in Canada, the latter may be the result of a general lack of language awareness among speakers of CanE. There is some truth in both, beyond doubt, but perhaps the latter scenario is the more pervasive reason for the purported linguistic tolerance of speakers of CanE.

Whatever the reasons, CanE has a sociolinguistically different status than American English (AmE). In an early article, the *raison d'être* for the study of CanE is found in the fact that "a knowledge of Canadian English is of importance in the investigation of the history of American English" (M. Bloomfield 1948: 4). This attitude has been echoed at times in the half-century since the publication of Bloomfield's article. Today, one can say that CanE plays an integral part in contributions to post-Early Modern English periods (e.g. Hickey 2004a).

Not too long ago, however, the treatment of CanE in its own right was a novel idea. In 1951, Partridge and Clarke published their book on 20th-century British and American English and broke with the tradition of "ignor[ing] the English spoken in Canada, South Africa, Australia and New Zealand" (1968 [1951]: 1), including a full chapter on Canadian English (Priestley 1968 [1951]). Twelve years later, Raven I. McDavid, the American dialectologist, rebuts opinions that deny CanE the status of a variety in its own right, when he says that

> it can no longer satisfy the serious student of North American English, whatever his nationality, and only a little knowledge of Canadian history is necessary to suggest that it [the confounding of CanE with AmE] was never an accurate statement of the facts. Like the English of the United States, Canadian English is far too complicated to be dismissed with a single categorical statement. True, Canadian English developed out of the familiar kind of colonial experience, borrowing new words and reshaping or recombining old ones to fit new experiences and new needs for communication. True again, there have always been currents of migration flowing in both directions across the border. […]
>
> But this is not all. At the same time there has been a continuous flow of immigration from the British Isles, some of it resulting in rather homogeneous settlements with strong British traditions in speechways […].

> And even this is not the whole story. One must reckon with Canadian na-
> tionalism, arising from autonomy attained not through a break with the
> Crown but by evolution within the Commonwealth and therefore less ob-
> vious than the nationalism derived from the autonomy which the United
> States achieved through armed revolt. (McDavid 1963: 469f)

These excerpts from McDavid's abridgement of Mencken's *The American
language* are more than 40 years old, but are more precise than some more
recent contributions on the genesis and status of CanE in the literature. Perhaps
the best-known such paper is Lilles (2000). Not linguistically trained as such,
Lilles exploits the catchphrase of the 'myth of Canadian English' in an assembly of misconceived bits and pieces of external language history and, what is
most important, without linguistic data. The fact that papers like these get published and still, seven years after its publication, feature prominently in radio
shows on language[1] is unfortunate. As will become clear from the review section, Lilles (2000) is little more than the linguistic equivalent of intelligent design theory or climate change sceptics in the field of CanE.

1.1 Colonial Englishes and Canadian English

Research into colonial and postcolonial Englishes is, with the exception of
American English, a comparatively recent activity. As late as the early 1990s,
Merja Kytö (1991a: 186) had to state that the study of "extraterritorial varieties
of English [is] a field of study still largely neglected by the mainstream of historical Anglistics". While this is certainly true for European English linguistics, to which the term *Anglistics* refers, American linguists have, per definition, always focussed on their own (post)colonial varieties of English.

   In comparison to other colonial Englishes, research on CanE is a late comer,
and CanE itself is considered by some as the "least documented of all major
varieties of English" (Halford 1996: 4). Australian English can show a considerable research history and has received scholarly attention even before WWII
(Partridge 1968 [1951]: 85), at a time when research on CanE was practically
non-existent. More recently, research on New Zealand English has gained
momentum with the discovery of tape recordings representing the speech of
late 19th-century speakers (ONZE tapes) (Trudgill 2004, Gordon *et al.* 2004).

---

[1] An episode of the CBC Radio show *And Sometimes Y* on CanE, aired 24 Feb. 2007, used
Lilles' article as a starting point. It can be accessed at:
http://www.cbc.ca/andsometimesy/pastshows.html?episode8 (16 Aug. 2007).

Amidst these trends, it seems that the study of CanE, despite considerable efforts since the mid 1950s, has been relatively neglected.

Since the late 1990s increased research efforts into what is generally referred to as Late Modern English (LModE), i.e. English varieties between c. 1700 to 1900, and its logical extension of focus to colonial varieties of English, has provided a new context for the study of diachronic CanE. Hickey (2004a) is a collection of essays that focusses on the "core 200-year period" (Hickey 2004b: 1) from the early 1600s to the mid-1800s that lay the foundation for post-colonial Englishes (reviewed in Dollinger 2005). The recent work on English varieties reflects a departure from a research paradigm that has usually focussed on the dominant varieties of English, BrE and AmE. As Watts and Trudgill (2002: 2) put it, histories of English have usually been largely "anglo-centric and based on Standard [British] English", but today there is no excuse for the treatment of one or even two dominant varieties at the expense of other LModE varieties, and the rising number of conferences and workshops on language history "from below", socially speaking, attests these fortunate new developments.

In line with this widening perspective, it is becoming more and more customary to include references to Canadian English in work on North American English. The most recent periodical report by the American Dialect Society on *Needed Research in American Dialects* (Preston 2003) frequently mentions the necessity to study CanE in its own right (e.g. Ash 2003). In terms of Ontario English, the present study aims to contribute its share.

1.2 Ontario English

Chambers (1991: 92) states that both Newfoundland English (NE) and mainland Canadian English "appear to have established themselves as autonomous national varieties". For historical reasons, the distinction between NE and mainland CanEs is sound on both external and internal grounds: Newfoundland only joined the Canadian Federation in 1949, after having remained a British colony under self-government for centuries, which is reflected in the island's distinct linguistic varieties (e.g. Clarke 1991: 108).

There is a general consensus for the separate treatment of mainland Canadian English and Newfoundland English as distinct varieties of an umbrella concept of CanE, which is reflected in the organization of major reference works (cf. Algeo 2001b: xxvi). In the present study, with the exception of one chapter, Canadian English is used here as a synonym of the English of Ontario, Ontario English. Only chapter (2), in which the literature is reviewed, will address the regional character of CanE and use 'CanE' as a hyperonym in the sense of an umbrella term including both mainland CanE and NE.

Ontario English (OntE) is a historically important variety in the Canadian context. While it was not the first mainland Canadian variety of English, since parts of the Maritimes were settled earlier, it is a variety of long standing. Most importantly, with the coming of the railway, OntE was carried further west in the second half of the 19th century. Given its historical importance, it is likely that OntE played a key role in the formation of Standard Canadian English, which is best shown in a uniform accent across mainland Canada (Chambers 1998a: 252). It seemed, therefore, a natural choice to focus on the probably single-most important Canadian regional dialect: early Ontario English.

1.3 Aims of the present study

This study attempts to shed light on the formation of early OntE by providing a description of the modal auxiliary complex from 1776-1850 and comparisons with both historical and contemporary varieties of English. The study is organized into two parts. Chapters (2-5) comprise the background and theoretical basis, while chapters (6-10) present the empirical data.

Chapter (2) reviews the literature on CanE and puts the present study in relation to previous research. It provides a research report that strives to incorporate as many studies as possible since the existing overviews are all rather concise reviews (Avis 1973a, Chambers 1979c, Chambers 1989, Chambers 1991, Chambers 1998a, Brinton and Fee 2001, and Chambers forthc.b). While from some perspectives one might consider the research review as in disproportion to the immediate needs of the empirical part of the study, it is the author's firm belief that a more thorough review might serve as a starting point for newcomers to the study of CanE. Certainly, a broader review is bound to miss some contributions in areas that are more remote to the core agenda of this study, I hope it will serve the intended more general purpose to some extent at least.

Chapter (3) provides an account of Ontario's external language history from 1776 to 1850. Wherever possible, special focus is given to demographically different immigrant groups and their numerical strengths. At the end of the chapter, the theories on the origins of OntE will be reviewed. Chapter (4) introduces the *Corpus of Early Ontario English*, whose *pre-Confederation section* is the empirical base of the CanE data in this study. This is followed by the presentation of a theory of new-dialect formation in chapter (5) (Trudgill 2004), which is the most detailed account of the formation of new varieties in colonial settings to date. New-dialect formation theory will be tested against the empirical data in chapters (6-10). The LModE data allow us also to test a recent theory of the development of modal auxiliaries that seeks to explain the distinctiveness of the English modals within the modal systems of other Germanic languages (Abraham 2001). The CanE data bridge to some extent the data gap between the well-studied periods of English from OE to EModE and the numerous studies on (late) 20th-century varieties.

The empirical part of this study deals with ten core modals and one semi-modal. Chapter (6) provides the general methodological background, lays out the rationale behind the choice of variables and introduces the research methodology. Chapters (7), (8), (9) and (10) present the data on eleven modals in OntE and other, non-CanE varieties. Each empirical chapter matches the data to the theoretical predictions of new-dialect formation theory (Trudgill 2004) and sketches the development of each modal in later periods until the present day. This will allow for the examination of the theory of root loss (Abraham 2001) in the broader context of modal auxiliary development since LModE times. In chapter (11) both parts, empirical and theoretical, will be synthesized and compared to previous findings. In the context of the study of Late Modern English (LModE), which has attracted considerable attention in recent years, the modal auxiliaries have not yet received the attention they might deserve (cf. recent collections with little mention of these variables, e.g. Kytö, Rydén and Smitterberg 2006). It is therefore hoped that this study, beyond the immediate Canadian agenda, may help to re-adjust the focus on the modals, which have been studied extensively in other periods. Chapter (11) attempts to answer five basic questions:

1) How can the use of modal auxiliaries be characterized in early CanE and how does this development comply with the known semantic trajectories for modals (Traugott 1989) and the theory of root loss (Abraham 2001)?

2) How conservative is early CanE modal usage? Does it undergo a colonial lag (Marckwardt 1958, Trudgill 2004)? How far does the founder principle apply (Mufwene 1996)?

3) Which of the existing theories on the origin of CanE (Bloomfield 1948 or Scargill 1957), to be reviewed in chapters (2) and (5), fits the data better?

4) To what extent do the modals in CanE provide evidence for existing models of new-dialect formation (Trudgill 2004)?

5) When did CanE focus (Le Page and Tabouret-Keller 1985), i.e. become a distinct variety that began to be perceived as distinct by some of its speakers?

It will be shown that the modal auxiliaries in early OntE show an array of phenomena that cannot be captured by popular notions of colonial lag. The modals in OntE are the product of a diverse set of influences, including parallel and individual developments in comparison to other varieties of English. While existing developmental scenarios for CanE focus on one or two factors as the major source of influence, we will see that CanE, often described vaguely as a mélange, a hybrid of features, can be described and traced in its development more accurately. Recent models of dialect development in colonial settings provide a useful theoretical underpinning.

Finally, based on these findings, an attempt is made to date the origin of CanE as a distinct, i.e. focussing, variety. We will see that early OntE, as an important early CanE variety, displayed a number of modal distributions not found in other varieties in the early 1800s and that by the second half of the 19th century CanE is probably best described as a new, focussing, colonial variety of English.

2 CANADIAN ENGLISH: A RESEARCH HISTORY OF THE 'OTHER' VARIETY OF NORTH AMERICAN ENGLISH

This chapter aims to introduce the reader to the available research on CanE and to some large-scale projects that were designed to gather CanE data but have not been completed or published. It will present research across Canada and will not be confined to OntE. What justification may there be to extend the necessary research review for this diachronic study of the modals beyond the geographical and temporal boundaries of the variety to be surveyed in the empirical part?

There are a number of reasons for doing this here: first, no comprehensive overview of studies on Canadian English has yet been released (CanE). The two monographs that come closest are Orkin (1970), an outdated, popular account that was never intended as a scholarly introduction to CanE, and McConnell (1978), a textbook, which is brilliant for its purpose but cannot fill this gap.

Second, overviews on CanE in article format are either outdated or very concise, or both: Walter Avis, who could not complete his monograph on CanE (McDavid 1981: 125), produced one substantial overview (Avis 1973a), which, just as Chambers (1979c, 1989), is outdated today. Chambers (1991, 1998a, forthc.b) and Brinton and Fee (2001) have been written in the context of larger volumes, which made it necessary to concentrate on the most prominent points. Clarke's (1993c) collection of essays on CanE covers the country from east to west. Most recently, another substantial collection of essays in a special issue of the *Canadian Journal of Linguistics* (volume 51, issues 2&3) makes available 13 papers on the theme of "Canadian English in the Global Context" in the broadest sense. Collections of essays, however, can hardly substitute for a coherent overview of CanE (but see Clarke 1993a and Avery *et al.* 2006 for the common thread in their contributions). Edwards (1998) is a collection of papers on languages in Canada, which includes chapters relevant for Canadian English.

Third, this review strives to include discontinued projects that figure prominently in CanE research and may provide valuable information and data. And fourth, while the survey of this chapter does not aim to fill the void of a monograph-long treatment of CanE in any way, it is intended to provide the reader with a reasonably comprehensive overview of work on CanE. While it has become impossible to discuss all aspects of work on CanE in any greater detail, it is attempted to identify trends and foci of the discipline and provide points of departure for future research.

It was pointed out earlier that linguistic research on CanE gained momentum relatively late. The foundation of the Canadian Linguistic Association (CLA) in 1954, which focussed on dialectological studies and the development of Canadian dictionaries in the early years (McDavid 1981: 123), would become the driving force behind scholarly research into the variety and its variants (cf. Chambers 1975c: vii). While research before 1954 is rather sparse, some of the early studies are notoriously difficult to obtain, as they were never published (see also Wanamaker 1981: 89).

There are several print bibliographies on CanE studies that provide a good point of departure. Avis and Kinloch's bibliography ([1978]) document writings on CanE from 1792 to 1975,[2] which is carried further by Lougheed (1988) to 1987. Bähr's bibliography (1977) includes references until 1976, while Schneider (1984) covers the period from the 1960s to early 1980s. More recently, Görlach (2003) extended and updated the documentation with an annotated print bibliography. There is, however, still neither an up-to-date electronic database, nor a fully indexed bibliography for CanE. The bibliography at www.canadianenglish.org is a step in the right direction, but has not gone past an embryonic stage at the time of writing.[3]

This chapter is organized in five sections. Section (2.1) introduces a number of basic terms, such as Canadian English, Standard Canadian English, and regional CanEs. Section (2.2) reviews the research available before 1954, while section (2.3) details the advances of the field since then. The presentation of studies is arranged along the linguistic levels of lexis, phonetics and phonology, morphology and syntax, which is completed by a section on language attitudes, usage and pragmatics. Regional dialects are discussed under phonetics and phonology, as most studies have dealt with this aspect to a considerable degree. Contributions that treat more than one linguistic level are listed under the heading where they place a certain emphasis, or where they have had their

---

[2] Avis and Kinloch ([1978]) is, with 723 items, much more comprehensive than Avis ([1965]), which contains only 172 items. The yearly bibliographies in the *Canadian Journal of Linguistics*, e.g. Avis 1969b, 1964, 1960, 1958, 1957, 1956b, are integrated in both book publications. Both bibliographies also include popular writings (news coverage) on CanE.

[3] This web portal was launched by Elaine Gold on the occasion of the first International conference on *Canadian English in the Global Context* in Honour of J. K. Chambers, Toronto, January 2005.

greatest influence. Findings are summarized in section (2.4). Finally, section (2.5) reviews diachronic language studies on CanE, which is the area of focus in the present study.

Before basic concepts in CanE are defined, the notion of the term *dialect* will need to be addressed. Consistent with the use of the term in North American dialectology, *dialect* is to be understood here as "any variety of speech, regional or social or both, that may be set off from other varieties by identifiable characteristics" (McDavid 1954: 3). As such, the term does not carry any pejorative connotations, which, in a European context, it may have, but is simply equivalent to *variety*.

2.1 Identity, standard and variation in Canadian English

CanE has not long been in the public consciousness of Canadians, and even today some of its speakers have failed to acknowledge their 'own' variety of English. Görlach (2003) attributes rising public awareness to some milestone research on the variety, such as the publication of the *Dictionary of Canadianisms on Historical Principles* (Avis *et al.* 1967), that "can be said to have established the entity 'CanE' in the minds of Canadians as well as lexicographers world-wide" (p. 111), or Clarke's (1993c) collection of essays that helped to further its identity among linguists (p. 118).

However, despite the strong evidence of research that we are going to see in this section, it is striking, as noted in chapter (1), that many Canadians seem to be unaware of the features of their own variety of English. So much so that even today one may find some ill-informed rant against the very existence of CanE in the linguistic literature. While Lilles' (2000) article in *English Today* disputing the existence of CanE was met with harsh criticism in one of the journal's next issues (Sutherland 2000, Upward 2000), the discussion testifies to the lack of language awareness among English students at Canadian universities[4] and to a doubtful attempt of the editor to prompt discussion without identifying Lilles' article as part of a Canadian complaint tradition (e.g. M. 1936 for an early example). As Harold B. Allen remarks in a 1980 review, al-

---

[4] Lilles, a literature graduate from the University of Toronto, obviously has not received any linguistic instruction or information on CanE. In this academic context, it is interesting to see how many Canadian universities offer courses on CanE. According to www.canadian english.org (2 August 2005) (and adding St. Mary's College, Halifax), seven universities and colleges offer courses in CanE. When compared to the more than 100 public and private universities and university-degree colleges in Canada, the number of institutions offering a course on CanE is, with around 5%, surprisingly low.

ready the first generation of linguists (Henry Alexander, Walter Avis, Matthew Scargill, amongst others) working on CanE proved

> that the English language in Canada has its own distinctiveness and that [...] it demands the serious study and research which for too long it has been denied but which is beginning to appear. (Allen 1980: 36)

More than half a century after perhaps the first treatment of CanE as a national variety of English in Partridge and Clark (1968 [1951]), this discussion shows clearly that the concept of pluricentric languages (Clyne 1992), which distinguishes between dominant (BrE and AmE) and non-dominant varieties (CanE, AusE, NZE etc.), is not firmly established. Not too long ago, Görlach (1991a [1987]: 108) considered CanE as "an entity that may not exist at all", while he acknowledged only four years later "a growing acceptance of the identity of CanE by Canadians themselves" (1991a: 121).

Even among North American experts, some statements may be found that deny CanE the status of a national variety. Based on these assumptions is the opinion that the 3,000-mile international border that separates Canada from the United States, has never been a linguistic boundary (Mackey 1998: 13). Such statements have been disproven many times, as the review section will make clear.

The view taken in the present study stands in contrast to such opinions. Recent studies, e.g. contributions in Clyne (1992), especially Leitner (1992) on English, Ammon (1995) and De Cillia (1998) on German, continue to show that national boundaries constitute not only legitimate, but useful lines for the delimitation of language varieties.

2.1.1 Homogeneity and evolving notions of Standard CanE

By accepting the present-day national boundaries of Canada as the geographical borders for the variety under review, we may look at different ways to stratify this variety internally. One recurring topic in many observations and studies of North American Englishes has been their reported homogeneity, spanning larger areas than anywhere in Europe. For CanE, this has received special attention and is found in much of the literature, in some even as a defining feature. First alleged by early commentators to the USA and Canada (Mencken 1936: 90, qtd. in Orkin 1970: 28f, MacMahon 1998: 398, Lighthall 1889: 581 on CanE opposes the notion), statements on the homogeneity in CanE are found in Priestley (1968 [1951]: 75), Avis (1973a: 62), Chambers (1973, 1975a, 1991, 1998a), Woods (1999 [1979]), Kinloch [and Avis] (1989), Kinloch (1983a), Brinton and Fee (2001: 422f), to list but a few.

The notion of homogeneity is connected with concepts of standard CanE, whose names, definitions and scopes have changed over time. First, geographical delimitations were central for what was called 'General Canadian'. Avis defines 'General Canadian' as a dialect "from Ontario westward" and connects it to early OntE

> The speech of this extensive area [from Ontario westwards] has its roots in old Upper Canada, or Ontario, and might be referred to as 'General Canadian', a dialect closely related to what is often called 'Northern American' in the United States. (Avis 1973a: 62)

The term is used in Woods' (1999 [1979]) PhD version of his Ottawa Survey (DAI-A, 40/11, p. 5846) but seems to have fallen into disuse since.[5] Another closely related term is 'heartland Canadian English'. Chambers (1973) defines 'heartland Canadian' as the

> large, supposedly homogeneous dialect triangle bounded by an imaginary line from Kingston, Ontario, to Edmonton, Alberta, on the northeast, the Rocky Mountains on the west and the Canadian-American border on the south (Chambers 1973: 84).

Later in the 1970s, British Columbia was included in the dialect triangle of the heartland[6] region, due to new research results (cf. Chambers 1975c: viii). At the same time, the notion was redefined socially, bringing it close to what is best referred to as a standard variety. It needs to be pointed out, however, that the definitions of the standard variety in CanE have been almost exclusively based on phonological descriptions. On this basis, Chambers (1975b: viii) redefined 'Heartland Canadian English' as "a standard dialect which is spoken *throughout Canada*: roughly, the dialect of broadcasters on our national networks, and increasingly the majority dialect of our urban centres" (italics added) (cf. Bailey 1991: 21 for an acknowledgement of the social dimension).

Chambers (1979c) compares linguistic data with the existing definition of 'heartland Canada'. Basing his argument on data assembled by Gregg, Chambers (1979c: 190) realigns the heartland Canadian region as *including* Vancouver:

---

[5] Interestingly, Brinton and Arnovick's (2006: 402) introduction to the history of English reintroduces the term for "educated, middle-class urban Canadian" speech for the area from the Ontario-Quebec border to Vancouver Island (Cf. the definition of a standard Canadian accent in Chambers 1975b, 1998a to follow).
[6] This is a term of long standing, but its origins are unknown (Chambers 1973: fn2).

> There seems to be no doubt that the boundaries of "heartland Canada"
> must be extended to take in Vancouver if the term is to be meaningful for
> Canadian English dialectology. (Chambers 1979c: 190)

In Chambers (1998a), one finds the most precise definition of the term standard CanE, limiting it to a "standard accent" in CanE. In his contribution, Chambers (1998a: 252) describes only one aspect of a Canadian standard variety of English, i.e. the standard accent, and defines it as the

> urban, middle-class English as spoken by people who have been urban,
> middle-class, Anglophone Canadians for two generations or more [...].
> (Chambers 1998a: 252)

As the Canadian middle class (MC) comprises the majority of the population and new immigrants tend to become members of the MC rather quickly, this definition is broader than it may appear at first. One exception is the standard accent of Newfoundland, which is explicitly excluded. Even in Newfoundland, evidence has since shown that mainland speech ways are becoming the model of prestige speech (Hampson 1982, Clarke 1997b). In any case, the notion of a standard accent or dialect has sprung from the observed homogeneity in CanE, which continues to be an important factor in the sociolinguistics of CanE. As Chambers (1991: 100) puts it: "At present, the best available evidence suggests that the tendency towards homogeneity remains a sociolinguistic force", which is echoed by Davison's statement that "Homogeneity is an active force in Canadian English" (1987, qtd. in Chambers 2006: 114).

For the purposes of the present study, we may define standard CanE as the middle class variety of urban Canadians (with a Canadian Anglophone lineage of two generations or more) from the Maritimes to British Columbia, spanning an area from Halifax to Victoria, or more than 6,000 km.[7]

This definition of standard CanE is supported by depictions of CanE in Canadian novels. Tilly (1980) found in his study of 25 novels from the 1970s that there are no "deeply etched regional differences in Canadian English" represented in the works, and that major linguistic differences are instead illustrated by "rural and urban speakers in every region, including Newfoundland". The fictional characters "are deeply aware of rural/urban, generational, social class and ethnic variations in Canadian English" (Tilly 1980, in DAI-A, 41 p. 4387) instead of regional markers.

---

[7] While Victoria has a reputation as a stronghold for some British variants, recent results (Hung, Davison and Chambers 1993: 266) reconfirms its place within the Standard Canadian speech area.

There has been some criticism, however. Standard CanE, as a notion that includes all of the Canadian mainland has held considerable currency until today, although one researcher defines what he calls "Central and Prairie Canadian English" as spanning "from Toronto (excluding Kingston, Ont.) to the Rockies but only possibly extant thence westwards" (Kinloch 1983d: 131 and Kinloch, in Kinloch and Avis 1989: 407). This opinion is visualized in Kinloch's map (1983c: 115) as showing B.C. outside of the General CanE speech area and excluding most of the northern shore of Lake Ontario.

Bailey (1982: 151) implies some elements of a "scholarly fiction" in the notion of General Canadian, a criticism which is based on lexical regionalisms, as he quotes examples such as *bluff* and *lumbering* and their uneven distribution across Canada. The notion of a homogenous speech is, however, mainly based on the mainland Canadian phonological system and allows for some variation in lexical items. Another reason for this criticism may be that the notions of *General Canadian* and *heartland Canadian* were yet to undergo some fine-tuning.[8]

Since the 1980s both the terms *heartland Canadian* as well as *General Canadian* have been employed less often than the new term *Standard Canadian English*, which emphasizes the social dimension more than the more regionally defined other terms. Occasionally, however, one can find *General Canadian* in more recent publications. Whatever the term used, however, it has become clear that Hamilton's (1964: 459) prediction that standard CanE phonology would collapse with AmE to form a "general North American standard" has not been borne out.

2.1.2 The 'standard' in reference works

The notion of standard CanE that we have discussed so far is bound to language description. There is, however, another notion of a 'standard' that is associated with prescriptive language behaviour, a notion that Canadians have hitherto only unwillingly adopted. Wanamaker (1976/77) investigates the question of prescribed standards based on questionnaires to Canadian newspaper editors and school boards. He documents a mixed practice in relation to the reference books used, and that "some school administrators do not wish to be prescriptive in connection with spelling and dictionaries" (p. 51).

---

[8] Trudgill and Hannah (2002: 48), and Brinton and Arnovick (2006), define *General Canadian*, as ranging from Victoria to Montreal, and place the Maritimes, besides Newfoundland, outside of the speech area. Labov, Ash and Boberg (2006: 224) define a Canadian "central region" from Eastern Ontario to the Rocky Mountains as including all typical CanE phonological features.

Only fairly recently have Canadian dictionaries and grammars gained wider currency, and even today one can still see *Webster's Third* or the *Shorter OED* on lecterns in public libraries for quick reference, while the *Canadian Oxford Dictionary* (CanOx) (Barber [2]2004, [1]1998) is safely tucked away in the reference section. The CanOx is apt to set the standard for CanE in terms of spelling, but is not the only attempt at doing so. The *ITP Nelson Dictionary*, published in 1997, as well as the 5th edition of the *Gage Canadian Dictionary*, which is the Canadian dictionary of the longest pedigree, are serving different market segments. The graded Gage dictionary series is the leader in Canadian schools, while the CanOx has been the most successful Canadian reference dictionary for the last ten years. These developments in the publishing industry point towards an increasing language awareness among the Canadian public, which is tried to be met by these publishing projects.

In the mid-1980s, the Strathy Language Unit was founded at Queen's University, Kingston, Ont., by the bequest of the businessman J. R. Strathy as "a unit for the continuing study of standard Canadian usage" (quoted in Chambers 1986). The exploration into the nature of the adjective *standard* resulted in what may be considered the first conference on Canadian English, which brought together an array of Canadian experts dealing with language professionally (cf. Lougheed 1986). The Strathy Language Unit (SLU) is dedicated to define a standard in CanE, which is done by keeping a synchronic electronic corpus of CanE writings and through the publication of a usage guide to CanE (Fee and McAlpine [2]2007).

A direct result of this first conference is Lougheed (1986), a highly interesting contribution to language policy in Canada, and to some extent a reflection, of the Canadian situation with its multiple standards and split usages, which have been influenced by both British and American usage. Sociolinguists, lexicographers, teachers, journalists and editors give their points of view on notions of a standard, as the volume testifies to the multitude of opinions in Canada. One gets the impression by some of the contributors that the time for codification has already passed, the time when, one work was considered as authoritative by some influential circles (e.g. Johnson's dictionary, Webster's speller, Konrad Duden's speller for German orthography) and quickly adopted by school boards on a national level and therefore spread throughout the country. At the same time, it shows that democratic principles have evolved since the 18th and 19th centuries to an extent that in Canada the mere search for a standard of orthography and usage triggers off a fear of imposition that runs counter to some of the core features of Canadian society, such as multiculturalism and tolerance – culturally, linguistically or otherwise (cf. Chambers 1986: 3).

One aspect that has been at the centre of linguistic awareness for more than one and a half centuries is spelling,[9] which I would like to single out from Lougheed (1986). The concept of a hybrid spelling in Canada, which blends BrE and AmE standards, has become widely known. Chambers (1986: 6-8), using Ireland's (1979) newspaper data from 1867-1967, shows that BrE and AmE spelling standards are prevalent in different parts of the country. Pratt (1993: 59) concludes that Canadian spelling expresses a tolerance for various kinds of spelling standards, which is the "kind of thing Canadians do best". Richards' (1988) survey on the associations of prestige and standard in CanE in Vancouver, produces a finding that is at odds with much of the sociolinguistic thinking of a standard. While she finds that a standard in Vancouver English exists, this standard is no prestige variety in the usual sense of the variety of an upper class, since Vancouver English features, apart from geographical homogeneity, also social homogeneity across different classes (DAI-A 49/12, p. 3708).

Other attempts to set a standard, whether through description or prescription, have been made via the print media. For the Canadian press, guidelines have been in existence since 1983 (Cobden 1986: 121) and since 1987 the stylebook *Editing Canadian English* (2000) has been available. Some studies have surveyed spelling practices in Canadian newspapers, such as Ireland (1979) and Bondesen (2004), both drawing from a sample of newspapers across the nation and revealing varied spelling patterns from province to province.

Living up the Canadian reputation of tolerance, whether linguistic or otherwise, Chambers (1986: 3) sees "any hint about standards in the sense of things imposed" as "repugnant" to Canadian society. The recommendation of a standard is, however, inevitable in reference works: although the Canadian usage guide by Fee and McAlpine (2007) aims to recommend rather than impose, it is in the hands of the users how to use the book – be it as a mere guideline or as a strict doctrine.

2.1.3 Regional Canadian Englishes

So far, several notions of standard CanE have been discussed, while in this section, proposals for linguistically distinct regions within in Canada will be

---

[9] Cf. first Canadian spelling book (Davidson's (1845 [1840])), or Mencken (1936: 396), who reports of Canadian governmental bodies urging "every loyal Canadian" to use British spelling in the early 1930s.

reviewed. Map (2.1) provides basic geographical information on Canada's provinces and territories, as well as their major urban centres:

Map 2.1: Provinces and Territories of Canada

One of the first articles on CanE, Chamberlain (1890), approached the study of CanE from a regional dimension. Today, regional CanE is often equated with linguistic enclaves. These linguistic enclaves exhibit relic dialects, such as Lunenburg Dutch, Cape Breton English, both in Nova Scotia, or the English in Peterborough, Ont. As standard CanE covers most of the country today, regional CanEs are spoken by relative minorities.

Early fieldwork was focussed on traditional dialectology, while sociolinguistic methods and sociolinguistic dialectology took a foothold in the mid-seventies (cf. Chambers 1991: 90). For some researchers, regional dialectal variation within CanE is still what is really important, since, in the opinion of one researcher,

> Canadian English doesn't really exist: it is still coming into existence. Or rather, there are an undetermined number of Canadian Englishes – and perhaps thousands of them. (Pringle 1983: 119).

While the statement is understandable from Pringle's engagement with the dialectal survey of the linguistically highly complex Ottawa Valley, it does not reflect the amount of attention that these regional varieties have received.

These gaps will be made explicit in the following subsections, while this short overview is limited to attempts to structure the regional variation within Canada. In the absence of a completed national dialect survey (Chambers 1994 comes closest to it), a combination of language external and internal reasoning is the basis for most studies.

It is important to point out that dialect boundaries in Canada do not coincide with Canada's provincial boundaries (Chambers 1979c: 177, Mackey 1998). The *Survey of Canadian English* (Scargill 1974), however, neglected this fact and left the location of respondents within a province unspecified, making the "isoglosses here coincide with provincial boundaries" (Scargill & Warkentyne 1972: 104). The lack of a complete, adequate dialect survey is the main reason why convenient labels based on provincial or regional borders, such as Ontario English, Montreal English or Saskatchewan English (see map 2.1) have become customary, instead of linguistically-defined areas. The reader is asked to treat terms like these accordingly in the present study, unless explicitly stated. These labels are not only convenient, but also necessary, as research has traditionally focussed on areas promising to produce significant differences in comparison to standard CanE, leaving aside other localities (but see section 2.3.2.3).

The notion of Canadian dialect boundaries has evolved over the years. One of the earliest studies that explicitly lists some dialect areas of Canada is Lighthall (1889). Applying external settlement criteria, Lighthall (1889) discusses the following dialects: Acadian English-speaking Loyalists (in the Maritimes), Acadian-Scotch (influenced by Gaelic), Lower Canadian dialects (i.e. Quebec), and Ontario. Moreover, Lighthall predicted the formation of Prairie and Rocky Mountain varieties in the areas that were by then largely uninhabited. Newfoundland had at that time not yet become part of Canada and was therefore not discussed.

Taking a big leap in time, Bailey (1982, 1991) lists the following dialect regions in Canada: the West – equivalent of British Columbia and the Prairies (Alberta, Saskatchewan and Manitoba) –, Southern Ontario (from Windsor to Toronto and Kingston), the Ottawa Valley (a prominent linguistic enclave), Quebec, and the Atlantic Provinces (including Newfoundland) (1991: 21-25). We can see that Bailey applies mostly geographic criteria, taking the provincial boundaries as a baseline. He subsumes Newfoundland under the heading of Atlantic Provinces, but not without stating its distinctive nature (p. 25). A quite different approach is taken in Wells (1982), who distinguishes, from a phonological point of view, merely three dialect regions: Western Canada, Eastern Canada and Newfoundland. More recently, Labov, Ash and Boberg (2006), in another large-scales survey, identify two dialects: a 'Canadian' dialect, from Quebec to British Columbia and the Atlantic Provinces.

Among the studies focussing on Canadian varieties, a balanced summary is found in Brinton and Fee (2001: 422f), who list the following major dialect areas: Newfoundland, Maritime English (Nova Scotia, New Brunswick, Prince Edward Island), Quebec (Montreal and the Eastern Townships), the Ottawa Valley, and "minor variants" in the West (British Columbia), the Prairies (Alberta, Saskatchewan, Manitoba) and the Arctic North. This delimitation is in accord with findings based on local accents, with some idiosyncrasies in Prince Edward Island (PEI) English (Chambers 1991: 97, based on Pratt 1982).

Recently, Boberg (2005b) has produced new evidence based on 53 lexical variables in context of the *North American Regional Vocabulary Survey*, which, unlike most previous attempts of classification, does not rely on settlement history. His study leads Boberg to state that

> In Canada, the strongest lexical boundaries were found to divide the English-speaking community of Montreal from neighboring regions to the east and west. These were followed in importance by the bundle of isoglosses that divides Newfoundland from the Maritimes. The boundaries dividing the Maritime provinces one from another—with the exception of Prince Edward Island—were found to be less important, as were those delimiting regions within western and central Canada from British Columbia to Ontario, suggesting a fairly homogeneous kind of English spoken by most people across this large region. (Boberg 2005b: 53)

Boberg identifies six dialect regions in Canada: the West, Ontario, Montreal, New Brunswick-Nova Scotia, Prince Edward Island, and Newfoundland. When synthesized with more traditional regional labels in CanE, four basic dialect regions are suggested here:

- Newfoundland
- Maritimes (Nova Scotia, New Brunswick, and including Prince Edward Island)
- Quebec (including Montreal)
- Central Canadian English (Ontario, Manitoba, Saskatchewan, Alberta, British Columbia)

It goes without saying that within these regions, further, possibly patterned variation is to be found. These four bigger regions will be divided on a provincial level, where necessary, in the absence of more precise labelling (cf. Chambers 1991: 93-95 for a short list of research desiderata in regional CanE). As shown earlier, Standard Canadian English spans across these regional zones as a socially defined variety/accent, spanning from Victoria, B.C. in the west to Halifax, N.S., in the east (excluding Quebec), and is by now extending its reach to St. John's, Nfld (Clarke 1997b: 31).

2.2 Research on Canadian English prior to 1954

A good amount of early articles and reports are writings in popular newspapers and other written media prior to 1954. While only a few scholarly articles exist, some are important documents of early 20th-century CanE. Two contributions in *American Speech*, Ahrend (1934) and Ayearst (1939), describe phonetic features of Ontario. Ahrend (1934) includes a transcription of Ontario speech, and, more importantly, is the earliest known description of the phenomenon now known as Canadian Raising (Chambers 1973, Chambers 2006). Joos (1942) formulated the basic phonological rule for Canadian Raising in an article that was "easily the most frequently cited article about Canadian English in the literature" at that point in time (Chambers 1975a: 78). Ayearst's article (1939) investigates differences and similarities between Canadian and American English, for phonological, lexical, syntactical and usage (spelling) variables. Generally, data are sparse from the pre-1954 period, which makes Henry Alexander's fieldwork a notable exception. As one of the early Canadian dialectologists, Alexander includes remarks on Canada in his introduction to the history of English (1940) (e.g. p. 187 on short *o*), mostly on German/Dutch and Gaelic influences in Nova Scotia (e.g. p. 206, 222f). Mencken (1936) includes very few remarks on CanE in *The American Language*, which were added in McDavid's (1963: 468-472) abridgement.

A number of early studies have been made more widely available in Chambers (1975a), which provides a springboard and bridges the gap between the disparate pre-1954 research and later work. Emeneau (1935), and more recently Trudgill (2001) investigate the dialect of Lunenburg County, Nova Scotia, where some German influence could be found until after WWII, while M. Bloomfield (1948) discusses the origins of Ontario English. Besides these important early studies, miscellanies such as McLay (1930), who reports very briefly on some disparate lexical variables, can occasionally be found.

Orkin (1970: 3-19) discusses the research and linguistic remarks prior to 1900, and quotes some early reports on linguistic features, all of which are of an impressionistic nature (ibid: 12f). While Orkin's informal account was much criticized by linguists (McDavid 1971), it was also praised (Urion 1971) in its attempt to provide a compendium on CanE, both historical and synchronic. Two nineteenth-century contributions are worth special mention in this context. First, a study by Chamberlain (1890) is remarkable as an early stock-taking of language research in Canada for French, English and other non-First-Nations languages. He assesses that towards the investigation "of the spoken English of the Dominion little indeed has been done" (Chamberlain 1890: 45). Another early study is Lighthall (1889), who delivers a concise overview of some CanE varieties and focusses on the fictional work of Thomas Chandler Haliburton from Nova Scotia, which would become the material for one of the earliest linguistic case studies on English in Eastern Canada (Avis 1950, 1969a). Besides characterizing what little research existed, Chamberlain focused on lexical items in various CanE dialects.

Lighthall (1889), whom we took as a starting point for the brief discussion on regional CanE above, is a remarkable piece of late 19th century scholarship, as he broke with popular notions that CanE is close to British English, as expressed below:

> It would probably surprise the average British Canadian to hear it suggested that the language of his people presents any very distinctive features, so widespread are the certain half-conscious notions that, excepting a few French, the language of the home-born people of our country is some very British and very un-American and practically uniform dialect, and that, though English, Scotch and Irish immigrants have individually imported their several variations, these never long remain without melting into that uniform dialect. These general impressions, which were not long ago proclaimed unchallenged in the Dominion Parliament by a leading member, are not correct. (Lighthall 1889: 581)

Today, it is self-evident to any Canadian, that Canadians sound more American than British. Lighthall discussed several regional dialects which he deemed important, such as the Nova Scotian dialects of the Acadian Loyalists, the Acadian Scotch English in Cape Breton and Pictou, and the Bluenose dialect; outside of Nova Scotia, he considers, amongst others, the Ontario and Quebecois English dialects. Lighthall also addressed French influence on Canadian English (1889: 582) and, surprisingly from today's point of view, pointed to the danger of French imperialism in the Northern parts of the country, describing the "very serious question of territorial displacement for the Saxon tongue" in this area (ibid). Lighthall (1889) and Chamberlain (1890) can be considered the earliest scholarly contributions to CanE and CanE dialectology.

Finally, the earliest study that explicitly mentions 'Canadian English' needs to be briefly discussed here. Reverend Geikie's (1857) article, a speech read before the Canadian Institute, was published in *The Canadian Journal of Science, Literature and History* in the same year. Geikie expressed his despise for all things Canadian, an attitude that is so well documented in Susanna

Moodie's *Roughing it in the Bush* (cf. Chambers 1993: 6f). While Geikie's report was unquestionably meant to curb the "way of appropriating what is worthless in the word coinage of our [American] neighbours" into CanE (Geikie 1977 [1857]:44), he apparently coined the term 'Canadian English', or at least "single-handedly discovered Canadian English, even though he was against it" (Orkin 1970: 11).

2.3 A survey of linguistic studies on CanE

As mentioned earlier, there are some brief overviews on research on CanE. Avis (1973a) provides an overview of research until 1970, while Chambers (1991, 1998a) and Brinton and Fee (2001) take the field into the 1990s. About half-way between the founding of the CLA and today, Chambers (1979c) commented that the literature on CanE was still "quite manageable" and evaluated the accumulated research. Earlier research had been largely void of focussed debates on research methodology. Chambers (1979c) diagnosed a "lack of evaluative and critical commentary on the material that has been accumulated" (p. 168) in a field that had grown enough to be scrutinized for its more general merits for linguistic theory, and beyond the level of regional interest. By criticizing methodologies and challenging some analyses, Chambers (1979c) added a new level of debate to a field that had reached the 'critical mass' for scientific discourse in the proper sense. This evaluative approach paved the way for first generalizations in CanE that were abstracted from empirical studies, instead from impressionistic ideas.

Since the late 1970s, the main focus of research on CanE has been dominated by synchronic sociolinguistic studies with a phonological focus. Up to the 1970s, lexis (cf. Avis 1972b: 239) was the area best researched, an activity that was soon matched in the field of descriptive phonology and pronunciation. At the first meeting of the *Canadian Linguistic Association* in 1954, plans were made to create a dictionary of words unique or in high currency in Anglophone Canada (Anon. 1955: 2). This work, Avis *et al.*'s *Dictionary of Canadianisms on Historical Principles* was published in 1967 on the occasion of Canada's Centennial and produced a body of lexicological knowledge (e.g. Lovell 1955a, 1955b, 1956, Harris 1975). As a result, vocabulary and phonology are the best-researched areas in CanE today.

The establishment of the *Journal of the Canadian Linguistic Association*, later renamed *Canadian Journal of Linguistics*, soon served as a platform for scholarly research and debate on CanE.[10] The early issues of the journal feature a considerable number of studies on CanE, with Avis setting the tone in a three-part contribution on vocabulary (Avis 1954), grammar and syntax (Avis 1955) and pronunciation (Avis 1956a) of CanE. Empirical studies, e.g. Scargill (1954) on Alberta vocabulary, Gregg (1957a, 1957b) on the pronunciation of adolescents and young adults in Vancouver, Story (1957) on Newfoundland place names, as well as plans for a nation-wide survey were conceived to define CanE by way of "a complete survey of the habits of speech of English-speaking Canadians across the country" (Scargill 1955: 27).

While the first volumes of the journal were entirely dedicated to Canadian English and Canadian French, subsequent volumes included a greater diversity of topics, so that by issue 7/1 (1961), the first one to appear under the new name of *Canadian Journal of Linguistics*, the journal was more diverse at the expense of the early Canadian focus. Reaching out to include other linguistic areas in the journal may have had negative effects on the study of CanE.

Avis (1973a: 57) concludes his section on writings on CanE saying that "the 1950s and 1960s reflect a remarkable upsurge of interest in the field of Canadian English".[11] The body of research has become quite substantial over the last fifty years, and the following sections are an attempt to present the research organized along linguistic levels. This should make apparent the lack of research in some areas, while others will be clearly shown to be at the centre of attention. We begin with lexis – vocabulary.

2.3.1 Lexis

The lexicographical work around the *Dictionary of Canadianisms on Historical Principles*, DCHP-1, is responsible for the bulk of our knowledge.[12] The term 'Canadianism' has evolved over time. Early on, Lovell (1955b) avoids the label Canadianism on account of the "overlapping vocabularies of American English, Canadian English, Jamaican English, etc." (1955b: 4), and prefers the term 'New-World Englishes'. Later, Lovell adopts a broader notion than had been customary, by paying account to the Canadian extralinguistic situation.

---

[10] Avis (1973a) cites the Massey report on the development in the arts, letters and sciences (1951), commissioned by the federal government, which included an article by Henry Alexander on Canadian English. This report is purported to have had a profound influence on the public (Avis 1973a: 56).

[11] Avis' most central recommendation, however, the establishment of a central location to store all data gathered on CanE (1973a: 58), was partially implemented in 1985 with the foundation of the Strathy Language Unit (SLU) at Queen's University, Kingston, Ont. With very limited financial resources, the SLU can serve this function only suboptimally for the time being.

[12] For a concise history of CanE lexicography and some of its problems see Gregg (1993).

His notion of a 'Canadianism' was incorporated into the final definition in the DCHP-1:

> A Canadianism, then, is a word, expression, or meaning which is native to Canada or which is distinctly characteristic of Canadian usage though not necessarily exclusive to Canada; Winnipeg couch falls into the first category, chesterfield ("sofa") into the second. (Avis 1967: xiii)

This definition, as broad as it is, makes sense in the Canadian, and indeed most former colonial, contexts. A consequent continuation of this line of thought is the introduction of the term 'North Americanism' (Avis 1967: xiii), which the editors suggest as well (cf. Toon 1981: 143).[13]

There is no doubt that the DCHP-1 must be considered a milestone in CanE research. Harris (1975) includes a statistical analysis of the entire dictionary and provides valuable insights into the makeup of CanE lexis by providing percentages of compounds, loans, coinages and so forth in the dictionary. DCHP-1 has, however, become seriously outdated. This becomes even the more prevalent, as there are indicators that its compilation was more focussed on the earlier stages of the variety than on the more recent vocabularies. Lovell, who was until his death the DCHP-1's first editor-in-chief, for instance, states that

> [s]ince the earlier examples of more settled words are ordinarily hardest to locate and, of course, more prized, the consequences of an inexperienced researcher overlooking, say, an 1856 example of Confederation (for it was used anticipatively well before 1867) are rather more serious than would be the skipping of more recent words. (Lovell 1956: 23)

While the DCHP-1 remains an indispensable document for earlier Canadian lexis, we are currently confronted with a gap of more than half a century of materials, between the DCHP-1 and the *Canadian Oxford Dictionary*, a project commenced in 1992. In August 2006, a project to revise the DCHP-1 was started at the University of British Columbia (Dollinger 2006c, Dollinger and Brinton forthc.). This project, DCHP-2, aims to update DCHP-1 for the 21st century and extend its historical coverage (see www.dchp.ca).

The DCHP is, however, not the only historical dictionary of CanE (Fee 1992b for an overview). Story, Kirwin and Widdowson's *Dictionary of Newfoundland English* ([2] 1990, [1]1982), DNE, adopts a definition of 'Newfoundlandisms' that seems to be derived from the DCHP. The DNE documents "the regional lexicon of one of the oldest overseas communities of the English-

---

[13] S. Hamilton (1997) compares the treatment of Canadianisms in various dictionaries.

speaking world: the lexicon of Newfoundland and coastal Labrador" (1982: xi). While the study of terminology in Newfoundland and Labrador has a long tradition (e.g. Patterson 1895, 1896, 1897, England 1925, Evans 1930, Greenleaf 1931), the DNE provides an organized and balanced look at the word-stock.

Terry Pratt's *Dictionary of Prince Edward Island English* (1988), documents the "non-standard words as used, or once used, on Prince Edward Island" (PEI) (p. xi), and applies a very carefully selected set of criteria for the inclusion of terms (p. xii-xiii). Pratt and Burke's (1998) dictionary of proverbial sayings on PEI is, just as Pratt (1988), based on both a reading programme as well as fieldwork surveys (1998: xx-xxvii). These two regional dictionaries, together with the DCHP, are the scholarly dictionaries on CanE regional varieties. Davey and MacKinnon (1995) is an early research report towards the planned *Dictionary of Cape Breton English*, i.e. the northern tip of Nova Scotia (cf. map 2.1), which was commenced in 1993 at the University College of Cape Breton and has recently completed the data collection phase (Davey: personal correspondence, see also Davey and MacKinnon 2002).[14] Other regional vocabularies have not yet been surveyed in any comparable detail.

At another level of accuracy and reliability, a surprising number of popular dictionaries, all of them more jocular than useful, can be found. A tidbit is provided in the following citation from Davis (1967), a booklet aimed to help British English speakers to understand Canadian English, which reiterates some misconceived reasons for linguistic differences between Britain and Canada:

> [t]he English of North America is derived from Elizabethan English spoken by the earliest settlers and Canadian English proclaims this heritage. If anyone has changed, it is the British in the last 100 to 200 years. Examples of British words that have fallen into disuse or had their meanings changed but which survive in Canadian English in their original sense are: **closet, deck of cards, hundredweight, presently, store, yard.** (Davis 1967: 2, original emphasis)

This is a good instance of the popular notion of colonial lag, which will be addressed later on in chapter (5). Popular works like this one are not limited to a national dimension, as there are a number of books on local CanEs. Poteet's (1988) South Shore Nova Scotian dictionary and phrasebook is such an example. It fails to provide any reasoning behind its inclusions apart from the im-

---

[14] http://www.capebretoner.com/archives/04-12-03b.html (31 Aug. 2005).

pressions of the editor. For rural Quebec, Campbell (1986) collected lexical words and phrases of Quebec's Gaspé Peninsula.

Other attempts are exclusively intended to entertain the reader, such as Orkin's (1973) booklet on all things Canadian, Stewart's (1999) expressions from rural New Brunswick, Mazerolle's (1993) *Moncton Dictionary* for urban New Brunswick talk or Thain's humorous collection of western Canadian sayings (1987, reprinted 2003). All of these publications, however, as funny as they may be, cannot replace more thorough scholarly investigations.

From a historical perspective, the *Western Canadian Dictionary and Phrase Book* (Sandilands [1913]), first published in 1912, is interesting as it allows us glimpses into what may otherwise have been lost, e.g. the entry for "Dad" is reported to be "frequently used when addressing an elderly man, as 'Hello, Dad!'". With around 1,500 headwords, it is also more comprehensive than most modern-day word lists and, it seems, also more reliable, as it was meant to be helpful, not entertaining (John Orrell in the introduction).

The influence of languages other than English on the CanE vocabulary has at irregular intervals received some treatment, so that only the most recent developments are discussed here. Apart from studies on the historic French influence on CanE (e.g. Avis 1978b, Yuen 1994), a number of other languages have left their marks on CanE. Most recently, Gold (2004b, 2003) has investigated Yiddish loanwords in CanE. She shows (Gold 2004b: table 1) a general increase of selected words of Yiddish origin such as *schmooze, schlep* and *schmuck* in CanE print media in the 1990s.

There are a number of studies on the lexis of regional varieties of CanE. Scargill (1954) reports on single usages of lexical items in Alberta that would justify a more complete survey. More recently, Nylvek (1993b: 218-222) deals with some semantic variation in Saskatchewan English, and Burnett (2006, 1992-2003, 2001) has researched the English dialect of New Brunswick, placing considerable emphasis on lexis. The lexis of the English language in Quebec is studied in Hamilton (1958a, 1958b), an early study on differences between Montreal and Ontario English. More recently, McArthur (1989) is a study that deals, despite its title, with vocabulary only.

A general tenor of these studies can be seen in statements of increasing American influence on CanE vocabulary, a finding that has recently been qualified (e.g. Boberg 2005b). McDavid (1951) is an early reminder that not all influences come from AmE, but that AmE itself is influenced. McDavid studied, among other things, the lexical influence of CanE on upstate-New York AmE and suspected CanE to account for the distribution of some lexical items (1951: 255).

Apart from general lexicography, onomastics has played a significant role in earlier research. Seary (1958) investigates the French influence on Newfoundland place names, which culminated in his onomastic dictionary of an area of South-Eastern Newfoundland (Seary 1971). Recently, Harry (1999) has focused on the place names of Nova Scotia, while Poteet (1999) deals with idiosyncrasies of Nova Scotian English along the south shore, to name just a few examples.[15] Rayburn (1997) is a dictionary of Ontarian place names, which also serves very well as a socio-historical research tool.

By and large these dictionaries and lexicological contributions have an inherent historical slant. Most of them illustrate regional variation in word choice and concepts, drawing from different domains, e.g. fishing, fur trade and so forth. Scargill (1977) goes so far as to write, based on lexical items, what he calls a *Short History of Canadian English*, which would have been more aptly named a short history of CanE *vocabulary*. With nine pages on grammar, it hardly deserves the title, even if we were to take Harris' (1975) statement at face value that "it is in its vocabulary that the English spoken in Canada differs from British English on the one hand and American English on the other" (DAI-A, 37 p. 3589).

Recently, new attempts have been made to revive the linguistic study of vocabulary usage in North America. Boberg (2005b) and the North American Regional Vocabulary Survey (NARVS) is one project in vocabulary studies that may revive the somewhat faded interest in geolinguistic studies in lexicology in CanE, even more so as some of the results provide answers to some of the perennial questions of CanE. What is important is that Boberg, based on a national survey of c. 50 lexical items, finds quantifiable evidence that

> Canadian dialect regions have more in common with one another than any of them has with the United States and that no region of Canada could be characterized as consistently more or less American in its lexicon than any other. (Boberg 2005b: 53)

Findings like these give further support to the proponents of a pluricentric language concept (e.g. Clyne 1992).

In general, however, research agendas since the 1970s have not focussed on lexical variables. While the focus has abated, some staples of CanE lexicological research, such as the distribution of *chesterfield* 'couch' (Chambers 1995a), *dresser* 'chest of drawers' (Berger 2005: 83-102) and *runners* 'running show, sneakers'(Wick 2004, Berger 2005: 102-119) have remained popular as a result of the DTC project (Chambers 1994).

---

[15] Cf. Clarke and MacKenzie (2001) for more sources on Newfoundland lexicology.

The field of CanE descriptive phonetics and phonology, on the other hand, has seen much progress. A field which has figured prominently in CanE research from early on, phonology is a prosperous field in CanE studies and is the next linguistic level presented here.

2.3.2 Phonetics and Phonology

Phonetics and phonology have been key areas in much of early 20th-century linguistics. While phonetic observations have been made in early linguistic studies on CanE, a lot of these observations were made outside of a theoretical framework so that the data do not allow for cross-comparisons (Chambers 1979c). Wells (1982, III: 491) summarizes the situation in CanE of the early 1980s by saying that phonology "is not discussed but taken for granted". While descriptive phonetics was included right from the outset in the research agenda of the CLA, e.g. Avis (1956a), "an urgent need for more material based on first-hand phonetic observation" (Gregg 1957a) was identified at the same time.

2.3.2.1 Canadian Raising

An impressive number of phonology papers deal with a phenomenon that has become known internationally as Canadian Raising. The phenomenon, which is not exclusive to Canada, is usually considered "the most distinctive feature of Canadian English" (Trudgill and Hannah 2002: 48), at least as far as phonology is concerned. Canadian Raising and related phenomena have vexed phoneticians and phonologists and have been a very proliferate area for the last three decades (see Chambers 2006 for a recent overview).

Some of the early papers were written from a generative point of view. The earliest one, Chambers (1973), is probably the most influential paper in Canadian English. Although the phenomenon was discovered and described much earlier (Ahrend 1934, Joos 1942), Chambers (1973) reviewed the phenomenon from a theoretical perspective and coined the name 'Canadian Raising'. Related papers include Gregg (1973a) on diphthongs in three varieties, Picard (1977) and Paradis (1980).

Characterized briefly, Canadian Raising is a phenomenon affecting the modern reflexes of the ME long vowels $\bar{\imath}$ and $\bar{u}$, which, affected by the Great Vowel Shift, are usually realized in (BrE) standard speech as the PDE diphthongs /aɪ/ and /aʊ/. Canadian Raising affects the onsets of these diphthongs before voiceless consonants, which are raised to qualities in the vicinity of [ʌɪ] and [ʌʊ] before voiceless consonants. This accounts for the diverging diphthongs in the sets *house* [hʌʊs], with a raised first part, vs. *houses* /haʊzɪz/, where the onset of the diphthong remains low, and likewise *wife* [wʌɪf] vs. *wives* [waɪvz]. As Vance (1987: 195) reports, some claims have been made that the Canada-U.S border is an isogloss for Canadian Raising in the area of Ontario, while Vance's own research and data produce evidence contradicting such statements. Vance (1987: 207) shows AmE evidence for the existence of a phonetic distinction between the two variants [aɪ] and [ʌɪ] in some dialects of Northern New York State. Allen (1989) complements Vance's picture with linguistic atlas data from the 1950s, spotting raised onsets in Minnesota and in North Dakota. Thomas' (1991) paper on the historical dimension of the phenomenon is based on unpublished linguistic atlas data and shows, while Canadian Raising occurs on both sides of the Canada-U.S. border, that the onsets are markedly more raised in the Canadian areas than in the USA (1991: 150f).

The number of studies dedicated to Canadian Raising is beyond the scope of the present study. Chambers (1979c), Chambers (1989) and Chambers (2006) provide an assessment of the state of research and the development of the phenomenon at the respective time of writing. Rosenfelder (2005: 8-29) provides a more basic introduction to the phenomenon. What is significant for the study of CanE is that Canadian Raising is considered, together with the LOT-THOUGHT merger, which results in homophones for *cot* and *caught*, as the single feature that most clearly defines Canadian English (e.g. Chambers 1991: 93).

Canadian Raising and (aw)-fronting
The raising of /aʊ/ has been identified as a sociolinguistic variable and a change in progress in CanE (Chambers 1980, Chambers and Hardwick 1986). Instead of being raised, the diphthong is more fronted. This has become known as (aw)-fronting, i.e. the fronting of the first element, first identified in Chambers (1980: 17; 1987a), as the key factor of a new change in progress first observed in North Toronto young females (p. 21-23). This phenomenon was reported in such diverse communities as Toronto, Vancouver (both in Chambers and Hardwick 1986), Victoria (Davison 1987) and Montreal (Hung 1987), with some indicators that fronting is in stable variation in Montreal (Hung 1987: 136), while Toronto, Vancouver and Victoria exhibit both age- and gender-grading (Chambers and Hardwick 1986, Davison 1987). First, findings in Chambers (1980: 25; 1981a) indicated an "Americanization of Canadian Raising" (p. 33), since fronted realizations were usually non-raised, i.e. working against Canadian Raising, and thus approximating AmE pronunciations. Hypotheses of an Americanization of the Canadian diphthong, however, turned

out to be, in hindsight, not warranted: fronting continued, while non-raising did not (Chambers 2006: 117).

Canadian Raising was tested against various independent sociolinguistic variables, as in Chambers (1981a), which found a "gross correlation" "between the linguistic change and the sociopolitical attitudes measured by the political heteronomy indices" (p. 20) for (aw)-fronting in a North Toronto sample, which "reduces the confidence in the hypothesis that the linguistic change in progress in North Toronto [(aw)-fronting] represents the Americanization of Canadian Raising" (p. 33). Chambers (1985) is a micro-study on North Toronto (aw)-fronting among younger urban Canadians in comparison to older speakers. This aspect is further pursued in Chambers (1989) for Toronto, Davison (1987) for Victoria and Chambers and Hardwick (1986) for Vancouver, which provide very profound data for a pan-Canadian sound change in urban contexts. Kinloch and Fazilah (1993) investigate the phenomenon of Canadian Raising for /aʊ/ in Fredericton, New Brunswick. Cichocki (1986: 60-76; 116-124; 1988) demonstrates the phenomenon on Toronto English data. The extent of fronting may have social implications in CanE. Esling (1991) investigates vowel and consonant quality in Vancouver along various independent variables, of which gender as well as socioeconomic class prove indicative of socially salient speech patterns. While middle-class speakers demonstrate fronting and nasality, working-class groups exhibit retraction tendencies of vowel realizations (Esling 1991: 131).

The idea of a "general Americanization of Canadian English" (Davison 1987: 120) has been in the air of much of the research and was reconfirmed in many studies across the country,[16] while other studies show the continuation or innovation of specifically CanE features.[17] Burnett (2006: 172f) suggests that as soon as "good data" is available, studies show that "the simplistic notion that Canadians are allowing themselves to be subjugated by their neighbours has fallen flat".

---

[16] E.g. Clarke (1993b) on the tendency of a highly salient variable in Newfoundland and its approximation towards a trans-continental North-American English value; Woods (1993) shows that out of eight typically Canadian phonological variables, six decrease in frequency in his apparent-time Ottawa study, while two increase, confirming a "general trend toward less distinctive Canadian speech patterns" (p. 171); Zeller (1993), on border effects along the line from Toronto to Milwaukee, shows that Canadian border dwellers tend to adopt AmE lexical and phonological variants; Stevenson (1977) finds that the Lower Mainland in B.C. shows a tendency towards some American variants of pronunciation.

[17] E.g. Esling and Warkentyne (1993) on the retraction of /æ/, which stands in opposition to the fronting of this phoneme in northern U.S. cities, or De Wolf (1993: 288), who finds "a conformity to the wider pattern of Canadian urban usage" in Vancouver pronunciation variables.

Chambers (2006) provides ample evidence from various researchers, most recently Rosenfelder (2005), and shows that Canadian Raising is not vanishing, but that it is undergoing some slight modifications. Today, it can be said that "Canadian Raising is intact and unscathed, albeit slightly altered in the phonetics of the onset vowel for the /aw/ diphthong" (Chambers 2006: 117), as a result of the fronting process. Moreover, we have reason to hypothesize that Canadian Raising is being exported to parts of the Northern United States (ibid). From today's point of view, it not only seems that the highly salient CanE feature Canadian Raising is alive and well, but that it will remain to be seen whether changes like these will reverse the prediction that CanE and AmE will merge into a "continental standard" (Chambers 1998b: 31). Canadian Raising plays a role in theoretical linguistics concerning the phonemic vs. allophonic status of the diphthongs (Idsardi 2006)

Thomas' (1991) article on the origins of Canadian Raising in Ontario is one of the few studies on pre-1900 CanE. Based on materials from linguistic atlas research in the mid-1900s, he comes to the conclusion, on the basis of quantifiable data, that Canadian Raising is a Canadian phenomenon not found to the same extent in the adjacent American regions. He dates Canadian Raising to around the year 1880, extending its documentation for two generations prior to what had been attested by synchronic real-time studies. Moreover, Thomas suggests that Canadian Raising may have been an independent Ontarian innovation (Thomas 1991: 162), challenging Trudgill's (1985: 43; 1986: 159) assessment that Canadian Raising shows signs of a mixed British Isles origin and is the result of dialect mixing.

In recent years, research in a pan-North American context has unearthed another very important change in progress, which has been labelled Canadian Shift, to which we shall turn now.

2.3.2.2 Canadian Shift

There is no doubt that the study of CanE research has come of age. The best proof is its contribution to important theoretical issues, such as the discussion revolving around Canadian Raising and vowel shifts in North America. Clarke, Elms and Youssef (1995) identify a phenomenon they call 'Canadian Shift', a phenomenon first reported in Vancouver by Esling and Warkentyne (1993) (Boberg 2005a: 134). This phenomenon involves the lowering and retracting of front vowels. This chain shift is suggested to be the result of the low-back vowel merger, with a pull chain of the low-front vowel /æ/ to a more low-central position /a/. This shift is followed by the tendency of /ɛ/ to lower towards the vacant position, which is again followed by a lowering of /ɪ/ as well

(Clarke, Elms and Youssef 1995: 212). One reason for the chain shift might be the low-back merger of the THOUGHT and LOT vowels /ɔː/ and /ɒ/ (Labov, Ash and Boberg 2006: 220; Wells 1982, I: 132, III: 493). The phenomenon is also reported for rural Ontario, where the same constraints are reported to be operational as they are in urban centres (De Decker 2002). Originally believed to not occur east of Montreal, there is some evidence for the Canadian Shift spreading into the Atlantic Provinces (Hollett 2006: 159).

The Canadian Shift serves as evidence against previous claims that CanE is part of a larger dialect area (Labov 1991), encompassing all of continental North America that is not affected by the Northern Cities Shift or the Southern Shift, i.e. Eastern New England, Western Pennsylvania, the Western United States, and the Midlands. Labov's trichotomy would put Canada in a "Third Dialect" group (Ash 2003: 60, Labov 1991: 30f). However, as Boberg summarizes, the

> operation of the Canadian Shift reinforces not only Canada's unique linguistic identity, but more generally the enduring strength of regional dialect differences in North America. (Boberg 2005a: 135)

The Canadian Shift contrasts sharply with the Northern Cities Shift in the area of the Ontario Golden Horseshoe: while from Toronto to Niagara Canadians lower their front vowels, Americans across the border in Buffalo or Detroit, in both cases just across a bridge, *raise* and/or retract their low-front vowel /a/, /ɛ/ and /ɪ/. It is therefore the best criterion for distinguishing Canadian from Northern Inland speech (Labov, Ash and Boberg 2006: 220).

Boberg (2005a) extends and slightly adapts the picture of the Canadian Shift with data from a Montreal English perspective, while in Boberg (2000), phonological differences and similarities between the Canada-U.S border are investigated, and observations on geolinguistic models of spatial feature diffusion and spread are tested. These tests are based on much more sophisticated tools than were available to Avis half a century earlier, and their results suggest that geolinguistic models of diffusion developed in Britain (Trudgill 1974) do not hold in the U.S.-Canadian context (Boberg 2000: 23f).

2.3.2.3 Regional surveys
One of the most pressing desiderata in CanE is the lack of a complete national dialect survey that is based on sociolinguistic principles. While the project initiated and reported first in Chambers (1994) is becoming one such survey, only some parts of the country are covered to date. However, much research has been organized along regional lines as a lot of the data has been collected on various, variably defined, regional varieties of CanE. This section portrays

these surveys, and while it must be added that most studies include non-phonetic variables, the large majority of variables are of a phonological nature, which warrant their treatment here.

2.3.2.3.1 Early linguistic atlas data

The earliest systematic data on regional Canadian Englishes was part of the linguistic atlas projects of the United States and Canada, which was commenced in the 1930s. Most data, however, was not published until much later. Kurath's (1972 [1939]) atlas of New England is the exception here. It includes New Brunswick data from the 1930s collected by Guy S. Lowman (Kurath 1972 [1939]: before map 1, verso). Allen's (1973-76) atlas of the Upper-Midwest includes data from five CanE speakers, one each from Estevan, Sask., Sprague, Man., Killarney, Man., Fort Francis, Ont. and Fort William, Ont. (Avis and Kinloch [1978]: 3). An analysis based on these data is Kinloch (1995). McDavid et al.'s (1980b) atlas of the middle and south Atlantic states contains Ontario samples, also collected by Guy S. Lowman from the late 1930s to around 1941, and includes fieldwork by McDavid from the 1950s. This provides mid-20th century data by CanE informants along the Ontario waterway from Cornwall to Port Colbourne, Ont. The work by McDavid was carried out for Marckwardt's linguistic atlas of the north-central states, material that has not yet been published but which was used in Thomas (1991), yielding important insights into the genesis of Canadian Raising.

Other dialect surveys include the Maritimes dialect survey, which was commenced in 1968/69. This survey comprises fieldwork from Nova Scotia, New Brunswick and Prince Edward Island (http://www.lib.unb.ca/archives/-kinloch/series4.html, 15 Aug. 2005). It seems that the survey was never finished, but that data, including the replication of New Brunswick interviews from work on the linguistic atlas project from 1931-32, is available in the Kinloch collection at the University of New Brunswick (http://www.lib.unb.-ca/archives/kinloch/series2.html, 15 Aug. 2005). Perhaps the earliest systematic fieldwork in Canada was carried out by Henry Alexander in the 1930s in Nova Scotia. This project ground to an early halt during WWII and was never revived. There do not seem to be any published accounts of this early research (cf. Avis and Kinloch [1978]: 1, McDavid 1954: 5, Wanamaker 1981: 88, Wilson 1958: ii).

Starting in the 1970s, a number of sociolinguistic or sociolinguistically inspired studies were conceived. These studies are the Survey of Vancouver English (SVEN), the Ottawa Survey, the Ottawa Valley Survey, the St. John's, Nfld., Survey, and a national usage survey (Scargill 1974), all of which were carried out roughly between 1970-1985. Both the SVEN data and the Ottawa Survey were not published until recently (Gregg 2004, Woods 1999). For the Ottawa Valley Survey, apparently, no final results were produced.

A number of surveys have a national character. The *Survey of Canadian English* (SCE), while being the "first attempt at a nation-wide English language survey" (Scargill and Warkentyne 1972: 104) and carried out swiftly, bears a number of design limitations that do not allow for examination of the data. Chambers' national *Dialect Topography Project*, commenced in the early 1990s (Chambers 1994), is still in progress but can already deliver reliable information on seven Canadian areas (cf. section 2.3.2.4).

The SCE is based on a postal questionnaire that was administered with the help of the Canadian Teachers' Association across Canada in early 1970. Unfortunately, the SCE is deemed as a survey of "questionable design" (Pringle 1983: 100), since it followed the linguistic atlas methodology employed by Wenker in 19th-century Germany, and did not attempt to include newer methodological approaches. It surveyed 104 variables (Warkentyne 1971) in the areas of pronunciation, lexis, and grammatical usage, all variables that were easily administered in a postal questionnaire. Scargill (1974), Scargill and Warkentyne (1972), and Warkentyne (1971) present findings based on the SCE, while Bähr (1981) is considered the most comprehensive analysis of the data (Görlach 2003).

Finally, some dialectological research has been carried out by students for course credit, at times producing highly significant findings. McConnell's (1978) textbook for students aims to simulate small-scale usage surveys of CanE. This Canadian tradition of student research is continued in courses on CanE throughout the country and undergraduate level in-course research from Queen's University and the University of Toronto is made accessible by the SLU.[18]

The discussion of surveys that follows does not explicitly refer to the various sections dedicated to the Canadian provinces in SCE, as they are easily found in Scargill (1974) or Bähr (1981) and are only of limited interest by today's standards. As with Canadian Raising, increasing Americanization is a recurring theme of some of the studies to be discussed. Apart from this tendency, the decline of regionalisms is also accounted for as giving way to standard CanE, which is documented in Newfoundland English (e.g. Clarke

---

[18] Cf. the *Strathy Undergraduate Working Papers on Canadian English*, published annually since 2000 by the Strathy Language Unit, http://post.queensu.ca/~strathy/ topics/other_publications.html, 15 Aug. 2005), or Rodman (1993) for a report on three student projects.

1997b). Starting in the west and moving eastwards, we begin with research in British Columbia.

2.3.2.3.2 British Columbia

British Columbia, the most westerly province, joined the Canadian confederation in 1871. The Survey of British Columbia was a postal survey of the 1960s and early 1970s. While the border regions of B.C. are reported to have been covered (Gregg 1973b: 106f), the findings were not published. Gregg's (1973b) plan and results for the Kootenay region, just west of the Rocky Mountains and the traditional dwelling area of the Kootenay First Nation, was part of the Survey. It seems that most of the material, apart from Polson (1969) and Stevenson (1977), was never made accessible. Earlier studies include Gregg (1957a, 1957b) on Vancouver English.[19] Much of the original Survey can today be found in the Archives of the University of Victoria. The most prominent study of B.C. English is the Survey of Vancouver English, to which we now shall turn.

Survey of Vancouver English

The Survey of Vancouver English, SVEN, was commenced in 1978 as a result of an earlier pilot study (1976-78), and continued into 1981, with its final report submitted to the funding body (SSHRC) in 1984 (Gregg 1992: 250, De Wolf 1995: 329). However, it was not until 2004, when Gregg's study was published by the *Strathy Language Unit* (Gregg 2004), that the comprehensive results were made available to a wider public. The SVEN database, now based at three locations (UBC, UVic and SLU), consists of detailed interviews and tape recordings of 300 informants (Gregg 1992), including a wide array of independent variables and subsections of a stratified sample of the Lower Mainland that allows the quantification of all queries. This project has had, with some "50 to 60 papers" (Gregg 1992: fn9), a remarkable turnout that is, however, mitigated by the very late publication of the main study (Gregg 2004). De Wolf (1992) is a monograph on mostly phonological (and some lexical) variation in Vancouver (based on the SVEN data) and Ottawa (based on Woods' 1999 [1979] survey). These two data sets allow the testing of predictions on homogeneity on the basis of these two major Canadian centres, thousands of kilometres apart from each other.

The SVEN studies span a wide field. De Wolf (1995) investigates the accents of teachers in Vancouver in relation to sex, age and socio-economic

---

[19] Woods' unpublished 1970 survey of the British Columbia Kootenay region is mentioned by Chambers (1979b: 171).

status, showing a general conservatism of Vancouver teachers (1995: 331). De Wolf (1988b) and De Wolf (1983) exploit phonological variables in Vancouver in comparison to Ottawa. Gregg (1992) examines lexical and grammatical variables, mostly those identified by Avis *et al.*, while the focus is clearly on phonological variables (nine out of ten phonological variables are on vowels and diphthongs). Gregg (1983) is on lexis, Gregg (1984, 1988) on phonology, lexis and grammar, while Gregg (1985) focuses exclusively on the latter. De Wolf (1990a) discusses grammatical variation in Vancouver and Ottawa English, while De Wolf and Hasebe-Ludt (1988) present methodological considerations for SVEN. Richards (1988) is also based on the SVEN data, investigating prestige and standard forms in CanE.

Taken together with studies on the methodological problems and principles of SVEN (Gregg 1985, Murdoch 1985, De Wolf 1985, Hasebe-Ludt 1985, Esling 1986 on vowel variants, Murdoch 1981, Hasebe-Ludt 1981 and De Wolf 1981), we may say that the 'gold mine' SVEN has been quite impressively exploited and that the data is gaining more and more importance as a resource for historical real-time studies.

The next variety has not been systematically studied in the framework of a large-scale study, but is so intricately bound to British Columbian history that it warrants a brief treatment here.

A Canadian pidgin: Chinook Jargon

Chinook Jargon is a now extinct contact language based on native languages, most prominently the language of the Chinook Nation, which was enriched with some English and French elements after the arrival of the European settlers. The pidgin is reported to have been spoken by around 100,000 people in the 1870s and 1880s in the Pacific Northwest. A basic overview of its features can be found in McConnell (1978: 226-237). Harris (1981, 1983) examines the lexis of Chinook Jargon, which gave British Columbians such words as *skookum* 'big', *saltchuck* 'ocean' or *tyee* '[1]chief, [2]a species of fish', which are loanwords that are still in use today (McConnell 1978: 227).[20] While some borrowings remain part of B.C. English, the 'knowledge of old-timers' (ibid.) of Chinook Jargon must be considered gone by now. Apart from these lexical vestiges, Chinook Jargon is today extinct.

---

[20] Cf. also www.thetyee.ca, the name of a recently founded weekly online newspaper.

2.3.2.3.3 The Canadian Prairie: Alberta, Saskatchewan, Manitoba

Alberta and Saskatchewan are rather young provinces in the Canadian context, both celebrating their first centennial in 2005. Alberta has been studied early on (Scargill 1954, 1955), but no surveys beyond the level of pilot studies have materialized. Edmonton has been a centre of attention for some time; Avis (1972b) is a phonological analysis of the speech of an educated Edmontonian, which is prompted by a paper by Walker (1975). Both studies are based on the speech of one, but not the same, informant that was born and educated in Edmonton. Other surveys include the description of the speech of black settlers in the Albertan Amber Valley (Emery 1971), and, more recently, of the phonology of Albertan Mormons (Meechan 1999), making these studies extraordinary in the sense that they deal with a CanE variety of Albertan minorities.

The province of Saskatchewan has largely escaped scholarly attention for some decades after initial studies by Lehn (1959) on phonology and Graham (1957) on L1 influence from German. It was not until the 1980s and 1990s when new studies appeared, which were by then conducted in a fully-fledged sociolinguistic, variationist framework. Nylvek (1993a, 1993b) is based on a postal questionnaire from 2,000 native-born, non-mobile Saskatchewanians in Saskatoon and Regina and two rural centres. Her results in phonology and vocabulary show, for the early 1990s, that Saskatchewan English showed a strong tendency to adapt to AmE pronunciation patterns (cf. also Nylvek 1992, 1984).

The next province to the west is Manitoba, which joined the Canadian confederation in 1870. While Manitoba has a considerable French and Métis (mixed French and Indian ethnicity) component among its populace and is interesting from a language contact perspective, it must be considered one of the least studied areas. Scott (1939) is an early account of the LOT-THOUGHT merger based on the speech of a Winnipeg informant. Recently, Hagiwara (2006) presented a complete, acoustic study of the Winnipeg vowel system, comparing it to other Canadian phenomena such as Canadian Raising. Apart from these studies, the Manitoban variant best known is a dialect named Bungee (or Bungi). Bungee is the name of a contact variety that came into existence in the 19th century in the Red River area. An early, but informal description is Scott and Mulligan (1951), who portray Bungee as a mix between Scottish and Orkney English with Cree with "the occasional use of a few French words and other languages" (p. 42). Blain (1989: 14) portrays Bungee as a contact language combing features of "Cree, Salteaux, Gaelic and Lowland Scots English and perhaps a bit of Norn" [i.e. a variety of Old Norse on the Orkneys]. Judging from transcriptions and examples, Bungee seems to have been code-switching based on Cree syntax. One prevalent feature of

Bungee phonology seems to have been variation between the voiceless alveolar fricative /s/ and its alveolopalatal relative /ʃ/.

Bungee is reported to have been used by "almost anyone in the Red River county", including the well educated (Blain 1989: 42), although the latter "could and did speak perfect English, or with a barely perceptible accent" (p. 42f). Stobie (1967-68) examines the history of the dialect from an external point of view. In the late 1980s, a small group of elderly speakers still used this variety (Blain 1989), which is thought to have left some traces in the phonology of English in the area (Blain 1989: 210). Recently, Gold (2007) categorized the aspectual system of Bungee based on existing material.

2.3.2.3.4 Ontario

Quite in contrast to Manitoba, neighbouring Ontario has attracted considerable attention, as is evidenced in the discussion of Canadian Raising. The most important data today come from the *Dialect Topography of the Canada* project (Chambers 1994), which includes data from the Golden Horseshoe from both 1991 and 2000, allowing for real-time comparisons, which will be treated in Section 2.3.2.4. Starting with earlier studies, one can say that systematic research on OntE began in the 1930s, with the fieldwork for the *Linguistic Atlas of the United States and Canada*. South-western Ontario was then surveyed as part of the New York State project (McDavid and McDavid 1952: fn1). McDavid and McDavid (1952) present maps in relation to the pronunciation of *h* before semivowels, which include data from the border regions in Ontario.

Ahrend's (1934) article, entitled 'Ontario speech', is one of the earliest linguistic papers on the variety. Besides giving external information, a transcription of OntE is part of the study. While remarks on pronunciation are found in the literature, they are mostly of an impressionistic character (e.g. McLay 1930). Avis' (1954, 1955, 1956a) studies from the 1950s are based on a comparison of Ontario with neighbouring AmE regional varieties, as is Allen's (1975 [1959]) study on differences along the 'middle border'.

A number of studies have been conducted from the viewpoint of experimental phonetics. Léon and Martin (1979) is an edited volume of several contributions in a more descriptive, and less theoretical, paradigm based on 17 high-school students born in Toronto and vicinity. The contributors to the volume investigate the vocalic and consonantal system of Torontonian English, as well as its prosody. These studies provide quantifiable information on vowel heights, degrees of nasality and the like. A. Thomas (1979), for instance, shows that [h] in <wh> clusters had almost completely disappeared in Toronto. Jack Chambers' studies on Toronto English are close phonetic observations that detect sound changes in their early stages (e.g. 1979c: 171-177, 1980, 1981a, 1985), which include language acquisition scenarios for phonetic variables in Canadian born teenagers whose families live abroad (Chambers 1988) as well as children of immigrants in Canada (Chambers 2002).

A certain cluster of description of First Nation English is also found in Ontario. Darnell (2005) summarizes work in Southwestern Ontario and states that, primarily from a pragmatics and discourse perspective, varieties of different First Nations English often times share enough features to set them apart from standard Canadian English. Matsuno (1999) examines the vowel system of the Ojibwa First Nation in Sault St. Marie, Ontario, and across the river in Sault St. Marie, Michigan, at the crossroads of two changes in process: the U.S. Northern Cities Shift and the Canadian Shift. She concludes that younger Ojibwa's vowel system resembles the Northern Cities Shift, while the older generation uses a system close to the Canadian Shift.

Continuing this focus on rural Ontario, Chambers (2005: 227-229) reports on vernacular features of the English of Prince Edward County, a peninsula in Lake Ontario near Kingston. Because of its relative isolation, Prince Edward County may be considered, simplifying drastically, the Canadian version of Martha's Vineyard in the linguistic context.

Ottawa and Ottawa Valley Surveys

Two important sociolinguistic surveys in Ontario are Howard B. Woods' Ottawa Survey, a study of considerable importance for CanE, and Pringle, Padolsky *et al.*'s survey of the Ottawa Valley. Both surveys, much like SVEN, were conceived in the late 1970s, but in contrast to the Vancouver survey, neither of them produced a comparable publication output.

The two surveys are quite different, however, despite their geographical proximity. While the Ottawa survey is a study of urban CanE in Ottawa, the Ottawa Valley survey deals with a linguistic enclave area along the banks of the Ottawa River, not too far from the city of Ottawa. Several contributions discuss the methodological problems of the Ottawa Valley (Pringle and Padolsky 1983, Padolsky and Pringle 1981, Pringle, Dale and Padolsky 1985), but no final report has been made available.

The Ottawa Survey (Woods 1999 [1979]) on metropolitan Ottawa investigated, above all, phonological features, besides some morphological, syntactical and vocabulary variables (pp. 184-198). Based on a questionnaire, a hundred interviews were conducted, recorded and computerized in punch card format (Woods 1999: 70f). Woods (1991: 146-8) reveals a fair amount of stylistic variation in Ottawa English phonetics, while socioeconomic variation is less pronounced in comparison to other phonological studies. This result indirectly corroborates the egalitarian pattern in Canadian society and notions of homogeneity attached to it. One of the more general results of the Ottawa Survey was, once more, that "American English is exerting an influence on Canadian English" (p. 265).

2.3.2.3.5 Quebec

Farther east, the predominantly francophone province of Quebec has also been home to a sizeable community of Anglophones since the fall of New France in 1759. Research on CanE has focussed on Montreal, the Eastern Townships (east of Montreal, bordering Ontario), and Quebec City, the areas where by far most English speakers live. Montreal, which, in much of applied linguistic research, is usually associated with the attitude studies by Lambert *et al.* (1960), has been surveyed in two monographs with respect to CanE. Hamilton (1958a) surveyed the English of Montrealers in the late 1950s, studying both lexical and phonological variables, besides some disparate items from morphology, syntax and usage (based on a four-page questionnaire). More recently, McArthur (1989) focusses largely on lexis in his Quebec study, and Fee (1991) examines French lexical loan words in English newspapers.

Recently Montreal's English-speaking ethnic minorities of the second and third generations have been investigated phonologically. Boberg's (2004a, 2005a) work in Montreal's ethnic communities prove to be a fruitful ground for systematic variation in CanE. Boberg (2004a) is one of the first contributions that specifically investigate the phonetic and phonological features of ethnic groups in Canada. His data come from Montrealers of Irish, Italian and Jewish ethnicity, which makes this study one of the first ones to explore the long-term effects of heavy immigration of non-native speakers of English to Canada.

2.3.2.3.6 Maritimes – New Brunswick, Prince Edward Island, Nova Scotia

While the Maritimes were one of the first areas surveyed, this early interest faded. Most studies are either unpublished theses or appeared in the proceedings of a regional linguistic conference that do not get the wider distribution they deserve.[21]

A number of studies deal with New Brunswick. Bateman (1975) compares the usage of New Brunswick university students to those of regional results for New Brunswick based on SCE data. In phonology, Davey (1985) compares the

---

[21] The Proceedings of the *Linguistic Association of the Atlantic Provinces*. The contents may be viewed at http://www.unb.ca/apla-alpa/papers.html, 6 Sept. 2005.

vowel system of one New Brunswick informant to Ontario and Central Prairie speech and detects some differences, while Drew (1979) surveys the phonology of St. John, N.B., based on four informants and concludes it to be similar to General Canadian, with only minor differences in the low back vowels (Lougheed 1988: 16). Holder (1979) notes a structural pronunciation feature in the Maritimes and Newfoundland in the devoicing of /z/ before stressed vowels, such as in *represent, position*, or the proper name *Zeller's*, where [s] is pronounced. House (1985) examines the situation of English in New Brunswick's Francophone areas. Kinloch (1972/73) presents some New Brunswick findings as a part of the SCE. More recently, New Brunswick English grammatical and lexical features have been studied by (Burnett 1992-2003) and border studies between New Brunswick and Maine have been carried out (Burnett 2001, 2006)

For New Brunswick and Prince Edward Island a research review is available up to the late 1970s, identifying some desiderata (Kinloch and House 1978). Prince Edward Island, the smallest province, has been surveyed on a lexical level during the preparation for the DPEIE (Pratt 1988) and Pratt and Burke (1998), as well as the phonological level (Pratt 1982). Cullen (1971) reports specifically on early dialect research on Prince Edward Island.

Nova Scotia has received some attention early in the 20th century, as it was among the first provinces to be studied, when Henry Alexander carried out his unpublished fieldwork in 1939/40. Wilson's (1958) study on Nova Scotian English, based on the counties of Lunenburg and Queens, is both an early and quite comprehensive treatment of a Nova Scotian relic variety, with some German substratum (Lunenburg was founded by German protestants). Starting with the external settlement history, the volume deals not only with lexis and phonology, but also with grammar, although he concludes that the patterns of both standard and non-standard morphological usage "is not noticeably different" in Southwest Nova Scotia, when compared to the Eastern United States (1958: 103). Wilson's "fruitless search for characteristic Lunenburg syntax" is indicative of the fading German vestiges of the area (1958: 108). This work is complemented by Wanamaker's (1965) dialectological fieldwork on Nova Scotia's King's County. Alexander's, Wilson's and Wanamaker's (DAI-A, 26, p. 2741) studies make Western Nova Scotia a linguistically better documented area than many other Canadian regions.

Falk (1985) examines the idiomatic vocabulary in Nova Scotian youth literature. Falk (1984) investigates regional differences in Nova Scotia on the basis of a mostly lexical questionnaire. In phonology, Kinloch (1999 [1980]) describes the vowel system in Halifax. More recently, Nova Scotian black settlers of long standing have become the focus of attention (e.g. Poplack and Tagliamonte 1994).

Falk and Harry (1999) is a volume on Nova Scotian English, and while the contributions contain valuable insights, their informal character and idiosyncratic descriptions somewhat mitigates the outcome of this innovative enterprise. Poff and Arnold (1999: 183), in their research of gender-based differences, report on an apparently unpublished 1972 paper by Richard Bauman that documents what they call the fading "sociability and verbal art" in the General Stores of rural Nova Scotia.

Recently, the phenomenon of yod-dropping, or deletion of the palatal glide in words such as *new, student or Tuesday*, has gained some attention as it has been studied over much of Canada. Pi (2006) uses Dialect Topography data (see section 2.3.2.4) to assess the spread of the phenomenon from Ontario to the Maritimes. Clarke (2006) uses the same variable in a comparison between Vancouver, Ottawa, St. John's, Nfld., and CBC newsreader data and interprets it as a marker of linguistic identity. This brings us to the easternmost province of Newfoundland and Labrador, a markedly different variety within CanE.

2.3.2.3.7 Newfoundland (and Labrador)

The youngest Canadian province, Newfoundland, which includes both the main island and coastal Labrador, joined the Canadian confederation in 1949, after more than four centuries as a British colony. As a linguistic enclave, Newfoundland has attracted considerable scholarly attention. Kirwin (1968) accounts for earlier studies, while Clarke and MacKenzie (2001) provide an online bibliography and a good point of departure for any study on Newfoundland English. Seary, Story and Kirwin (1968) is one of the first linguistic surveys in Newfoundland. They limit themselves to the South-Eastern Avalon Peninsula, the island's economically most important area, and identify four dialects in this confined area alone, for each of which they describe the phonological inventory (p. 57-73). For a complete dialect survey of the island, see Paddock (1982). Good and succinct overviews of the variety, which highlight important areas of research, are provided by Clarke (1997b, 2004a, 2004b), while Kirwin (1993) approaches the variety from a more historical perspective.

More detailed accounts are available for a number of areas. Paddock (1981, Paddock 1966) is an empirical study of 24 informants from Carbonear, Newfoundland, that treats morphology, phonological and lexical variables. It is conducted in a pre-Labovian paradigm, following basically the approach of the linguistic atlases (Kinloch 1983b: 186). Noseworthy (1971) deals with phonology, grammar and lexis, including place names, while Dillon's (1968) study on the south shore, i.e. the Avalon peninsula and vicinity, is largely concentrated on the external language history of the area, with some concluding remarks on phonology and lexis (p.111-126). Whalen (1978) constructs the phonetic context of *h*-dropping in the remote Northeastern Newfoundland area of New World Island. Two important studies in a sociolinguistic framework are Colbourne (1982) and Lanari (1994), which allow hypotheses about changes in progress.

St. John's Survey, Newfoundland

One of the first studies of Newfoundland English in a sociolinguistic framework was the St. John's Survey (Clarke 1985, 1991). Research based on this and other data has shown that Newfoundland dialects are moving closer towards mainland CanE, as younger speakers differ significantly from pre-1949 generations (Clarke 1991: 119, Clarke 1993b). A number of studies of St. John's English have appeared since, among the most recent ones are D'Arcy (2005b), which documents phonological innovation in St. John's English and Hollett (2006), which is an acoustic study of the Canadian Shift.

This completes the overview of regional CanE studies. Wanamaker's assessment (1981: 89) that one of the biggest problems of research on CanE is "that so little of it has been made public", still holds, as a considerable number of studies referred to could not be located in major Canadian research libraries.

One current project appears to remedy the dire lack of adequate regional data. This project, the *Dialect Topography Project of Canada*, is a sociolinguistic national survey of Canada that has been carried out since the mid-1990s. While it has not yet covered half the Canadian land mass from east to west, it has already produced a substantial body of data on CanE from several provinces and urban centres that facilitates, and in many cases enables for the first time, dialectological research. Equally important, the data are accessible online to researchers world-wide free of charge.

2.3.2.4 The Dialect Topography of Canada Project

This project, first introduced by Chambers (1994), sets out to kill two birds with one stone: to remedy the lack or proper data in Canada equivalent to linguistic atlases (called for by Gleason 1982: 29), and to provide sociolinguistic data on a given region. By using a new methodology, Dialect Topography shortens the time span between the conception of a survey and the publication of findings from several decades (as with linguistic atlases) to a few years. The first such survey, the *Dialect Topography of the Golden Horseshoe* (the region from Toronto to Niagara around the head of Lake Ontario), was carried out in the early 1990s, as a result of Zeller's (1993) pioneering study.

The Dialect Topography of Canada (DTC) has introduced a number of important methodological considerations that have altered CanE research. While the sociolinguistic studies of the 1980s on CanE usually excluded non-native-born speakers of CanE (Gregg 1992: 252; Woods 1999 [1979]: 2), dialect topography specifically opened up the field to non-native influences.

Chambers (2000: 178-181; Chambers and Heisler 1999) demonstrates this novel approach based on a regionality index, which renders dialectological research less dependent on region as its prime variable. The regionality index labels each informant on a scale from 1 to 7. Someone who is native-born to a region and has lived there all her life would be a 1, while a recent immigrant from abroad would be a 7. Other independent variables includes the standard features of age, sex, social class, education, but also language use and occupational mobility. Another distinct feature of the DTC is its innovative data sharing technology, which makes the database publicly available for online searches free of charge (http://dialect.topography.chass.utoronto.ca/, 21 Aug. 2007), and which should, it is to be hoped, set an academic precedent for the future.

Dialect topography, however, is not limited to phonological variables, as lexical, as well as grammatical variables are included. In comparison to traditional usage surveys such as the SCE, DTC avoids traditional design limitations of postal questionnaires as it solicits sociolinguistic information on the informants and thus provides a more detailed view of dialectal variation, which includes residents that are not native-born to a given region, while keeping the time spent for data collection at bay (Chambers 1994 for its principles).

So far, CanE data from seven regions has been completed and made available online. These regions are New Brunswick, Quebec City, Montreal, the Eastern Townships, the Ottawa Valley, the Golden Horseshoe and, most recently, the Greater Vancouver Regional District. To allow for cross-border studies, DTC also includes smaller samples from upstate New York and Maine. It is clear that every completed sub-survey adds a piece to the description of CanE and extends, and possibly revises, the sociolinguistic description of CanE across the nation. Berger examines and tests some principles behind DTC and concludes that DTC has helped to "enlarge the knowledge on [sic] Canadian English" (2005: 120) in important ways, including mobility by way of the regionality index.

This concludes our section on phonology and regional CanEs. Having discussed studies based largely on lexis and phonetics/phonology, we shall move to an area that has not yet attracted much attention: morphosyntax.

2.3.3 Morphology and syntax

The study of morphology[22] and syntax has not received the same amount of attention as phonology and lexis, which may be explained by the fact that there do not seem to be too many categorical differences in English grammar between standard varieties, especially in syntax, which is "probably the part of English grammar that is most homogeneous throughout the world" (Görlach 1991b: 25). The variation that does exist is usually considered part of non-standard varieties (Butters 2001: 327f). In terms of the distribution of features, however, a much larger number of grammatical patterns can be found, some of which may be distinctive features of a given variety.

2.3.3.1 Disparate morphosyntactic variables

The morphological structures studied in CanE centre on non-standard past tense and past participle formations. These forms have been surveyed in usage surveys since the 1950s and include the verbal paradigms of *to dive, to sneak, to get, to drink, to write, to see, to eat, to bath*, some of which have shown variation in other varieties of English since the LModE period (cf. Oldireva 2002, Avis 1955: 14f). New sociolinguistic methodologies, such as the Dialect Topography of Canada presented above, have made it possible to track changes in more precise ways (see Berger 2005: 68-82 for studies on *dived/dove, sneaked/snuck*; Creswell 1994, Murray 1998). Other usage studies include relatively confined changes in the verbal paradigm, which are often related to semantic changes. The form of the verb signifying the notion of borrowing money from someone, may be either *to lend* or *to loan* in CanE, with the latter one being the standard form. There is a preference reported for the 'shorter', i.e. older, forms of *spelt/spelled, dreamt/dreamed, learnt/learned, knelt/kneeled* (Brinton and Fee 2001: 432).

Moving on to syntax, we can note a more prominent part of the research tradition which has produced a number of variables. First, the choice of prepositions in (partly) lexicalized phrases has been researched in OntE and in other varieties. These expressions, such as *sick at/to/in the stomach*, have been suggested to be the result of original settlement patterns, as *sick to* is typical in

---

[22] The term morphology is confined here to inflectional morphology, as derivational morphology is considered part of lexicology (word-formation).

New England, while *sick at* is more a midland and southern AmE variant (Avis 1955; McConnell 1978: 179). Another example is the preposition used when telling the time, such as *a quarter to/till/of eleven* (Avis 1955: 16f). Since expressions like these tend to be partly lexicalised, they could also be treated as lexical items.

Second, a more central syntactic difference concerns *do*-periphrasis in questions. Avis (1955: 16) noted that *do*-use in questions such as *do you have any marmalade?* was the American interrogative form of *have you any marmalade?*, the latter of which Avis witnessed in OntE in the 1950s. Today, the change towards *do* in OntE is likely completed.

Four syntactic features have been identified in Chambers (1986) in the context of CanE to illustrate the cline of "standardness". The standardness in the four examples is the lowest in (2.1) and increases to (2.4). While the examples in (2.1), (2.2) and (2.3) are of local usage in various communities across Canada, construction (2.4) is a candidate for standard CanE grammar.

The most colloquial variable is a construction that is attributed to Irish origin (Trudgill 2004: 16). It is *after* + V + ing, meaning that the action of the V+ing has been recently completed (all examples are taken from Chambers 1986: 9f):

> (2.1)   a. He's after coming home from the mainland.
>   b. He is after telling me all about it.

Sentence (2.1a) would be equivalent to *He's just come home from the mainland*. McCafferty (2004) shows, however, that the *after* construction was also used in future constructions in Irish English until the mid-1800s. Both the perfective use described by Chambers and the futuritive use provide clues for future research, while the latter would yet need to be identified in CanE.

In second position on the informal-formal cline is a construction called positive *anymore*, where *anymore* is equivalent to 'these days, as opposed to some previous time' (Butters 2001: 331). The examples in (2.2) give some idea of its use:

> (2.2)   a. He complains a lot anymore.
>   b. Anymore, they usually call it 'cottage cheese'.
>   c. War, anymore, is genocide.

Positive *anymore* is found in a number of varieties of Midland AmE, in the Northern Irish English (Butters 2001: 331f), and has been reported in southern

Ontario and the West. Chambers (forthc.b) disagrees with theories that the phenomenon is due to a contact scenario with Scottish or Northern Irish English because of different function positive *anymore* fulfills in North America and should be considered an "independent development in New World grammar rooted in eastern Pennsylvania" (ibid.: section 6).

Third, *ever*-exclamations are constructions that occur throughout North America. (2.3) shows the use of *ever*-exclamations, which make the action habitual, i.e. occurring at all times:

> (2.3)   a. Does he ever drive fast!
> b. Is he ever stupid!

Fourth, initial *as well* is a construction that may be found in Canadian term papers, theses or newspaper editorials. Sentence-initial *as well* may be "a true Canadianism" (Chambers 1986: 10), as shown in (2.4):

> (2.4)   He told Mary to be careful. As well, she has asked all four of us to help her.

The special attention is merited here by the unusual position of *as well*, used as a 'normal' sentence adverbial such as *therefore* or *hereafter*. It has been claimed by Gleason (Chambers 1986: 10) that *as well* occurs in sentence-initial position only in CanE. In the *Strathy Corpus* of present-day CanE, *as well* occurs 11,477 times, and more than 450 times in sentence initial position (following a period). In this respect, with a frequency of almost 5%, it could be a sound part of standard CanE syntax. What is more important, however, is that the British National Corpus does not include sentence-initial *as well* at all. It seems as if, while not exclusively limited to Canada, as American examples are found, sentence-initial *as well* is part of standard CanE.

A minor issue in CanE syntax, and one of uncertain origin, is the practice of placing adjectives *after* nouns. This is a very confined practice, but is often found in attributives in names of entities and institutions in Canada (Brinton and Fee 2001: 432), such as *Revenue Canada* or *Parks Canada*, a practice that is also used beyond the official nomenclature, e.g. the governmental institution called *Ontario Parks* is found in a number of hits on non-official websites as *Parks Ontario*.

There have been very few more comprehensive studies of morphosyntax. De Wolf (1990b, 1990c) surveys variation in verb morphology and in some syntactic constructions, such as negation, variation of objective *who/m*, the use of subjunctive *was/were*, and *do*-periphrasis in interrogatives in Ottawa and Vancouver. Drawing from Wood's and Gregg's data, De Wolf attempts to establish the Canadian majority usage in both segments and correlates it with a number of independent sociolinguistic variables. Moreover, De Wolf (1992: 115-140) includes, besides a morphological discussion of verb forms, a number of syntactic variables, including tense choice and verbal agreement.

Concerning the latter variable, an interesting finding is produced by Falk (1979) for noun-verb agreement. She claims that as early as the late seventies, *they* was used as a generic pronoun, rather than *he*, in indefinite singular contexts. Scvr and Kasatkina (1977) discuss synthetic forms of the subjunctive and analytical *should* in a range of CanE written sources (Lougheed 1988: 42). One syntactic variable that was reported early in its development in CanE is the use of *cep'fer* in southern Ontario youth (Chambers 1987b). *Cep'fer* is a new complementizer, which, while deriving from *except for*, is largely synonymous with *although,* and possibly comparable to the conjunction *but* in function and use.

Recently, studies based on the Toronto English Corpus have added new findings on morphosyntax. The apparent-time developments of modals WILL, GOING TO, HAVE TO and SHALL have been traced over much of the second half of the 20th century (see Tagliamonte 2006a), allowing comparisons with other varieties of English.

One area of syntax that has been discussed more extensively with CanE data is the origin of African-American Vernacular English (AAVE) verbal agreement and third person –*s*, which opens the next section of ethnic minority varieties.

2.3.3.2 Syntax and ethnic minorities of CanE

The AAVE verbal –*s* debate is part of the discussion on the origins of African American Vernacular English (AAVE), and as such not confined to black CanE speakers. However, CanE data have been used quite extensively to investigate this phenomenon, which warrants a treatment within this survey.

The research in the Canadian context revolves around early black settlements in Nova Scotia. The history and linguistic resources of black ex-slaves in Nova Scotia are well documented (e.g. Poplack and Tagliamonte 2001: 39-87, Poplack and Tagliamonte 1994), and issues of early Nova Scotian AAVE are frequently treated in contributions on AAVE (e.g. Rickford 1999, Mufwene *et al.* 1998). A discussion on the origin of the verbal –*s* concord rules in AAVE is found in Clarke (1997a), with evidence from Newfoundland, and Poplack and Tagliamonte (2004) with non-Canadian evidence. Poplack and Tagliamonte (2000) also survey the grammaticalization of *going to* structures in their analysis of an early Nova Scotian black loyalist settlement.

Apart from this very focussed discussion in the broader context of AAVE, only a handful of studies have been carried out on the syntax of Englishes of minorities of long standing. One example is Inglis (1999), who surveys aspects of syntax in the English of L1 speakers of Mi'kmaq. At times CanE data are discussed in generative studies. Carroll (1983) explicitly focuses on infinitival complements of the *for-to* type in Ottawa Valley English from a government and binding point of view. Falk (1990, 1989) has worked on syntax, word order and morphology in Cape Breton Island, N.S.

2.3.4 Language attitudes, pragmatics and bilingualism

The linguistic levels dealt with in this section are what may be called 'soft'-levels in comparison to the traditional trinity of lexis, phonology, and grammar. As such, however, they have received only occasional attention by researchers until the 1980s. Considering the apparent shortage of morphological and syntactical studies in relation to lexis and phonology, it seems little surprising that pragmatics has not been a prime focus in CanE, with the exception of attitudinal studies that have gained some attention.

2.3.4.1 Language attitudes

The importance of attitudinal studies for CanE has been recognized relatively early, but on the whole, and partly due to the more sophisticated research methodologies that are required, attitude studies have not figured prominently in English Canada until fairly late in the 20th century.

First attempts were made in the early 1980s. Warkentyne (1983) surveys linguistic attitudes among a B.C. student population, and Owens and Baker (1984) establish an index of linguistic insecurity in Canada based on Manitoban data. Warkentyne and Brett (1981a) interpret practices of grammar teaching in schools as evidence for linguistic insecurity in Canada. The most widely available attitude studies on CanE are probably Pringle (1985) and Chambers (1991: 100-102), who write on national tendencies, followed by Halford's (1998) attitude study of the Canadian west coast. Falk (1980) takes a different methodological approach, as she studies language attitudes toward CanE dialects as expressed in three novels. Clarke has surveyed language attitudes quite extensively in some Newfoundland communities. On the basis of these data, she documents the influence of standard CanE and AmE on the Newfoundland vernacular (Clarke 1997b: 24-30, 1982, 1981). Edwards (1999) studies language attitudes towards rural dialects in Antigonish, Nova Scotia. For the use of English in areas with a French language component, Mazurkewich *et al.* (1984) replicate Lambert *et al.*'s (1960) language attitude study in Montreal on the connotations of English and French dialects in a matched-guise framework.

There have also been attempts to investigate more specialized aspects of language attitudes, such as King and Clarke's (2002) discussion of the expression *Newfie* for a person from Newfoundland. The functions and connotations of the term can be considered as an exploration of language attitudes and its effects to group labelling. Oscillating between an in-group term and a 'racial' slur, the word illustrates the sociolinguistic problem of identities and regionalisms in a larger nation, as *Newfie* is perceived as derogatory by Newfoundlanders, but is considered merely an informal, possibly also endearing term, in the rest of Canada, a usage that is sanctioned by dictionary entries (p. 551). A similar approach is applied by Davey and MacKinnon (1999) in their treatment of nicknames of people and places in Cape Breton Island, Nova Scotia.

Findings on language attitudes also surface in traditional usage surveys. Some of the results of these surveys have been incorporated into Fee and McAlpine's (2007) usage guide. Spelling, for instance, can be interpreted as an expression of linguistic preference by adhering to a more BrE or AmE standard, and thus allows inferences on language attitudes. Ireland (1979) surveys spelling practices in Canadian national newspaper for the first century after confederation, 1867-1967, and attitudinal aspects have some prominence in his discussion. Warkentyne and Brett (1981b: 306f) use the data from the SCE to show on the basis of 22 variables (phonetic, vocabulary and spelling) that, while some Canadian individuals may attest to prefer either AmE or BrE variants, the CanE mean scores for each variable differ significantly from both AmE and BrE variant distributions, which points towards an increasing awareness among CanE speakers at the time of data collection for the SCE in 1970.

Generally speaking, attitude towards one's variety has always been addressed in a more qualitative manner in studies that sought to establish whether CanE was becoming more American or not (e.g. Nylvek 1992a). Today, attitude as a quantifiable independent variable figures prominently in some sociolinguistic studies. Poplack, Walker and Malcolmson (2006) include an attitude dimension in their sociolinguistic approach on Quebec English, while Clarke (2006) interprets yod-dropping, as in news pronounced as /nu:z/ vs. /nju:z/, from the background of linguistic identity.

2.3.4.2 Pragmatics 'proper'

Pragmatics proper, i.e. the study of meaning in context beyond the levels of phonology, vocabulary and morphosyntax, has not yet produced a rich literature in relation to CanE. Until recently only a few contributions were available.

Perhaps the best known Canadian discourse feature is discourse marker *eh?* Avis (1972a) is the first study on the uses and functions of the discourse marker *eh*, /eɪ/, which focuses on literary works from Britain, the USA and Canada. Gibson (1976) is a related master's thesis on the discourse marker *eh*. And while Avis concluded that *eh* was not Canadian, as it is in the same functions in BrE and AmE sources, over the last three decades *eh* has "expanded its function from an oral discourse marker to an icon of Canadian identity" (Gold and Tremblay 2006: 262).

Recently, the discourse marker LIKE has gained scholarly attention: Tagliamonte and Hudson (1999) compare its use in British and Canadian youth as a quotative device, Tagliamonte and D'Arcy (2005, 2004) deal with various aspects of the discourse marker LIKE, which has gained considerable public awareness. D'Arcy (2005a) is a monograph on the development of LIKE that draws heavily on CanE data.

Tagliamonte (2005) identifies JUST as a discourse marker in present-day CanE. Other discourse markers include devices such as *I think, I would think* and so forth, which were surveyed as an adjunct to Woods Ottawa survey (1991: 145f), showing a positive correlation of the number of opinion openers used with socioeconomic status.

In the area of politeness studies, Hofmann (2003) is a cross-linguistic comparison of non-dominant varieties, where CanE is reported to be the "most formal and indirect" variety in request patterns (DAI-A 64/09 p. 3270), giving empirical support to stereotypes of Canadian politeness. This finding suggests that impressionistic observations on the politeness of CanE speakers may prove correct and warrant a comprehensive approach to the pragmatics of CanE, as recently explored for Irish English by Barron and Schneider (2005). Such a study would be bound to reveal a number of possibly unique CanE features in respect to distance, face, and the indirectness of speech acts.

There are few studies on disparate pragmatic phenomena. Intonation in spontaneous conversation in CanE has been surveyed in Seguinot's (1976) dissertation on the intonation patterns of bipolar questions (DAI-A 39, p. 1521f). Halford (1996) surveys features of post-segmental prosodic patterns of spoken CanE. While she provides detailed prosodic transcriptions of her spoken corpus in an impressive appendix, Halford does apparently not specify the regional provenance of her informants. A related aspect is investigated by Falk

(1999a), who writes on the pragmatics of emphasis by way of verb choice in Cape Breton English.

Haggo and Kuiper (1985) take a discourse perspective in their study of discourse structure, formulae and prosody of stock auctioneers in the Ontario Stock Yards. Arthurs (1988), Kuiper and Haggo (1985) investigate hockey terms on the one hand and hockey commentaries as an oral, highly formulaic variety on the other.

2.3.4.3 Bilingualism: code-switching

One area of increased interest in sociolinguistics in recent years concerns the change from one language to another within the same speech act. Multicultural societies such as Canada represent a treasure trove for instances of code-switching. On the whole, however, most studies that examine bilingual phenomena deal with lexical loanwords and less with code-switches proper.

French-English contact phenomena have perhaps received the bulk of attention, and contributions include Grant-Russell (1999), Chambers and Heisler (1999), Palmer and Harris (1990), McArthur (1989) and Manning and Eatock (1983). Poplack (1985) was one of the first projects that surveyed French influence on Quebec English from the theoretical perspective of code-switching (see also Poplack, Walker and Malcolmson 2006). Butler and King (1984) illustrate phenomena between French and English in bilingual communities in Newfoundland.

Virtually all studies of bilingual phenomena are based on synchronic data. Dollinger (2007a) approaches code-switching between English and German in British Columbia from a historical dimension. While there are a number of studies on code-switching, their focus is less on the fact that they may be partially based on CanE data, but rather on the corroboration of theoretical concepts underlying code-switching. Despite the plethora of immigrant languages in Canada, it seems that most studies limit themselves to the two official languages, English and French.

2.4 Summary of synchronic research on CanE

As a result of this review of almost exclusively synchronic studies of CanE, we can identify a number of achievements as well as some desiderata. A visual reference point is Chambers' research map of Canada, which shows the work in regional CanE until the late 1970s (1979c: 178f). Map (2.2) is an update of the original map, with the light grey shaded areas depicting work done until the 1970s and solid black indicating studies carried out since. Map (2.2) only pro-

vides a rough overview, however, disregarding the amount of studies carried
out and their quality. Moreover, it does not consider the national postal questionnaire of the SCE, just as was the case in the original map provided in
Chambers (1979b).

On the whole, compared to the two dominant varieties, BrE and AmE, CanE
"remains relatively understudied" (Brinton and Fee 2001: 424). It is striking in
map (2.2) that the English of the North remains virtually unstudied, except for
a brief chapter in McConnell (1978) and Inuit loanwords in CanE (Avis 1978c)
that cannot be located more precisely geographically.

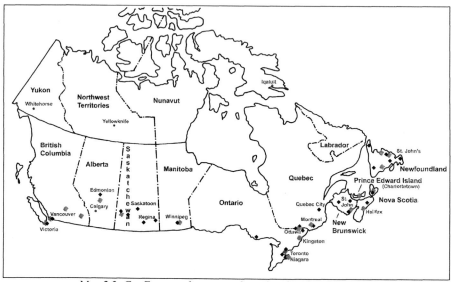

Map 2.2: CanE research areas; adapted and updated for 2005
Grey diamonds = research until 1979, black diamonds = research since 1979. Based on
Chambers (1979b: 179), map by H.A. Gleason, Jr. Reproduced by permission of the author

With the occasional exception, much research carried out since has focussed on
previously studied areas. However, some gaps could be filled. Nylvek's studies
in Saskatchewan figure very prominently in the map, which does not represent
the number or depth of studies carried out. The Golden Horseshoe area around
Toronto, for instance, is much better known linguistically than Saskatchewan,
which is not shown in the map. The gaps in CanE dialectology are slowly being filled, but it remains clear that some areas of New Brunswick and western
and northern Ontario, most of Manitoba, Saskatchewan and Alberta, the interior of British Columbia and parts of Nova Scotia, remain understudied.

Two desiderata are not shown in map (2.2). First, communities founded by L2 speakers of English, such as Ukrainian, Dutch, German, French, Polish and other groups throughout Canada, remain largely a desideratum that was first identified in Chambers (1991: 95). Work has commenced in this area, above all, in Montreal. Second, which is of imminent importance for the present study, the amount of diachronic work done on CanE is also not shown in map (2.2).

2.5 The shortage of diachronic studies on Canadian English

That CanE must be considered an understudied variety becomes especially clear for studies of diachronic development. This is the result of two tendencies in much of the existing research: (a) much of it has been conceived along syn-chronic lines, and (b) studies with a diachronic perspective have employed an apparent-time design to remedy the lack of real-time data, but do not reach beyond the early 20th century. Brinton and Fee (2001: 426) capture the present situation clearly saying that "studies of the development of linguistic features of Canadian English over time do not yet exist". Any attempt to write a history of CanE is, therefore, severely hampered, if not rendered impossible. The first (and so far only) 'history' of Canadian English (Scargill 1977), which was characterized to in chapter (1), illustrates this clearly.

Apart from a substantial body of lexicological work on earlier Canadian English, which was discussed in the context of the DCHP, the DNE and the DPEIE, language studies based on real-time data hardly exist. As a result, most statements on earlier varieties of CanE are based on the external language history and are at best extrapolated with what is known of the input varieties to CanE.

There is, however, some irony concerning the lack of diachronic research into our variety. Early on in his career, Gregg (1957a) pointed out that by the late 1950s

> [i]n the studies of Canadian English which have appeared up to date, emphasis has largely been placed been [sic!] on the social-historical factors which account for the distribution of different groups of English-speaking settlers. (Gregg 1957a: 20)

Gregg takes this as an impetus to draw attention to phonetic variables, which were to become the major research agenda in CanE, possibly at the expense of diachronic studies.

As mentioned in chapter (1), there are two textbooks that provide basic information on the genesis of CanE. McConnell's (1978) textbook has been reviewed in the scholarly literature. It must be considered an essential component in the literature on historical CanE, as it was approved by Avis (McDavid 1981: 125) and is preferred by McDavid (1980a) over Scargill's 'short history' (1977) in both approach and scholarly detail, which speaks for McConnell's text. McConnell's original subtitle, *Canadian English and how it came to be*, emphasizes the diachronic dimension it entails, a title that was later changed to *Canadian English and how it is studied*. As an introductory textbook, however, it cannot provide the depth required in specialist literature.[23] There is a need for a linguistic history of CanE that deserves its name.

2.5.1 Apparent-time and real-time studies

A number of researchers have employed apparent-time studies on CanE that have provided most of the internal language data for developmental studies of CanE. Chambers (various studies, e.g. 1995a), Poplack and Tagliamonte (in their discussions of verbal *–s* in Nova Scotian black communities, e.g. 1991; 1993) or Tagliamonte (2006a), based on the *Toronto English Corpus*, are apparent-time studies that reach back to the early 1900s. Thomas (1991) examines linguistic atlas data from the 1950s, whose oldest speakers reach back to the 1880s, and provides highly interesting insights into early Canadian Raising. It is clear, however, that most of the 19th century remains beyond the reach of apparent time studies. Kirwin (1993), in like manner as Poplack and Tagliamonte, combines the external language history with synchronic data to reconstruct earlier stages of Newfoundland vernacular English. Walker (2005) is based in part on the *African Nova Scotian English Corpus*, consisting of interviews conducted in the 1990s, which reaches back some decades.

Real-time studies of earlier CanE, which are of imminent importance to the present study, have been carried out for some varieties.[24] Most of these real-time studies are based on Maritimes and Newfoundland English and their sources are either literary depictions of rural speech in early novels or early governmental documents.

Fictional representations of folk speech in or relating to early CanE have provided some windows into the past. Avis' (1950, 1969a) work on language

---

[23] Baeyer [1977] is a textbook for advanced adult learners of English with a challenging scope for the audience and, while it is well written and researched, cannot meet scholarly standards.

[24] Lexical studies on older varieties are excluded here to the extent that they provide word histories which are not the focus of the present study, e.g. Sledd (1978), Dollinger (2006c) on *Canuck*.

in *The clock-maker*, a novel by Nova Scotian writer Thomas Chandler Haliburton (1836) characterises the literary depiction of the New-England 'Yankee
dialect' of Sam Slick, the novel's protagonist, comprising phonology (Avis
1950: 14-69), grammar and syntax (71-128), as well as vocabulary (130-190).
By implication, these data allow hypotheses on the nature of early 19th-century
Nova Scotian English.

Avis' work (1950) focuses on the speech of the fictional protagonist Sam
Slick and does not systematically consider the relationships between other literary dialect depictions in Haliburton's novel and their implications for the
representation of vernacular features in the novel (Avis 1950: 205, qtd. in Bailey 1981: 92). Bailey (1981) investigates the reliability of the literary depictions of various non-native English dialects in Sam Slick and finds it worthy
for further study. Bengtsson (1956), apparently independently of Avis (1950),
also investigates Sam Slick's language. Her approach compares an earlier
study on the *Biglow Papers* by James R. Lowell (first published 1848), who
depicts rural characters from New England, with Sam Slick's speech and de-
cides that the latter represents early New England speech "faithfully" (p. 41),
but see Schneider (2002) for a methodological framework and critique of such
approaches (cf. Wilson 1973). Bengtsson presents the phonological and grammatical information along various categories and compares Haliburton's with
Lowell's renderings. However, she does not explicitly mention the conventions
of the literary depictions of folk-speech, so her study reveals little of actual
spoken 19th-century New England, and by careful extension, Nova Scotian
speech.[25]

G. Clarke (1999) also employs fictional representations of language in his
study of attitudes towards 19th-century Black English in Nova Scotia, an approach that is also employed in Falk's (1999b) study on early Nova Scotian
English. For the Maritimes (N.S., N.B. and P.E.I.), Kinloch (1985, 1983e)
charts the external language history and illustrates some early features. Mackey
(1998: 22f) briefly reports on some attitudes of local Canadians to 19th-century
newcomers.

Early documents provide the other window into historical CanE. Scargill's
(1956) miscellany of one page provides a very short list of linguistic features
of early 18th-century documents from Nova Scotia. A more comprehensive
study is Babitch (1979), who studies the English of French-Acadians in the 17th
century. Hultin (1967) surveys historical sources for attitudes of Canadians
towards AmE, beginning in the mid-19th century. Concerning the variety of
focus in the present study, early Ontario English, and given its historical im-

---

[25] Nova Scotia was settled by English speakers in the first half of the 18th century.

portance as the nucleus of what was to become standard CanE, surprisingly few diachronic studies are available.

2.5.2 Diachronic studies on Ontario English

Textbook knowledge states that the

> English used in Canada's central provinces, Ontario and Quebec, is essential for understanding many facts about Canadian English in general, for it is from this region that western Canada drew most of its English-speaking settlers (McConnell 1978: 176).

In this context, it is striking that most of the discussion on early Ontario English relies, given its importance, on the interpretation of external history with surprisingly little real-time data at hand. Overview articles are one source of information. King (1998) reviews languages in Ontario, including a brief historical account, and a slightly more detailed account of the development of OntE is found in Chambers (1998a).

As a consequence of this lack of documentation, this section will review discussions in which forms of earlier OntE, prior to the reach of apparent-time studies (pre-1920), have played a significant role. To facilitate geographical orientation, map (2.3) shows southwestern Ontario in greater detail. The district, county and township borders of 1837, roughly around the middle of the period under investigation, are depicted to provide a point of reference for the following chapters.

Findings based on internal language data are few and far between. Chambers (1993, 1981b) work on 19th-century language attitudes, which adds a Victorian point of view on variation, is one important source on early OntE. Thomas (1991) on Canadian Raising, pre-dates the origins of Canadian Raising to around 1880 and shows that it is significantly more often used in Ontario, as opposed to neighbouring New York. With this finding, he opens up the field for a discussion of the origins of the phenomenon and addresses the question whether is it the result of a Canadian innovation (Thomas 1991) or dialect mixture (Trudgill 1985, 1986: 159, 2006).

Pringle (1981) is based on early 20th-century novels by Ontarian writer Ralph Connor, who depicts the Gaelic-influenced Glengarry dialect (cf. map 2.3 in the northeast). Spelling has received some attention. The historical part of Ireland's (1979) survey of spelling deals with pre-1846 spelling books, i.e. the year before the introduction of authorized school books from Ireland (Parvin 1965: 24). Gold (2004a) surveys early spelling practices in connection to

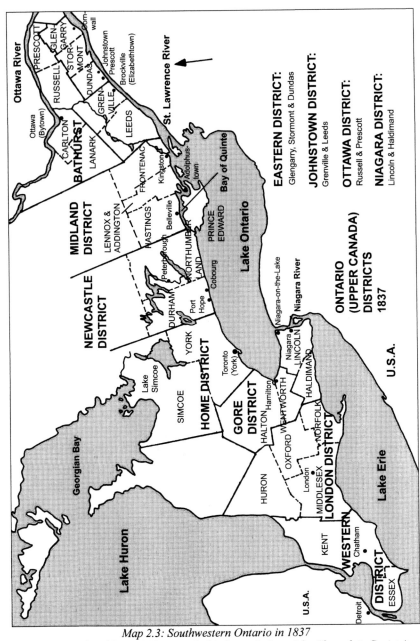

Map 2.3: Southwestern Ontario in 1837
(source Read and Stagg 1985: xvii, by kind permission of the Champlain Society)

schooling in early Ontario for the Upper Canada period, i.e. 1791-1841. She examines 15 words in four 18th- and 19th-century spelling books of British, American and Canadian provenance and finds that AmE influence on early CanE in the area of spelling has been exaggerated and that it is "unlikely that American spellers had much influence on early written Canadian English" (§ 5). Most recently, Chambers (forthc.a) traces the history of positive *anymore* in Southwestern Ontario.

The work of Pringle and Padolsky in the Ottawa Valley has produced a number of historical studies that relate directly to historical CanE linguistics, although no final results have been published from the project and surprisingly little linguistic information has been matched with the very carefully researched demographic details of the region. The exception here is Padolsky and Pringle (1984: 268-271), which correlates mostly phonological variables to the demographic input varieties in the Ottawa Valley.

Padolsky and Pringle's (1981) preliminary work on county histories in the Ottawa Valley in the form of a 'source book' contains demographic information from every township from 1851 to 1971 to a degree of detail that is of relevance to sociohistorical linguistics. It is important to stress that the historical source book was written by and for linguists and provides the kind of information that historical dialectologists would wish for.

The early history of the Valley up to 1855, which is of more importance to the present study, is documented in Reid (1990) from the social historian's point of view. Given this difference in focus, it may be worthwhile supplying specific historical background information from a linguistic perspective for other areas based on the model by Padolsky and Pringle (1981).

The contributions (foremost Bloomfield 1948 and Scargill 1956) on the origins of early CanE include a discussion of Ontario. Since their lines of thought are based on external language reasoning, they will be discussed in chapter (5) on new-dialect formation.

2.5.3 Summary

This overview has shown that the study of CanE has come of age in terms of the relevance of its synchronic findings for linguistic theory. It has become an established branch within North-American linguistics and provides important insights on several questions, such as AAVE, phonology or North American dialect areas. At the same time, there are some problems related to CanE research. First, the relative inaccessibility of earlier fieldwork is a logistic problem. Second, and more fundamentally, a focus on select geographical areas and

linguistic phenomena can be seen for much of the research history, with diachronic, real-time studies representing one of the biggest desiderata.

The present study explores diachronic CanE in a variationist, sociohistorical
research paradigm. Before introducing the linguistic data at the core this study,
the language-external history of the province before 1850 will be presented in
the next chapter.

3 ONTARIO 1776-1850:
AN EXTERNAL LANGUAGE HISTORY

The external language history of Ontario is usually included in overview articles on CanE (e.g. Chambers 1998a, 1991, Brinton and Fee 2001). However, only very few studies have attempted to link the external history with linguistic phenomena (e.g. Chambers 2004, 1993, Padolsky and Pringle 1984). On the whole, one can say that the external history of Ontario has not been an integral part of the study of CanE in general and of OntE in particular.

For the purposes of the present study, the settlement patterns of the Province of Ontario need to be reviewed more closely from its early days to the end of the period under investigation in 1850. This account will be necessarily more detailed, both in terms of the political, but, more importantly, the demographic developments, than what has been customary in the literature on CanE. This socio-political account of early Ontario will provide the basis for (a) the reasoning and choices behind the *Corpus of Early Ontario English*, the tool at the base of the empirical part of the present study (cf. chapter 4), and (b) the sociolinguistic situation of early Ontario from the viewpoint of new-dialect formation.

While the socio-political circumstances of early Ontario are interesting in their own right, the reader is asked for some patience, as the *linguistic* relevance of some of the historical details will only become fully apparent in the subsequent chapters. The present chapter provides the background for the distributions and developments of modal auxiliaries in chapters (6) to (10) and the synthesis of the arguments in chapter (11).

3.1 Preliminaries: settlement in waves

The area now referred to as Ontario had a number of different names before 1867, the most important one of them was, from 1791 to 1841, Upper Canada, (for other names, see appendix 2). While there were also areal changes during the period, these changes were never substantial and will be addressed in chapter (4), on corpus compilation, where needed.

The following account of immigration to early Ontario between 1776 and the mid-19th century takes the external accounts in the linguistic literature on CanE (e.g. Chambers 1991, 1993, 1998a, Avis 1973a) as a starting point and extends them with findings from a number of histories and case studies, as well as some (near-) contemporary documentation.[26]

Chambers (1991: 91f; 1993; 1998a) divides immigration to central Canada into four major waves from the 18th century to today. The first wave consisted of a "wholesale movement" (Chambers 1991: 91) of immigrants from the USA, from about 1776 to 1793, with a small trickle continuing until the War of 1812. The second wave was triggered off by British government legislation to allow emigration from the British Isles after the War of 1812. Its aim was to 'dilute' the American base of Upper Canada and, for some time, not only legally enabled, but actively promoted immigration from the British Isels (England, Scotland, Wales, Northern and Southern Ireland). The third wave began with the opening of the new provinces of Manitoba (1870), British Columbia (1871), and Saskatchewan and Alberta (1905). This wave, peaking around 1901-1911, was made possible by the newly-built transcontinental Canadian railroad. The third wave consisted, apart from more British settlers, of central and eastern Europeans. The fourth wave started after World War II, and is probably best described as a diverse mix of people, with some thousand-strong contingents of Italians, Ukrainians, German speakers, Greeks, Chinese, Portuguese and other immigrants who moved to Canada's urban centres. In recent years immigrants from various Asian countries have provided one of most profound influences.

For the present study of pre-Confederation Canadian English, waves I and II are of relevance and will be dealt with in this chapter.

3.2 The first wave: American immigration

While there is a wealth of work available on the settlement of Ontario, historians regret the lack of documents allowing an accurate assessment of the exact size of early American immigration (e.g. Landon 1967: 18, MacDonald 1939: 87), which was a crucial component in the formation of Ontario English. On the whole, the Ontarian records must be considered "inaccurate and confusing"

---

[26] The following studies figure most prominently: Smith (1813), Gourlay (1824), Canniff (1869), Cruikshank (1900), Cowan (1961), Landon (1967), Cowan (1978), Bothwell (1986), Ladell (1993), Akenson (1999), Wood (2000), J. Clarke (2001), Douglas (2001), Campey (2005).

(Landon 1967: 2).[27] As a result, researchers are forced to employ indirect means, such as the assessment of early travel reports and other evidence, to quantify early immigration movements with reasonable accuracy.

At the outbreak of the American Revolution in 1776, some sources speak of some 25,000 English speakers in *all* of Canada, with the overwhelming majority living in the area east of the Ontario-Quebec border. Orkin gives a tangible account of the demographic situation at the time:

> The territory south of the St. Lawrence River [in Quebec], now known as the Eastern Townships [close to Ontario's eastern border], had been reserved for future settlement and was virtually uninhabited. As for the rest of the country [west of the townships], primeval forest stretched west of Montreal and along the northern shores of Lakes Ontario and Erie, broken only by a handful of trading posts which had been established by the French at strategic points: Fort Frontenac, where Kingston now stands, Toronto (called by the French Fort Rouillé), Fort Niagara, Detroit, Michilimackinac at the entrance to Lake Michigan, Sault Ste. Marie and a fortified place where now stands Thunder Bay. [...] There were probably not more than a few hundred English-speaking persons in all of what is now Ontario. (Orkin 1970: 52f)

Before the late 1770s, Ontario was a vast bush land sprinkled only with trading posts and manned by voyageurs of French or Métis origin, who were moving goods in the economically dominant fur trade. A notable exception of a sizeable community is Detroit, founded in 1701, and perhaps some French outposts that flourished on Georgian Bay on the southeastern shores of Lake Huron (cf. map 2.3). These posts, however, were generally short-lived, except in the Detroit-Windsor area (Joy 1972: 117). Less than 1,000, probably even less than 500 English speakers were spread out over this vast area so that we cannot speak of a viable English-speaking community in Ontario. Craig (1963: 1) considers Ontario in the 1770s "nearly empty of settlers", while Avis (1973a: 46) speaks of "no settlements prior to the [American] Revolution in Ontario". This situation, a vast land with almost no English-speakers present may qualify, perhaps, as what Trudgill calls a *tabula rasa* situation, which is the precondition for his dialect-mixing theory (2004: 28). We will have to return to this question in section (5.3.1).

The first wave of immigrants was an immediate result of the American Revolution. It was comprised of people unwilling to remain in the newly proclaimed republic of America and those who were merely hoping for better

---

[27] Meseck (1995: 37) argues that the demographic input cannot be gauged as precisely as needed, for both American and British immigrants. This must be considered an exaggeration, as will be shown in the present chapter.

prospects in the British possessions. These early immigrants from the USA are usually referred to as United Empire Loyalists.[28] The loyalists came early, some even before the outbreak of the first skirmishes in the USA. For the sake of simplicity, the start date of English in Ontario will be 1776. These early settlers moved northwards to British territory either to wait for passage to Britain, or to move further west, taking advantage of government land grants. Some of the letters in period 1 of the CONTE corpus are correspondence related to early land grants (see appendix 1, chapter 4).

The first peopling of Ontario is linked with land surveys. While surveyors' accounts provide one of the best starting points for early Ontarian demographics, in some cases these documents are also interesting for linguistic purposes. The settlement of the province started in the early days of the war of independence, first in the Detroit area, then in British possession, and in the Niagara peninsula (Ladell 1993: 61). One of the first pieces of firm evidence of early land taking is a document relating to lots in the Detroit area that are reported to have been occupied in 1774. In the winter of 1777 the Butler's Rangers, an army corps, was formed at the Niagara Peninsula (more precisely on the American New York side), whose soldiers were among the earliest settlers in the area (Ladell 1993: 58).

This early immigration by what must be considered anti-republicans, was a slow trickle at best, which intensified quickly. By 1778 refugees were already becoming "a serious problem" (Ladell 1993: 61) for the colonial government, a problem that was partly remedied by temporary housing in camps. By the mid-1780s we can already speak of two classes of American immigrants: on the one hand those monarchists who would not live in the 'rebel' republic, and on the other those American immigrants who are usually euphemistically called 'late loyalists' and who came after 1783 in search of free land and British governmental assistance. By early 1783, when the colonial government received orders to prepare for the pending peace treaty between Britain and the USA, some 6,000 to 10,000 people – men, women and children – (Ladell 1993: 61, cf. Bothwell 1986: 20) were waiting to move out of temporary accommodation to their own stretches of land.

The lack of precise data results in diverging assessments here. White (1985: 56) states that by 1786 "less than 6,000 'United Empire Loyalists' had arrived in what is now Ontario". In 1784 alone, however, 6,000 Loyalists are reported to have settled in "western Quebec", which is roughly congruent with present-

---

[28] Historians distinguish between (real) United Empire Loyalists and Late Loyalists. The assumption is that the early American immigrants were loyal to the Crown, while the latter came predominantly for free land (Francis, Jones and Smith 2000: 238).

day Ontario (Bothwell 1986: 20). By 1800 historians estimate the population
between 10,000 (Bothwell 1986: 21) to "probably not more than 12,000"
(Landon 1967: 2), while historical commentators speak of up to "nearly twenty
thousand" in one case (Weld 1968 [1807], II: 63). Since the international
boundary was no significant obstacle at that time, the real Loyalists were des-
tined to become an ever-decreasing part in the demographic makeup of the
province. Already by 1796 the "proportion of Loyalists to the whole population was decreasing, ten years later they were in a minority" (Landon 1967:
14).

While settlements in the Detroit and Niagara regions existed, regular, gov-
ernmentally-conducted settlements started at Kingston and on the Upper St.
Lawrence (appendix 3.3 depicts the earliest surveyed town lots). Contemporary
documents state that 3,776 men, women and children were settled in the area
by July 1784, and by Nov. 1784, immigrants counted already 6,152 loyalists,
of which 5,576 drew full governmental rations (Ladell 1993: 72). Using
White's data on New York immigrants who settled in the Bay of Quinte area
west of Kingston (1985: 56), we would add 2,125 men and women with 1,500
children, which brings up the figure to at least 7,401 by late 1784.

These figures show that the number of immigrants must have been considerably higher than 6,000, since peak migration was to continue until 1793. An
estimate of 7,500 – 12,000 Loyalists by the end of the century (Chambers
1991: 91) seems to be a plausible figure for the upper end of the spectrum only.

With the coming of the loyalists, administrative structures had to be set up
quickly. Upper Canada was partitioned into four original districts, which were
named Luneburg, Mecklenburg, Nassau and Hesse (east to west). These four
districts were soon after rezoned and renamed, when the German names were
abandoned for the more "domestic", English, ones of Midland, Home, London
and Western in 1792 (Macdonald 1939: 86). Subsequently, they were further
divided as the need for smaller units grew with increasing immigration (cf.
appendix 3.4 for the districts of 1788 and 1802; cf. map 2.3 for the districts of
1837).

3.2.1 Demographic input until 1812

For scenarios of new dialect-formation it is not only important to establish the
demographic input in terms of the numbers of the settlers, but also their origins
as precisely as possible. Chambers (1998a: 259f) identifies, based on Canniff's
(1869) study, two settlement movements: first, people from New England, who
arrived via the Maritimes, and a second group from Pennsylvania, New Jersey,
New York and Vermont, who arrived over inland routes. This tallies well with

more recent historical studies such as Wood (2000: 25), who states that "overland settlers from western New England, up-state New York, New Jersey and Pennsylvania moved into Ontario".

This settlement from two American region also means that two dialectally distinct groups, one from the American middle colonies (New York, New Jersey, Pennsylvania) and one from western New England moved to Upper Canada. Map (3.1) shows the settlements in Ontario around the year 1800 and marks the three major points of entry into the province, which acted as gateways for the loyalists. In the following sections, the groups migrating to Ontario before 1812 will be discussed, and, wherever possible, their numbers will be provided. In section (3.3), the post-1812 immigration will be presented in detail, which will allow us to gauge the numerical influences of both migrations.

3.2.1.1 American input

As mentioned earlier, authoritative and reliable figures that separate the flows immigrants into Upper Canada by provenance are somewhat elusive for this first movement wave. Gentilcore's (1993) data of American immigration to New Brunswick, however, provides clues to the origins of the Ontarian immigrants. Gentilcore (1993: plate 7) details the following data for the year 1783:[29] of all refugees from Pennsylvania c. 80% moved to Canada, of the New England and New York refugees c. 30%, and from other mid-Atlantic colonies c. 40%. Moreover, almost 75% of the Pennsylvania immigrants were farmers. Of these immigrants, some 14,000 in total, roughly 20% (c. 2,800) did not stay in New Brunswick. Ontario was the most popular out-of-province destination for them, with one third of them moving there.

If the make-up of Gentilcore's New Brunswick sample was similar to the overall movement to Ontario, the mid-Atlantic immigrants, including New York, comprised the lion's share of immigration. This reasoning is corroborated by White (1985: 57), who assesses that "the largest number of Loyalists in Ontario were farmers from the back parts of New York and Pennsylvania".

While the majority of immigrants spoke, beyond much doubt, a mid-Atlantic dialect, early migrants tended to fall into two political categories and settled, which is of sociolinguistic importance, in different areas. Landon notes that until the 1820s, a "western tilt" in terms of political allegiances existed in the Ontarian populace (1967: 18). This imbalance was caused by the growing number of either neutral settlers or immigrants that were openly hostile to-

---

[29] Gentilcore's case study is based on c. 3,000 New Brunswick immigrants, i.e. almost a quarter of the total immigrant population of that year.

wards the Crown, such immigrants that were lured by the prospect of free land after taking the oath of allegiance to the British Crown. This development resulted in two camps of immigrants. The first one, the 'real' loyalists came during or right after the American Revolutionary War and tended to settle mostly in Kingston and east thereof on the Upper St. Lawrence (cf. appendix 3.3). The second, and potentially more opportunistic group settled on the western frontier of the 1790s, west of the head of Lake Ontario (present-day Hamilton). In the eyes of the Lieutenant-Governor of the day, Francis Gore, the region from York [Toronto] to Long Point and Lake Erie was the non-loyal, unreliable area of the province (White 1985: 70). Political allegiance as an independent variable is of linguistic interest, but needs to be relegated to future study.

The more important variable, from the view point of new-dialect formation, however, is the linguistic input. It was shown above that two major AmE dialects, mid-Atlantic and New England English, were brought by these wave I immigrants. In the following section, it will be attempted to disentangle these 'American immigrants', the loyalists and late loyalists, along their first language backgrounds. Here, one is confronted with a number of serious limitations of the data, as contemporary documents usually only record the ethnic origin, which reveals at best indirect clues to the immigrants' language competencies. However, in some cases meaningful assessments of language use in early Ontario can and will be made, which will allow us to reconstruct the linguistic characteristics of early OntE.

3.2.1.2 German speakers

Among the early settlements at Niagara and along the Upper St. Lawrence (close to the Quebec-Ontario border) were not just loyalists whose L1 was English. Contrary to Ahrend's assessment in an early linguistic article (1934: 137) that German speakers resided only from the 1830s in the province, they were, as a matter of fact, among the earliest immigrants. The early German immigration into Ontario is usually only referred to as "Loyalist" and is, probably as a consequence, often overlooked (an exception is Orkin [1970: 104f].

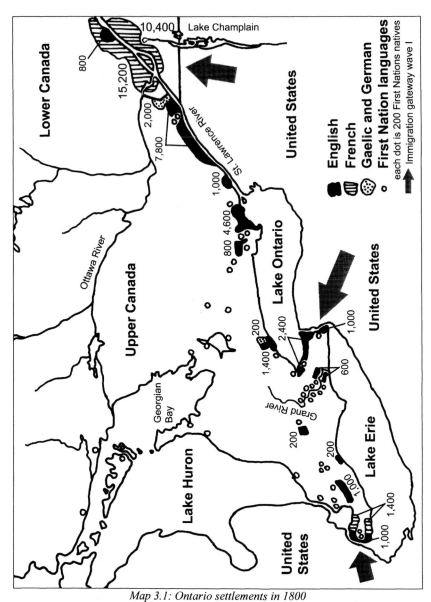

Map 3.1: Ontario settlements in 1800
(source Gentilcore 1993: plate 68, by kind permission of University of Toronto Press)
Figures for English, French, Gaelic or German speakers are provided. Each dot represents
200 First Nations language speakers in an area. Grey arrows indicate the three major points
of entry for immigrants: in the east via the Hudson River and Lake Champlain to the Upper St.
Lawrence, and the inland routes, via the Niagara Peninsula and via the Detroit region.

A considerable component of the British troops in the American Revolutionary War, which totalled around 12,000 (Bausenhart 1989: 26), were hired mercenary and auxiliary troops from various German states. These troops were German native speakers, and as many as 1,450 disbanded soldiers settled in Quebec, while around 1,000 permanently settled in Upper Canada and the Maritimes (ibid: 26). These numbers were in any case significant for early Ontario as German speakers comprised up to one sixth of the early population. Most disbanded German troops settled in the earliest surveyed townships in eastern Canada in complete militia units (cf. appendix 3.3), which helped them preserve their L1 for some time. One disbanded mercenary corps at Niagara, however, included only a contingent of German soldiers (ibid.: 19), which would have accelerated the loss of German in comparison to the St. Lawrence settlements. In map (3.1), the dotted areas on the St. Lawrence show the German (NB: and Gaelic) speakers in 1800, while at Niagara no indication for German is given.

The German identity of these immigrants tends to disappear rather quickly in early documents. Major Henry Merkley was the mayor of the loyalist settlement of Williamsburg in Dundas County (midway between Brockville and Cornwall, see map. 2.3). Merkley, however, who served in the Legislative Assembly from 1804-1808, was originally called Heinrich Märkle and is one of those loyalists that are generally assumed to have been speakers of one of the two AmE dialects imported to Ontario. A characterization of Merkley from the early 1860s, refers to his language competence and reveals a different picture. He was, we are told,

> a German of the Lutheran creed, and a blunt and honest farmer; possessed of limited education, and speaking very broken English. His homespun suit of Canadian grey, and his ofttimes ludicrous pronunciation of the English language, added to the energetic, and at times vehement style of this delivery, frequently elicited bursts of mingled laughter and applause from the House. [...] Respected by all parties as a man of sterling integrity, he was also of jovial as well as humorous disposition, and was a frequent guest at the governor's table. (Croil 1861, qtd. in Bausenhart 1989: 30)

This document provides evidence both for the loyalty of the early German immigrants, but, what is more important of their struggles with the English language: 'very broken English', the 'ofttimes ludicrous pronunciation' and the bursts of laughter of the delegates offer a vivid impression of the limited linguistic competence of one of the most respected members of society. This implies that in the early 1800s until the end of our period in 1850, a considerable substratum of German would have been present on the upper St. Lawrence, and phenomena such as bilingualism and code-switching would have occurred[30]. By the late 1820s, however, signs of language attrition are reported. In 1833, for instance, due to the problems of maintaining a German-speaking Lutheran minister, worship was conducted in English only in the Williamsburg church (Bausenhart 1989: 31f).

After the disbanded soldiers from the American Revolutionary War, Mennonites from Pennsylvania and immigrants from Germany were the next ones to arrive. The Pennsylvania Mennonites were erroneously called Pennsylvania *Dutch,* when in fact they were Pennsylvania *Deutsch,* or Pennsylvania German, who, including some Swiss German speakers, were overwhelmingly speakers of a High German dialect (Bausenhart 1989: 42) – as opposed to Plattdeutsch, which is, like Dutch, a Low German variety.

German-speaking Mennonites settled in three main areas, the Markham settlement, the Niagara settlement and the Grand River settlement. A number of families who came to Ontario directly from Germany in the 1790s founded Markham Township (cf. map 3.1, the dotted area NE of Toronto) (Bausenhart 1989: 110, fn18; Wood 2000: 47). A group of Mennonites settled in Vaughan township near Toronto. As early as 1802, "more than thirty Pennsylvania Mennonite families", German speakers, had settled along the north shore of Lake Ontario.

The Pennsylvania Dutch also came early. In 1803, Mennonites from Pennsylvania purchased a vast stretch of land in what came to be known the German Company Tract (English and McLaughlin 1983: 5), to which Richard Beasley's writings in the CONTE Corpus are linked (chapter 4). The settlement of the German Company Tract was administered independently of the colonial government: loans were paid through the communities in Pennsylvania, and the land was usually sold and allotted there. The earliest census data from 1871 shows that the birthplace of almost one third of the population of Berlin (807 people), i.e. present-day Kitchener,[31] was Germany, and that more than 2000 people, or 73%, claimed to be of German origin (English and McLaughlin 1983: 244-6). Berlin was a significant inland settlement in the early days of the 19th century, especially for a settlement some 50 km removed from an easily accessible waterway. Similar figures are available for Markham: of its 2,306 inhabitants later in the period, around 70% were Germans (Bausenhart 1989: 54).

---

[30] See Dollinger (2007a) for English-German code-switching in early BC.
[31] Berlin was renamed during WWI (in 1916).

3.2.1.3 Scottish Gaelic speakers and Scots speakers

Scottish immigrants were early settlers in Ontario. As early as 1784 Highland Scots moved to the old province of Quebec. The earliest Scots came to Ontario via the United States, where they had settled only a decade earlier from Glengarry, Scotland, in the vicinity of Inverness. They included some Germans and English (Campey 2005: 20), who settled near the Highlander settlements in Glengarry and Stormont Counties (cf. map 2.3, map 3.1 collapses German and Gaelic speakers as one group). From then on, a steady stream of highlanders came to meet their people in Upper Canada; between 1801 and 1803 alone 4,000 left the highlands (ibid: 27). At that time, the emigrants' "language of [...] ordinary local conversation" was still Gaelic (McCrum, Cran and MacNeil 1986: 141), which they took to Ontario's lakefronts and the Ottawa Valley (cf. Padolsky and Pringle's 1981 historical resource book). The earliest passenger list in Campey (2005: 183) shows 87 people from the Scottish highlands and islands off Inverness-shire. These immigrants left for Quebec in the summer of 1790 and, with the exception of two blacksmiths, all of them were tenant farmers or servants. By 1791, 1,285 Highland Scots lived in Glengarry County, which amounted to 13% of the Upper Canada population at that time (Campey 2005: 24). Map (3.1) shows both the Gaelic and the German speakers collapsed. As can be seen from the numbers for German and Gaelic immigration, the majority in the NE corner of Ontario were Gaelic speakers.

3.2.1.4 The Irish before 1815

The Irish were not as significant as the Scots in the early days. Detailed studies such as Akenson (1999) on the Irish in Ontario – based on two townships – do not even record pre-1812 Irish immigration. While some Irish were undoubtedly in the province, they did not, unlike the Scottish, cluster in groups but remained a small minority, until immigration slightly increased after the Irish Rebellion in 1798 (Dept. of State 1979: 124). Examples of early Irish immigrants are Irish Methodists moving to the Bay of Quinte region in the 1780s and in the first decade of the 1800s (see map 2.3, Canniff 1872: 285; 295). The Methodists came via the USA, as did Patrick McNiff, a prominent early Irish immigrant who lived near Saratoga, New York, before he fled as a loyalist. McNiff was licensed as a land surveyor as early as 1784 and became the seventh surveyor in Southern Ontario, of which we have evidence in the CONTE correspondence section. While Irish individuals like McNiff were more the exception than the rule before 1815, the Irish were to gain significant importance among the second wave immigrants.

3.2.1.5 French speakers

The French had been present in the Detroit region since the early 1700s. For the year 1800, Gentilcore (1993) provides an estimate of some 1,400 French speakers in Ontario, all of residing in Essex County in the extreme southwest (map. 3.1). Other permanent French settlements were in the border region with Quebec along the banks of the Ottawa River at the confluence with the St. Lawrence.

Individual small groups are reported in between the major French areas in the extreme southwest and southeast of Ontario. A rather small contingent of French loyalists are the Huguenots, French Protestants, who came with the first wave around 1783 and settled in the Detroit and Niagara regions (Reaman 1957: 59f, 204f). While some of these immigrants were descendants of French-American Huguenots from the USA and probably English monolinguals, others, as indicated by their French first names, may still have been French speakers. Some Belgian Walloons are reported to have been in the province of Quebec at the time of the American Revolution (Dept. of State 1979: 29), but they do not seem to have been of significance in Ontario.

Generally speaking, however, French had given way as a lingua franca of the fur trade since 1759, when the British acquired the territory; map (3.1) shows no indication of French-speaking areas (of more than 200 people) apart from the areas discussed above. Early CanE borrowings from French are documented from the early fur trading period (cf. Avis 1978b), e.g. *coureur de bois* 'bush ranger', first attested in 1703; *bat(t)eau, battoe* 'type of vessel', 1760; *coulee* 'dry river bed', 1802 (Avis *et al.* 1967).

3.2.1.6 Dutch settlers

The Dutch are another group of early settlers. Bloomfield (1948: 5) mentions "Dutch and Germans" among the early immigrants to Ontario. While there is always the danger of a confounding of *Dutch* with *Deutsch*, i.e. German, as much as 5 % of the early Ontario population are considered as having been not only of Dutch descent (Potter-MacKinnon 1993: 15), but also speakers of Dutch. Nelson (1961: 89) says that the loyalist Dutch moved to Ontario and tended to preserve their language, while the Dutch who remained in the USA were more likely to assimilate and lose their L1. The early Dutch input, taken together with a small number of wealthy families who came directly from Holland (Schryer 1998: 19f), must have had some presence in early Ontario, but happened to leave no "durable traces" (Schryer 1998: 20) as they adapted quickly into mainstream society.

3.2.1.7 Loyalist First Nations

Another loyalist group were the Six Nations Indians, who, siding with the Crown, relocated north of the border after the American Revolutionary War. Some 2,000 people settled along the Grand River at the time (see map 3.1; Gentilcore 1993: plate 68, Ladell 1993: 71 speaks of 1,840 in 1785). Around the Bay of Quinte, another large group of some 800 Six Nations Indians took homestead (Gentilcore 1993: plate 68), in the Detroit-Windsor area around 1,500 First Nations are documented (ibid, Wood 2000: 45), while the hinterland would have been home to some 2,000 to 3,000 natives (Wood 2000: 45), who were, however, far removed from the other settlers. Their influence on early OntE has not yet been studied, but work is currently being carried out on the lexical influence of native languages on early CanE (Derek Irwin: email, York University).

3.2.1.8 Other immigrant groups

Other early immigrants include religious congregations that tended to cluster in groups. Quakers located early near the Bay of Quinte, on Yonge Street south of Lake Simcoe, in Pickering and Uxbridge townships, in the Niagara peninsula and two groups further west (Wood 2000: 47). The Quakers were generally of English background (Reaman 1957: 23), had lived in the USA for some time and were part of the American North-West movement in the late 1780s. While the bulk of them went to the American Northwest (esp. Ohio), Quakers from New Jersey, New York (including a strong contingent of Dutch-American Quakers from Dutchess County) and Pennsylvania, came to Upper Canada (Dorland 1968: 50-61). An example is the township of Norwich, which, although first named in 1795, was known as 'Quaker Village', since Quakers from Dutchess County settled there in 1811 (Rayburn 1997: s.v. Norwich).

While the Quakers were an important group in early Canada, they are also known for their social idiosyncrasies, which become manifest linguistically most clearly in the use of obsolete pronoun forms such as *thou* and *thee* in the second singular. Willet Casey's use of *thee* as a term of address and the opening formula "Respected Friend" in a letter to an official in the CONTE Corpus make him a prime candidate as a Friend, or Quaker. The Quakers were mostly English speakers and assimilated quickly.

African-Americans are another group of early immigrants, which made early AAVE part of the early Ontarian mélange. While the migration of African Americans on a bigger scale came into full swing only after 1815, there were some black settlers in the province from the early days on, including a number of slaves of Loyalist immigrants of the 1780s. Black loyalists were, moreover, employed by the British army in the American Revolutionary War, mostly in supplementary functions such as boatmen, labourers, or buglers. However, there was one fighting corps, the Black Pioneers, which was formed entirely from free blacks (Winks 1997: 31). While some of the soldiers stayed in Upper Canada after the war, their numbers could hardly have been significant enough for the province as a whole (Wood 2000: 47) to have had a linguistic influence beyond their immediate communities.

3.2.2 The size of the population in 1812

While estimates by historians diverge to a considerable degree, a fairly reliable estimate is that by 1812 Ontario had a population of somewhere in the vicinity of 83,000 inhabitants. Landon (1967: xvi) reports of a populace of 75,000 (ibid.: 1; also Francis, Jones and Smith 2000: 243), while other figures are as high as 136,000 (Bothwell 1986: 28, likely based on Smith (1813: 63) and as low as 'just below 70,000' (Wood 2000: 24, figure). Perhaps the best source is Gourlay (1822), which is a contemporary survey based on questionnaires sent out in 1811, polling all ten Ontarian districts at the time. Gourlay calculated a total population of 83,250 (1822: 612).

What is more important for our linguistic profiling than the exact number of inhabitants is the ratio of American vs. British immigrants. This ratio is usually given as Americans outnumbering the British by 4:1 in much of the historical literature and appears to be based on Michael Smith's study (1813: 62) (Francis, Jones and Smith 2000: 228; Landon 1967: xvi)[32]. Since Smith's figures seem to be far off in terms of total population, which he lists as 136,000 at the time (1813: 63), there remains at least some doubt as to the precision of his widely accepted ratio of 4:1. A slightly more detailed assessment of the general population is offered by Akenson (1999: 111), who divides the population of Upper Canada by 1812 into ten parts, producing 6:2:2 as the ratio between non-loyalist Americans, British Isles immigrants, and American loyalists (and their respective offspring),[33] but he does not depart from the 4:1 overall figure.

Ideally, to gauge the linguistic situation of early Ontario, we would wish for exact percentages of immigrant groups in Ontario, as this would improve the possible scenarios of new-dialect formation in chapter (5). The best data come from two contemporary studies of the Ontario population that both aspire to provide exact, in one case strictly empirical, information. These are the above-

---

[32] A later edition of Smith, published in 1814, provides the ratio 3:2 for US to British immigrants (Akenson 1999: fn117).

[33] For a critical evaluation of the sources for population demographics before the outbreak of the War of 1812, see Akenson (1999: ch. 2, fn117).

mentioned studies by Gourlay (1822) and Smith (1813), which are worth looking into in greater detail.

Michael Smith's *A geographical view of the Province of Upper Canada* was researched and written in the years 1810-12, and, as a result of the outbreak of war, somewhat hastily and haphazardly published in 1813. Moreover, most of Smith's manuscripts were seized at the U.S.-Canadian border since the information had become of military significance, and, therefore, Smith was forced to rely on his memory and the few notes he had left in Buffalo (Smith 1813: 3) when writing the account. Nevertheless, Smith, himself an American, claims that he "ha[s] wrote from experimental knowledge, and not merely from what has been suggested by others" (ibid: 4f). The lack of the complete manuscript may account for the fact that Smith devotes his attention disproportionally to the London District in the west, while other districts are only dealt with in short paragraphs. At the time of Smith's writing, big parts of the Western District (cf. maps 2.3 and 3.1) were still unsettled. Smith's discussion was intended as a guide for the prospective settler and is, on the whole, less structurally balanced than the second contemporary source by Robert Gourlay.

Gourlay's book *Statistical account of Upper Canada* was published in 1822 and meets the expectations of its title. Gourlay bases much of the demographic part of his survey on tax declarations from 1811-1817, which is within a range of six years contemporary with Smith's data. Gourlay uses estimates only if questionnaire data was unavailable (1822: 269).[34] With more than 600 pages, Gourlay's report is almost six times as comprehensive as Smith's and offers superior information; it is an impressive work of early demographic scholarship.

The general picture that emerges from these two studies can be summarized as follows, while appendix (4) provides the outline results in greater detail: The Ontarian west (London and Western Districts), had been settled shortly before 1812 by American immigrants who came, like earlier first wave Americans, from New York, New Jersey and Pennsylvania. Some settlers from New England (Vermont) and other states are found there as well, with a significant Quaker component, and the French settlement in the Detroit area. In the east, the data for Perth, half way between Kingston and Ottawa, shows that the majority were Scottish immigrants. Apart from the occasional Irish migrant (cf. the mill owner in the Ottawa District in appendix 4), no pre-1815 Irish migra-

---

[34] Gourlay's results did not suit the governing class of the day, the Family Compact, as it revealed details about ineffective government, which were used to accuse colonial administrators (Douglas 2001: 109). This not only put Gourlay in jail, but resulted in his being exiled from the province in 1819 (Bothwell 1986: 41).

tion is recorded. Scottish immigrants (cf. Campey 2005: 4) were the second most prominent group in that period after AmE speakers. These two case studies provide some insights into the overall demographic pattern around 1812. The second wave of immigration, however, was to bring significant changes to this demographic mélange.

3.3 The second wave

The War of 1812, which had lasted for three summers and ended in 1814, coincided with the beginning of a new era in Europe. Napoleon was finally defeated in 1815, and Europe's massive armies were no longer needed. In Britain, thousands of disbanded soldiers were joined by early losers of the Industrial Revolution, especially from Northern England, and formed new masses of unemployed. It is this historical background that started a new wave of immigration into the New World, and Upper Canada took a very big share of it. Before the War of 1812, legislation was aimed to restrict emigration; as of 1815 the British government not only made immigration legal (Cowan 1961: 41), but in some cases actively promoted it.

Regardless of the exact ratio of American to British inhabitants in Ontario, it is clear that the Ontarian population was predominantly American by origin. Post-1812 Ontario, therefore, had two major problems in the eyes of the Crown: largely unsettled land next to a potentially aggressive neighbour and an American population, which, despite having defended the province successfully against American intruders in the war, did not earn the trust of the Crown. Immigration from Britain was seen as the solution to both of these problems. After the War of 1812, anti-American prejudice was instilled in large parts of the Ontarian population (Landon 1967: 41), and American immigration was forbidden after the war (Landon 1967: xvii), a law that was watered down over the years to come.

The wave of immigrants from many parts of the British Isles was triggered off by British legislation in 1815. The members of the British Parliament were undecided on the issue of assisted emigration. While some proposed assisted emigration as a solution for the masses of discharged soldiers, others were opposed to active assistance. As a consequence, the British government's attitude towards emigration changed a number of times, allowing for assisted emigration schemes between 1815 and 1825, but none of them for a longer period (Cowan 1978: 6). The bulk of immigrants came without official help, sometimes assisted by self-appointed 'emigration officers' such as Lord Selkirk or

Colonel Talbot (Bothwell 1986: 49), the latter one being of considerable importance for settlements along Lake Erie. The foundation of the Canada Company in 1826, promoted by the Scottish writer John Galt, coordinated land sales for British immigrants on a bigger scale (e.g. for the vast Huron Tract, some Clergy and Crown reserves, Lee 2004).

Cowan's surveys (1961, 1978) of these immigration movements have served as a source for linguistic studies on CanE (e.g. Chambers 1991, 1998a, 2004). In total, over one and a quarter million immigrants came between 1815 and 1865, averaging almost 25,000 a year. Absolute figures for immigration in those years, grouped by year and port of departure are provided in appendices (3.1) and (3.2).[35]

From a linguistic point of view, this second wave of immigrants is usually considered – with the exception of language attitudes and some prescriptive norms – as having had only little linguistic influence (Avis 1978d: 4). As Chambers (1998a: 263) puts it, "linguistically, the long-term influence of the British immigrants was highly restricted". In areas where these second-wave immigrants formed the original population of a settlement, such as the early Scots and the thousands of later Irish immigrants in Peterborough or parts of the Ottawa Valley (Chambers 1998a: 263), some of their linguistic idiosyncrasies can still be heard today (Avis 1978d: 4; Chambers 1998a: 263).

To inquire into the linguistic background of early Ontario, we again need to establish the precise origins of these immigrants. Immigration from 'the British Isles' can be a very misleading term, as it includes speakers of many regional dialects. There are a number of dialects of English that play a major role in the settlement of the New World. A distinction between southern English and non-southern English is a crucial dichotomy in LModE new-dialect formation (Trudgill 2004). Hickey (2004d) and Macafee (2004) highlight the importance of the Ulster Scots of Northern Ireland in this context. Ulster Scots is a development of 16th- and 17th-century Scots in Northern Ireland and played a significant role in the formation of American dialects on the eastern seaboard (Hickey 2004d: 87). It is, therefore, aimed in the present context to discriminate between Ulster Scots and Southern Irish wherever possible. This distinction has not traditionally been made in the study of CanE, but has great potential to help track the development of the new variety.

---

[35] Only direct immigration from Britain to Canada is recorded, and no figures for immigration via American ports and inland routes to Ontario are included.

3.3.1 Disentangling dialects: Scottish, Irish and regional English English

In this section an attempt is made to disentangle the speakers of various varieties of English that migrated to Ontario from 1815 to 1850. As immigration data do not include some demographic distinctions, such as Northern vs. Southern English immigrants or Northern Irish Ulster Scots vs. Irish Catholics, supplementary data will be used to quantify the immigration movements. Figure (3.1) shows the overall immigration to Canada from Great Britain and Ireland.

We see that immigration saw a first peak in 1819, a second in 1832, as a consequence of the cholera pandemic in Europe and, towards the end of our period, the climax in 1847, which can also be readily interpreted as a result of the Irish potato famine. While these data provide the base for further demographic reasoning, we need to keep in mind that figure (3.1) depicts the overall departures for Canada, including immigrants who moved further to another Canadian province or to the United States. Moreover, it does not show others who came via American ports and settled north of the border.

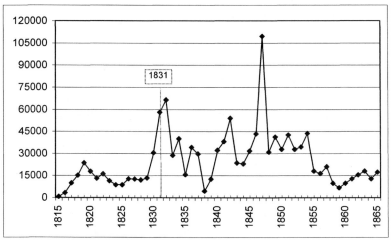

Figure 3.1: Emigration from the British Isles to Canada, 1815-1865
(British North America) (data from Cowan 1961: 288, appendix B, table I)
NB: direct sea passages only, immigrants via the USA not included

It is fairly safe to say, however, that the great majority of immigrants in figure (3.1) chose Ontario as their final destination. For the years after 1829, we have data on the composition of these immigrants, as shown in figure (3.2):

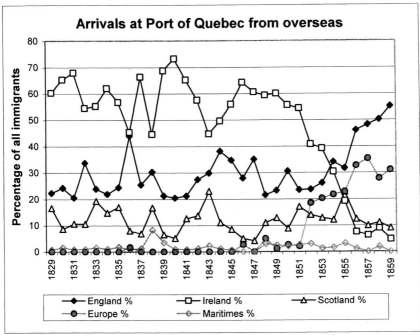

Figure 3.2: Arrivals at the Port of Quebec 1829-1859
(data from Cowan 1961: 289, table II, for absolute figures see appendix 3.2)

Figure (3.2) shows that immigration from 1829 to the early 1850s was dominated by the Irish, followed by the English and Scottish. Continental European immigration was picking up significantly only in 1852, and domestic immigration from the Canadian Maritime Provinces, with the exception of 1838, was below the five percent mark of overall immigration.

For immigration in the years prior to 1825 only hypotheses exist. While Akenson (1999: 139) believes that the Irish are likely to have also dominated early post-1815 migration to Canada, this view is implicitly challenged by Cowan (1961, 1978), who places more emphasis on the Scottish (1978: 6), followed by the English and Irish (1961: 44) in the early years.

In the following, the major immigrant groups are discussed, with a particular focus given to English-speaking immigrants. One of the most elusive groups, the 'English', who included speakers of many different regional dialects, will make a start.

3.3.1.1 English and Welsh immigration

The term 'English' may, like in other situations, lead to some confusion. In mid-19th-century Ontario, the 'English' could denote people from three places: someone from England, someone from Wales, or an English Canadian (that is a Canadian of English or Welsh origin), which is problematic for immigrant data.

Immigration from Wales is especially hard to gauge. As potential Welsh speakers subsumed under the 'English' label, they would have contributed to the language mix of early Ontario. According to a publication of the Department of the Secretary of State (1979: 230), Welsh regiments fought in the War of 1812, which, once disbanded, settled in Kingston and London. In the 1830s, some Welsh migrated to Queenston on the Niagara peninsula (ibid.: 231), but no figures are provided. For the bigger part, however, the Welsh seem to have been classified as English once in Canada. Data from British emigration ports, which is the basis for the following discussion, is expected to present a somewhat lesser problem in this respect.

As for the English, it can be considered as established that their rate of immigration did not equal that of the other groups in the early years. By 1819, the first peak year in figure (3.1), "perhaps one half of the British subjects" who sailed for North America were English (Cowan 1978: 7). While this quantitative assessment is a start, it does not specify the regional origins of the English immigrants. In Trudgill (2004), to be further discussed in chapter (5), it has been shown that discriminating between South-Eastern and Northern English speakers in the broader sense is crucial to assess the influence of dialect mixing, which requires us to break down the data further.

Cowan (1961: 291-293, table iv) provides a list of ports of departure for arrivals from 1831 to 1860 with detailed tables compiled from the London Public Records Office (Cowan 1961: 290-293). In Dollinger (2007b), these data are rearranged by the emigrants' ports of departure for 1831, a year of a particularly high intake. Table (3.1) shows that of a total of around 10,300 English emigrants that year, 66 percent of emigrants departed from northern, northwestern and Yorkshire and Lancashire ports, which indicates the emigrants' non-southern provenance. Only one third, however, left from southern, southwestern and southeastern ports in that year (no Welsh ports are reported). This leaves us with almost 6,900 'Northerners' in the broad sense, and some 3,500 'Southerners' in a likewise broad interpretation. Among these 3,500 were, due to their proximity, also Welsh who were likely subclassed as English. Completing this input scenario for 1831, we need to add some 5,300 emigrants from Scottish ports (Cowan 1961: 292) and an astounding 34,000 from Irish ports.

EXTERNAL LANGUAGE HISTORY 83

Port of departure (in British Isles)	Number of emigrants	Percent of annual total
'Northern' England (N, NW, Yorkshire & Lancashire; East Anglia)	6,900	13.9
'Southern' England (S, SW, SE)	3,500	7.0
Scotland	5,300	10.7
Ireland	34,000	68.4
SUM TOTAL	49,700	100.0

Table 3.1: Emigrants departing from the British Isles in 1831
(input data from Cowan 1961: 288, appendix B, table 1; c. one third, i.e. 20,000 immigrants are unaccounted for)

The percentages are highly interesting: while Irish immigrants account for more than two thirds of the Canadian intake, Northerners, in our definition of the term, are the second most prominent group, followed by Scottish immigrants, which leaves far behind speakers of a form of Southern English with a ratio of less than 1 in every 14 immigrants, or about 7 %. This low figure even includes some Welsh. In comparison with the overall picture of departures from Britain from 1815 to 1865 in figure (3.1), 1831 was one of the peak years for the second wave of immigration, ranking third within the time frame: this suggests, given that no significant changes of composition took place over the years, that speakers of varieties farther removed of the southern English standard immigrated to British North America at a percentage of more than 90 %. These proportions stand in a contrast to public perception of 'English' immigration. Edited volumes on mostly southern English speakers (e.g. Cameron, Haines and McDougall Maude 2000) also tend to be on the southern minority .

The question remains, however, in which respect these data from one year are representative of the entire period of second wave immigration, or at least of the pre-1850 part thereof (The issue will be addressed in section (5.3.6) on new-dialect formation). For the present it shall suffice to say that speakers of Southern British English were a small minority in early Ontario.

3.3.1.2 Scottish immigrants: Gaelic, Scots and Scottish English
Immigrants from Scotland were vital in the early years of the province and continued to have a strong impact later on. Predominantly, Scottish settlements came to be known as the 'Scotch Block' or 'Scotch Line' in this period. While case studies of single townships are manifold, an overall picture of early Scottish immigration has only been compiled recently by Campey (2005), who sur-

veyed the migration from Scotland to Ontario from 1784 to 1855 by examining an impressive number of 963 ships and 99,434 emigrants (p. 170).

Concerning the relationship of immigrants of English and Scottish provenance, Cowan (1961: 47) reports that the free emigration movement after 1815 "picked up more quickly from Scotland than from England". In some cases, immigrants departed late in the year and had to live until the next spring in temporary accommodation at Kingston, Brockville, Cornwall or other local centres (Campey 2005: 44, see map 2.3). Since the Scottish, just as the Irish, in general preferred to settle in Upper Canada (Landon 1967: 44), we may assume a rate considerably higher than 50% who established themselves in Ontario and only a minority relocating elsewhere. In the first couple of years since 1815, both Highlanders, who were usually Scottish Gaelic speakers, as well as Lowlanders, who were speakers of Scots, were equally presented, while later Lowlanders comprised the majority of Scottish input.

The Scottish immigrants were the first choice of emigrants for the British government and promoted immigration to Canada among them. Advertisements for assisted emigration to Ontario were run in newspapers across Scotland (Campey 2005: 37). Immigrants responding to these calls were first directed to eastern Ontario, where the area between Kingston and Ottawa, the Rideau River Valley, was aimed to be settled. In the assisted and governmentally funded sailings from the summer of 1815, some 350 Highlanders and an equal number of Lowlanders (Campey 2005: 36) sailed to Upper Canada. Although Gaelic-English bilingualism was common for the early period, one may equate the Highlanders with a Scottish Gaelic linguistic background and the Lowlanders with Scots linguistic roots, both of which decreased as a consequence of increasing Anglicization (McCrum, Cran and MacNeil 1986: 152). It soon turned out that Highlanders preferred to live among other Highlanders and they were persistent enough with the authorities to gain permission to relocate to Glengarry or to the Highland communities in the Maritimes (Campey 2005: 40).

As a consequence, the Rideau River Valley was settled in the 1820s by Lowland Scots. Their purpose, in the eyes of the British government, was to provide a 'second line of defence' against American invasion behind the settlements to the south. These Scottish immigrants developed the inland water way from Kingston to Ottawa (then Bytown), which would maintain inner-provincial communication lines in case the St. Lawrence waterway would be blocked by a second American invasion. Perth, the Lanark County settlements and the Rideau Canal, were also settled by Lowlanders. In 1820 and 1821 alone, 3,000 Scottish, largely Lowlanders, migrated to the Lanark area, and by

1822 "sizeable Scottish communities" had become established (Campey 2005: 52; 61). By 1817, Perth counted 1,900 inhabitants, by 1822 already 4,700, almost all of which came from Scotland. The Lowland Scottish emigration societies also left their imprint on the new colony, as the Scottish tended not only to emigrate in groups with their families, but sometimes

> [w]hole communities were effectively transplanted from the Clyde region [in western Scotland, incl. Glasgow] to Upper Canada. Sometimes the inhabitants of a street – like Abercrombie Street in Glasgow, which formed four different emigration societies, moved en bloc to the Rideau Valley Townships. (Campey 2005: 65)

Ramsey and Smith Falls (both named in 1823) on the Rideau River had become Scottish strongholds by 1832 (Campey 2005: 63), from where some letters are included in the CONTE Corpus.

Scottish immigrants were also directed to locations in the western peninsula and in central Ontario along the lakeshore between Kingston and Toronto. In the west, many Scottish settled in Talbot's settlements on the north shore of Lake Erie, a settlement that was 75 miles removed from any inhabited part (Macdonald 1939: 131). Others settled farther west along the shores of Lake St. Clair in the Detroit-Windsor region in townships started up by the Scottish before the War of 1812 (Campey 2005: 110; 120).

Map (3.2) summarizes the results of Scottish immigration by the end of our period in 1851. Light grey shaded areas show moderate concentrations of Scots, while black shadings mark Scottish strongholds. In central Ontario, Scottish centres included townships around Lake Simcoe, north of Toronto in Ontario County, York County and Victoria County, and west of Toronto in Halton County (Campey 2005: 99). While other centres such as Cobourg or Colborne also had "appreciable Scottish populations" (ibid.: 96), percentages were lower than in other places. A patchwork of settlements is found in the western part of the province. In contrast to the east and the areas west and north of Toronto, where Scots dominated "entire township blocks, the central region they were mere components of ethnically mixed population centres" (ibid.: 97), which were mostly dominated by recent Irish immigrants.

The social makeup of the Scottish immigrants was more diversified than for other groups. While the majority were also farmers, tradesmen, and labourers of very modest means (Campey 2005: 144), a sizeable minority of Scottish immigrants were what Cowan (1978: 7) calls "the very sinew of the country's [Scotland's] strength" and not members of the lower class.

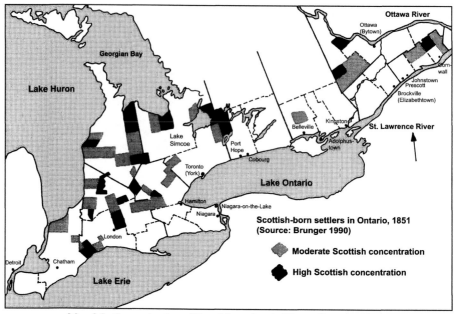

Map 3.2: Concentration of Scottish settlers in Upper Canada, 1851
(source Brunger 1990: 252).

Two remarkable cases are the townships of Fergus and Bon Accord, represented by the little black triangle just west of Hamilton in map (3.2). Both were founded by highly educated Scottish emigrants and could not only boast a decent school in the Ontarian back woods of the 1830s, but, in the case of Bon Accord, also 'excellent amusement' for both old and young, such as a library, a temperance society, a singing school and a debating society (Campey 2005: 143). These towns, which were only a few kilometres apart, developed a 'reputation for intelligence' and attracted some exceptionally well educated people (ibid.: 144). These townships must have been centres of high culture in an unexpected place.[36]

---

[36] John Langton, a diary writer in central Ontario's Newcastle District, describes another settlement from the 1830s on Sturgeon Lake, 30 km east of Lake Simcoe. Of the six settlers in the area, we learn that

> four of them have been at an University, one at the Military College at Woolwich, and the sixth, though boasting no such honours, has half a dozen silver spoons and a wife who plays the guitar. (John Langton, qtd. in Langton 1950: xi)

British emigration assistance was indirectly provided for these exceptional pockets in early Ontario. Until the Atlantic passage became cheaper as a by-product of the timber trade in the 1820s (shipping timber to Britain and emigrants on the return journey), members of the lower class were not as numerous as one would expect. In the early years, the government was funding only those who could have afforded to emigrate, by introducing compulsory deposits that "ensured that no paupers would be selected" (Campey 2005: 39). While these deposits were primarily intended to provide an incentive to stay in Ontario and not relocate elsewhere, they also prevented the poorest from leaving Britain in the first place.

It is important to put the social standing of the Scots into perspective, however. Some passenger lists include the emigrants' profession and allow insights into their social positions. The shipping lists from two early promoted immigrations from 1815 and 1820 can be divided into lower and middle class emigrants (table 3.2):

Emigrant's social class	1st assisted emigration, four vessels, Edinburgh 1815		Vessel *Commerce*, Greenock 1820	
	Numbers	%	Numbers	%
Lower class (labourer, farmer; shepherds, weavers)	124 families	81.6	40 families (159 people)	80.0 (84.6)
Middle class (skilled trades, e.g. joiner, blacksmith; and professions: e.g. doctors, teachers)	28 families	18.4	10 families (29 people)	20.0 (15.4)
	152 families[37] (757 people)	100.0	50 families (188 people)	100.0 (100.0)

Table 3.2: Two lists of Scottish emigrants under Government Regulations (raw data from Campey 2005: 191-196).

The families classified as middle class represent around 20% in both cases. Among the 1815 emigration was one surgeon and one schoolmaster; the rest of the middle class were members of the skilled trades in both the 1815 and the 1820 data. This comparison relativizes the higher status of Scottish immigrants somewhat. While, as shown above, some people with good education and of some financial means emigrated, the majority of early Scottish settlers appears to have been, nevertheless, members of the lower class who managed to provide the necessary governmental deposits.

---

[37] Includes four English families form the North and Midlands.

3.3.1.3 Irish immigration

As shown in figure (3.2), Irish immigration dominated from 1829 to 1853, never falling below the 40 percent mark. Linguistically, however, the Irish represent three distinct groups. One distinction is between Irish Gaelic speakers and Irish English speakers. Most Irish born between 1771 and 1801, those from roughly the western half of the island as well as a pocket midway between Dublin and Belfast (McCrum, Cran and MacNeil 1986: 183) were *Gaelic* speakers.

The Irish *English* speakers are comprised of speakers of two distinct varieties of English. As has been pointed out by historical linguists, e.g. Hickey (2004d), an important dichotomy in input of New World Englishes is based on Northern Irish, i.e. Ulster Scottish , and Southern Irish input. While these groups are not distinguished in census or port authority data, a feasible way to assess their ratios is to approximate the Catholic Irish with immigrants from Southern Ireland and the Protestant Irish with the Ulster Scots from the north (Akenson 1999: 349).[38] What is interesting to note is that prior to the Great Famine in the late 1840s, the Irish population of Ontario was – contrary to the popular perception of Irish immigrants as Catholics – mostly protestant (Wood 2000: 46), with a ratio of Catholic vs. Protestant Irish of 1:2 in Upper Canada before the Great Famine (Akenson 1999: 26). Akenson argues (1999: 20f) that the Protestantism of the Ontario Irish was the reason why they were largely 'absorbed' into Ontarian society, when compared to the Catholic Irish of the United States. Ontario Irish are thought to have been largely of the 'wrong sort', i.e. Protestants, who blended in more easily than Irish Catholics, who, promoting Irish nationalism, stood out in protestant New England.

As shown in figure (3.2), the Irish came prior to the infamous famines of the late 1840s. As early as 1818, some 15,000 Irish are reported to have arrived in British North America (Cowan 1978: 8), which is a surprisingly strong contingent even when compared to the 26,500 leaving Ireland in the post-famine year of 1849 (Cowan 1961: 293). Figure (3.2)[39] shows clearly that "well before the Great Famine, the Irish were the single most important group of migrants to British North America" (Akenson 1999: 15).

The question where the bulk of the Irish immigrants settled in Ontario, whether in urban or more remote rural areas, is of importance for the dialect formation process. It has been claimed in the literature on CanE that "most of

---

[38] This method is somewhat compromised by the presence of Southern Irish of Anglican background, however.

[39] Cf. also appendix (3.1), where Irish migration is quantified between 46.3 to 81.8 % of the overall migration.

these [second wave] immigrants settled, naturally, in towns and villages founded by the Loyalists" (Chambers 1998a: 262). Assessments like these seem plausible in much of the historical literature, since the Irish in the USA, one of the most prevalent groups of the Irish diaspora, clustered in major cities and towns. This preference for urban areas is often presented as a result of the outdated agricultural methods of the Irish, which made them inept for farming in the New World. It is little surprising that this argument, which has been put forward "scores, perhaps hundreds of times by serious scholars" (Akenson 1999: 346), is also found in the CanE literature. The demographic facts reviewed here, however, cast a different light on the Irish in Ontario: for the bulk of the second wave immigrants considerable evidence shows that they did *not* settle in towns, but rather in the still vacant, more remote lots and townships. Akenson state this very clearly:

> The unavoidable fact is that, even employing the broadest possible definition of "urban," one has to conclude that the overwhelming majority of Irish migrants to Ontario settled in the countryside. In 1851, 78.9 percent of the Irish-born lived in rural areas, and in 1861 the percentage was 74.4, and that by the most narrow of definitions of rural. (Akenson 1999: 36)

What are the implications of the newcomers settling in rural, less populated areas rather than in towns and villages? Based on 20th-century data, the linguistic influence of the second wave immigrants is considered as "highly restricted" (e.g. Chambers 1998a: 262). If these immigrants did not have, as a result of their rural residence, very close contacts to the settlers who had established themselves earlier in urban centres, one would expect more variation in 19th-century OntE than the few relic areas in late 20th-centry OntE would suggest. The theoretical 'choice' of land of the newcomers between 1808 and 1840 is shown in map (3.3):

The darker areas represent settlements of high density, while lighter shading depicts more loosely settled areas (white = unsettled, uncleared bush land). A comparison of the maps in (3.3) shows that plenty of land was available for settlement in the first half of the 19th century. It is in these vacant bush lands that the majority of the Irish, and likely also of other newcomers, settled.

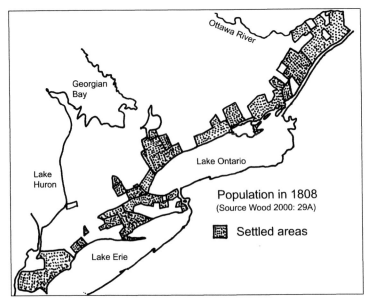

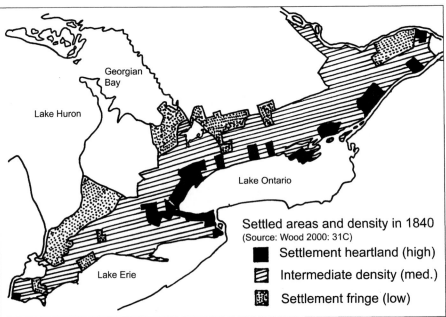

Map 3.3: Population in Ontario, 1808 (top) and 1840 (bottom)
(source: Wood 2000: 29A & 31C)

3.3.1.4 Post-1815 American immigration
In this period immigrants from the USA are almost insignificant in terms of absolute numbers and are often times ignored in some accounts. However, much of the political discussion in the post-war years was dominated by fierce arguments on the status of non-naturalized immigrants from the USA (Bothwell 1986: 39), some of whom had not only been living in the province for decades, but also fought in the Upper Canadian militia corps in the war against the American forces. The issue of naturalization would produce a rift between the political establishment, i.e. the "Family Compact", and big parts of the population that should culminate in armed rebellion in 1837/38 (ibid.: 45).

When finally, in 1820, political steps were taken to loosen the strict regulations for acquiring British citizenship (seven years of residence plus a series of oaths) more than half of the population was naturalized (Landon: 1967: 46): all people who had had ties in the province were declared British citizens. This included not only those who had received land grants, held public office, or had taken the oath of allegiance to the Crown (a requirement to settle in Ontario at some times), but also those who had merely settled in the province in or before 1820 (Landon 1967: 47). The new naturalization law, however, singled out prospective American immigrants and made them aliens.

In the 1815-1867 period there "continued to be a considerable American element" (Landon 1967: 47) relocating to Ontario. Although it could not match British immigration in numbers, these American immigrants reached socially important positions, as they tended to be, in the words of Landon (1967: xvii), of a " superior type, including as it did men with capital and technical skills, also professional men who had hitherto been few in number". While no numbers are available to quantify these immigrants, it is safe to say that post-1815 American business and American capital were instrumental in the industrialization of the province (ibid.: 51): iron mines in the east of the province, gypsum mining at the Grand River, tanneries across the province, American axe-makers, and, in the linguistic context most important, print shops (Landon 1967: 53) were founded and run by these middle class American entrepreneurs from the mid 1820s to the 1840s.

3.3.1.5 German immigration
For almost the entire period under investigation, immigrants from Germany travelled to Upper Canada. Before 1846 no direct sea route existed from Germany to Canada, when finally a route from Hamburg and Bremen to Quebec was established (Bausenhart 1989: 64). Until then, however, most German immigrants came via New York City. This explains the small intake from con-

tinental Europe in Cowan's data before the mid-1840s, and showing a marked increase by 1852 (cf. fig. 3.2).

In the 1840s immigration from Germany intensified considerably. "Most of the 36 German states were involved in dumping their surplus populations", as Bausenhart (1989: 66) puts it, and Canada was willing to take the able-bodied all too willingly. By 1848 for instance, many thousands of German immigrants had found homes in Waterloo County, with its urban centre Kitchener (ibid: 69f). European Germans not only immigrated to the German centres in Ontario, as "German settlers could be found throughout Ontario by 1850" (Dept. of State 1979: 91).

3.3.1.6 Other immigrant groups
Black immigrants increased considerably in numbers in the post-1815 period and settled mostly in western Ontario (Dept. of State 1979: 35). In the 1820s black immigrants arrived "in substantial numbers" (Winks 1997: 142); and by 1835 anti-black sentiments were being heard in the province that had officially abolished slavery just two years earlier (ibid.: 148). The first sizeable black groups in the province presumably triggered these complaints; by 1860, some 60,000 blacks had come to Ontario (Dept. of State 1979: 35).

Generally speaking, immigrants other than Scottish, Irish, English, American and German did not migrate in significant numbers before 1850. One exception before 1850 are Norwegian immigrants who settled in the Detroit-Windsor region (Magee 1985: 27). On the whole, however, Scandinavian migration was also sparse before 1850. While immigration from continental Europe is first documented in 1836 in figure (3.2), cf. also appendix (3.2), those who came most likely travelled via American ports and are harder to track.

3.3.2 Social stratification of second wave immigrants
The social stratification of these immigrants may have had, depending on one's model of dialect formation, profound influences on language. While American immigrants in this period were much less significant in numbers, they tended to be members of the middle class. We can say little that compares to the British Isles immigrants, with the notable exception of the Scottish. Their settlement strongholds were shown in map (3.2).

For the English, mostly unskilled labourers emigrated, although a very small number of "persons of some means" came as well (Cowan 1978: 7). Susanna Moody, author of *Roughing It in the Bush*, is a good example of the latter. For the Irish, however, it seems implicitly likely that the overwhelming majority were lower class immigrants.

Overall, data from Gentilcore (1993: plate 9) provides a quantitative picture of immigration at the end of our period. Of the immigrants between 1846-1851, only 6.5% had a learned trade and would make them members of the middle class, while the rest were common labourers or farm labourers, i.e. members of the lower class. Compared to the Scottish data from two early immigration schemes shown in table (3.2), where middle class immigrants comprised around 20%, we may say that the middle class component was somewhere in the range of 6.5-20%, depending on the ethnicity and time of emigration. This, on the other hand, renders immigration to Upper Canada predominantly a lower-class phenomenon, of 80% or more.

3.3.3 Benchmarks of Early Ontarian society
So far we have discussed the various dialectal and L2 input varieties to early Ontario. There are some more general aspects of early Ontarian society that need to be considered: the amount and quality of schooling that new generations received, and the demographic development over the period and the mobility of the populace. All these factors had a bearing on the formation of a new dialect.

3.3.3.1 Schools and education
It is self-evident that a pioneer society like Ontario prior to 1850 places a different emphasis on education than a more developed society. Landon (1967: xix) reports that public education "made little advance before the period of the rebellion" in 1837. Canniff (1872: 329) states that the "majority of refugees possessed but limited education", and even some half-pay officers "were void of education". While the first school already opened in 1785 in Kingston (ibid: 330), the state of education did not improve for some time to come. Some farmers considered education to have a negative effect on the work ethics of the young,[40] and, in many cases, the limited instruction people received was during an occasional evening by a family member (Canniff 1872: 329f).

Before 1846, the situation in Ontarian schools was uncoordinated. While teachers were required to be licensed as of 1799, secondary schools were established in 1807, and then only one per district. The Common School Act of 1816 finally provided for elementary schools in each district (Parvin 1965: 7).

---

[40] One of the diarists in the CONTE Corpus, Benjamin Smith, testifies to this occasional school attendance, as he reports of children going to school a mere four days in the winter of 1812/13.

In the early days, curricula were synonymous with textbooks, and 1821 data from Toronto shows that Lindley Murray's grammar and related books "occur on almost every list" of textbooks used, acting as some form of standard. While Murray's books were allegedly chosen from their British provenance – they were published in Britain (Parvin 1965: 15) – Murray was an American expatriate from Pennsylvania who lived in England and produced highly successful textbooks for the English market. In some way, Murray may have brought about or reinforced American forms through the backdoor.

Despite some early school legislation, common standards in Ontario's schools were introduced only in the 1840s by the reforms of Egerton Ryerson. The Common School Act of 1846 provided the foundation for the Provincial Board of Education, which introduced "the use of uniform and approved text books in the schools" (Parvin 1965: 21). An attempt by the board to ban "foreign Books, in the English branches of education" throughout Upper Canada (ibid.) was a move against American textbooks. In 1846, the provincial school board adopted the Irish National School Books for classroom use and settled the issue in favour of British texts for some time.

Comprehensive studies of the language textbooks of early Ontario do not seem to exist, and opinions diverge widely. Some (near-) contemporary sources state that Noah Webster's spelling book, the "blue-backed speller", first published in 1783, was "almost universally used" in Ontario schools (Chambers 1998a: 263), while others admit only limited influence of Webster's spelling book (Canniff 1872: 333f). In more recent studies, however, Ireland (1979: 89) concludes the historical part of his spelling survey that "Webster's speller was not nearly as popular in Canada as were [Mavor's, Cobb's and Carpenter's]", which were works of British origin. Ireland's finding is corroborated by Gold (2004a: §4), who studied four 19th-century spelling books, and concludes that "American spellers [...] would have had little influence on Canadian English in the years of Upper Canada, 1791-1841". All this points towards the use of British books and a less prominent role for Webster's works than is often assumed.

Contemporary anecdotal evidence certainly confirms the results of these two studies. Canniff (1872: 331f), for instance, reports of four schools in Adolphustown around 1800, all of which used Dilworth's (British) spelling book, which was, next to the New Testament, "the only book[] possessed by these academies". Histories like the monumental 28-volume *Documentary history of education in Canada* (Hodgins 1895), and an analysis of some sample data would probably reveal a strong regional component of spelling conventions in early Ontario, as a result of local school traditions and textbook use.[41]

Apart from textbooks, the origins of the teachers in early Ontario schools would also have been important. Gold (2004a: §4) concludes that the influence of American teachers in the province seems to have been exaggerated for political reasons, while Parvin (1965: 13), like Avis (1978a: 41), acknowledges the dominance of American English teachers in Ontarian elementary schools of the day, an opinion which is expressed in Thomas Rolph's statement from the 1830s:

> It is really melancholy to traverse the Province, and go into many of the Common Schools; you find a herd of children instructed by some anti-British adventurer, instilling into the young and tender mind sentiments hostile to the Parent State [...], false accounts of the late war in which Britain was engaged with the United States; geography setting forth New York, Philadelphia, Boston, etc., as the largest and finest cities in the world; historical reading books, describing the American population as the most free and enlightened under heaven; [...] and *American spelling-books, dictionaries, and grammar, teaching them an anti-British dialect, and idiom*; although living in a Province, and being subjects, of the British Crown (Hodgkins 1895, III: 3 fn; emphasis added).

The term "Anti-British adventurer" is a pejorative label for American teachers, who were significant in numbers. Apart from American teachers, the Scots, some of whom being highly educated, would have been apt for teaching. While Bloomfield (1948: 6) specifically refers to Scottish school teachers in early Canada, Irish also are mentioned (Canniff 1872: 331). Wilson (1978: 12) draws a more detailed picture and concludes that Americans taught in rural areas, moving from place to place, since the grammar schools of the towns were staffed by "Anglican clergymen from Great Britain" from 1807 on. This regulation would give the Scottish and Irish school masters mentioned above an invaluable advantage for those positions.

The picture that emerges from this brief review of studies on education in early Ontario is one that does not allow for quick generalizations apart from the prevailing heterogeneity of norms, standards and textbooks, but it also suggests that some of the perceived wisdom, such as the dominance of Webster's books or the ubiquity of American teachers, are in need of revision.

---

[41] Ireland's (1979) study of 20th-century CanE in the printing press shows marked regional variation between the provinces in this respect.

3.3.3.2 Demographic developments and mobility before the railway

The coming of the railway coincides with the middle of the 19th century in Ontario and provides a useful cut-off point for historical studies. Wood (2000: 41) identifies three key aspects of pre-1850 Ontarian society: first, Ontario was a pioneer society and "perhaps the most fundamental element was the ratio of women to men". In the first few years it was not unusual for "twice as many men as women" living in towns and settlements and "unmarried women were rare" (ibid). This ratio naturally changed over time, after 20 years it was less than 120 men to 100 women. Second, a "central feature was the rapid increase in the number of children" in the first half of the century (Wood 2000: 41f), which resulted in nearly 60% of the population born in Ontario by the end of 1851. This would imply that the demographic basis for a potentially quick formation of a new dialect would have been laid by a large percentage of children in the crucial periods (see chapter 5). While third, and possibly most importantly, "a readiness to move was a dominant characteristic of the population throughout the period under study [pre-1850]" (Wood 2000: 42).

This means that even before the coming of the railway, and despite very inconvenient modes of transportation into the hinterland, Ontarians were moving about. For the later period, the canonical example of Wilson Benson, a Northern Irish from Ulster who moved to Ontario in 1841, illustrates this well (Norris 1989: 179f, Wood 2000: 42). From 1841 to 1850, Benson moved seven times, and two more times after that, within the province. First, he moved along the north shore of Lake Ontario by boat, and later into different areas in the hinterland NW of Toronto, where he died in 1911. The mobility of the pre-1850 Ontarian, however, tended to remain 'within the district' at first, before moving farther afield.

The quality and speed of overland travel is a factor that gave the boat a considerable advantage in early Canada, as overland travel was no quick, let alone convenient form of transport. Around 1800, at the when Jane Austen wrote her novels, we know that carriages could travel 50 miles on "a good road" in "little more" than half a day (*Pride and Prejudice*, chapter 32). To travel from Toronto to the US border by land, one would therefore have spent close to two days on the road for the 180 miles around the lake head; from London to Niagara, one would have travelled three days on this 300-mile track. These estimates show that overland travel times were considerable, and are likely to have been longer, especially from more interior locations such as London where the tracks were not as developed as the English roads Jane Austen referred to. This means that the absence of a waterway to a given destination was a serious problem hindering the mobility of the populace.

3.4 Summary

As was shown, the immigration to Ontario in the period 1776-1850 was ethnically and linguistically diverse. The Loyalist input of the first wave, consisted not only of American English speakers and speakers of native languages, but to a considerable degree of German and Dutch speakers, and to some extent of French speakers. American immigrants came predominantly from New York, New Jersey, Pennsylvania, i.e. the middle states, with some from New England (Vermont) and a smaller contingent from the Atlantic seaboard (e.g. Delaware and further south). The immigration of Quakers and other groups continued until and during the War of 1812, which brought more American English and German speakers. The Scottish, a good part of them Gaelic speakers, were a considerable element of early Ontario society, while only few Irish are recorded before 1812. As immigration increased, First Nations groups became numerically less and less important. Finally, British colonial personnel complete this pre-1812 head count.

After 1815, the proportions of immigration changed considerably. Scottish immigration continued and while Scottish Gaelic speakers came early, Lowland Scots speakers soon outnumbered them. Irish immigration, which consisted of Irish Gaelic, Ulster Scots as well as Southern Irish English speakers, became numerically very important. English immigration, however, was to pick up more slowly after 1815. Hickey (2004b: 10) expresses the mismatch in Irish English and English English speakers very clearly saying that English was more often exported "out of Ireland rather than directly from England". It is important to note that among the Irish, however, the Ulster-Scots and Irish Protestants were in the majority. For the English, the non-Southerners comprised the overwhelming majority. German immigration continued on a proportionally smaller share than before the War of 1812, but picked up again in the late 1840s. Little is known of the Dutch, who seem to have integrated more quickly than the German speakers. Finally, black immigrants were to become a sizeable minority from the 1820s onwards.

In short, early Ontario was a linguistically rather diverse area and the present study can only attempt a first global look at the situation, without a close-up of these disparate communities. Specialized data from these immigrant groups, e.g. the German or Dutch on the upper St. Lawrence, for instance, would provide highly interesting cases for studies of language contact in early Canada. Additionally, one might attempt to establish the origins of the first wave American English speakers by their time spent in the Thirteen American Colonies rather than their place of departure when hostilities broke out. It may well be, it is even likely, that some of the immigrants which we characterized as mid-Atlantic or New England English speakers had moved to America only after their formative years which would have resulted in (near-) British English dialects being present in wave I. However, this very focussed scope will have to be left to future enquiry.

With this demographic background knowledge we can now move on to discuss the electronic corpus at the heart of the empirical sections of this study: the *Corpus of Early Ontario English, pre-Confederation section.*

4 THE CORPUS OF EARLY ONTARIO ENGLISH, PRE-CONFEDERATION SECTION (CONTE-pC)

As we have seen in the concluding sections of chapter (2), the study of histori-cal stages of Canadian English, and Ontario English in particular, has been based on the external language history. Other studies rely on present-day evi-dence as a base for educated hypotheses on the characteristics of early CanE. The lack of a proper research tool in form of a machine-readable corpus of early CanE has hitherto made diachronic studies rare exceptions.

The *Corpus of Early Ontario English* (CONTE) is designed specifically to help alleviate this lack. While CONTE, commenced in December 2002 at the University of Vienna, is still work-in-progress (see Dollinger 2006a [2003]), the pre-Confederation section of the corpus was completed in June 2004 and provides the data for the present study.[42] The pre-Confederation section, CONTE-pC, covers the years 1776 to 1849. The lines of reasoning behind the various choices made during the design and compilation processes are made explicit in this chapter. While the design principles apply to the complete cor-pus, examples for illustrations will be taken from CONTE-pC unless stated otherwise.

CONTE aims to facilitate studies of early OntE and beyond and is expected to be useful in a number of different ways, as it should

- allow linguists to define Ontario English from a historical perspective and answer questions pertaining to it.
- help researchers to gain insights into the spread of English, especially in North America.
- help to delimit Canadian English, differentiating it from American Eng-lish and British English on the one hand, and differentiating Ontario Eng-lish from other varieties of Canadian English, on the other.
- help to clarify Canadian French influence, which has been considered as being fairly small when compared to English influence on Canadian French (Orkin 1970: 50); French influence, on the other hand, is seen to

---

[42] As soon as resources allow, the pre-Confederation section will be made available via the Oxford Text Archive.

have been considerable in the early years of the province (Avis 1978b: 158).

- allow researchers to gain further insights into the development of fairly recent national varieties of (Late Modern) English.

CONTE is comprised of texts from three genres: diary entries, letters and local newspapers. These three genres represent some of the best data in the Canadian context. Given the fact that no drama or fiction is available in the early CanE periods and that parliamentary debates were written in reported style[43], diaries and letters may be used as indirect indicators of more informal language use.

4.1 External periodization

The periodization of CONTE is the result of historical events that shaped Ontario as well as some more pragmatic considerations. The starting point represents the peopling of Upper Canada with the arrival of the first sizeable group of Anglophones after 1776 (cf. section 3.2).

In light of three possible start dates for the temporal dividing line (1776, 1783 and 1791)[44] the internationally more significant date of 1776 was chosen. As was shown in chapter (3), the outbreak of the American Revolutionary War is causally linked to the first sizeable English immigration into inland Canada, i.e. Ontario (cf. Canniff 1971: 52-63). The start date, beginning with the "5th of July" 1776, so to speak, is therefore the theoretical chronological beginning. However, documents from the early years prior to 1780 may be almost elusive to be obtained.

At the other end of the temporal spectrum, the recent subperiodization of Late Modern English (cf. Görlach 1999: 5, Bailey 1996), which includes the 19th century as a whole, provides a conventional cut-off date. For the present study, a cut-off point in the middle of the 19th century proved to be a good choice for various reasons for CONTE-pC, since a number of language-external events took place around 1850 that irreversibly changed Ontarian society. These events are related to technological innovations, demographic and

---

[43] Cf. an excerpt from the *Journal of the House of Assembly of Upper Canada*, e.g. 1st Session of the 12th Provincial Parliament in the 5th year of William IV, March 19, 1835, p. 262:

"On motion of Mr. Lount, seconded by Mr. Always, Ordered, That the petition of Ronald Fraser and others, be referred to the Committee of Supply. On motion of Mr. Duncombe, of Oxford, seconded by Mr. Rymal, Ordererd, That [...]".

[44] 1783 marks the year of the Peace of Paris, which settled the American Revolution; 1791 marks the foundation of Upper Canada in the western part of the old Province of Quebec.

political developments. The most important technological advances at the time include:

- the advent of the railway and with it easy inland transportation (Wood 2000: passim, Sautter 2000: 54f). Increased mobility is a major linguistic factor that needs to be considered.
- the introduction of telegraphic communication in the late 1840s in Ontario (Wood 2000: xxi), which changed the ways of communication.

Changes in the demographic make-up of the province, include developments pertaining to:

- Population demographics: Ontario counted almost one million settlers by 1850 (Wood 2000: 24, Sautter 2000: 53). The present study thus investigates a sample of the speech ways of the 'first million +' of inhabitants that reached Ontario.
- Scottish immigrants: the early Scottish immigration is fully included in CONTE-pC (cf. map 3.2).
- Irish immigration: streams of Irish newcomers reached a first heyday at the end of the period (Cowan 1961: 292).
- Public education: public education "made little advance before the Rebellion [of 1837]" (Landon 1967: xix) and "no real advance came until 1844" (ibid.), when Egerton Ryerson became superintendent of Upper Canada.

The final reason for a cut-off date in mid-century is of a political nature: while the province was booming by the 1840s, no voices were yet heard for more independence from Britain, which should eventually result in Confederation in 1867 and the beginning of Canada as a country (e.g. Sautter 2000: 57). Therefore, the present study is concerned with Canadian English from an exclusively colonial point of view. For the Ontarian situation, therefore, an end-date of 1849 seems to be a good choice for CONTE-pC.

In corpus linguistics, however, yet another element needs to be borne in mind which seems to make an end-date in the middle of the century a logical choice. Methodological considerations from the viewpoint of a variationist, cross-dialectal study of English requires accurate data that are comparable to the CONTE-pC design. By choosing the cut-off for 1849, it will be possible to compare the CONTE data sets with already existing corpora of the period, such as ARCHER-1, *A Representative Corpus of Historical English Registers*

(Biber, Finegan, Atkinson 1994; Biber and Finegan 1995), Version 1. ARCHER-1 includes both comparable British English (BrE) texts in 50-year intervals (e.g. 1750-1799, 1800-1849, 1850-1899), and more limited American English data.

4.2 Internal period division

In the pre-Confederation Canadian context prior to 1850 one is dealing with an overall time span of not even 75 years, and, therefore, with less time overall than most periods alone in the *Helsinki Corpus* (Kytö 1996). By transferring the principles applied in Labov's work on changes in PDE, one can derive a principle for how to structure the corpus internally. According to Labov, one should divide a corpus in a

> [...] span of time large enough to allow for significant changes but small
> enough to rule out the possibility of reversals or retrograde movements:
> we might say from a minimum of a half generation to a maximum of two.
> (Labov 1981: 177)

Adhering to this principle, the 25-year periods in CONTE fall into Labov's window and are roughly equivalent to the smallest periods to detect real, non-lexical, language change (cf. also Mair 2002: 106, or Nevalainen & Raumolin-Brunberg 2003: 11, who list 20-year periods as a minimum figure). CONTE-pC is divided into three periods:

- period 1: 1776-1799
- period 2: 1800-1824
- period 3: 1825-1849

This design should enable the researcher to trace language change in real-time at a temporal scale between generations. For comparison, the British English *Corpus of Nineteenth-Century English* (Kytö, Rudanko and Smitterberg 2000) use with 33-year period divisions a similar figure. In order to compare the CONTE-pC data with other corpora, one may combine two periods of CONTE-pC to match them with one period in ARCHER-1. The *Corpus of Late Eighteenth-Century English Prose* (CL18P), compiled by David Denison *et al.*, is another LModE corpus that will serve as a basis for comparison for the letter section in period 1, 1776-1799. The precise approach will be laid out in the methodology section in (6.3). Before discussing the corpus design and genres in more detail, one first needs to address an even more fundamental issue: What is an Ontarian text?

4.3 What makes a text Ontarian?

There are several ways to define the 'Ontarianness', or 'Canadianness', of a text. The *Dictionary of Canadianisms on Historical Principles* (Avis *et al.* 1967) confined its source materials to those

> written by persons native to or resident in Canada who were writing about Canadian life or by travellers and other visitors to Canada who were commenting on their experiences in this country. (Avis 1967: xiii)

Although this definition was an "important innovation" (Story, Kirwin and Widdowson 1982: xi) in lexicography, it would be too broad for the present study. Pringle (1986: 26f) discusses similar problems in relation to present-day English and the definition of a standard for Canadian English. Without offering solutions, he surmises that, although the exclusion of people not Canadian-born would be desirable for reasons he does not specify, he admits their importance for their historical input (p. 27). On the other hand, in section (2.3.2.4) it was shown that Chambers (2000, 1994) explicitly *includes* immigrants in his dialect topography studies, and approaches their language behaviours with the help of a regionality index (RI). While the latter approach is desirable, the extralinguistic situation of the data does not yet allow the calculation of an RI for the informants in CanE at this point. Definition of Canadianness, or, in our context, Ontarianness, therefore, cannot be taken over unchanged from the RI. Two issues seem prevalent here: first, geographical provenance and life centres of a speaker and second, questions of allegiance to the British Crown.

4.3.1 Geographical considerations

Geographical boundaries serve as a first step. By employing a geographical definition, we may delimit potential candidates to texts written in what is now Ontario. However, this criterion is straightforward only after 1796. From 1776 to 1791, which is part of the earliest period of CONTE, the geographical area known as Ontario was part of the colony of Quebec, then encompassing the vast area from the lower St. Lawrence to Hudson's Bay. In 1791 the colony was divided into Upper Canada (today's Ontario) and Lower Canada (today's Quebec). For this earliest period, not many texts from what is now Ontario exist, but early documents pertaining to Ontario were written in what is now

Quebec. Until 1791, we may include this material, as Ontario was only in the making: settlers had just started to move there from the USA and the east, and the administrative bodies of the colony were still located in Montreal or Quebec City. Moreover, the military forts around Lake Ontario and farther west, Oswego, Niagara, Detroit and Michilimackinac, also remained in British possession (Bothwell 1986: 26) and only fell into American hands in 1796.

In sum, CONTE includes texts written in what is present-day Ontario – except for the period between 1776-1796, when Ontarian English texts from the neighbouring areas outlined above are also included.

4.3.2 Questions of allegiance

We next need to address the question of *whose* texts may be considered Ontarian. Two major waves of immigration are of importance here: the original immigration from the United States after 1776 and immigration from the British Isles, including Wales, Scotland, Ireland and Northern Ireland, after 1815. Even from the beginning of settlement, however, the population was a heterogeneous assemblage of groups from different homelands. As shown in the previous chapter, apart from English speakers, Scots, Gaelic, German, Dutch, African-Americans, French and various Amerindian groups round off the linguistic mélange.

The question then remains, what people of what backgrounds should be considered in a corpus of early Ontario English. While obvious cases such as the British traveller in the Canadas who published a travel report would have to be ruled out, the definition of 'Ontarianness' should not be taken too narrowly to account for the complex Canadian extralinguistic history. A case study of three diarists should serve to demonstrate the principles applied here.

4.3.2.1 Anne Powell

Anne Powell kept a diary of a journey from Montreal to Detroit in 1789, which was one of the forts still in British possession. Her brother William Dummer Powell, who became district judge of Hesse District (see appendix 3.3), is the key to our knowledge about Anne (cf. *Dictionary of Canadian biography*, VI: 605-613). Anne was born into a well-to-do, upper-middle class merchant family in Boston. In 1789, she travelled with her brother as part of his entourage from Montreal to Detroit, where he was to establish a new district court. Her travel diary survives in a reliable typescript.

The Dummer-Powell family was divided both denominationally as well as politically. Since Anne was living in Canada after 1776, she belonged to the family's loyalist wing. The last detail we know about her is that she died tragically in Montreal in 1792 while giving birth.

Can Anne's text be considered Ontarian? Anne was an upper middle-class woman, probably born around or before 1770 and partly raised in Boston. She most likely lived on Canadian territory since the American Revolution. As a first-generation immigrant, she was one of the United Empire Loyalists, who are considered the historical core of English-speaking Canadians. Because Anne belonged to the group of people that constituted the first major wave of English-speaking immigrants to Ontario, she has a strong claim to being an early Ontarian.

Anne's case is fairly clear-cut, since we know quite a lot about her. For the next two cases, standard reference works may not help us much to unearth biographical information.

4.3.2.2 Eleanora Hallen

Eleanora Hallen was only a little girl when she wrote her diary, a version of which has been published for use in schools[45] (cf. Parry 1994, from which biographical details are taken). The diary tells the story of a girl who started to write in 1835 at the age of 12. She was born in Rushock, near Birmingham, England, and started writing in England. She emigrated to Ontario with her parents shortly after, where members of the family still live. Eleanora continued to write in her new country. Is her writing Ontarian? And if so, did it start being Canadian with the first line she wrote on Canadian soil?

In Eleanora's case, again it would be hard to exclude her writing from the corpus after her arrival in Ontario. Clearly, she did not change her writing abruptly, but like Anne, Eleanora represents a typical group of migrants who formed early Ontario, since she came with the second big wave of immigrants, this time comprised of people from the British Isles. Since this second wave of immigration was just as typical of early Ontario as the first, we need to include Eleanora's writing from the time of her arrival in Ontario. Although Eleanora did not change her writing drastically with her passage, she was no less Ontarian nor less Canadian than Anne.

4.3.2.3 Ely Playter

That early Ontarian ways of life are very diverse is further illustrated by Ely Playter. Ely kept a diary from 1801 to 1853 with entries pertaining to almost every day for over 50 years, documenting his daily activities. He was a home-

---

[45] Eleanora's diary is not available in CONTE-pC, as no reliable version could be obtained in time.

steader who lived in Ontario for many decades. During the War of 1812, he fought the American invaders and recruited new soldiers for the king to defend the homeland.[46] This, however, did not keep him from retiring to upstate New York in the years around 1840.

Although we do not know where or when he was born and raised, we have a 53-year-long documentation of his life, almost all of which he spent in Ontario, for some time he even served in the Ontario Assembly. To exclude Ely would be unthinkable: he was Canadian, although he did not seem to bear too much of a grudge against the former enemy. In some respect, we might say that Ely is perhaps typically Ontarian, exemplifying a somewhat pragmatic and ambivalent attitude to all things American.

4.3.3 Summary

It is clear that this approach of text selection has its limitations, but there is no better means at our disposal. If we look at Canadian society, where migration has been the norm rather than the exception since the early days, nothing different than personal histories with periods of relocating and moving on could be expected. Original plans to include only those people born and raised in what is now Ontario were dropped for many reasons, but above all, because this criterion would have failed to take the external history of Ontarian English into account.

In summary, we arrive at a guiding principle to define a pool of potential texts for compilation, i.e. the corpus 'universe'. Provided that the texts were composed within the time frame from 1776-1849, all texts that were written by people who had been living, or were to live, for a considerable time in what is now Ontario *and* who composed the texts while living there, are potential candidates (including Ontario-related texts from Quebec until 1791 and from the British forts until 1796). We therefore include people who may have seen themselves as "British," "British North-American," "American", "Canadian" or otherwise.[47]

---

[46] The biographical information on Ely Playter is taken from file F556, accompanying the microfilm of his diary at the Archives of Ontario.

[47] In light of the long process towards Canadian independence, which was not completed until after World War II, English-Canadians (as opposed to French-Canadians) regarded themselves British.

4.4 Corpus design

CONTE is divided along temporal and social criteria. Chronologically, the corpus is split into five periods from 1776 to the end of 1899, each period spanning 25 years, with the exception of period 1, which lasts only 24 years (cf. appendix 1 for a complete outline). CONTE-pC, which is the basis of the present study, comprises the first three periods, from 1776-1849.

4.4.1 Source materials: genres selected

CONTE includes three genres: diaries, (semi-)official letters, and local newspapers. Although all three genres are non-speech-based genres, they may be classified according to their level of formality to allow statements about written, as well as hypotheses about spoken Ontario English. Following the classification by Kytö and Rissanen (1983), diaries belong to the informal register and may be considered to reflect some features of spoken language on this account.

Newspapers are an obvious choice in the written, formal category, as these data are readily available. This genre is comprised in CONTE-pC of local Ontario newspapers and is, by definition, the only genre in the corpus that has been entirely compiled from printed texts. As a consequence, some regularization on behalf of the printers is expected.

Diaries offer a window into private, personal writing and are therefore to be placed more on the informal side of the continuum. Letters are an interesting source of information, but have often been excluded by scholars as legitimate data. Brown and Gilman (1989: 170) decidedly rule out letters, as they "cannot inform us about the colloquial spoken language" and therefore resort to plays in their study "[p]rimarily because there is nothing else". Research has since recognized the merits of correspondence, e.g. the Helsinki *Corpus of Early English Correspondence*, from ME to EModE and increasingly so for LModE texts. The available corpora of correspondence, are, however, generally based on print editions, which do not include letters by semi-literate, minimally-schooled (Fairman 2006), writers, or, in the context of colonial Englishes, of emigrants, which are of particular interest in variationist studies such as the present one.

Surprisingly, emigrant letters have only recently been subject of linguistic study (Montgomery 1995, Montgomery 2003, Van Herk and Walker 2005, Walker 2005), with Eliason (1956) as an "early but sole exception" (Schneider 2004: 268). Montgomery (2003: 10) is one of the most vocal advocates of the superiority of emigrant letters on the cline from spoken to written language as "it is manuscript documents – in particular, letters from semiliterate writers – [...] hold the most value" for linguistic study. As Van Herk and Walker (2005: 116) point out, letters represent "a *direct* (albeit written) view" of the variety in question, which is the most imminent advantage over fictional accounts or renderings of speech in drama. Tieken (1987: 187, table 1) shows that for some syntactical variables[48] in 18th-century sources, no genre-specific tendencies can be found between informational prose, letter writing (epistolary prose) and direct speech in fiction or drama, as their occurrence varies on an idiosyncratic level, which confirms Van Herk and Walker's assessment concerning these particular variables.

Some of the letters in CONTE-pC are written by people with little schooling, where more influence from the informal register is to be expected. For this reason, these letters are termed *semi-official letters*, as opposed to the official letters by the more proficient writers who were usually working out of governmental offices in the Ontarian context. On the basis of this observation, one can assume semi-official letters to be closer to spoken language than the official ones.

4.4.2 Social stratification

In the period under investigation sufficient background information is usually available to identify a large number of informants and their social backgrounds. CONTE is divided into two social classes in the diary and letter sections: lower class and middle class. The lack of third tier, an upper class, is documented in the history of early Canada. The first governor of Upper Canada, Colonel John Graves Simcoe, is reported to have said that he could not find "enough 'gentlemen' in the province" (Landon 1967: xv) to set up an elite class on the British model.

The two social classes are applied to CONTE, with the exception of the newspaper genre. While it may be assumed that printers, as members of a trade, are members of the middle class, they would have followed printing conventions regardless of their social standing. The diary and letter sections are split into middle and lower class writers. Wherever possible, this distinction is based on external information, such as the *Dictionary of Canadian Biography* or archival information on the texts. In the case of some letter writers, however, this was not possible. In such cases internal criteria were chosen to assign class membership. The criteria are (a) absence of an author's name in the *Dictionary of Canadian Biography* to rule out any affiliation with the more estab-

---

[48] In her case *do*-periphrasis in negative sentences.

lished members of the society in early Canada, (b) format and style of hand-writing and (c) the content of the correspondence.

4.4.3 SIN speakers
The letter section is additionally divided along the provenance of the writers. Table (4.1) shows the data for the three periods in CONTE-pC. While most writers could not be clearly identified at the time being, those who could be tracked down provide a glimpse into the make up of early Ontario:

Place of origin	Period 1	Period 2	Period 3
Scottish	2	4	1
Irish	1	2	4
English	3	3	3
American	3	12	4
Canadian	1	2	3
Welsh	0	0	1
unknown/uncertain	38	25	48
TOTAL	48	48	64

Table 4.1: Origins of letter writers in CONTE-pC[49]

As we have seen in chapter (3), the Scottish, Irish and Northern English (SIN) are of special numerical importance in periods 2 and 3. The material from those writers has been regrouped in a SIN-section to determine whether their input was different than that of Southern English speakers.

The SIN-label is not to suggest that these groups were linguistically coherent, apart from their being speakers of a non-southeastern (standard) English variety. The label, however, alludes to the discrimination against speakers from these regions for committing the two sins against prescriptive linguistic propriety, i.e. infractions against 'proper' pronunciation and grammar (cf. Beal 2004: 97f). Another remarkable feature is the high proportion of Americans in period 2, 25% overall, which indicates both the continuing immigration before 1812 and their social importance in post-1815 Ontario.

4.4.4 Corpus size and sampling
Texts from specific genres were selected differently from the general 'universe' of potential Ontario English texts: quasi-random selection was only possible in the case of letters on microfilm, allowing the compiler to select every

---

[49] Women are only a small minority in CONTE-pC, as only six of the 160 informants are female (3 female writers in period 1, one in period 2 and two in period 3).

fifth or seventh letter to reach the targeted number. For diaries and newspapers a different method was applied.

While in section (4.3) the theoretical boundaries of Ontario English were considered, in this section we are faced with the more pragmatic problems of the corpus compiler. This is especially true for the earliest texts in CONTE-pC, which could have been composed as early as the "5th of July 1776". However, the earliest body of texts that was found were letters from the Archives of Ontario, some of them undated, with the earliest dated letter from 1788. While *de facto* we are dealing with data from 1788 onwards, we shall nevertheless stick to the methodological demarcation date of 1776.

Concerning the selection of texts, another potential drawback must be noted here. While corpora that are based on published material allow a more balanced division within periods in the case of CONTE-pC, the sampling includes longer stretches of texts, due to the lack of verbatim print editions. For diaries, the scarcity of verbatim editions and manuscripts prevented any random method of selection. The procedure applied for the selection of texts took the holdings of the Archives of Ontario and the University of Toronto Libraries as a starting point.[50] Anne Powell's travel diary of 1789 and the beginning of Benjamin Smith's diary from 1799 serve as evidence for the first period from 1776 to 1799. In this genre, what was found and proved to be reliable data is included. Two problem cases are the diaries of Benjamin Smith and Charlotte Harris. Owing to the general scarcity of data, both Smith's and Charlotte Harris' diaries are distributed over two periods. Other texts are included for these periods to ensure varied coverage, but this design limitation will need to be kept in mind when researchers use the corpus for study.

With newspapers, however, we are in a better position, since data are readily available for all periods except the first. Again, the holdings of the Archives of Ontario and the University of Toronto Libraries served as a starting point. Generally, newspapers from smaller villages were preferred over those from bigger ones. Therefore, we find the *Wingham Times* and not the *Toronto Star* in the period from 1875 to 1899. The preference for small local newspapers, as opposed to large national ones, arises from the presumably higher amount of linguistic variation that local papers seem to offer.

All in all, CONTE-pC contains 125,000 words of running text, while CONTE will comprise some 225,000 words, in three genres. It features ap-

---

[50] While good inventories are available for female diarists (Carter 1997, Buss 1991, Gerson 1994), the information provided is often not sufficient to discriminate Ontarian diarists from other Canadian writers. For this reason, the quest for documents started with the library catalogue.

proximately 10,000 to 20,000 words in at least two texts for each genre and period. The goal was to include samples between 5,000 and 10,000 words and where this was impossible, for diaries and newspapers one chunk of at least 2,000 words is included, which should provide a minimum to carry out a variety of studies. The letter component always include full letters, which vary in length between 38 and 900 words.

Extracted from this overall sampling of texts, the subsections pertaining to social class, divided into middle and lower class, and the subsection on SIN-speakers are smaller, however. Appendix (1) provides a complete list of the texts included in CONTE-pC, sample sizes and the projected texts in periods 4 and 5 (1850-1899).

4.5 Text samples

In this section each genre will be illustrated with data from CONTE-pC. We will start with the genre that is expected to yield the least variation: newspapers.

4.5.1 Local Ontario newspapers

Newspaper data are readily available, and data after around 1830 is available online through the innovative text-sharing policy of *Canadiana Online*, published by the *Canadian Institute of Historical Microreproductions*.[51] The earliest data, however, are still found in archives only (Dec. 2004).

Ontario's first newspaper, the *Upper Canada Guardian*, was founded in 1793. Until 1826, printing was an extraordinarily expensive business in the Canadas, as there was no domestic paper production (Stabile 2002: 271, Burant 1985: 1483). The early days of printing were therefore restricted to governmental proclamations, or, which is of greater interest for variation studies, advertisements for land sales or businesses, such as the following, taken from the *Canada Constellation*:

---

[51] The database, an astonishing, searchable collection of early Canadiana in pdf-format, can be partly accessed free of charge at http://www.canadiana.org/eco.php?doc=home, 27 Aug. 2007.

> CHARLES FIELD respectfully informs that he has taken the noted house and stand formerly called Wien's, sign of the Lyon, and com-menced the business in it of a tavern. He has an assortment of the best of liquors, and will keep constantly supplied with every article the country will afford for the pleasure of this customers. The strictest attention will be paid to man and horse, and favors most thankfully received by him. Niagara, July 26.

Figure 4.1: Advertisement from the Canada Constellation
(31 August 1799, title page)

Despite being a printed source text, a number of features are noteworthy. The disregard for concord in the phrase 'this customers' is interesting, for instance. Moreover, the placement of the prepositional phrase 'in it', referring back to the premises, also strikes the modern reader. It is known that in early 19th-century BrE pronominal objects could follow the verb, e.g. *when I gave it him* (Denison 1998: 239), but the sentence position of prepositional phrases is less explored. While two similar occurrences are found in BrE data, one in ARCHER-1 and one in CL18P, none occurs in the American data (ARCHER-1). The question arises whether this word order feature in CanE is imported from BrE, a result of dialect-mixing or even L2 influence in Ontario. These few thoughts show that interesting features can be found even in short newspaper excerpts such as the present one and provide points of departure for linguistic analyses.

4.5.2 Diaries
Data for diaries provide an interesting window into past verbal behaviour. The data, which are to a large extent unpublished diaries in CONTE, are not only from a linguistic point of view highly interesting. Here is a sample of Ely Playter's handwriting:

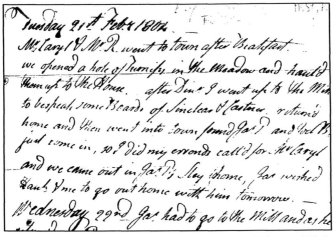

Figure 4.2: Scan of a diary entry by Ely Playter (21 February 1804)

This is as good as quill script gets. Ely's hand is relatively easy to read, and it should not be too hard to compare the manuscript with the transcription.[52] (NB: superscript is omitted in CONTE):

Tuesday 21st Feb.y 1804
Mr Caryl & Mr. R. went to town after Breakfast. we opened a hole of
Turnips in the Meadow and haul'd them up to the House. after Dinr I
went up to the Mill to bespeak some Boards of Sinclear & Casterer,
return'd home and then went into town found Jas. P. and Joel B. just
come in, so I did my errends call'd for Mr Caryl and we came out in
Jas. P.'s Slay home, Jas wished Hank & me to go out home with him
tomorrow. – Wednesday 22nd Jas. had to go to the Mill and as he

Figure 4.3: Transcription of Ely Playter's diary entry from CONTE

For manuscripts like these, the question of upper and lower case, which is linked to punctuation, is highly interesting. The second sentence starts with a lower case 'w' in 'we', but it seems clear that a full stop is preceding it (cf. Ely's commas in the fourth and third lines from the bottom in fig. 4.2). In general, however, it is not always clear whether writers discriminated between

---

[52] Some problematic characters exist even in clearly written, well-preserved texts, such as initial 'J-' in Ely's diary. In many cases, this character is indistinguishable from initial 'G-' and the preference for 'J-' in the name "Ja^s." is based on extra-linguistic criteria, e.g. Ja^s for Jason or Jasper.

upper and lower case for all letters. It may be that there was only one grapheme in their graphemic system for certain letters.[53] However, at least for 'w-', Ely knew both forms, as we can discern from his use of 'W' in 'Wednesday' in the last line in the scan. The same question applies to 'after' in the third line, but an analysis of the following pages of the manuscript reveals that Ely used 'A-' as well.

Only for the longer texts, such as diaries, is a more thorough analysis of the graphemic inventory of a writer possible. In letters, we frequently only have half a page by a certain writer, which is often too little data to establish his or her graphemic inventory. Where possible, the peculiarities of handwriting are noted in the text headers.

4.5.3 Letters: the 'letters received' at the Archives of Ontario
The letters under the heading MS-563 (Reel 1 - 36) in the Archives of Ontario, Toronto, are the sociolinguistically most diverse data. The 36 rolls of microfilm contain a wealth of texts by people who wrote to the Government of Upper Canada. They asked for land grants, reported as land surveyors on their work, and argued over the proper implementation of a settlement policy. These letters, which are all manuscripts, may be classified into two groups:

- semi-official letters: petitions from private persons applying for land grants or support
- official letters: intra-governmental communications and letters by authorities (government officials, including Church of England)

While the second group is rather uniform, the first allows not only for an immense amount of linguistic variation, but provides a window into language use from the lower strata of society.

One example of a semi-official letter is the following transcription of a letter by Margaret Lessiel. Lessiel writes from Hamilton to the Governor General of Canada at the time, the Earl of Gosford, to find out the whereabouts of her husband, who fought in the British forces. She needs part of her husband's pension to feed her six children (words in [ ] could not be clearly read, while < > mark up the corpus annotation):

---

[53] An example of a writing system that does not discriminate between upper and lower case for one letter is shown in Dollinger (2003: 31f).

To the Honorable The Governor of Upper Canada

Sir, my Husband Michael Lessiel was a Soldier in his Majestys
27th Regiment of foot out of which [Ricd.] he obtained the
pention 6 P day he Served in the victories in Ireland - he went
to America about four years 1/2 ago. he Sold out his pention
received 16 Sterling and was to get land in Upper Canada, I
got no Amount from him Since he went away I am a desolate
woman having Six Small Children I awry bad way to Support
them. I therefore humbly beg your honour will cause him to
be proclamed in the publick news papers for no other purpose than that

please turn over

I might know whether he is dead or alive that I might right
<write> to him of my desolate Setuation And that the Lord
may lay it up in Glory for your eternal Salvation will be the
Constant prayer of your most obedt. <obedient> humble Ser-
vant
<sign> Margaret Lessiel

Hamilton
12th January 1836

<other hand>
Michael Lessiel 27 Foot at 6 p Day received the Balance of his
Commuted Allowance [of] 16.13.4 - at Quebec in the month of
October 1831 - <sign illegible>

Figure 4.4: Transcript of Margaret Lessiel's petition to the Governor General
(12 January 1836, from CONTE-pC, sheets no. 13473 & 13474)

Texts like these are rich with features, some of which may be found to be more
commonly shared among Ontarians and Canadians. Lessiel's spelling is highly
regular but has its oddities: 'proclamed', 'Setuation', or the confused spelling
of 'right' for 'write.' It is, as yet, unclear whether these features were Lessiel's
idiosyncrasies or whether they shared wider currency among the Ontarian
lower classes. For this reason, features like these were preserved throughout
the corpus, and annotated with the PDE form (in angular parentheses).

In terms of manuscript form, letters present their challenges. An example of
an official letter, written by George O'Kill Stuart, a Church of England cleric,
addressed to Thomas Ridout, a clerk in the surveyor general's office, is repro-

duced in figure (4.5) and shows a letter of poor visual quality that was a bor-
derline case in terms of decipherable.

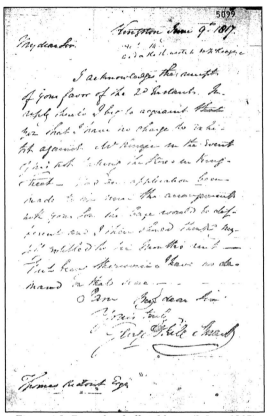

Figure 4.5: Example of official letter (9 June 1817)

Figure (4.5) shows a good example of a letter that is typical in form, layout,
and content of a middle class writer (here, the process of taking possession of a
store on Toronto's King Street by Mr. McKenzie is discussed).

Figure (4.6), in contrast, shows one of the challenges of LModE letter
writing in the form of cross-diagonal writing, here in a letter from 1836 (not
included in CONTE for problems of transcription):

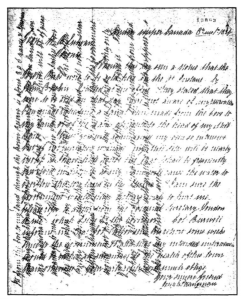

Figure 4.6: Excluded letter for reasons of illegibility

O'Kill's letter is a MC letter, while Lessiel's a LC letter. However, as the transcription shows, Lessiel was not an entirely unschooled writer. The class of semi-official letters therefore contains a continuum of writing skills, from writers without hardly any training to fairly proficient writers such as Margaret Lessiel.

4.6 Coding and text headers

During the mark-up process, special emphasis has been paid not only to a considerably close transcription of the source texts, especially the manuscript sources, but also to the biographical and social data of the authors, which is implemented in the text headers. Lessiel's letter is an example where we can discern some plausible sociolinguistic information. Table (4.2) illustrates CONTE's descriptors at the example of Lessiel's letter:

Extralinguistic data:	
Author's name	Lessiel, Margaret
Author's sex	f
Age	@30-39@
Date of writing	1836
Place of provenance	@Britain@
Place of residence at time of writing	Hamilton, Ontario
Remarks concerning provenance/residence	wife of a soldier who abandoned his family in 1831. @In Canada for 5 years.@
Education	unknown, @some schooling@
Profession	@housewife@
Social status	lower class
Political affiliation	unknown
Linguistic data:	
Genre	letter, semi-official
Style overall	prose
Style specific	non-speech based, formal
Linguistic remarks	one grapheme for initial s-

Table 4.2: Example of a text header in CONTE
Providing linguistic and extralinguistic information on M. Lessiel's text
(Assessments are within @ @)

The transcriber's observations are documented in the category 'linguistic remarks,' as is the case here with Lessiel's use of word-initial 's-.' While the external data is not as detailed as in the (hitherto unpublished) sender database of the *Corpus of Early English Correspondence*, which includes 27 items (Nevalainen and Raumolin-Brunberg 1996b: 50), it contains the information essential for microlinguistic studies. Other data such as the number of words or letter content can be easily obtained by the users of CONTE.

Annotation codes have been kept to a minimum. In total, there are five codes, which appear within < >, in one case within [ ]: first, all abbreviations of words at the end of a line are preserved throughout the corpus, and annotated with <le>, for 'line end', followed by the unabbreviated word form to facilitate searches.

(4.1) They were wholly cover'd with their blankets and sought not by the effects of ornaments either to attract or frighten the other sex, for I cannot determine whether the men mean to make them-selves <le:

themselves> charming or horrible by the pains they take with their persons. (Anne Powell's diary, 1789)

The reflexive pronoun 'themselves' is abbreviated at the end of a line in the original, which is preserved in CONTE. Second, the code <nw>, for 'rendered now as', was added after a word with different spelling in present-day English, as in example (4.1):

(4.2) [...] you will se <nw: see> sir, by my Petition wich <nw: which> I have Enclosed, se <nw: see> my request, [...] (letter 359)

Insertions or corrections in the manuscripts are not rendered in these ASCII-based transcriptions, and only the 'final' corrected version is considered in CONTE. While this would have been desirable for some types of studies, the simplicity of a plain ASCII transcription with few codes was given prevalence here. Third, words that could not clearly be deciphered, are rendered in the text, followed by the code <il>, for 'illegible':

(4.3) to ascertain what quantity <il> of land that tract contains to compare with the Grants made therein (letter 13899)

And fourth, a word that could not be deciphered at all, was transcribed with '[xxx]' for each occurrence.

(4.4)   28th Went to rickmans and to adam greens St home
         29th Went to hatts took 6 bushels to Hatts for [xxx] and to mill
         30th Sunday Went to Joseph houses to meeting. C Do
         (Benjamin Smith's diary, June 1799)

This concludes the introduction to CONTE and CONTE-pC and their design principles. Having outlined the research history of CanE, the external history of Ontario for the period under investigation, and the design principles and features of CONTE-pC, there is now only one piece missing before we can embark on the case studies of the modal auxiliary complex in early OntE. The focus of the next chapter is on recent theories of dialect-mixing and new-dialect formation, which will provide the theoretical framework for the empirical part of this study.

5   NEW-DIALECT FORMATION IN EARLY ONTARIO

In this section, we shall review two scenarios brought forward to account for the development of OntE which complement, and in some sense complete, the review of historical work on CanE in section (2.5). Because of their immediate relevance for new-dialect formation, however, both approaches are discussed in the present chapter.

The two theories, Bloomfield (1948) and Scargill (1957) were published long before recent advances in the field of new-dialect formation, and both still figure prominently in accounts of the development of CanE (e.g. Fee 1992a, Woods 1999: 23, Boberg 2004b: 353f). A review of these theories will serve as a springboard for a discussion of two conflicting scenarios in dialect contact situations, dialect mixing vs. swamping, which includes the central notions of the founder principle and colonial lag. One approach, Trudgill (2004), will then be presented in detail, as it offers the most specific scenario. This approach will be tested in the Ontarian context and will serve as the theoretical backbone for the empirical case study chapters (7-10).

We have seen in chapter (3) that the external language history of early Ontario allows for considerable amounts of dialect contact between different varieties of English as well as language contact between English and other languages. Dialect contact is defined here as a type of language contact that involves mutually intelligible varieties of a given language, a criterion that is not met in language contact.

5.1 Two scenarios for the origin of CanE

Section (2.5) illustrated the shortage of diachronic studies in CanE, which has a serious impact on hypotheses of the development of early CanE. While sociolinguistic apparent-time studies from the 1990s provide a window in the past back to the 1920s, linguistic approaches have not yet been consistently used to reconstruct language and language use in early Ontario. Chambers summarizes the state-of-the-art concerning the formation of early CanE:

> Around the time of Confederation [in 1867], Canadian English, unmistakably a branch of North American English, must have been nearly in-

distinguishable from varieties spoken in the states of Pennsylvania, New
Jersey, New York and Vermont, to which it, not coincidentally, had direct
historical ties. Then, in the early years of this century, certain linguistic
features which had co-existed alongside variants shared by Americans
became dominant. In the 1920s, they apparently became general, or standard. Among them were Canadian Raising and the generic term *chesterfield*. The life cycle of Canadian English as a focussed, unified variety
appears short-lived. Within fifty years, by the 1970s [...] it was audibly
losing some of its more distinctive features. (Chambers 1995a: 165, un-
derscore added.)

This assessment is based on apparent-time evidence, which suggests that the
days of Canadian linguistic identity from the 1920s to the 1970s were tied to
Canada becoming a sovereign nation. For the 19th century, however, no comparable data have been available, which confines enquiries to language-
external reasoning, contemporary commentary, sporadic early CanE attestations, in combination with back-projection from present-day evidence and the
available knowledge on related, early AmE varieties. While at the time of Confederation in 1867, and thus 17 years after the end of our period, OntE is considered as having been 'nearly indistinguishable' from American varieties, it
would be surprising if no particular distributions of forms and functions were
found after four generations of settlement in Ontario when compared to the
input varieties. To what extent these distributions may be considered as characteristic for an emerging CanE variety will need to be established in each case.
The earlier one of the two contributions, Bloomfield (1948) has a clear stand-
point on the issue, which has since developed into the majority opinion.

5.1.1 Bloomfield (1948)

Morton W. Bloomfield's article focuses on the importance of the Loyalist immigration from the United States and is one of the early papers arguing for a
scenario that came to be known as the 'Loyalist base theory'. While acknowl-
edging other migratory movements, Bloomfield states clearly that the Loyalists
shaped the linguistic patterns in Ontario and connects the political conservatism of the Loyalists with linguistic conservatism:

> The important group, both in number and prestige, were the Loyalists,
> who, hardy and industrious, opened up Ontario [...]. They were conserva-
> tives who had suffered for their loyalty. Hence, to the normal conserva-
> tism of emigrating linguistic groups there was added, in this case, a strong
> political and psychological conservatism. This frame of mind was to have
> its effect upon Canadian English and Canadian life. (Bloomfield 1948: 5)

We have said earlier in chapter (3) that not all of these immigrants were die-hard monarchists and some of them (as is acknowledged by Bloomfield 1948: 6) were speakers of different native as well as second-language varieties of English. While Bloomfield (1948: 6) explicitly allows for contact phenomena and "speech mixture" in early Ontario, he maintains that the speech of the Loyalists had set the patterns that later arrivals assimilated to:

> Canadian English then is basically eighteenth century American English modified by other influences, notable among which are the Southern Standard English and the English taught by Scots school teachers. (Bloomfield 1948: 6)

The usefulness of this very broad generalization is limited. While one might say that, for instance, LModE is the result of EModE modified by other influences, we are not gaining many insights from this statement, except to suggest a general historical lineage. In Bloomfield's citation, however, one is struck by the apparent importance of Scottish teachers in Canada, which probably exaggerates their real share (cf. 3.3.3.1). As one of the first Loyalist base theorists, however, Bloomfield (1948) is an important development in the study of diachronic Canadian English.

5.1.2 Scargill (1957) and (1985)

Scargill (1957) is a rebuttal of Bloomfield (1948), stressing the regional character of CanE as "it is dangerous for an investigator to assume that an influence that can be dated for one area will necessarily be valid for another area" (Scargill 1957: 14). While Bloomfield does distinguish between Canadian regions, he includes very general statements that seem to violate a regional approach to CanE. Scargill offers eight points of criticims of Bloomfield (1948), which may be re-grouped in four categories:

I. Late 18th-century American English dialects, which served as input varieties in Ontario, were subject to dialect formation themselves, i.e. in a state of flux, exhibited considerable variation, and were no readily formed varieties (Scargill's points 1, 5 and 7).

II. British English influence is marginalized: what today is perceived of as an Americanism may have been an 18th-century variant of BrE instead (Scargill explicitly mentions Northern English varieties), which were introduced by British officers, clerics and teachers. The existence of Americanisms in CanE today are therefore no proof for AmE influence (2, 3 and 4).

III.   The influence of later immigrant groups, most notably the Scottish and Irish, is not adequately accounted for (6).

IV.   Innovation in CanE is marginalized (8).   (after Scargill 1957: 13f)

While Scargill's criticsm has its merits, it offers no evidence for points (I) and (II). Unless it can be shown that late 18th-century American English was more heterogeneous, possibly on account of continuing in-migration, and not yet focussed, (I) becomes meaningless as all varieties are subject to variation at all times.

While (III) will ultimately need to be clarified on the basis of LModE corpora of Irish and Scottish varieties, point (IV), which was a valid criticism at the time of writing, has been remedied since (see Avis *et al.* 1967) and must be considered as proven today. Apart from a massive body of evidence for lexical innovations in CanE (cf. DCHP-1; Dollinger and Brinton forthc.), other features also testify to CanE innovations. Canadian Raising, for instance, may be the result of dialect mixture in 19th-century Canada (Trudgill 1986: 159, see Thomas 1991 for a diverging view and Chambers 1989: 85 for a balanced assessment of both scenarios).

Point (II), however, is the result of different developmental stages of linguistic input, sometimes referred to as 'layering' (Lass 1990: 268) and a highly valuable point. The diachronic dimension and relative chronology of changes needs to be kept in mind, since some changes that appear to be Americanisms from a PDE perspective may in fact be the result of early BrE variants and therefore little proof for American influence. As figure (5.1) shows, -*or* spellings became categorically used in AmE only in the second half of the 19th century. Figure (5.2) shows the uses in BrE[54]. We see that *honor** (* stands for a wildcard) occurs in 20% of all cases in BrE, and *favor** is found in 1750-99, while *neighbor** even gains ground in 1800-49, which indicates changes in both AmE (towards –*or*) and BrE (which held on to –*or* spellings for some time). We conclude that the use of this variable as an idicator of AmE influence on CanE would have to be ruled out before 1850.

---

[54] Please note that periods are not entirely congruent between AmE and BrE.

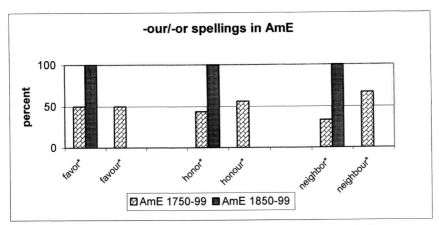

Figure 5.1: Diachronic development of -our/-or spellings in AmE

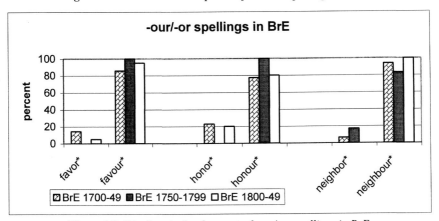

Figure 5.2: Diachronic development of -our/-or spellings in BrE

The equivalent variables in CanE illustrate a rather extreme change in the direction of BrE. Spelling variables show a high degree of awareness in literate societies and, while early Ontario was not a society where reading and writing were standard skills, the data in figure (5.3) show a clear scenario:

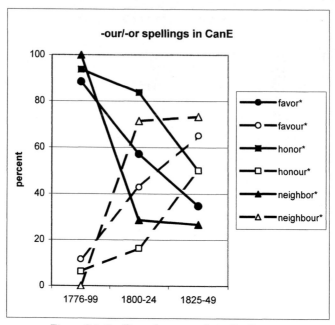

*Figure 5.3: Spelling of –*our *words in CanE*

We see that in 1776-99, *-or* spellings were the norm in Ontario. In 1800-24, however, during the time of the War of 1812, their percentage decreases and continues to fall in 1825-49, when *-our* spellings prevail. It seems that Ontarians changed their spelling habits as a result of the War of 1812 and shed their American roots, so to speak, by converging closer to a BrE norm; at the time, *-our* spellings had already been the majority form in BrE (see figure 5.2). In empirical case studies, the use of parallel corpora from Britain provides some safeguard against a neglect of the diachronic development of donor varieties. As this spelling example shows, the parallel data are also a protection against Scargill's criticism from point II, i.e. the neglect of a diachronic dimension in BrE.

Overall, Scargill's theoretical take on the development of CanE is probably most important for emphasizing the British influence. For Ontario, Scargill concedes that the "immediate basis of Canadian English is to be found in Loyalist speech", but adds that the

> later and more extensive pioneer settlements may have destroyed Loyalist speech influence; and [exisiting] Americanisms may have to be traced to

> a more modern source. Moreover, [...] eighteenth-century British
> influence must be given some consideration. (Scargill 1957: 15)

Scargill (1957) reached a considerable number of readers, as it was chosen as an introductory essay on CanE in Klinck's (1976) literary history of Canada. Scargill's view, which serves well in conjunction with Bloomfield (1948), but much less so as an essay on its own, therefore gained some currency even beyond linguistic circles. Scargill's valid criticism of the Loyalist base theory, however, got pronounced more and more over the years and mutated into something coming close to a monogenetic input scenario of BrE varieties. Scargill's introductory article in the *Canadian Encyclopedia*, for instance, opens with the following surprising statement:

> Although English was used in Canada before the 19th century, there were
> neither enough speakers nor enough significant features in the language
> for it to be regarded as anything other than British English. (Scargill
> 1985: 582, reprinted in subsequent editions [1988] and [2000])

Clearly, this view, which renders any AmE influence before 1800 as irrelevant, is untenable. Given Ontario's external history and the scarcity of 18th- and 19th-century internal evidence to support such a claim, Scargill's view must be considered as inadequate for standard reference works, let alone very recent ones. In chapters (7-10) the real-time data will reveal what, if anything, is tenable of this statement. The external history would certainly point towards AmE and not BrE.

5.2 Polygenetic theories of colonial Englishes

Both Bloomfield's and Scargill's points of view must be considered as mere hypotheses of the development of English in Ontario, since they were formulated in the absence of language internal-evidence. Recent years have seen the development of theories of the formation of new varieties that specifically address colonial contexts. Trudgill (2004) categorizes developmental theories of colonial varieties broadly into monogenetic and polygenetic approaches. On the one hand, monogenetic theories, which have considerable currency in Romance linguistics (Trudgill 2004: 7f), assign little or no role to contact scenarios in the development of colonial varieties, while, on the other hand, polygenetic theories maintain "that colonial varieties are the consequence, at least in part, of dialect mixture" (ibid: 11).

The basic concept of dialect mixture, i.e. the formation of a blend of a number of dialects in a newly settled place into a new variety, is intuitively plausible and far from new as it appeals to popular notions of a cultural *melting pot* or *mosaic*. In the CanE context mixing scenarios are explicitly addressed in an early contribution by Lighthall (1889: 583), which leaves its processes unspecified. In recent years, dialect contact and mixing scenarios have gained considerable scholarly attention, which reflects the increasing adoption of mobility into models of linguistic change (Chambers 1995b: 66).

Polygenetic approaches can be considered the consensus scenario in contemporary sociolinguistics (Trudgill 2004: 11) so that here, I will discuss the two conflicting views expressed by Bloomfield and Scargill in relation to two *poly*genetic theories of dialect-mixing[55]. These are the theory of swamping on the one hand (Lass 1990) and the theory of new-dialect formation on the other hand (Trudgill 2004).

5.2.1 Notions of swamping

The first point of view is argued for by Roger Lass, who, in an early and influential paper on the phonologies of colonial Englishes, attempts a typology of these varieties that leads him to reason that

> ETEs [extraterritorial Englishes] grow out of multiple migrations, and each component wave tends to have a distinct regional character. But it is not normally the case that all sub-migrations contribute equally – or at all – to the character of the final product. *Nor does this product necessarily reflect in any very close way the demography of the original wave, or any particular one, or even all of them put together.* There is a peculiar sort of development in most cases, in which the overall profile of the 'finished' ETE tends to be of one regional type – southern – regardless of what other types are represented in the settlement history. (Lass 1990: 267, italics added)

Lass (1990: 268) basically suggests that colonial Englishes "for complex and not very well understood reasons" are not the expected result of a mixing process in the general sense, i.e. each of the ingredients contributing some features. Instead, colonial Englishes reflect the dominance of one regional input variety, which is southern English English.[56] One is tempted to link this finding to the social prestige of southern English English, a connection that Lass (2004: 367) considers in a later paper.

---

[55] For some strengths of monogenetic scenarios see Trudgill (2006: 270-280).
[56] Lass defines the English South as including a good part of the English Midlands, which is roughly equivalent to the area south of a line from Bristol to Northampton and Peterborough.

At first glance, one of the two Canadian developmental scenarios seems to support Lass' theory of swamping. Scargill's point of view of a prevalence of BrE features in CanE would certainly point in this direction. However, Lass' *Law of Swamping* makes it clear that Scargill and Lass talk about two different processes. While Lass refers to an abstract process, to a language-internal predisposition (which he describes from a phonological point of view), Scargill is arguing from demographic numbers alone. Lass' and Scargill's differences can be seen in the following citations. Lass' *Law of Swamping* says that:

> (i) In cases of mixed input to an ETE, whatever the original demography, the output is (a) southern, and (b) more eastern than western.

> (ii) Whatever the size of the non-southern input, it will normally leave only unsystematic relics (e.g. odd lexical items, idioms, or minor constructions); there will rarely be larger-scale structural effects (e.g. in the system of phonemic oppositions). (Lass 1990: 269)

The *Law of Swamping* suggests that "evolutionary and sociolinguistic" features are more powerful than demographic influences (Lass 1990: 249), which relegates the role of contact to minor effects. Lass' swamping will be called here *typological swamping*.

In contrast to this view, Scargill's point (6), discussed in section (5.1.2, under III), illustrates the notion of swamping that is inherent in his work. In contrast to Lass' notion, Scargill's swamping is conditioned by large-scale demographic input. The following quotation shows that Scargill is arguing language-externally, when he introduces the term 'swamping' from a historical context:

> Between 1815 and 1850 some 800,000 people from the British Isles came to British North America. As a Canadian historian said: 'The Great Immigration completely changed the Nature of the British North American colonies, swamping the old Loyalist and American communities with Irishmen, Scotsmen, and Englishmen …'. (Scargill 1957: 13)

Scargill argues from numbers and uses the term in an entirely different way than Lass and is therefore better referred to as *numerical swamping*.

Notions of *numerical swamping* play a role in recent developmental scenarios of varieties of English. Two approaches which refer to the concept explicitly are Kiesling (2004: 423) on AusE and Sudbury (2004: 405) on Falkland Island English. Lass' *typological swamping*, in contrast, does not figure prominently in recent accounts, which is of little surprise. While it is a useful construct for long-term phonological developments, *typological swamping*, which relates phenomena back to motherland English and relegates variation to the sidelines as relics of linguistic input, can hardly serve as a theoretical backdrop for variationist grammatical studies. Notions of typological swamping may well be the *result* of the interpretation of variationist accounts, but it cannot be their theoretical underpinning. Since variationists aim to identify differences between varieties, one cannot start with the concept that are varieties are ultimately descendants of one, socially prestigious, BrE dialect. We will therefore abandon Lass' notion and focus on polygenetic scenarios that focus on the actual mixing process and not on its typological outcome.

5.2.2 Dialect mixing proper

While dialectologists have traditionally focussed on non-mobile speakers, colonial varieties, with their typically mobile populations, defy a meaningful description based on the immobility of speakers. Immigration can be perceived as an extreme case of mobility (Chambers 2002), which plays a special role in language change and its powerful effect has been stated as a "natural linguistic law: mobility causes people to speak and sound more like people from other places" (Chambers 1995b: 66). Face-to-face interactions play a crucial role in language change, much more so than other, more indirect forms of communication. A number of approaches to describe processes of linguistic change have been developed for contact scenarios, which may be categorized as micro- and macrolinguistic scenarios.

The microlinguistic approach figures most prominently in social network studies (L. Milroy 1987). Social network concepts have recently been applied to various historical stages in the development of the English language.[57] These settings include medieval settings (e.g. Bergs 2005 for ME), EModE ones (e.g. Nevalainen 2000) as well as LModE scenarios (e.g. Tieken 1991, 1996, 2000b). As LModE studies focus largely on literature circles of the middle and upper middle classes in Britain, the concept has yet to be applied to dialect formation studies in colonial settings, however.[58]

Macrolinguistic approaches to contact scenarios in the history of English comprise the second category and represent the bulk of research (e.g. the contributions in Algeo 2001a, Hickey 2004a). While contact phenomena, most notably borrowing, have always played a role in English historical linguistics, precise descriptions of historical bilingual linguistic phenomena and sociolinguistic processes have been available only fairly recently (e.g. Schendl 2002).

---

[57] See Tieken (2000a) for a workshop report on social networks in the history of English from ICEHL-10, Manchester (1998).
[58] While this task is beyond the scope of the present study, the reader is referred to appendix (5) for a basic question concerning the reconstruction of social networks in early Ontario.

Due to the nature of our data (see chapter 6), contact scenarios in early Ontario will be treated from a macrolinguistic perspective in the present study.

Two notions resurface in the context of dialect mixing scenarios in different guises, and it seems worthwhile to discuss them before we turn to the application of a specific model of dialect-mixing to the early Ontario data. These concepts are the founder principle and the notion of colonial lag.

5.2.2.1 Founder principle

The founder principle is a concept from biology that was adapted into linguistics in Mufwene (1996). It offers a guiding principle to gauge the historical ties of colonial varieties and their donor varieties when various settlement waves complicate the matter. In some sense, however, it merely provides a label for the observation of long standing that early migratory inputs seem to be more important to the actual outcome of a dialect mixing process than later migrations. The founder principle is used to

> explain how structural features of [varieties] have been predetermined to a large extent (but not exclusively!) by characteristics of the vernaculars spoken by the populations that founded the colonies in which they developed. (Mufwene 1996: 84)

In the Ontarian context, the founder principle is of particular importance, as the Loyalist base theory is congruent with it: after the coming of the first-wave Americans, the massive British input, which was trailing by roughly a generation, is suggested to have had only marginal linguistic effects. M. Bloomfield expresses implicitly the idea of the founder principle in the following passage:

> During and after the time of the American Revolution, the military importance of Canada increased [...].
>
> Most of the military population was a floating one, but some soldiers settled permanently. During their stay, the officers led a dashing social life, and the men mingled with the masses. But neither they nor the small number of civilians from Great Britain affected the basically Loyalist nature of English-speaking Canada. *This Loyalist frame had been firmly fixed by 1830* when immigrants from Great Britain, mostly poor, began to settle in increasingly large numbers. *The Loyalists had moulded Canada*, created its ruling caste and set its social standards, *among which was its language.* (Bloomfield 1948: 6, italics added)

It is clear that Bloomfield expresses the idea of the founder principle in the italicized passages. Interestingly, he specifically refers to dialect and language contact situations in early Canada:

> [In early Canada] There is, of course, speech mixture due to large-scale migration during the [19th] century. Southern [BrE] Standard, Northern [BrE], Scots, and Irish English, for instance, are spoken in Canada among first and second generations of immigrants from Great Britain, as well as "foreign" English dialects, *but gradually all varieties of English are being assimilated to the Canadian English of the Loyalists,* which, in turn, has been modified to some extent by the process. (Bloomfield 1948: 6, italics added)

Bloomfield's description of the processes of dialect formation in early Canada is remarkable, as it captures the essential points of what we now know as the founder principle. As the Loyalist base theory has become the majority view among linguists, M. Bloomfield is perhaps the first in a long line of transmission to express this idea for the formation of Canadian English.

5.2.2.2 Colonial lag

Directly linked to the question of historical ties and their relative importance is the concept of colonial lag, the phenomenon that transplanted societies are linguistically more conservative than the motherland variety. It appears that the term was coined by Albert H. Marckwardt, and, despite popular perception of a general conservatism in colonial speech, Marckwardt defines the notion as the survival and retention of linguistic structures for a *limited* period of time:

> These post-colonial survivals of earlier phases of mother-country culture, taken in conjunction with the retention of earlier linguistic features, have made what I should like to call a colonial lag. I mean to suggest by this term nothing more than that in a transplanted civilization, such as [US-American] undeniably is, certain features which it originally possessed remain static over a period of time. (Marckwardt 1958: 80)

While Marckwardt leaves the time frame for a lag unspecified, it becomes clear from the definition that he does not consider colonial varieties as inherently conservative, but more for in a transitory manner. Recently, Trudgill (2004: 26) defines this temporal dimension more precisely and limits the phenomenon to the time depth of the first generation of settlement. Moreover, and equally important, he introduces the precondition of what he refers to as *tabula rasa* situations[59]. Tabula rasa situations are geographical settings where no dialect of the language under investigation had been spoken before. Trudgill

---

[59] It has been pointed out (e.g. Görlach 1987: 43) that in situations where dialect mixing does not occur, colonial lag may extend beyond the first generation, such as in the case of Icelandic or the German *Sprachinseln* in northern Italy (see Trudgill 2004: 35 for more exceptions).

views the concept as a by-product of the demographics of newly settled areas and uses colonial lag

> to refer to a lag or delay, which lasts for about one generation, in the normal progression and development of linguistic change, and which arises solely as an automatic consequence of the fact that there is often no common peer-group dialect for children to acquire in first-generation colonial situations involving dialect mixture. (Trudgill 2004: 34)

In both definitions, Marckwardt's and Trudgill's, the aspect of a limited time effect plays a major role that has not always been considered in discussions of the phenomenon. Görlach (1987) investigates the history of the notion on several linguistic levels, concluding that

> the term and phenomenon described by [colonial lag] are largely myths as far as the hard linguistic facts of language varieties of English are concerned (1987: 55),

but adds that "they can still be true as far as attitudes go" (1987: 55). Put in Labovian terms, it seems that Görlach confines the notion of colonial lag to changes that are essentially changes from above the level of consciousness. Clearly, we have two diverging assessments: while Görlach limits the phenomenon of colonial lag to attitudes, Trudgill confines it merely on a temporal scale in *tabula rasa* settings.

In the empirical chapters (6-10), both Trudgill's and Görlach's notions will be investigated and matched against the data. To corroborate Görlach's concept, our results would have to show that only modals that are subject to change from above should show conservative behaviour in comparison to BrE varieties. To confirm Trudgill's notion, all modals should display more conservative behaviours in period 1 than periods 2 and 3.

In each case, however, conservative and progressive behaviour would need to be established first for each variable and variety separately, as we cannot assume that one variety is more conservative – across the board – than another one. As Wolfram and Schilling-Estes (2004: 197) have shown, even conservative communities "are indeed dynamic and cannot be described simply by appealing to dialect conservatism". In other words, since conservatism is a relative notion, so is its twin notion colonial lag.

The idea of generally more conservative and more progressive linguistic varieties, however, remains appealing to linguists. Krug (2000: 256) considers the possibility of a general ranking of entire varieties by degrees of conservatism, once adequate data is available:

If, say, regional (national or intranational) patterns were recurrent, one
might rank varieties in terms of progressiveness more confidently than is
possible at the present stage. (Krug 2000: 256).

Until now, corpus studies (e.g. Kytö 1991a, Kytö 1991b) relate temporal lags
to a given variable in a given context. In the present study, it will be aimed to
show to what extent the varieties examined may fit a more general conservative or progressive pattern in the central modals and one semi-modal. An ac-
cumulative assessment tool, to be introduced in the final chapter, will be used
in this respect.

5.2.3 Dialect mixing in early Ontario

In introductory articles on CanE (Fee 1992a: 180, Boberg 2004b: 353f) reference is frequently made to the two original views expressed in M. Bloomfield
(1948), for the American Loyalist base theory, and Scargill (1957) for numerical swamping.

The majority view today, as expressed by Avis (1978d) and Chambers
(1991, 1998a), is that CanE has an American base that was influenced by later
British mass migration. However, the British influence is deemed to have been
severely limited and confined to language attitudes and norms (cf. Chambers
1998a, 2004). The majority view therefore suggests a contact scenario for
OntE as a mixed dialect with heavy emphasis, in accordance with the founder
principle, on the first wave migrants. Early writings by British travellers who
visited Ontario before 1812 have been characterized by historians as
"abound[ing] with references to the 'Yankee' manners and habits of speech,
even among those of other than American origin" (Landon 1967: xv),[60] which
would point towards the dominance of loyalist speech.

The exact nature of this mixing process, however, has hitherto been left unaccounted for. Woods (1999: 23f), for instance, summarizes the argument for
the years until 1850, saying that "both American and British immigration and
settlement contributed jointly to the development of Canadian English […]",
but leaves their respective shares unspecified. The recent theory of new-dialect
formation, brought forward by Trudgill (2004), provides for the first time a
fairly detailed theoretical backdrop for contact scenarios in colonial settings,
which also bears great potential to shed light on the dialect-mixing process in
early Ontario. Trudgill (2004), as the hitherto most precise scenario, will be

---

[60] Probably one of the earliest transcriptions of OntE is found in Campbell (1937 [1792]: 157),
a Scot travelling the country with a "note-book in hand" (p. vii). He renders four lines by an
Ontarian resident near Hamilton, who was "an old Yankee rascal", spoke the "twang peculiar
to the New Englanders" but had not yet lived in Ontario for a year.

tested against the modal data in the subsequent chapters and will be introduced, discussed and, where necessary, adapted in the next sections.

5.3 New-dialect formation theory (Trudgill 2004)

The theoretical underpinnings of the empirical part are to a large extent derived from Trudgill's (2004) model of new-dialect formation. While the model is compatible with other researchers' approaches, such as Mufwene (2001) or social network studies (e.g. Tieken 2000a), Trudgill (2004) is the most detailed account for dialect mixing scenarios. The theory was first outlined in Trudgill (1986), but has recently been refined on the basis of unique recordings of elderly New Zealand English speakers from the 1940s (ONZE tapes). Since the late 1990s, the ONZE recordings have resulted in a number of contributions on the origins of New Zealand English in particular and southern hemisphere Englishes in general (cf. e.g. Gordon *et al.* 2004; Trudgill *et al.* 2000, Trudgill, Gordon and Lewis 1998, N. Woods 1997).

After introducing the stages and processes in Trudgill (2004), the scenario will be applied to the Ontarian situation, first to the language external history in this chapter, and then to the internal data in chapters (6-10). We will see, to what extent the state-of-the art of historical corpus linguistics allows for the empirical testing of dialect mixing scenarios.

5.3.1 *Tabula rasa* situations

Trudgill's theory of new-dialect formation applies to a special type of contact situations. The theory has hitherto been applied almost exclusively to New Zealand English or southern hemisphere English, which developed in relative isolation to other varieties. Trudgill's theory is confined to *tabula rasa* situations, which are carefully defined as situations

> in which there is no prior-existing population speaking the language in question, either in the location in question or nearby. (Trudgill 2004: 26)

It is clear from the discussion in chapter (3) that the level of isolation of English speakers in early Ontario is not as extreme as is the case for New Zealand. Tabula rasa situations need to meet two conditions: early Ontario meets the first condition of *tabula rasa* situations, of 'no prior-existing' English speaking population, apart from the insignificant numbers of transient fur traders in the region. The second condition, however, concerning the remoteness of other English speakers does not seem to apply to Ontario. As was shown in section

(3.3.3.2) on mobility, most early Ontarians could complete a journey in three days to American settlements such as Buffalo or Detroit, and only early settlers further inland residing in place with no access to navigable rivers would face a considerably longer journey. Because of these communication lines between Ontario and the U.S., early Ontario is no *tabula rasa* situation *per se* in the sense of Trudgill's definition. We may say, however, that the intensity of communication was limited because of physical barriers (the Great Lakes) or the costs of a passage by boat and bad roads, especially early in the period. Moreover, at some points in time, the ties between the countries were downgraded or even temporarily severed, especially after periods of armed conflict (1776, 1812, the 1837 rebellion), which would have discouraged travel.

It is likely that the intensity of contact with the United States varied greatly by region. Landon (1967: 2f, 14) suggests that political allegiance was unevenly distributed in the province: while western Ontario was more pro-American, eastern Ontario, with its early loyalist settlements, was openly hostile towards the U.S., which would imply, other factors being equal, fewer contacts down south. On the whole, contact with outsiders, i.e. Americans, were more frequent than in Trudgill's prototypical *tabula rasa* situation in New Zealand, but less intense than between, for instance, the original thirteen American colonies. This would imply that we are likely to see a somewhat different process of new-dialect formation in Ontario than in New Zealand.

We conclude that early Ontario cannot be considered a *tabula rasa* situation *per se*, as it had intermediate to low-level contact with its American neighbour. This might be referred to as a *semi tabula rasa* situation. It would be reasonable, perhaps, to expect a kind of hybrid new-dialect formation process as a result. In addition to tabula rasa phenomena, we would expect types of language change that are typically found in established speech communities, such as processes of diffusion of linguistic features and geographical spread between centres (e.g. Chambers and Trudgill 1998: 178-186).

5.3.2 Some other models

While other scholars have also focussed on contact scenarios in the formation of colonial Englishes, no other model matches the detail and testability of Trudgill (2004). Two of them, Mufwene (2001) and Dillard (1985), will be discussed here to illustrate this assessment.

Mufwene (2001) is a model developed for creole languages and is interesting in the present context for two reasons. First, it opens up avenues between sociolinguistic contact scenarios (e.g. Chambers and Trudgill 1998, Trudgill 1986) and models of evolutionary linguistics that view language as complex adaptive systems (e.g. Gell-Mann 1994, Ritt 2004, Ritt 1995). Second, and more importantly in the present context, Mufwene stresses the importance of the input as "[d]iffering mixes [of input dialects] in the colonies would also have yielded different outputs to restructuring" (2001: 159). What Mufwene, however, refers to rather globally as restructuring, is explicitly formulated in Trudgill (2004), as will be shown below.

Dillard (1985) focuses on the transportation of dialects to overseas locations and discusses the levelling of BrE dialects prior to their arrival in America. As will be shown below, Dillard effectively only deals with phase (Ia) (see section 5.3.4), leaving most other aspects aside. While this point, however, is well illustrated with many examples, e.g. the Puritans' passage to Massachusetts after their extended stay in Holland, Dillard (1985: 51) draws an extreme conclusion by suggesting to "give up the notion that British regional dialects hold the key to the history of American English". As such, Dillard (1985) is less a model of dialect convergence than a scenario which raises awareness of independent developments in colonial Englishes; but it certainly goes too far when some of the best data for inquiries into the formation process, British input varieties, are categorically ruled out.

The importance of input, or donor varieties is widely acknowledged today. All contributions in Hickey (2004a) on colonial Englishes not only (a) "bring into focus just what input varieties were probably operative in individual colonies" but also (b) "examine the extent to which dialect mixing and/or language contact have been responsible for the precise structure of overseas varieties" (Hickey 2004b: 1). The input varieties in early Ontario, including non-English varieties, have been identified and discussed in chapter (3), which leaves us to attempt to answer question (b) as to the role of dialect and language contact in the formation of early Ontario English.

But how does the formation of a new variety come about? Mufwene (2001: 12) refers globally to the formation process as a form of restructuring, which is defined as "the reorganization of the mechanical system of a language and/or of the pragmatic principles regulating its use". Trudgill (2004), on the other hand, is rather specific in his postulation of three consecutive developmental stages and six processes that comprise new-dialect formation. Trudgill's model is not only more precise, but offers a scenario to spell out the formation process in early Ontario that is unparalleled in other models. It remains to be seen in chapters (6-10), whether Trudgill (2004) will need to be adapted to the Ontarian situation, or whether the model may be extended unaltered to the *semi tabula rasa* situation found in Ontario. The theory employs the processes of mixing, levelling, unmarking, interdialect development, reallocation and the focussing of the variety, which will be discussed next.

5.3.3 Six key processes

The six processes at the heart of Trudgill (2004) exploit concepts from different linguistic schools and approaches. As the processes are arranged and modified, and in some cases redefined differently than in other approaches, they will be presented here as laid out in Trudgill (2004: 84-89). The processes are:

1) mixing	4) interdialect development
2) levelling	5) reallocation
3) unmarking	6) focussing

Process (1), mixing, is the *sine qua non* of all contact scenarios, i.e. speakers of different dialects must interact in a given location. Process (2), levelling, is understood here as an effect of mobility and defined as the "loss of demographically minority variants" (Trudgill 2004: 84). As speakers from different regions bring their different variants to the colony, it is predicted that, by and large, the majority variant will, other things being equal, be selected as the variant of the new dialect. Process (3), unmarking, however, influences the purely arithmetic outcome of dialect mixing in process (2), as more basic, unmarked forms tend to be preferred over more marked ones (e.g. non-nasal vowels over nasal vowels).

Process (4), interdialect development, is a real contact phenomenon as it produces "forms which were not actually present in any of the dialects contributing to the mixture" (Trudgill 2004: 86). Interdialect forms can be considered the colonial equivalent of mixed or fudged forms between two primary competing forms, e.g. variable (u) realized as /ʊ/ and /ʌ/ in words like *hundred*, *some* in Northern East Anglia (Chambers and Trudgill 1998: 111). Fudged forms, i.e. intermediate forms (ibid: 110), will occur as a result of the mixed input in the colonial context and may prove to be good contenders for survivors, despite their minority status, "simply as a result of their linguistically intermediate status" (Trudgill 2004: 87).[61]

While usually only one variant is selected from a pool of variants, occasionally "more than one competing variant left over from the original mixture may survive" (Trudgill 2004: 87). These forms are candidates for process (5), real-

---

[61] It is clear that Trudgill (2004) is a description of the formation process. On a more abstract level, however, neo-Darwinian models provide a fairly convincing theory to account for changes in the direction of intermediate forms.

location, and may be redistributed as social, stylistic or systemic variants in the new dialect. Canadian Raising is a case in point for system-internal reallocation by redistributing existing input diphthong variants to phonetic environments that allow for more ease of articulation (Chambers 1973; 1979c: 196). Process (6), focussing, goes back to work by Le Page and Tabouret-Keller (1985) and is the "process by means of which the new variety acquires norms and stability" (Trudgill 2004: 88). Trudgill further distinguishes between koinéization, comprised of processes 1-5, and new-dialect formation, which includes focussing, i.e. processes 1-6 (2004: 89). New-dialect formation necessitates therefore not only levelling and reallocation processes of various sorts, but also the construction of a local identity. While the notion of 'focussing' figures prominently in the recent literature, the nature of the process is not well understood. We will see in the next section what 'focussing' might entail.

A final point needs to be raised before discussing Trudgill's three stages of formation. As the theory is largely based on sound change, it is concerned with the selection of (phonetic) *forms*. For a scenario of grammatical change, such as in the present study, we therefore need to extend the theory to capture *forms and their functions*. If a certain form, e.g. *must*, is used to express a certain function, e.g. an obligation as in *You must submit the paper by tomorrow 4 pm*, and this form competes with other forms for that function, e.g. *have to* as in *You have to submit the paper by tomorrow 4 pm* (also an obligation), then new-dialect formation makes predictions concerning these forms and their competing functions, but not necessarily for other functions of a form, such as *She must be there by now* (subjective inference), where must faces no competition from *have to* at the time.

This concludes this brief introduction of the six key processes. They are operative in differing degrees at the three stages of Trudgill's theory (2004), which are discussed next.

5.3.4 Three stages in new-dialect formation

The cornerstone of Trudgill (2004) are three developmental stages, which "roughly correspond to three successive generations of speakers" (2004: 89). Under normal circumstances, we would therefore expect focussed varieties to emerge in colonial *tabula rasa* situations in about 75 years, or in less than a century. For the sake of convenience, I divide each stage into phases, which is only meant to facilitate the discussion and does not indicate an additional stratification of the developmental process. Each of the three stages consists of two major phenomena, as can be seen in table (5.1):

STAGE I	a) rudimentary levelling	and	b) interdialect development
STAGE II	a) extreme variability	and	b) apparent levelling
STAGE III	a) choice of majority forms	and	b) reallocation

Table 5.1: Stages in Trudgill's new-dialect formation theory

5.3.4.1 Stage I: when adults accommodate

In phase (Ia), rudimentary levelling, accommodation happens during the first encounters of speakers of different dialects, e.g. in the port town, on board of a ship, and in intermediate camps either in the colonies or at a transient location. In this earliest stage, accommodation would have occurred mostly between adult speakers, which resulted in limited types and frequencies of accommodation processes (Trudgill 2004: 89). As we have seen in chapter (3), the first wave of loyalist immigrants from Pennsylvania, New York and New England, had to wait several months before taking up their own lots. Likewise, the passage from Britain, and the journey inland to Ontario would have been the scenarios for rudimentary levelling for the second wave immigrants.

The crucial factor of rudimentary levelling is, however, that mostly stereotypical features are accommodated to (Trudgill 2004: 93). Accommodation in face-to-face communication between adults has been shown to be usually limited to the salient features of a dialect, i.e. those features that are "most prominent in the consciousness" of speakers of other varieties (Trudgill 1986: 12).[62] In other words, those features that are stereotypical of a given dialect other than one's own are more likely to be accommodated to. It is clear, however, that stereotypical features are not necessarily the ones that are characteristic of a given variety.

Another feature influencing rudimentary levelling in the Ontarian context would have been by prescriptive norms. Normative ideas may have had an effect in phase (Ia), as it is here that adults are the prime agents (but less so in later stages when children become the key players). Dillard (1985) focuses on early processes of accommodation – during the trans-Atlantic passage and in temporary accommodation on the way to the New World –, which are subject to 'rudimentary levelling'. Since rudimentary levelling is the cornerstone of Dillard (1985), we see that Dillard's approach stops short of other forms of accommodation, especially those involving the next generation.

---

[62] While Trudgill (2004: 89) considers this tendency as "biologically inherited", I would argue that this human tendency is not hard-wired in the genes, but an outcome of cultural evolution itself (e.g. Dawkins 1989).

Phase (Ib), interdialect development, involves the production of unusual, or even novel, forms that are not present in any of the input varieties. Interdialect forms are the result of partial accommodation and/or misanalyses by adult speakers (Trudgill 2004: 94). In our study of the modals, hypercorrection would affect, e.g., the use of SHALL in all three persons by non-Southern English speakers. As is evidenced in statements such as in Fowler and Fowler's *King's English* (1973: 142), the proper use of SHALL and WILL, while it "comes by nature to southern Englishmen [...] is so complicated that those who are not to the manner born can hardly acquire it". In early Ontario we would expect hypercorrections of this type towards the Southern-English norm, in stage I.

One striking difference in stage I between Trudgill's scenario in New Zealand and ours in Ontario is that the loyalists, the first generation immigrants and their children intermingled, among others, with speakers of more or less related languages, such as adult German speakers, and Scots and Gaelic speakers and their families. This adds a further layer of language contact and the possibility of some, albeit very restricted, influence from L2 and L1 varieties, if only for a transient phase.

What role might the first generation immigrant children have played in the formation of OntE? The crucial role of children in language change and maintenance is well known. In stable, focussed speech communities, young children of immigrants manage with ease to filter out the non-native parts of their parent's speech (e.g. the Ethan Experience, Chambers 2002: 121-123). This 'innate accent filter', in our case a more general 'dialect filter', was active for those children of first wave immigrants to Ontario, who were young enough, i.e. had not reached the critical period around puberty. The question is, however, what linguistic behaviour was filtered out in the context of a lacking peer variety that would, in the more stable situations, have served as a model.

Colonial lag and early immigrant children
As we have seen, Trudgill (2004: 34) sees a colonial lag only operative in stage I. Because immigrant children had no "common peer-group dialect" to accommodate to, they acquired forms of the older generation's speech. Apart from that, the role of these children is left relatively unaccounted for in Trudgill's model. Just as was the case later in New Zealand, the early Ontario loyalist refugees came as families, including children (Potter-MacKinnon 1993), as did the Scottish immigrants (Campey 2005), Irish immigrants and many groups after them. A head count in eastern Ontario in 1784 (Potter-MacKinnon 1993: 11), shows that of 3,463 immigrants (including 7 servants),

41 percent were male, 17 percent females, but 40 percent were children (usually under the age of 16). If we assume, conservatively, that half of the children were under 10, there would have been substantial numbers of young children in early Ontario to drive the formation process. In New Zealand, for the first decade of settlement between 1840-50, accounts show a slightly lower number of children, accounting for c. 38% of the input population, and a much lower ratio of men to women with 1.3 men to every woman (Mein Smith 2005: 59). The Ontario ratio was closer to 3:1. With women as the major caretakers at the time, average family size would be bigger in the Ontarian context, and these characteristics would have influenced the dialect mixing process, with different family-internal social network sizes.

While family sizes were big, schools and other institutions that promoted the face-to-face interaction between children were not numerous in Ontario. For the first generation of immigrant children, however, situations which facilitated communication with their peers outside of the family included, e.g. in the temporary camps and, once these families were settled in lots, e.g. among neighbouring families. Before stage II, however, when a new Ontario-born generation acquired language, rudimentary levelling and interdialect forms among adults would have had less significance in Ontario than in New Zealand. In Ontario, roughly one generation after the original settlement, around 1805, social structures had been set up and basic schools had been founded. Given the demographics of early Ontario, around 1795, i.e. 12 years after the first big waves of settlement, children under 16 would have already accounted for 55-60% of the population (Wood 2000: 25, table 3.1). This would have started the selection process of children on a grand scale already in the second half of stage I, which points to a more accelerated formation than in Trudgill's New Zealand scenario. In principle, the processes that we are to discuss in stage II must have, as a result of their high percentage among the Ontarian population, at least partly applied to children in stage I as well.

5.3.4.2 Stage II: Children select
In this stage, the native-born children of immigrants had to filter out forms during their own language acquisition from the multitude of dialect forms that they heard around them. The ONZE tapes provide apparent-time evidence for this stage and its high degree of variability (Trudgill 2004: 101).

Phase (IIa), extreme variability, occurs at this stage (Trudgill 2004: 101-108). Children select features from different dialects around them, which result in "new and hitherto nonexistent combinations". We said earlier that Canadian Raising is perhaps a good example of one of these new combinations, as the vowel onsets of diphthongs were relocated in a more economical way than in old world dialects.[63] The sociolinguistic situation would lead to two phenomena, which are evidenced in the ONZE tapes (Trudgill 2004: 106). First, the selection would include the acquisition of more than one form for a given function by one individual, i.e. intra-dialectal variation. Second, people growing up in the same place at the same time, who would under normal circumstances acquire the same linguistic features, "may differ markedly from one another in their linguistic use of variables", i.e. display inter-dialectal variation, in new-dialect formation scenarios.

The variability in stage II is already subject to some sort of levelling (Trudgill 2004: 109). This reasoning is the result of forms that are expected to have been part of the original input, but are not witnessed in the ONZE recordings. The lack of features prevalent in the original input varieties results in the proposition of a second type of levelling, *apparent levelling*. Apparent levelling operates below a threshold level that is based on a minimal discourse frequency of a given feature. According to Trudgill (2004: 110), any imported feature would have had to occur "in sufficient quantities" in order to be selected by a new generation of speakers. Features that are numerically underrepresented would not have met this precondition of language acquisition of the younger generation. Assuming that forms are equally distributed across immigrant groups, we can equate the frequency of a feature associated with a group with the group's demographic strength. In this way, 'apparent levelling' leads to a reduction of variants that do not meet the threshold, for which Trudgill tentatively suggests 10%.[64] As we have seen in chapter (3), southern English speakers accounted only for 7% of the Ontarian input demographic in the second wave, coinciding largely with stage II, and their forms would not have met the threshold.

Stage II, therefore, is the first stage of a more profound reduction of variants by way of apparent levelling, which is largely dependent on demographics. This stage shows more considerable changes in the newly-forming dialect – quite in contrast to stage I, which allows only for the accommodation of salient dialect features. Trudgill (2004: 108) characterizes this phase as a period of "variable acquisition, not accommodation", as children are "selecting at will

---

[63] It would therefore be of little surprise if the origin of the feature in Ontario could be predated by half a century from the 1860s (Thomas 1991: 148) to the early 1800s.

[64] For the adoption of phonological features in grade-school children a threshold of around 20% has been suggested in a different context (Chambers 1988: 664), which may be an alternative cut-off point.

from a kind of supermarket, as it were, of [...] variants with which they were surrounded".

5.3.4.3 Stage III: The majority principle

In the third generation after the original settlement the variants that are still left after rudimentary levelling and apparent levelling are further reduced to usually only one variant per function. To account for the process, Trudgill (2004: 114) proposes the principle of majority, which leaves aside more elaborate social concepts, above all notions of prestige and identity. By comparing the speech of ONZE informants to present-day New Zealand English, Trudgill states that

> the crucial explanatory factor for the way levelling takes place is the survival of majority variants [...]. The final shape of New Zealand English is the result of a levelling process which, for the most part, consisted of the loss of demographically minority forms. (Trudgill 2004: 114)

This approach lends itself well to empirical testing based on the distribution of forms and demographic information, which will be undertaken in the following chapters. Moreover, it relegates social concepts to the sidelines of the explanatory process. Trudgill makes this point explicit when he says the following:

> I do not find it at all necessary, in considering Stages II and III of new-dialect formation in tabula rasa situations, to call on the social factor of 'prestige' or related factors such as 'status' and 'stigma' as explanatory factors. Nor do I invoke 'identity' or 'ideology' as factors that were involved. (Trudgill 2004: 149)

Social concepts do not figure prominently in Trudgill's scenario. Consequently, ideas that a "patently non-English dialect" was chosen as a sign of a rejection of England by Irish and Scottish immigrant children in Ontario (Fee 1992b: 180f) would not fit well with the principles of the model, although they may have had some currency among adult immigrants, who would have been the major linguistics players in stage I alone, and not in subsequent stages.

M. Gordon (2005: 147) rightly assesses that this orientation towards a more mechanical, demographically controlled process is the most controversial aspect of the theory. At the same time, however, provided it can be applied to other settings besides those it is based on (e.g. Trudgill 1986; 2004), the theory would provide us with an empirically testable scenario for the birth of colonial varieties in general that supersedes previous accounts.

The outcome of the selection processes in stages I-III is also called koinéization (Trudgill 2004: 89). The koiné would still display a degree of variation and would need to undergo focussing towards a more unified variety. Chambers (1995a, 1989: 85) considers a "unified, focussed dialect of Canadian English" to be a product of the 20th century, but allows for some features to have been established earlier. Canadian Raising has been shown (Thomas 1991) to have existed in 19th century Ontario. Together with the low back vowel merger, as indicated by spellings of *sauce* as *sarce* in Susanna Moodie's writings (Chambers 1989: 86), we can list two features that would have been part of OntE by 1850.

5.3.4.4 Focussing

The product of stages I-III would then, finally be transferred into a socially stable, i.e. normed variety, which may be codified in some way. The process of focussing is usually referred to as applied by Le Page and Tabouret-Keller (1985: 5f), who briefly introduce the notion in their context of creole studies. Is focussing, one may ask, a largely conscious process? Le Page and Tabouret-Keller's work focuses on language and identity, which implies a conscious focussing process, at least in part, on behalf of the speakers. Trudgill (1986: 88) defines focussing as the process that provides "norms and stability" to a variety, which leaves it a rather fuzzy concept, but which has proven useful in recent work (e.g. Al-Wer 2003, cf. Kerswill 2002).

In contrast, Hickey (2004b: 20) points out that the emergence of an 'identity' is a "largely unconscious process", that sets focussed varieties apart from embryonic, i.e. diffuse, ones. Cooley (1992: 179) also characterises the process – at least implicitly – as an unconscious one, when she presents focussing as a feature that may or may not be noticed by speakers of a new variety:

> During the time of early focussing, some people would recognize these embryonic focused dialects and others would not. (Cooley 1992: 179)

Cooley (1992: 182) continues stating that AmE varieties were already "systematized and focussed varieties" before the Revolutionary War, but were only noticed as dialects of a common standard language by pre-revolution commentators. What kind of process are we to understand under 'focussing'? The emergence of a linguistic identity can either be the result of a conscious effort, or of an inherent process of human social interaction under stable situations (as a by-product of linguistic processes). A combination of both would perhaps be most plausible, with differing percentages of conscious and unconscious processes depending on the social circumstances.

In the Canadian context, which never included a political break with Britain, and only half-hearted or temporal ones with the USA, conscious attempts of establishing a Canadian identity were never as consistent as in other countries. In the wake of the World Wars, however, the period between 1920 and 1970 has been suggested as a period of conscious focussing. We have evidence that in the mid-1800s CanE speakers were linguistically more occupied – if they were concerned about their language at all – with *not* sounding American, that is, with adhering to British standards, which were conceived as superior (Hultin 1967; Chambers 2004). Reviewers in Canadian magazines, for instance, "warn[ed] the public of Americanisms and advise[d] Canadians to shun them" (from 1847, quoted in Hultin 1967: 249).

In this context, it is very plausible that an unconscious focussing process went unnoticed, similar to what Cooley reported of pre-revolution AmE. Given the proximity of CanE and AmE, any CanE feature that resembled an AmE one was likely to be discouraged, or, at best, went uncommented. Reverend Geikie (1857 4; 14), a visitor from Britain, referred to the emerging CanE in 1857 with the famous words of a "corrupt dialect growing up amongst [the Canadian] population" and to its forms as "lawless and vulgar innovations". The anecdotal evidence points to one direction: while Canadians tried to adopt British standards, they could not hide the American base of their language. It can be easily imagined that this kind of linguistic situation was not conducive for appreciating one's own, slowly focussing, variety of English. We will see in the empirical part, whether, and to what extent, the CONTE-pC data can provide support for this scenario of a largely unconscious focussing process in early Ontario.

There is one notion left that figures prominently in Trudgill (2004), which will be discussed before we address one practical problem of application of the theory. This is the notion of homogeneity and uniformity in 19th-century varieties of English, which is connected to the concept of drift.

5.3.5 Homogeneity and drift in CanE

The remarkable homogeneity of standard CanE has been addressed in chapter (2), and it is interesting to see that Trudgill (2004) provides an explanatory scenario for the homogeneity of colonial Englishes in general. Crucial to the spread of forms over a larger area in early settled colonies, e.g. the Atlantic USA, is the notion of drift, i.e. parallel developments in several varieties, and the increasing mobility since the late 18th century.

The notion of drift, going back to Edward Sapir (1949: 150), stipulates that varieties from a common source continue to evolve in similar directions by undergoing similar linguistic changes. This means that certain changes in colonial varieties had already been engrained in the linguistic system and would set the path for future developments for some time to come, even after the separation of the varieties. As Trudgill (2004: 130) points out, some changes since the 19th century in world Englishes appear to be a result of parallel development. The use of HAVE in interrogatives, requiring *do*-support in many varieties around the world today, is a development that Trudgill suspects as the result of a drift whose predispositions were established in LModE. Lacking an adequate survey, the following example can just be used to illustrate the idea of drift:

19th c.	Have you coffee with breakfast?	(habit)
	Have you any money?	(possession)
20th c.	**Do** you have coffee with breakfast?	
	Have you any money?	
21st c.	**Do** you have coffee with breakfast?	
	Do you have any money?	(Trudgill 2004: 130)

While the 20th-century situation appears to be modelled after BrE dialects, it is clear that AmE seems to have completed the change towards *do*-periphrasis rather early in the 20th century, with OntE only lagging a generation or so behind (cf. Avis' (1955: 16) evidence for CanE and AmE. While Avis attributes this emerging pattern to a dialect contact situation in which AmE influences CanE speakers, it could also be an instance of drift, an example of "changes in the language which have been set in motion and are continuing even after geographical separation" (Trudgill 2004: 131), a separation that was, in the OntE context, never complete.

Trudgill (2004: 132) differentiates between two types of drift that he finds in the ONZE data: *type 1 drift* is a result of changes which had already been underway at the time of separation and which were completed independently, while *type 2 drift* is characterized as inherited "shared tendencies or propensities" which can lead to similar changes in donor and receiving varieties after separation. Drift of type 1 will be referred to as *continuing drift*, while drift of type 2 will be called *directional drift*.

According to Trudgill, *directional drift* (type 2) in combination with speakers' unprecedented mobility levels in the 19th century are the two main reasons for homogeneity in colonial Englishes (2004: 161). We have seen in chapter (3) that the early Ontario population was characterized as a highly mobile one right from the beginning. As the Canadian west was settled in the 1870s with the newly-built railway lines as its backbone, remarks on the homogeneity in CanE across the continent were found. Lighthall (1889: 581) refers to the notion of a "practically uniform dialect" across Canada (if only to deconstruct it from a dialectologist's point of view) and by the beginning of the 20th century the notion of a homogenous CanE was firmly entrenched (Priestley 1968: 76).

It is a plausible scenario that high levels of mobility in early Ontario would have accelerated instances of drift and other changes by diffusing them more quickly through the province – with the possible exception of more remote or self-contained areas.

5.3.6 Some problems of applying new-dialect formation theory

We have seen that in Trudgill's theory colonial dialects come very close to statistical composites of the donor varieties with the majority principle as one of its cornerstones. Certain stages and phases, however, rely more heavily on the majority principle than others. The phases of apparent levelling (IIb) and stage III (a&b) rest on rather straightforward calculations based on the demographic input to explain why some forms have survived but others have not.

There are some practical considerations that would need to be kept in mind, however. Although the concepts seem rather straightforward and easy to be applied, a number of issues need to be considered when dealing with immigrant demographics. Data from immigration port authorities will serve to illustrate the problem of segregating migratory streams for one's calculations of majority input. Trudgill (2004: 160) defines the notion of majority rather loosely by saying that it can mean that a feature is "present in the speech of a majority of speakers" but also that it is "the most commonly occurring variant in terms of tokens".

Data for two sets of immigrant groups provide the backdrop for an illustration of the problem in our context: Northern and Southern English on the one hand, and Northern and Southern Irish on the other hand. Let us assume a divided usage between Northern and Southern English speakers for a given variable and apply the principle of majority based on input demographics. Strictly speaking, we would need to count the incidence of the forms in both Northern and Southern textual evidence, i.e. the tokens. While this would be the best methodological approach, it would necessitate text samples of the input varieties that are, at present, difficult to obtain (see Dollinger forthc.). An alternative approach is to gauge the incidence indirectly via the sizes of the population in relation to each other. While this is only an approximation, it is the best practicable method available to us with the historical corpora currently at our disposal and equivalent with Trudgill's first notion, i.e. the presence of features in the majority input.

Figure (5.4) provides the immigration data for the later years from 1831 to 1849, with the percentages provided for Northerners:

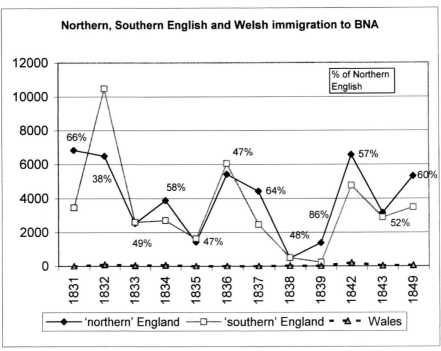

Figure 5.4: SIN and Southern English immigration to BNA
(based on Cowan 1961: 291, App. B, Table IV, absolute numbers per year)

In chapter (3) it was shown that Southern English speakers were a minority of the overall input. On the whole, the curves are rather parallel in our data, with some spikes, however, most notably in 1831; percentage figures are shown for Northerners. If one assesses the input on a year by year basis, we see that of the 12 years we have data of, Northern speakers provided only in seven cases the absolute majority in comparison to Southerners and that in five out of 12 years the difference between Northern and Southern input was rather marginal, i.e. between 47 and 52 percent for both of them, which must be considered as an equal distribution.

Figure (5.5) shows immigration from Northern Irish ports (& vicinity) and Southern Irish ports. Here again, we see the challenge of establishing a majority form. With the exception of the years 1834, 1836 and 1837, when Southern

Irish arrived in sizeable larger numbers than Northern Irish, immigration was again rather balanced and provides few clues for the establishment of a majority input. While the gap widens considerably during the Irish potato famine in the late 1840s, this migration takes place too late to show some influence by the end of our period.

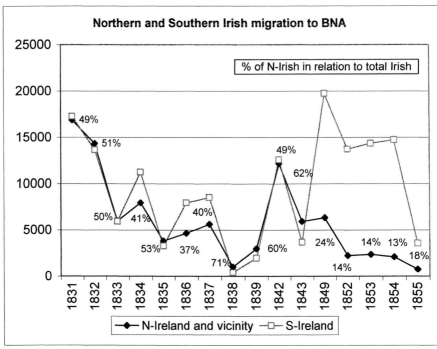

Figure 5.5: N-Irish and S-Irish immigration to BNA
(based on Cowan 1961: 293, App. B, Table IV)

The question here is whether immigration to Ontario was stratified enough to allow for a meaningful assessment of majority forms based on the demography of input varieties. As new-dialect theory grants large minority forms a good chance for being selected, provided that they are intermediate or unmarked forms and have a system-internal selection advantage (cf. Trudgill 2004: 160), we have few means to predict which forms would be chosen. We have to conclude, however, that the Ontarian immigration data in figures (5.4) and (5.5) do not help establish a dominant input pattern conclusively for the majority of the years shown, rendering the need for another principle that may assist in predicting the eventual form selection.

Another aspect of importance comprises the regional settlement patterns in early Ontario. We said earlier that the second wave immigrants "settled in the countryside, most commonly in the nineteenth century as farmers" (Akenson 1999: 5) and did not settle in the towns as much as in the United States. This would imply that older Ontarian towns and more recently settled rural areas would proceed at different speeds along the three stages of the model. One scenario predicts that the countryside would be lagging behind the centres by one stage, as the settlement in the fringe areas were opened roughly one generation after the loyalists took possession of their lands. Since one stage is completed in roughly one generation, the countryside is therefore expected to lag behind the towns by one stage in the new-dialect formation process. However, this scenario of a rural lag, so to speak, would apply foremost to settlements closer to the settlement fringe, as other rural areas would tend to look towards the urban areas for their linguistic models.

5.4 Summary

In this chapter the classic contributions by M. Bloomfield and Scargill were the points of departure for developmental scenarios of CanE. While both are essentially void of linguistic data to support their claims, they have dominated the discourse on the formation of CanE. The state-of-the-art concerning dialect development in Ontario is summarized by Walter Avis who states that

> American speech habits have been entrenched from the beginning, even though they may since have been somewhat modified by later waves of immigration from the British Isles. Avis (1978a: 40)

Both the mixing process and the modification process still need to be accounted for in a more complete developmental scenario, however.

Furthermore, basic approaches to the formation of colonial varieties were outlined and the model of new-dialect formation by Trudgill (2004) was adopted as the theoretical framework for the empirical part. It was pointed out, however, that the *semi-tabula rasa situation* in early Ontario would likely render it a hybrid scenario, with both the new-dialect formation stages *and* more traditional geolinguistic diffusion models occurring simultaneously. Moreover, the high percentage of children in the first wave of immigration, which was to increase in the years following, and larger family sizes would likely result in an accelerated progress through the formation stages.

The selection of forms is considered as guided primarily by the majority principle, which is only mitigated by three processes: first, the process of unmarking, second, the existence of intermediate forms and, third, the process of drift, which grants social concepts such as prestige and identity a less prominent role than in more traditional contact scenarios. Furthermore, Trudgill's original notion of the selection of forms for the new variety was extended to include forms *and their functions* to account for grammatical phenomena. The distributions of form in given functions will be used to account for grammatical and semantic change in the modal auxiliaries. It was also suggested that remote rural areas lag behind urban areas by roughly one stage, which is accounted for in two different layers, or speeds, of development.

The process of focussing requires special attention in early Ontario as the extralinguistic situation may have distorted the process of new-dialect formation. Since focussing is more likely a largely unconscious process in early Ontario, it is possible that the intermediate state of CanE – in between AmE and BrE influences, with the latter one being the norm of the social elite and the former closer to the vernacular – resulted in failure to recognize the embryonic and budding features of CanE. Instead, a potential CanE feature would likely have been viewed as yet another American 'barbarism'.

In the next five chapters, internal data from the period 1776 to 1850 will be employed to assess the theories, hypotheses and predictions of new-dialect formation theory. To explain the formation of OntE, the following factors would need to be considered (cf. Trudgill 2004: 1f):

1) dialect contact among the input varieties of OntE
2) linguistic changes in British and American input varieties that did not occur in OntE
3) linguistic changes in OntE (innovation) that did not occur in Britain or America
4) instances of drift and parallel development

Keeping these four major processes in mind, we will proceed to the empirical part of the present study.

6 LATE MODERN ENGLISH MODAL AUXILIARIES: METHODOLOGICAL CONSIDERATIONS

The diachronic development of the English modal auxiliaries involves both syntactic and semantic aspects. Although most changes in the modals' formal, syntactic properties, such as the change from full verbs to auxiliaries and their rise as a separate syntactic category, were completed by the beginning of our period (Traugott 1972, Lightfoot 1979), their semantic development did not stop by the end of the EModE period.

LModE syntax must be considered one of the most understudied linguistic levels of the period (Beal 2004: 66), which holds especially true in comparison to the syntactic literature on OE, ME, or EModE. Therefore, it is little surprising that the most comprehensive study on LModE syntax to date[65] opens with a remark on the pioneering nature of the enterprise (Denison 1998: 92).

This neglect of scholarly attention may be the consequence of the generally less dramatic syntactic changes in LModE – with only very few exceptions such as the spread of progressive constructions (Smitterberg 2005, Beal 2004: 78-82). Since most categorical syntactical features of English had been established by 1776, changes have been statistical in nature since then, which tends to make these changes "more a matter of stylistic than syntactic change" and less interesting for syntacticians. (Denison 1998: 67)

The English modal auxiliary complex is no exception here. In a framework such as Lightfoot (1979), which considers changes in the English modal system as the result of a spontaneous "wholesale re-analysis" (1979: 114), we cannot be surprised that generativist studies usually stopped short in the EModE period. More recent work on grammaticalization and subjectification (e.g. Fischer 2003, 1994, Krug 2000, Brinton 1991, Traugott 1989, Goosens 1987, Plank 1984), however, points, quite in contrast to Lightfoot's thesis, towards a gradience of changes in the English modals throughout their history. These changes, "form part of a reorganization that has been going on throughout the recorded history of that system" (Jacobsson 1994: 179) and make the

---

[65] i.e. Denison's (1998) chapter of monograph-length in the *Cambridge History of the English language*.

LModE modal auxiliary complex a well-suited complex for a corpus-based, variationist approach, such as in the present work. For EModE, the modals have been studied in a corpus-based framework. The work of Gotti and associates (2002), and most prominently of Kytö (e.g. 1991a, 1987), who surveyed the constraints and distributions of modal verbs in her EModE Corpus of *Early American English* (1620-1720), are key contributions that serve as waypoints for the empirical part of this study. Denison (1998: 165) identifies the LModE modal verbs as an area of "considerable changes in usage", an area which has largely flown below the radar of variation linguists.

Changes do not stop short of the 20th century, of course. Fuelled by high incidences across all genres and registers, modals continue to be in a state of flux and seem to be undergoing a series of changes (e.g. Smith 2003, Leech 2003, Mair and Leech 2006, Mair 2006: 100-111, Tagliamonte 2006b: 484-492). As Krug (2000) has shown in some detail, modal newcomers are constantly in the making, as can more readily be seen in the more recent grammaticalizations of HAVE TO > HAFTA, WANT TO > WANNA, GOING TO > GONNA.

6.1 Definitions and terminology

In any study that involves semantic features special emphasis must be placed on the illustration of the terminology used. While the latter will be carried out in the individual chapters on the modal auxiliaries, the more general terminology will be introduced here. Most generally, modals that are referred to in upper case characters, e.g. CAN, include all paradigmatic forms and (spelling) variants, e.g. *can, canst, cann* in the data. Likewise, CAN'T includes all negative forms, e.g. *can't, cant, cannot, can not*.

6.1.1 Formal characteristics

The NICE criteria (cf. Palmer 1990: 3 for their genesis) are a starting point for any study on the modal auxiliaries. They are shown in (6.1a) and comprise the tests of negation, inversion, coda, and emphatic affirmation. In combination with three additional criteria that serve as tests for their syntactic status as auxiliary verbs (Palmer 1990: 4), which are shown in (6.1b), the NICE criteria provide a set of tests to identify most modal expressions. Quirk *et al.* (1985: 317) identify nine central modals in present-day English: CAN, COULD, MAY, MIGHT, SHALL, SHOULD, WILL ('LL), WOULD ('D) and MUST.

(6.1) a. Negation with '*nt*:   I *can't*, I *cannot* come.
            Inversion: *Can* I come?
            Coda: I can come and so *can* you
            Emphasis: I *cán* come.

       b. no –*s* in 3rd p. singular   ** He *cans* come.
            no non-finite forms   ** to can, ** canning
            usually no co-occurrence   ** She may will come
            with other modals
            (except for restricted cases of double modals in some dialects)

Not all central modals meet all NICE criteria, however. For instance, MAY does not have a negative form in *mayn't*. Therefore, the NICE criteria cannot be considered as absolute tests, but as mere indicators that need to be assessed for each modals including other parameters. If we consider the historical core of the English modals, the OE preterit-present verbs, OUGHT, classified by Quirk *et al.* (1985) as a marginal modal, may be added to the list of nine central modals in the LModE context of the present study. OUGHT, in ME more frequently rendered with grammaticalized TO as OUGHT TO is a case in point. Table (6.1) shows the original core of the OE preterit-present verbs, which historically form the core of the English modals:

Infinitive	Present	Preterit
āgan 'to owe'	āh	āhte > *ought*
cunnan 'to know how'	cann > *can*	cūðe > *could*
magan 'to be able"	mæg > *may*	meahte > *might*
* mōtan 'to be allowed'	mōt	mōste > *must*
sculan 'to be obliged'	sceal > *shall*	sceolde > *should*

Table 6.1: OE Preterit-present verbs and their PDE relatives
(Pyles and Algeo 1993: 126)

Unlike OUGHT TO, which derives from preterit-present *āhte*, the predecessors of the core modals WILL and WOULD, *willan* and its preterit form *wolde,* derived – atypically – from a weak verb and were early additions to the core modals. This addition of OUGHT TO is intuitively appealing especially in the LModE context, which would have favoured certain forms considered obsolete today, such as OUGHT. This study will therefore survey Quirk et al.'s nine central modals plus OUGHT TO, i.e. ten core modals.

   While the criteria in (6.1) are useful to identify core modals, they also cannot identify structures that are on the way of becoming fully-fledged modal auxiliaries and which are potential rivals of the core modals. Generally speaking, these newer modal structures have been shown to undergo a steady increase in discourse frequency since the 1650s (Biber 2004: 201) in both AmE and BrE, and we would expect a similar scenario in other varieties. These forms include WANT TO, NEED (TO)[66], HAVE TO, (HAVE) GOT TO (cf. Krug 2000), which have been variously referred to as quasi-modals (e.g. Brinton 1991, Fischer 1994), semi-modals (Quirk *et al.* 1985: 137, Biber *et al.* 1998: 205), modal idioms (Quirk *et al.* 1985), marginal modals (Quirk *et al.* 1985) and emerging modals (Krug 2000).

In the following case studies, all modal structures that are not among the ten core modals (nine central modals as defined by Quirk *et al.* 1985, plus OUGHT TO) will be invariably referred to as semi-modals *without* any theoretical implications as to their status, i.e. no distinction is being made between, e.g. *got to* as a modal idiom and *have to* as a semi-auxiliary. They are, following my definition, both semi-modals. Moreover, the term 'modal expression' will be used as a cover term for all items conveying modality.

Quirk *et al.*'s nine core modals plus, for historical reasons, OUGHT TO, will be the area of focus in the following chapters. In the four empirical chapters, we will look at aspects, both syntactic and semantic, of CAN/COULD, MAY/MIGHT, WILL/WOULD, SHALL/SHOULD, MUST and OUGHT TO and, in the case of MUST, some of its semi-modal competitors in LModE. Other semi-modals were generally not as far advanced, and competitors of MUST were leading the development. The overall incidence in CanE of other semi-modal expressions, shown in appendix (6), shows that the incidence of expressions conveying modality was generally low at the time.

6.1.2 Modality: root, deontic, dynamic, epistemic and other concepts

Modality, as a cover term in a general sense, refers to the status of a proposition. A basic way of distinguishing propositions is in terms of their factual (realis) vs. non-factual (irrealis) content. In these basic terms, a sentence such as *John is in Port Alice* would be a factual proposition, while *John might be in Port Alice* would be considered non-factual (cf. Palmer 2001 for other distinctions). In most Indo-European languages two grammatical systems express this general notion of modality: 'mood' on the one hand and 'modality', in the narrower sense, on the other hand. Mood is an inflectional category of the verb and divides the spectrum in Indo-European languages in *realis* propositions,

---

[66] NEED, without TO, is a low-frequency form occurring in some dialects (with a possible link to Scottish influence), e.g. *The glass needs washed*, and has an intermediate status between core and semi-modals (cf. Quinn 1999: 191 for some examples).

i.e. the indicative mood, and *irrealis* propositions, i.e. the subjunctive mood (and related moods, such as optative or injunctive moods). While a distinction based on mood is usually binary (Palmer 2001: 4), modal systems that operate with other means than verbal inflections, such as the English modality markers (e.g. *perhaps, maybe, likely*), or modal auxiliaries, are typically gradient systems (besides modal adverbs and adjectives, which are not considered in the present study).

For present-day BrE, the semantic studies of the modal auxiliaries include the classic and ground-breaking empirical account by Coates (1983) and Palmer's (1990) monograph on the English modals, both of which provide a framework that will serve as a starting point for the semantic analyses in the present study. The problem of categorizing different semantic shades of the English modal auxiliaries is particularly notorious (Coates 1983: 13, Palmer 1990: 2), and a distinction between two basic types of meanings, deontic vs. epistemic meaning, has been applied successfully in historical work.

Defined loosely, we could say, following Palmer (1990: 7), that deontic modality is used to "express what is obligatory, permitted, or forbidden", while epistemic use "relates to an interference by the speaker, and is not simply concerned with 'objective' verifiability". A third category, dynamic modality, is closer to deontic uses. Palmer (2001: 9) summarizes the basic difference between deontic and dynamic modality, saying that "with deontic modality the conditioning factors are external to the relevant individual, whereas with dynamic modality they are internal" (see examples 6.3-6.4 below). For Palmer (1990: 2), epistemic and deontic are "the two most semantically fundamental kinds of modality".

While the scope of these definitions of modality is fuzzy, as the three definitions above have shown, they have proven to be sufficiently accurate for empirical studies. To illustrate the use of the terms, some pairs from Palmer (1990, 2003) are shown below:

(6.2) a. John *may* be there now.   b.   John *must* be there now.
                      (epistemic)
(6.3) a. John *may/can* come now.   b.   John *must* come now.
                      (deontic)
(6.4) a. John *can* speak German.   b.   I *will* help you.
                      (dynamic)

The examples in (6.2) illustrate epistemic uses, as they make "judgments about the probability of the truth of the proposition", while the examples in (6.3) "in some way influence the action" (Palmer 1990: 5) – by giving permission for

John to come in (6.3a), or by making his coming obligatory (6.3b), i.e. deontic readings. It is important that in the examples in (6.3) the control is external to the subject: in (6.3a) an authority is granting John permission to come now, in (6.3b) he is commanded to come now. In (6.4b), on the other hand, the control of the action is in the hand of the subject. In the present study on LModE in early Ontario, focus will be put on the distinction between epistemic and non-epistemic meanings, the latter often called root meanings, which is the most basic functional differentiation.

The term 'root meaning' "refers to the logic of obligation and permission" and "[t]ypical [r]oot modals, such as MUST and MAY, cover a range of meanings, of which 'Obligation' and 'Permission' represent only the core" (Coates 1983: 21). 'Root use' of modals, referring to their presumably 'original' functions, are a broader concept than deontic meaning and seem more workable as a classification system in a diachronic study such as the present one, which is why the term and concept of 'root uses' is given preference (but see Palmer 1990: 22 for the preference of dynamic meanings in present-day English). Root meanings also translate well into an epistemic vs. non-epistemic dichotomy, which is the most important delimitation in the modal auxiliaries, as they can be considered as a cover term for both deontic and dynamic uses. In this study, I will adhere to the basic distinction between 'root uses' on the one hand, and 'epistemic uses' on the other hand.

There is yet another reason for the exclusion of dynamic modality as a concept for the classification of the data. The more basic, binary classification system will ensure that the various studies of modal auxiliary verbs can be compared in relation to the spread of epistemic uses in English (see 6.1.3 below). Where needed, as in the case of CAN and its functions shown above, we will semantically subclassify root uses as 'ability' (as in 6.4a) and 'permission' uses (as in 6.3a), but adhere to the basic root vs. epistemic distinction. Example (6.4a) would be a prototypical example of dynamic modality, which we will classify as root (ability) (see chapter 7 for more examples).

There are a number of other concepts that are in some cases related to the two- or threefold distinctions outlined here, and in other respects expand on these notions (subjectivity ~ epistemic modality, Traugott 1989) or rearrange the semantic spectrum differently (e.g. prepositional modality vs. event modality, see Palmer 2001; extrinsic vs. intrinsic modality, see Quirk *et al.* 1985, Biber *et al.* 1999). Except for the concept of subjectivity, which we will refer to briefly in reference to OUGHT TO, these concepts are not part of the present study (see Depraetere and Reed 2006 for a summary of various categorization schemes in recent studies on English modality; Nuyts 2005 and de Haan

2005 for cross-language typologies, or Barbiers 2002). There is one concept, however, that we need to mention briefly as it plays some role in the next subsection: the notion of 'alethic' modality. Characterized as a notion at the margins of modality studies and hardly ever used today (Nuyts 2005: 8f), it is concerned with the "necessary or contingent truth of propositions" (Lyons 1977: 791), with the term itself deriving from a Greek root meaning 'true'. In practice, the difference between alethic and epistemic/root modalities may be characterized as a distinction between 'truth in the world' vs. 'truth in an individual's mind' (Nuyts 2001: 28). This would mean that sentences such as *He can run 100 metres in under 11 seconds*, can be root (dynamic; he told me so), epistemic (I suppose so: given his 200 metre time, I believe 11 seconds are in his range) or absolute truth (alethic – we saw him run the time at the last championships). Lyons (1977: 791) sees alethic modality closer to epistemicity.

The distinction between root modality and epistemic modality, the former of which has been referred to as the "most influential proposal" in modal semantics (de Haan 2005: 29), has been popular in early generativist theory (Lyons 1977: 792), and may be considered the most reliable means, if also somewhat rudimentary in light of more recent classifications into deontic, dynamic (or agent-oriented modality), and epistemic (or subject-oriented modality) of discriminating the semantic realm of modality. The basic differentiation adopted here, however, will facilitate, and in some cases even enable, the analysis of the LModE data, while limiting ambiguous or indeterminable cases to a minimum.[67]

6.1.3 Epistemic uses since LModE: increase, stagnation or decline?

As has been pointed out before, grammaticalization patterns are claimed to be unidirectional and have been identified for the English modals in the following clines:

Facultative > deontic > epistemic > futurity, conditional etc.
(Goosens 1987: 118)

main verb > premodal > deontic > weak epistemic > strong epistemic
(Traugott 1989: 43)

---

[67] Cf. for an opposing view Nuyts (2001: 25), who considers the confounding of deontic and dynamic uses as "unfortunate". Please note, however, that Nuyts is working with present-day data.

It will be shown to what extent the Canadian data fit in these clines for the English modals, which generally have been considered as showing a radically different behaviour when compared to the modals in other Germanic languages, especially Dutch and German (Nuyts 2001: 176). Recently, Abraham (2001, 2002) has proposed a formal account on the separate status of the English modals. While his account is conceived as a comparative study of English with German and Dutch (and Danish) reference points and presented in a formal syntactic-semantic framework, the Canadian data can be used to test Abraham's account of the English modals. Among the conditions accounting for the status of English modals, Abraham (2002: 45) claims the demise of the lexical aspect/aktionsart sensitivity of the English modals in Middle English to be responsible for a development that is distinct to other Germanic languages.

Abraham (2001: 34) suggests the loss of lexical aktionsart, to be more precise 'terminativity', and the development of a grammatical aspect system instead since the ME period (see Smitterberg 2005 for 19th-century developments), as "the trigger for the far-reaching auxiliarization of MVs [modal verbs] in English". Abraham (2002) finds that core modals in present-day spoken American English appear predominantly in epistemic readings, while root meanings of core modal verbs are replaced with new semi-modals such as HAVE TO or BE PERMITTED TO (instead of MUST, MAY), which are considered to be at a "final stage" in the diachronic development (2002: 46).

Function	WILL	MAY	MIGHT	SHALL	MUST
temporal	1655	--	--	0	--
root	24	0	--	0	0
epistemic	8	84	144	0	0
IS TO	**WANT TO**	**WISH TO**	**BE PERMITTED**	**SHOULD**	**HAVE TO**
59	267	4	6	100	222

*Table 6.2: Modals in present-day, professional spoken American English
(Abraham 2002: 20, tables 1&2)*

Table (6.2) shows Abraham's AmE data behind his claim, which will serve as one of our reference points for an assessment of the compatibility of the LModE data with this account. It is surprising that not one single root use is reported for MUST and MAY, functions which are apparently taken over by BE PERMITTED and the well-established HAVE TO. SHOULD, together with MIGHT, occur rather frequent in these data, with semi-modal WANT TO (see Krug 2000) as the most frequent modal.

While the full implications of Abraham's theory are beyond the scope of the present study, especially in relation to other Germanic languages, we might see if, and to what extent, his prediction is borne out in the English varieties. We will also be in a position to assess, whether these changes in the modal auxiliaries are spearheaded, once more, by spoken AmE, the "main driving-force of change in this area" of modality (Mair and Leech 2006: 328).

The direction of change, as suggested by Abraham, is headed towards epistemic readings in the core modals and towards deontic readings in the semimodals. It is clear that a full analysis of the complex interdependencies would necessarily involve a survey of the aspect/aktionsart and modality interface, which is beyond our scope (see also Ziegeler 2003, 2006 for English). In the present study, we will investigate how epistemic readings, an important indicator for the correctness of Abraham's theory, develop in the Canadian LModE data. We would expect to find some intermediate stages of development by referring to EModE and present-day data. Each of the following empirical chapters will include a section on the development of epistemic uses, which in some cases requires the reinterpretation of the semantic analyses in root (nonepistemic) vs. epistemic terms.

According to Abraham's (2001) theory, and as shown in Goosens' and Traugott's clines above, one would assume the steady expansion of epistemic readings, possibly with the exception of CAN. Abraham (2001: 8) characterizes CAN as to be excluded from "the root vs. epistemic split, since, due to [its] fundamental alethic status (von Wright 1951), such a split cannot be maintained effectively". We have seen in the preceding section that alethic modality refers to the absolute truth of a proposition, beyond the certainty of the subject, some objective truth. The exclusion of CAN revolves around the notion of 'ability' as shown in (6.5a):

(6.5) a. She must speak Danish.   b. She can speak Danish.

In (6.5a), there is either an element of obligation in the future (deontic reading) or a knowledge that is inferred by the speaker (epistemic reading). In (6.5b), one could argue, an objective, verifiable truth (alethic modality) is reported, whereas another way of looking at it would be to consider (6.5b) an instance of dynamic modality[68] (or subject-oriented modality), or simply another root use (and subcategorization 'ability'). The latter categorization will be applied in chapter (7), and it will be shown to what extent the LModE data suggest the exclusion of CAN; generally speaking, it seems that the basic classificational

---

[68] Some consider alethic and dynamic modality as interchangeable terms (van der Auwera 1986: fn 4).

dichotomy in root (deontic and dynamic) vs. epistemic would allow the integration of those 'alethic' functions of CAN along with other root uses.

6.2 Semantic areas: choosing variables

For the present study, the array of modal meanings needs to be divided. The central modals CAN/COULD, MAY/MIGHT, WILL/WOULD, SHALL/ SHOULD, MUST and OUGHT TO are the point of departure and can be subdivided along functional and semantics lines. Three variable complexes were chosen for this survey of modal usage in early OntE. In two cases, the main competitors will be central modals, while in one case the competition will involve a semi-modal. Coates (1983) surveys the modals in PDE empirically along functional and notional criteria, which provide the backdrop for delimitation of the modal complex. The areas identified for case studies take the following notions as a starting point:

- Permission, ability and possibility
- Obligation and necessity
- Volition and prediction

The first area, permission, ability and possibility, comprises the modals CAN, COULD, MAY, MIGHT (Coates 1983: 85-107). The modals of obligation and necessity are MUST, HAVE (GOT) TO, NEED (TO), SHOULD and OUGHT TO (Coates 1983: 31-84), of which MUST, HAVE TO and (HAVE) GOT TO are usually referred to as markers of strong obligation (Myhill 1995), which is our second key area. For volition and prediction – the latter is often referred to as pure futurity – SHALL and WILL are the two main variables. The discussion is complemented by SHOULD and WOULD, the historically related forms to SHALL and WILL, in hypothetical contexts and SHOULD, WOULD and OUGHT TO in hypothetical and non-hypothetical contexts. All of these complexes will also be surveyed for their developments in the area of epistemic modality. The next sections will focus on the choice of variables for each of these areas and provide the reasoning behind their inclusion in the present study.

6.2.1 Permission, ability and possibility: CAN/COULD and MAY/MIGHT

Coates (1983: 86) characterizes this semantic area along two poles: permission on the one hand, and ability on the other hand, with possibility in between (sometimes referred to as 'neutral possibility'). As with other modals, the borderlines between these functions are fuzzy, which is the reason why Kytö (1991a) introduces a class for 'indeterminate' cases in her study on the modals in EModE AmE.

What, however, are the LModE changes in this area? Earlier in the history of English, CAN is found beginning to infringe upon the territory of MAY in the domain of permission (Traugott 1972: 171f)[69]. In LModE, CAN and MAY have been identified as undergoing a change in progress in the 19th century (Simon-Vandenbergen 1984, Facchinetti 2002: 64). Simon-Vandenbergen (1984: 364), hitherto the only study of CAN and MAY that includes a large set of LModE data from the 19th century, finds that CAN was beginning to infringe on MAY denoting root possibility in 19th-century plays, which suggests that the change originated in the spoken language. These are findings that promise to make CAN and MAY a worthwhile object for study in our context: how were CAN and MAY used in early CanE in this respect? How did these changes, and possibly others, spread in CanE, as compared to other varieties? An attempt will be made to answer these and other questions.

CAN and MAY have parallel forms in COULD and MIGHT, which have developed functional patterns of their own as they serve mainly as epistemic markers. Their use is reported in Kytö (1991a: 216) to show differences in both AmE and BrE in the EModE period, which make them good candidates for a study of LModE (chapter 7).

6.2.2 Obligation and necessity: MUST and HAVE TO

Chapter (8) traces the LModE development of the modal expressions HAVE TO and MUST. MUST and HAVE TO, while having quite distinct histories and formal characteristics, are usually considered markers of strong obligation and necessity (Coates 1983: 31). While MUST, a central modal, formally meets all criteria in (6.1), it is an atypical case among the central modals with its change of meaning in MUST NOT. This defective paradigm, which is a legacy of its development, poses interesting questions in relation to the newcomer HAVE TO.

Krug (2000: 95f) has shown that arguments that emphasize the defective paradigm of MUST, which acted as a trigger for the suppletive form HAVE TO in negative and past tense contexts, do not seem to have been the driving force behind the increase in discourse frequency of semi-modal HAVE (GOT)

---

[69] Ehrman (1966: 12), analyzing a section of the 1961 Brown Corpus of AmE, still considers permission CAN as "relatively rare", but also mostly attested in the dialogue data, which supports this reasoning.

TO. This is somewhat counter-intuitive, but since HAVE TO appeared first in present-tense contexts, where MUST was doing fine, i.e. had no formal limitations; there must have been different reasons for the increase of the semi-modal. (Krug 2000: 81).

The late 18th and 19th centuries show a marked increase in frequency for HAVE TO. As a form that gained momentum first in the early 19th century, the effects of HAVE TO on MUST will be detailed. HAVE TO is compared with MUST in its functions, and the developmental patterns in CanE will be compared to other varieties.

6.2.3 Volition and futurity: SHALL and WILL

In contrast to the variable sets in the domains of both (a) permission, ability and possibility and (b) strong obligation markers, the area governing the use of SHALL and WILL has been subject to numerous comments by 18th- and early 19th-century prescriptivists. Sundby *et al.* (1991: 190-192) devote ample space to the subject and illustrate the great extent of language awareness governing the use of SHALL (SHOULD) and WILL (WOULD), so that they classify as linguistic stereotypes (Labov 2001: 196).

The discussion of SHALL and WILL will focus to some extent on prescriptivist norms and will be apt to shed light on *changes from above* in early Ontario, both in the sense of changes from the upper realms of society, and changes operating above the level of consciousness. In this respect, SHALL and WILL stand, in some ways, in contrast to CAN and MAY vs. MUST and HAVE TO, whose changes never acquired the same level of public awareness. An assessment of which changes were *changes from above* vs. *changes from below* will be provided for each of the variables in the final chapter.

6.2.4 SHOULD, WOULD and OUGHT TO

SHOULD serves a rather wide array of modal functions. In the present context, SHOULD will be compared to WOULD in two contexts. While previous studies (Kytö 1991a, Nurmi 2003) surveyed SHOULD and WOULD on largely the same independent variables as SHALL and WILL. SHOULD will be looked at in its use in hypotheticals, one of the core functions of WOULD, as well as in non-hypotheticals.

In non-hypotheticals SHOULD will be pitted not just against WOULD, but also against OUGHT TO. SHOULD and OUGHT TO are somewhat uneven competitors. While SHOULD has a number of functions and domains, it competes with OUGHT TO as a marker of necessity (Palmer 1990: 123). Both express a weaker notion than MUST and HAVE TO and will be compared in their use in non-hypothetical contexts.

A final section in each chapter will survey the development of epistemic meanings for all three variables. Before we embark on the first of four case studies, we will need to familiarize ourselves with both the data and introduce some methodological considerations.

6.3 Methodological considerations

CONTE-pC provides the Canadian data for this study. As the expected kind of changes lean heavily on the stylistic side, the comparison of incidence in CONTE-pC to other data is necessary. Our data for comparison come from two sources and comprise three historical varieties. ARCHER-1, *A Representative Corpus of Historical English Registers, Version 1* (cf. Biber, Finegan and Atkinson 1994; Biber, Conrad and Reppen 1998)[70] will provide the main benchmark for comparisons with late 18th- and early 19th-century BrE and a more limited set of AmE. Furthermore, the data is supplemented by *A Corpus of Late Eighteenth-Century Prose*[71], which is a letter corpus of considerable size from northwestern England (NW-BrE).

6.3.1 Comparing distributions: the parallel corpora

I will refer to the CONTE-pC data from Ontario as Canadian English, CanE, regardless of potential regional differences in early CanE. The letter, journal (diary) and newspaper sections of ARCHER-1 for periods 1750-1799 and 1800-1849 are used for comparison. Hereafter, the terms 'BrE' and 'AmE' will refer to these three genres in ARCHER-1 from 1750 to 1849 as they will serve as our BrE and AmE 'corpora'. The *Corpus of Late Eighteenth-Century Prose*, CL18P, a letter corpus transcribed from manuscripts from late 18th-century North-West England (NW-BrE), will be used as an additional benchmark in the earliest period. Table (6.3) summarizes the data from the four corpora:

---

[70] I am indebted to Christian Mair at the University of Freiburg, Germany, who kindly granted me access to ARCHER-1 (compiled by Douglas Biber *et al.*).
[71] Compiled by David Denison, Linda van Bergen and Joana Soliva Proud (cf. Van Bergen and Denison 2007). I wish to thank David Denison for granting me online access to the corpus; http://www.llc.manchester.ac.uk/subjects/lel/staff/david-denison/corpus-late-18th-century-prose/ (5 Sep. 2007).

	CanE (CONTE-pC)	AmE (ARCHER-1)	BrE (ARCHER-1)	NW-BrE (CL18P)
Genres	letters, diaries, newspapers			letters
Period 1	1776-1799	1750-1799	1750-1799	1761-1790
Period 2	1800-1824		1800-1849	
Period 3	1825-1849			
Period 4+5	1850-1899	1850-1899	1850-1899	

Table 6.3: Overview of corpora, periods and genres
(shaded areas: non-existent corpus data)

Data from four corpora in the letter genre in period 1, and three genres in CanE, AmE and BrE will be used. In the empirical parts, the labels CanE (data from CONTE-pC), AmE (ARCHER-1), BrE (ARCHER-1) and NW-BrE (CL18P) will be used in reference to the corpora as shown. For instance, BrE-1 refers to BrE data from ARCHER-1 from period 1, or CanE-3 from CONTE-pC data from period 3. Grey shadings indicate unavailable corpus data at the time being. We see that there are, despite of unfortunate gaps in the AmE data, plenty of opportunities for cross-comparisons. Additionally, period 4+5 is provided, as it will serve to pro-track later developments in AmE in one case. For all other studies, however, the cut-off point is 1849.

A note of caution as regards to methodological caveats seems to be in order here, as none of these corpora is bigger than 300,000 words. The Canadian data from CONTE-pC comprises some 125,000 words, in ARCHER-1 the corresponding newspaper, diary and letter sections count 51,000 words for AmE and 120,000 for BrE, while CL18P is the biggest corpus used here with 300,000 words in the letter genre alone.

When attempting to verify Trudgill's dialect formation theory, as outlined in chapter (5), we are at the mercy of the available data. Of the three stages and six phases presented in table (5.1), there are two phases that lend themselves most easily to be surveyed with these corpora. These are phase (IIa), extreme variability, and (IIIa), choice of majority form (and function). With the frequencies of variables from certain input varieties, the population demographics and the CanE data, we are in a position to make statements on the variability and the acceptance of a majority form or function. Other phases, such as inter-dialect development or apparent levelling, are, however, not as easily accessible with the present data.

The Canadian data poses some additional problems. Since before 1812, i.e. for about half of our period, there was "little English writing" in what is now Ontario (Talman and Talman 1977: 97), we cannot include some text types that are found in BrE and AmE for that period. As a consequence, no speech-related data, such as drama or trial proceedings are available in CONTE-pC, which renders the genres of letter, diary and newspaper text as the best type of data. The former two genres, and their tendencies for informal writing, should partly remedy the lack of speech-based text types in pre-1850 Ontario, however.

All frequency counts are based on concordance generated with the Word-Smith Concordancing Tool (1998), and statistical tests will be used to substantiate the findings where possible. Following the conventions in much of the linguistic literature, chi-square tests at the 95% significance level ($p < 0.05$) will serve as a benchmark to help distinguish chance fluctuation from potentially systemic variation, which will be complemented (indeed corrected) by Fisher's Exact Test in cases where on variable has less than five occurrences. However, as a result of the relatively compact corpus sizes and short period intervals, not all results that appear to be otherwise convincing, will reach statistical significance. This is especially true for data that tap into the early phases of changes, when very low token frequencies are ubiquitous. On the other hand, statistical significance alone does not guarantee meaningful correlations. An attempt will therefore be made to alleviate methodological caveats like these by way of accumulation of evidence, both internal and external, and considering both statistical significance *and* percentile changes of the distributions.

6.3.2 Methodological caveat I: the letter sections

While the corpora used are on many levels highly compatible and match each other fairly closely, there are two issues that need to be considered. First and foremost, while ARCHER-1 is largely, if not exclusively, transcribed from printed sources, the vast majority of CONTE-pC letter and diary data, as well as the entire CL18P corpus, are transcribed from manuscript sources. Therefore, CL18P and CONTE-pC limit editorial interference to a minimum for these genres, which cannot be claimed for ARCHER-1.

Second, the letter sections are the most diverse genres among the four corpora. CONTE-pC's letter section contains a number of semi-official letters by semi-literate writers. These letters, sometimes referred to as pauper letters, are not matched in the parallel corpora used here. The ARCHER-1 letter section is compiled from printed editions, which generally lean heavily towards educated usage and CL18P is comprised of mostly middle class data. While, depending on the variables, this imbalance must be kept in mind, it is not to be expected to distort the results beyond reasonable bounds, as the pauper sections in

CONTE-pC comprise only between 7 and 20 percent of each data subset (cf. appendix 1 for the sizes in the LC section). The benefits of these data from minimally-schooled writers (see Fairman 2003), which provide a prime window into speechways otherwise lost, far outweigh the slight distortions to be expected. While CONTE-pC was designed to allow for comparisons with ARCHER-1 data, the sociolinguistic value of the material in CONTE-pC should be taken into account, which is, in many cases, more interesting than most LModE texts in ARCHER-1.

This caveat is the result of practical aspects of corpus compilation that are to a certain degree unavoidable. The second caveat, however, concerns the more profound theoretical and methodological issue of establishing historical connections on the basis of incidence and distribution features of linguistic variables, which will be discussed next.

6.3.3 Methodological caveat II: how to trace historical connections

One of the most profound questions in historical linguistics is how to prove the relationship of a form or function in variety A with a form or function in variety B. Obviously, the external language history and settlement patterns may provide a first clue, but, beyond that, the question remains how to decide whether a given variant in dialect B is the result of its importation via dialect A, i.e. via contact, or rather an independent innovation in B, or the result of directional drift (as discussed in section 5.3.5). While the problem is not new, this question has figured prominently in the recent literature. Poplack and Tagliamonte (1989, 1993, 1994, 2004) focus much on this problem, as does, in one way or another, every contribution in Hickey (2004a).

Poplack and Tagliamonte's studies attempt to establish historical relationships by taking into consideration more factors than mere incidence. They say that

> the simple attestation of one or the other [feature or form] in a language variety is not revealing; this can only be accomplished by first ascertaining their distribution in the language, as determined by the hierarchy of constraints conditioning their appearance, and *comparing* it with that of the putative sources. (Poplack and Tagliamonte 2004: 205, italics in original)

At its core, the approach rests on the exact distribution of a given feature in two or more varieties and is, of course, also not new. The method employed by Poplack and Tagliamonte has been at the core of the comparative method from its beginnings. Classic sound laws such as Grimm's Law or Verner's Law were derived from meticulous distributional observation. The novelty of Poplack and Tagliamonte's approach, therefore, is that they have been arguing for a renewed effort to provide more detailed surveys of a feature's context before jumping to conclusions of historical relationship. Whether one wishes to perceive of the distributional constraints as a hierarchy, which is an outcome of extensive statistical modelling, is a hypothesis worth discussing.

Proposed hierarchies, however, are secondary in the present context, as even a feature distribution that matches a proposed donor variety in every respect can, strictly speaking, *not* serve as direct proof for a connection. While such result would provide strong evidence for a historical link, especially when combined with the external history, there would still be the chance of independent parallel development or an instance of directional drift.

It is therefore of little surprise that other contributors suggest even more thorough study is necessary to establish historical relationships between varieties. Wolfram and Schilling-Estes (2004: 182), for instance, argue that empirical verification of a historical connection between two varieties would necessitate a survey of *complete* dialect lineages of all varieties involved, which is elusive in almost all cases, given the present resources of historical corpora (see Dollinger forthc.). As we have seen in chapter (3), on external language history, and in chapter (5), on new-dialect formation, the input dialects are manifold, and, even if these data sets were available, we would still be hard-pressed to rule out independent development or instances of drift. Having said this, however, we should maintain that the outlook for establishing some connection is not all that bleak.

In the present study, it will be attempted to meet several aims. First, the distribution of a given form and its functions will be established. Because of the fuzziness of the semantics of the modal auxiliaries, this will not be as straightforward as with strictly grammatical variables such as third person *-s,* and we will focus more on the prevalent functions than on the occurrence of restricted forms. Second, the comparative data available in ARCHER-1 and CL18P is far from representing a continuous diachronic lineage, so the interpretation of results will have to rely to some extent on external reasoning and heuristic methods. Third, because of the unavailability of a complete set of input data, it is methodologically impossible to arrive at a direct proof of the relationship between two features. After the presentation of the data in relation to the importation vs. parallel development of a given feature, the most likely interpretations will be offered in chapter (11).

Having discussed the choice of variables, the methodological approach and the two most serious caveats, the complex involving CAN/COULD and MAY/MIGHT will be the first one to be studied, followed by a close analysis of MUST vs. HAVE TO, which will be succeeded by the most overt change involving SHALL vs. WILL before, finally, SHOULD vs. WOULD and SHOULD, WOULD vs. OUGHT TO complete the picture of the variable sets chosen in the present study.

7 CAN (COULD) vs. MAY (MIGHT)

The modal complex expressing notions of ability, permission and possibility has been studied intensively at the synchronic level and for older language stages up to EModE (e.g. Kytö 1987, 1991a: 81-258, 1991b, Warner 1993: 176-178, Traugott 1972, Denison 1993: 292-325). LModE in general, and CanE in particular, have not yet received a similar level of attention.

In this chapter, the two core functions of CAN and MAY, permission and root possibility uses, as well as the functions of COULD and MIGHT in various contexts will be investigated. Where relevant, the results will be put in relation to Kytö's pioneering studies (1991a, 1991b, 1987) on early modern BrE and AmE to identify long-term trends. Before we embark on the case study as such, it seems worthwhile to briefly review the histories of CAN and MAY from OE to EModE.

7.1 A diachronic sketch of CAN and MAY

In OE *mæg,* the formal ancestor of MAY, is prevalent in its historically most important sense 'to be able to'. Following a pragmatic/semantic cline of grammaticalization, this ability use was extended to denote possibility and was subsequently developed into permissive uses. Permissive uses can already occasionally be found in OE (Traugott 1972: 71f).

OE had two forms denoting permission: the older form *mot,* 'be allowed, may', which later lost its permission meaning and evolved into a marker of strong obligation. Both OE *mote,* the ancestor of MUST, and its rival OE *mæg,* 'be strong or able, have power' underwent semantic changes (Warner 1993: 94; 163). While traces of permissive readings of *mæg* can already be found in OE, *mot* was finally replaced by *mæg* in these contexts in ME (ibid: 118), but the "full performative use of *may,* as in *You may go* 'I permit you to go', did not gain wide currency until the sixteenth century" (Traugott 1972: 118).

OE *cann,* on the other hand, originally meant 'to know, be acquainted with, know how to'. Once CAN acquired the meaning of 'to be able to', MAY gave up the meaning of 'to be able, be strong' (Kytö 1991a: 65). After undergoing this semantic change, the meanings of 'possibility' and finally 'permission' were only a question of time to be developed by implication, i.e. pragmatic factors that trigger these interpretations rather than 'ability' readings (Kytö 1991a: 65).

In comparison to the long-term development from OE to EModE, the study of this area in LModE has not been pursued as rigorously. However, whenever more general works refer to some post-1700 developments, the area of permission uses of MAY and CAN is usually mentioned (e.g. Traugott 1972: 170f; Kytö 1991a: 65; Denison 1993: 303), which indicates that these variables were undergoing some changes for our period. Simon-Vandenbergen (1984) seems to be the only quantitative study on CAN and MAY that includes a sizeable proportion of LModE texts. He shows (1984: 364) that root uses of CAN, in the sense of permission, first occur in 19th-century plays and infringe upon the territory of root MAY.

In our corpora we find examples that illustrate this shift of functions of CAN, as shown in example (7.1):

(7.1)   a.   ability (usually with animate subject):
             *I fancy Kitty **can** do nothing better* ...
                                               (BrE-1, letters)
        b.   'neutral, root possibility' (ambiguous case):
             *I should like to by it if I **can** by it two Advantage*
                         (CanE-3, semi-literate letter writer)
        c.   permission:
             We have decided upon my sitting with Mamma
             every night during tea and Minnie during dinner
             *as then I **can** read Mamma's prayers to her.*
                         (CanE-3; a teenaged diary writer)

As pointed out by Coates (1983: 139 for PDE), functions (7.1 b&c) are the core functions of MAY, which means that CAN is apparently beginning to compete with MAY in these functions in the early 19th century. In relation to 'permission', we are therefore in the position to identify progressive and conservative forms – CAN as progressive, and MAY as conservative – with CAN conveying more informal undertones than MAY.

7.2 Sentence types

Previous research has shown a correlation between basic sentence types and these modals. Diachronically and regionally most relevant to the present study is Kytö (1991a: 210), where a high co-occurrence for CAN and COULD in negative contexts, accounting for around 90% in EModE, is shown.

In the present study, a basic distinction is made between affirmative and negative sentences (declarative) and interrogative sentences. Negative contexts are defined as clausal negation (verb negation and clausal negation by way of a negative particle).[72] In general, contractions in the verbal negation of CAN, MAY, COULD and MIGHT are rare in the data. *Can't*, the short form with apostrophe, occurs only once in BrE-1 newspapers and once in CanE-1 letters, while *cant* occurs 5 times in CanE, and once in BrE. The standard form for the negation of CAN is *cannot*. MAY is only negated as *may not*, and COULD usually as *could not*, while one contraction is found in Canadian letters in period 1 as *couldn*, without the final dental. MIGHT shows, just as MAY, no short form in the data, and is negated as *might not*. The higher incidence for contractions in CanE is likely the result of semi-literate writers, which are not present in the other corpora, and should not be interpreted as a possible feature of early CanE.

Table (7.1) shows the distribution of CAN/COULD and MAY/MIGHT according to sentence type across our period:

		Affirmative		Negative		Interrogative	
CanE	CAN	69.6	(112)	30.4	(49)	0.0	(0)
(1-3)	MAY	93.8	(180)	2.6	(5)	3.6	(7)
BrE	CAN	58.2	(89)	41.2	(63)	0.6	(1)
(1-3)	MAY	96.6	(168)	2.9	(5)	0.6	(1)
AmE	CAN	74.1	(20)	25.9	(7)	0.0	(0)
(1)	MAY	96.2	(50)	3.8	(2)	0.0	(0)
CanE	COULD	54.0	(74)	41.6	(57)	4.4	(6)
(1-3)	MIGHT	93.0	(53)	7.0	(4)	0.0	(0)
BrE	COULD	54.9	(73)	42.9	(57)	2.3	(3)
(1-3)	MIGHT	93.7	(74)	6.3	(5)	0.0	(0)
AmE	COULD	50.0	(26)	48.1	(25)	1.9	(1)
(1)	MIGHT	100.0	(11)	0.0	(0)	0.0	(0)

Table 7.1: Overall incidence of CAN and MAY; COULD and MIGHT by sentence type (AmE data from period 1 only), percentages (n)

The pattern that arises from these data is rather clear. While it was to be expected that, due to the exclusion of speech-based data, the vast majority of occurrences would be declarative sentences, the distribution of CAN and COULD in negative sentences is fairly parallel across the varieties. Between

---

[72] One case of a negative interrogative was counted as negative.

25.9 and 41.2 percent of all forms of CAN occur in negative clauses in CanE, BrE and AmE, and are the variant of choice in these contexts, as opposed to occurrences of MAY, which do not reach 4% in any variety in negative sentences. MAY, on the other hand, is prevalent in affirmative contexts with well above 90% across the board. Statistical testing yields no significant differences between CanE when compared to BrE and AmE, but shows a preference for MAY in positive and for CAN in negative contexts in CanE and BrE, and also in AmE (see appendix 7.1).

A similar observation can be made for COULD, which occurs in 41.6 and 42.9 percent of all cases in CanE and BrE in negative clauses, as opposed to around 7 percent of MIGHT. MIGHT seems to have specialized in affirmative contexts, with no less than 93% of incidences across the board. The distribution of MIGHT and COULD in both CanE and BrE is significantly influenced by sentence type and is highly similar in both varieties, reaching levels of significance (cf. appendix 7.2).

The conclusion that can be drawn from these data is one that corroborates Kytö's (1991a: 209) finding that the distributional tendencies for both CAN (COULD) in negative contexts and MAY (MIGHT) in affirmative contexts were already established in EModE and therefore occur in almost parallel incidences in the LModE data, showing no systemic regional variation for CanE, BrE and AmE.

7.2.1 Overall development in EModE and LModE

For a comparison of LModE CAN/COULD and MAY/MIGHT, EModE data can again be taken as a point of reference. This allows us to chart the long-term trends from 1500 in BrE and 1620 in AmE until just after 1700. [73]

Figure (7.1) shows the development of COULD and MIGHT in negative contexts. Apart from a decrease of CAN and an increase of COULD in AmE, all varieties employ CAN and COULD to a similar degree in the LModE and the EModE data. However, we need to consider that the AmE data are based only on period 1, which could account for the irregularity. Overall, this relative stability may be interpreted as the result of an EModE change that had been largely completed by the beginning of the LModE period, which suggests an instance of drift (continuing drift).

---

[73] British EModE data comprise the years 1500-1710; American EModE data range from 1620-1720.

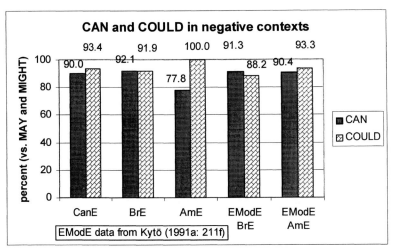

Figure 7.1: CAN and COULD (vs. MAY and MIGHT) in EModE and LModE varieties[74]

The scenario for MAY/MIGHT in affirmative contexts, shown in figure (7.2), seems to be rather different to the one for CAN/COULD. Here we see that MIGHT is used less frequently in AmE when compared to EModE data, and even the uses of MAY and MIGHT decrease slightly in BrE, with CanE showing a distribution that is in between AmE and BrE.

However, none of these differences in percentages, which appear to be considerable, reaches statistical significance in LModE (cf. appendix 7.3). The data in figure (7.2) is therefore a good example of how easily simple percentage calculations can be misleading. While this variation is influenced by the rise of CAN as a less formal variant of MAY in affirmative contexts (cf. Simon-Vandenbergen 1984: 361), we cannot rule out coincidence as the reason behind this distribution.

---

[74] Note that the EModE data comprise exclusively root uses for CAN and COULD. While Kytö's data do not contain occurrences of epistemic COULD (1991a: 203), in LModE this function is attested, as it is in PDE (Coates 1983: 165-7), e.g. expressing a tentative possibility, such as in the following example: *Oh well! It could be that it doesn't say where to change it here.*

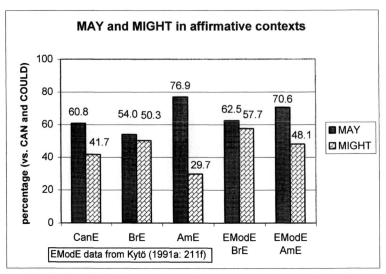

Figure 7.2: MAY and MIGHT (vs. CAN and COULD) in EModE and LModE varieties

For both cases, therefore, we have not found convincing evidence for changes that appear to distinguish CanE from BrE and AmE based on formal distributions. While the relative homogeneity of CAN/COULD in negative contexts is best interpreted as an instance of drift, MAY and MIGHT are confronted with considerable percentages of CAN/COULD in negative contexts. It seems that, if there is diatopic variation between these LModE varieties, we would need to consider the semantics of these auxiliaries, which we shall do next.

7.3 Semantic notions of CAN and MAY

Table (7.2) lists the categories used in the semantic analysis of CAN and MAY and provides examples for illustration. A total of 1,261 tokens was analyzed, including 341 occurrences of CAN, 435 of MAY, 322 of COULD and 163 of MIGHT, the latter two of which we will turn to in section (7.4). The semantic spectrum of CAN and MAY is divided into six categories:

Prototype Form	Notational Function	Example
MAY	Permission	If he show any Disposition to write me a penitential Letter, you *may* encourage it; not that I think it of any Consequence to me, but because it will ease his Mind and set him at rest. (BrE-1)
	Root possibility	Any person wishing to purchase *may* depend upon getting a great bargain. (CanE-2)
	Epistemic possibility	… and my ideas upon the several points which *may*, between this and then, occur to me. (AmE-1)
CAN	Ability	I fancy Kitty *can* do nothing better … (BrE-1)
	Permission	I have your Certificate that the land is not leased or vacant of course none [of the settlers] *can* be located without the sanction of the Lt. Gov. as in other cases. (CanE-2)
	Root possibility	Nothing *can* be more satisfactory than the readiness and unanimity with which the Legislature have applied to meet the emergencies. (CanE-3)

Table 7.2: CAN and MAY – Semantic categories and examples

The grey-shaded cells highlight the semantic areas in which CAN and MAY compete. As MAY had become obsolete as a marker of ability in ME and CAN was not used for epistemic possibility, the competition is limited to the areas of root possibility and permission. While there is some overlap between the functions, it was aimed, with the help of larger stretches of co-text and considering the historical context, to assign as many cases as possible to one distinct class. As a consequence, the number of indeterminate cases is kept at a minimum.[75]

7.3.1 Overall figures: distribution of functions

Figures (7.3) and (7.4) show the percentage results for MAY (all functions per genre and subperiod produce 100%)[76]. If we take a look at the CanE and BrE data for the overall diachronic trends of the functions of MAY by genre, we see some genre-specific trends, but no clear overall tendencies. In comparison to BrE, no general systemic geographic variation can be seen. The most obvious feature is the increased use of permission MAY in CanE letters, and its total absence in CanE newspapers, when compared to BrE:

---

[75] Apart from these notional criteria, a small number of cases could not be assigned and were, classified as indeterminate, removed from the total number of occurrences (n).

[76] See appendices (7.4) and (7.5) for the absolute figures of root possibility and permission uses for CAN and MAY.

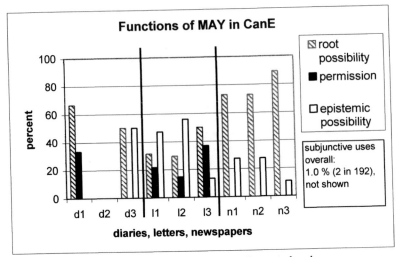

Figure 7.3: Functions of MAY in CanE by period and genre
(d = diaries, l = letters, n = newspapers)

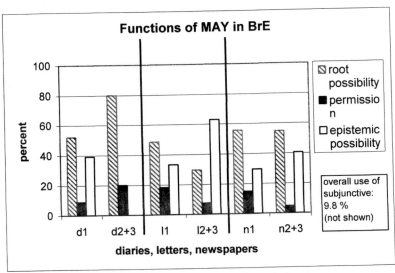

Figure 7.4: Functions of MAY in BrE by period and genre
(d = diaries, l = letters, n = newspapers)

Both varieties show no clear core function for MAY in the period, as epistemic as well as root possibility readings are used frequently in BrE and CanE. MAY, however, is used quite differently across the genres. In BrE, permission uses are found in all genres, while they occur less frequently in CanE diaries (d3) and not at all in CanE newspapers. It will be necessary, therefore, to survey CAN and MAY by genre.

7.3.2 CAN in Root possibility and Permission uses
If we take a look at the newcomer in this domain, CAN, we can see a more coherent diachronic short-term development. First, we will focus on root possibility uses of CAN, as shown in figure (7.5):

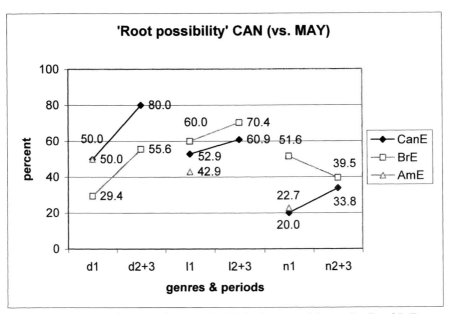

Figure 7.5: Development of CAN and MAY for Root possibility in CanE and BrE (AmE-1 for comparison)

By comparing the CanE and BrE data, we can see a picture that is largely parallel in incidence in the diary and letter genres for root possibility uses. Only in the newspaper genre the pattern diverges. The AmE data are closer to the CanE values across all genres, which indicates its loyalist base. Viewed in the larger diachronic context, we may say that CanE is more progressive in its use of CAN in diaries, but more conservative than BrE in letters and newspapers. The apparent tendency for an increase of CAN in diaries and letters is not confirmed by statistical testing, which yields no significance for the changes in figure (7.5) at the 95% level (appendix 7.6). This suggests a drift scenario for diaries and letters. The different developmental patterns in CanE and BrE newspapers could either be a result of chance, or alternatively, as they show the statistically strongest change, a stylistic change towards more BrE usage in Canadian newspapers. CanE uses more MAY in letters, but not in diaries, which indicates a more formal style in CanE than in BrE. It is probably best to interpret these figures as reflecting instances of directional drift and stylistic variation in CanE, with more formal, possibly more conservative tendencies in the letter and newspaper genres. This change can be perceived of as a change from above, as the use of CAN is found to be documented – and castigated – by 18th-century grammarians (Sundby *et al.* 1991: 211).

As for the second function in which CAN and MAY overlap, permission uses, we said earlier that a change in progress has been previously reported in LModE. Figure (7.6) shows the development for CAN denoting permission. In this function, all genres increase their use of CAN in both CanE and BrE over time. While differences in percentages appear in part to be considerable, again, no change is statistically significant (cf. appendix 7.7). What should we make of these results?

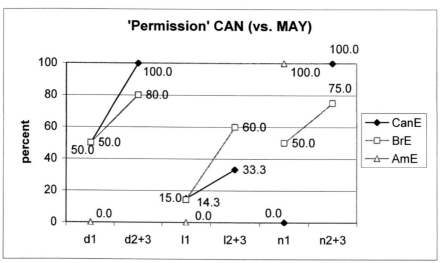

Figure 7.6: Development of CAN and MAY coding for Permission in CanE and BrE (AmE-1 for comparison)

It is clear that CAN is expanding its use in both CanE and BrE in the areas of permission (but note that in newspapers permission CAN was not attested, hence there is no interpolation line between periods 1 and 2+3) and, for diaries and letters, root possibility uses. However, neither the differences between CanE and BrE in each period, nor their increase from period 1 to 2+3 is significant, and statistical testing does not help us much to confirm a long-term change corroborated in previous studies. The change appears to be too slow to reach the 95% significance level in 25-50 year periods. We know in hindsight that in PDE, CAN is usually used for permission and not MAY, which conveys a formal undertone (Coates 1983: 103).

With this knowledge, we would interpret the diachronic changes in figures (7.5) and (7.6) as a LModE parallel development in both CanE and BrE leading up to the PDE distribution, even *despite* their lack of statistical significance. For LModE diatopic variation, we can say that 'root possibility' in newspapers tended to be expressed by MAY in CanE, as opposed to BrE, but with both varieties converging in the 30% range in period 2+3 (fig. 7.5).

7.3.3 CAN in 25-year periods

The comparisons of figures (7.5) and (7.6) are based on the half-century periods in ARCHER-1. While we could see some trends in this interval, we can zoom in closer, to 25-year periods, for the Canadian data. Figures (7.7) and (7.8) depict the variation for Root possibility and Permission in CanE. The uses of CAN and MAY for Root possibility are shown in figure (7.7) (absolute figures provided for CAN):

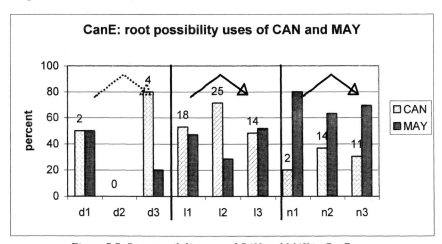

Figure 7.7: Root possibility uses of CAN and MAY in CanE

For letters and newspapers, the data show an increase of CAN, followed by a decrease, while the diary data do not allow for this comparison. However, the 25-year periodization suggests a pattern, which, if borne out in additional data, could indicate a short-term development pattern for CAN and MAY that is indicative of the dialect mixing process. It is interesting to point out that the increase of CAN in period 2 and its decrease in 3, this *inverse V-curve*, is, although not attested in d2,[77] theoretically also possible for diaries.

Extra caution will need to be exercised when interpreting these distributions, as, again, neither changes are statistically significant at the 95% level.[78] The second key area of competition, CAN denoting permission, may provide further clues.

Figure (7.8) shows the distribution for CAN as a marker of permission in CanE, again with absolute frequencies shown for CAN:

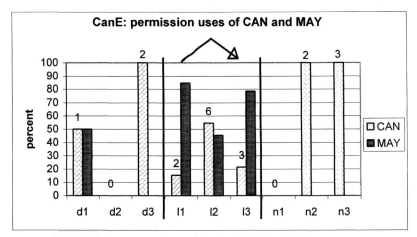

Figure 7.8: Permission uses of CAN and MAY in CanE

The data is somewhat disappointing due to the very low incidence in both the diary and newspaper genres. For the letter genre, however, the incidence is between 10 and 14 per period, which allows us to make some comparisons. Once more, an inverse V-curve can be seen; once more, statistical testing is not significant (see appendix 7.8 for absolute figures). Stage II in Trudgill (2004) is characterized by extreme variability and apparent levelling (cf. table 5.1). If we look at period 2, Root possibility in n2 and Permission in l2 can be inter-

---

[77] This is because of the absence of modals in much of Ely Playter's diary, as well as Benjamins Smith's factual, telegram-like writing style.

[78] The CanE – BrE contingency table can be found in appendix (7.8).

preted as such, with levels of CAN and MAY more equal than in periods 1 and 3. For Root possibility in l2, however, this is clearly not the case.

What could these data mean for the theory of new-dialect formation? A good point of departure seems to be to equate Trudgill's three stages with periods 1, 2 and 3. We said in chapter (5) that prescriptivism and norms would only play some role in stage I, when mainly adults are interacting. In our case of permission uses, prescriptive influences would have kept the incidence of CAN in check in period 1, which may have been applied to Root possibility functions as well. In period 2, stage II, this influence would have worn off, as more children would have spoken the language, while in period 3, genre-specific forms were selected in a focussing process. A drawback of this kind of interpretation is that – while it can be applied to the data – it is not the only scenario, since we cannot rule out chance variation. The next sections explore more data to make a stronger case for this scenario.

7.3.4 CAN vs. MAY and the three stages of new-dialect formation

We have said that CONTE-pC would in principle lend itself well to the testing of the new-dialect development process, and this section is primarily aimed to demonstrate how the predictions in Trudgill (2004) can be tested on the basis of 25-year periods in CONTE-pC.

Figures (7.7) and (7.8) provide the point of departure. If we rule out coincidence as an explanatory principle, what significance may the suggested *inverse V-curve* of CAN have for dialect-mixing theories in the Ontarian context? A first step would be to ascribe the decrease of the use of CAN in period 3 to BrE influence, since, as shown in chapter (3), the host of immigrants to Ontario after 1825 came from Britain. If this were indeed the case, some linguistic indicators for this theory should be found in the data. As BrE forms were minority forms under the 10% threshold suggested by Trudgill (2004: 111), southern BrE forms would not, if no other factors favoured them, be acquired by the next generation of speakers. One such factor, however, is the influence of prescriptive norms in period 1. MAY would be the more formal variant in this context and as such could have been accommodated to by the newcomers to a certain extent. This would decrease the incidence of CAN in period 1, which results in the inverse V-curve.

As southeastern English immigrants would not meet the demographic threshold, any input forms are likely to have come from Scottish, Irish and Northern English speakers and their forms (for convenience, the Scottish, Irish and Northern English emigrants were labelled SIN-speakers in chapter 4). The letter sections in CONTE-pC contain subsections for SIN-speakers, lower class

(LC) and middle class (MC) writers. For CAN and MAY, however, the SIN sample incidences are too small to be considered here (cf. appendix 7.9), which leaves us with the LC and MC sections. The following section discusses the new-dialect formation scenario for the best represented function, i.e. root possibility.

7.3.4.1 Middle vs. Lower Class speakers

Figures (7.9) and (7.10) show the data arranged by social class. For middle class speakers, shown in figure (7.9), CAN remains the majority variant over all three periods. The LC speakers, as shown in figure (7.10), however, start out in period 1 with a reverse ratio – MAY, the more formal, perhaps more submissive form, is the majority form. In period 2, this ratio is inversed (but only one instance of CAN is attested), while in period 3, LC shows very modest variation. While these changes do not meet the criteria for significance at the 95% level, both scenarios produce an inverse V-pattern for CAN, which we found earlier in the data for root possibility and permission.

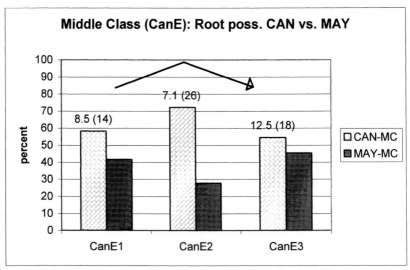

Figure 7.9: CAN vs. MAY in root possibility uses among CanE middle class speakers (occurrence per 10,000 words provided, n in parentheses)

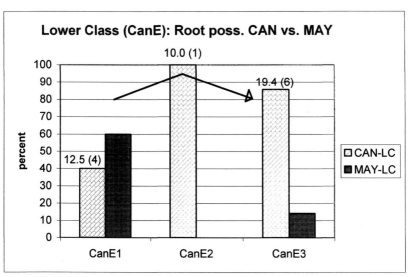

Figure 7.10: CAN vs. MAY in root possibility uses among CanE lower class speakers (occurrence per 10,000 words provided, n in parentheses)

How would these data match with the above interpretation of the SIN group? For MC speakers, extreme variability is not shown in period 2, as predicted in Trudgill (2004) (cf. table 5.1), but instead in periods 1 and 3. Taking a look at the LC data, we see that period 2 does show no variation at all. Trudgill's three stages do not seem to be matched in the data, and one would need to account for this development.

7.3.4.2 Different levels of development and a new stage I

So far, we have equated Trudgill's stages, which represent roughly one generation (Trudgill 2004: 89), with CONTE-pC's 25-year periods. By reconsidering the external language history, however, one can see a few points that would require a qualification of this generalization. The settled areas of Ontario in 1800 are shown in map (3.1). While the Ontarian centres had been settled since the 1780s or even before, and had had time to pass through Trudgill's three stages by 1850, the settlements founded after 1800 are shown as the vast empty land in map (3.1). The pre-1800 settlers are considered to have founded and remained in the major centres, such as Toronto, Kingston and the towns along the St. Lawrence and Niagara regions. These older settlements would be expected to have already gone through the first of the three developmental stages by 1800. For the newcomers after 1800, of whom we know from chapter (3) that they tended to settle on the vacant land and not in the towns, stage I would correspond to period 2, stage II to period 3 and stage III to a post-1850 period.

In this scenario, regionality in the sense of a dichotomy between urban and rural settings becomes an independent variable that would need to be considered in the new-dialect formation process. While ideally one would include this information in some sort of regionality index (Chambers 2000), the present study will have to work with the generalizations arrived at in chapter (3): post-1815 British immigrants tended to live in rural communities, while earlier immigrants, mainly from the USA, tended to live in the cities.

Overall, figures (7.9) and (7.10) suggest that period 2 is not equivalent with stage II in Trudgill's theory. Stage II is projected to display extreme variability and apparent levelling, the former of which is not attested here. Instead, period (1) exhibits considerable variation in both MC and LC, which suggests a regrouping of stage I as containing the original two phases, plus one phase from stage II. Stage I would therefore contain a) rudimentary levelling, b) interdialect development and c) *extreme variability*, which would produce the altered stage model in table (7.3):

STAGE I **NEW**	a) rudimentary levelling, b) interdialect development	and	**c) extreme variability**
STAGE II	a) extreme variability	and	b) apparent levelling
STAGE III	a) choice of majority forms	and	b) reallocation

Table 7.3: Trudgill's stages adapted for early Ontario
(cf. table 5.1 for the original stages)

We will see whether this adaptation provides an equal match with the data in chapters (8), (9) and (10).

7.3.4.3 CONTE-pC and Trudgill (2004)

CAN and MAY do not seem to exhibit significant diatopic variation between the varieties and the change from MAY to CAN, which is shown in all varieties to some degree for Permission and Root possibility readings, is better attributed to a parallel development in all varieties, i.e. an incidence of drift, apart from a stylistic preference in CanE to adhere to a more formal style in letters and newspapers.

The data suggest that the three stages of Trudgill's theory may not be applied as originally conceived. However, one finding to take from here to the next sets of variables is to allow for the introduction of different levels of development towards a more unified, focussed variety. This would entail in a first step a discrimination between earlier settled areas, which generally tend to be the urban centres at the time, and later settled areas, i.e. those settled after 1815. As a consequence, in a second and theoretically important step, the original stage I was extended with the notion of 'extreme variability' into a new stage I.

7.3.5 Long-term developments of epistemic and root uses

CAN does not occur in epistemic readings in the data, which is what was to be expected given that epistemic CAN seems to be a rather recent development. Coates (1995: 63) identifies epistemic CAN in an example from American academic English as in example (7.2) and asserts that BrE speakers would use WILL:

(7.2)   we hope this coding system **can** be useful [to other
         linguists working in the field]
                                        (Coates 1995: 63, ex. 17)

Facchinetti (2002: 235) in her study based on ICE-GB, finds, however, some instances of epistemic CAN also in BrE, as shown in (7.3):

(7.3)   We have displayed your posters in our college careers
         offices and hope that we can attract some good Lon-
         don students to the event.
                                        (ICE-GB, Facchinetti 2002: 235)

It is clear, however, that (7.3) is not clearly an epistemic instance (as Facchinetti acknowledges). One might better consider it as an instance of root possibility, such as in (7.4):

(7.4)   Britain's word can still be of value in some parts of
         the world.
                                        (Coates 1983: 90)

Facchinetti (2002: 239) semantically analyses 10% of the ICE-GB corpus and identifies 14 instances of epistemic CAN, or 4% of all instances of CAN. The three genres that come closest to diary, letter and newspaper data (which are written non-printed, written correspondence and written reportage/news reports) show four occurrences of epistemic CAN (p. 240, table 3a). Clearly, epistemic CAN is a recent phenomenon, not yet found in Coates' BrE data from the 1960s[79] (Coates 1983: 103), but is likely to reach more prevalent frequencies in the near future.

Negative forms of CAN, however, have been used epistemically for a longer period than positive CAN. Coates (1983: 102) notices 'infrequent' occurrences of epistemic CAN'T in her 1961 BrE data, which she considers as a suppletive form of MUST in the negative. Example (7.5) shows an instance of such use:

(7.5)   you can't have just given up painting completely, not
         if you had that kind of talent

                                             (Coates 1983: 101)

In the 1961 Brown Corpus of AmE, Ehrman (1966: 15) detects epistemic CAN'T under what she calls 'hypothetical force'. In the LModE data, however, some instances either lend themselves to a (near-) epistemic reading, as in (7.6), or that are clearly epistemic, as in (7.7):

(7.6)   a.   And as Major Wilmot has not yet been down for
               that purpose – I **cannot**, of course, think myself
               authorised to visit the Chantees

                                             (CanE, letters-3)
         b.   and yet, if the people have settled themselves according to these offsets, in front, they **cannot** near
               be disturbed, unless it can be clearly ascertained
               that with a view of encroaching upon

                                             (CanE, letters-2)

The examples in (7.6), from the CanE letter corpus, are classified as instances of permission, but it can be seen that an element of the speaker's judgement is present, an element of speculation, although downtoned by the parenthetical *of course* in (7.6a) and with heavier undertones of a 'permission not granted' in (7.6b). While overtones of permission prevail in (7.6), they indicate a cline towards more epistemic uses. In (7.7), from a teenage diary writer in period 3, there is no doubt that the CANNOT must be considered epistemic:

---

[79] The LOB Corpus (1 million words, written BrE) and the Survey of English Usage Corpus (c. 550,000 words, spoken BrE).

(7.7)   I laughed & ran away. Fortunately, Mamma, Mr Pear
         & all were there so he **cannot** think it was a tender
         scene going on between us...

                                             (CanE, diary-3)

Examples of epistemic CAN'T are already found in period 1 in BrE. In total, there is one example in AmE-1, two in CanE (both from the diary-3 section), two in BrE-1 (letters) and three in BrE-2+3 (diaries, letters and also newspapers). The data suggest that CANNOT acquired epistemic meanings long before CAN, at least by some 200 years.

In comparison to CAN, the case of MAY, with its well-established function as a marker of epistemic possibility, should prove easier to trace in the LModE data. Figures (11, 12 and 13) show the development of root vs. epistemic MAY in CanE and BrE, with AmE-1 for comparison. The figures provide both percentages (Y-axis) and absolute figures (on top of columns). Figure (7.11) shows that epistemic uses of MAY are on the increase in BrE, as would be predicted by grammaticalization theory (Traugott 1989), but they show a decrease in CanE between period 1 and periods 2+3.[80]

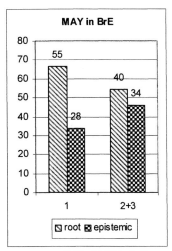
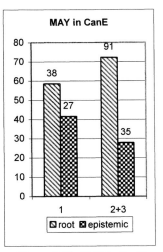
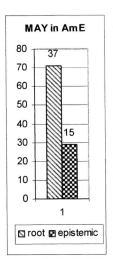

Figure 7.11: MAY in BrE   Figure 7.12: MAY in CanE   Figure 7.13: MAY in
                                                               AmE (period 1)

Percentages shown on Y-axis, n above columns

---

[80] This decrease generally occurs in period 3 across all genres, while period 2 is divided.

This decrease is attributable to a good proportion of Root possibility and Permission uses in the CanE data, both of which, as exemplified in (7.8a) and (7.8b), are frequently employed in the letters of land surveyors reporting back to the surveying office. They therefore represent a peculiar bias in the CanE data when compared to the AmE and BrE material:

(7.8) a.   The deeds may be forwarded to me at your convenience

(CanE-3)

b.   return to the Town of [xxx] in the Western District, in order that you may offer it for Sale

(CanE-3)

The percentages of epistemic MAY in the figures above, however, do not quite reach the levels found in present-day BrE (ICE-GB), which Facchinetti (2003: 305) quantifies at 61% of all uses of MAY. For spoken BrE, Coates (1995: 61) classifies almost three quarters of her sample as epistemic, and Leech (2003: 232) sees a sharp increase of epistemic uses between the early 1960s and 1990s in BrE, accounting for roughly three quarters of all instances today (see also Biber *et al.* 1999: 491, figure 6.12, 'extrinsic-possibility'). When compared to Kytö's (1991a: 106) data on late Early American English prior to 1720, one can see that epistemic uses (for both MAY *and* MIGHT combined) accounted for roughly only two percent of all instances, while in our LModE data, epistemic MAY comprises between 28% (CanE) and 71% (AmE) of all instances of MAY. Myhill (1995: 179) identifies epistemic MAY as the majority use in his pre-Civil War American data with 47% of all instances. While this development, an increase in epistemic readings, is not borne out in our CanE data for MAY, we may nevertheless conclude that the epistemic function was generally expanding its functions in LModE, with occasional fluctuation, somewhat influenced by the prevailing letter subgenre in CanE.

7.3.6 Summary

To summarize the data on CAN and MAY, we can only make few generalizations. We have seen, however, that statistical testing might provide a criterion that is too strict to identify some types of changes. The corpus sizes that are customary in English historical linguistics at present and the relatively small 25-50 year periods fail to produce significant results, as we can see, in hindsight, for the increase of permissive CAN. We have also seen that the comparison of percentages, which has been used excessively in much of historical corpus linguistics and statistical testing produce different results. The disadvantages of the two methods could be characterized as follows: if we take percentile changes at face value, we are more likely to arrive at an interpretation; if we make statistical testing our sole criterion, we may fail to identify important changes. On the whole, we have to say that CAN and MAY are subject to drift in CanE and BrE, with AmE and CanE sharing similar percentages. Changes in the percentages of COULD and MIGHT by sentence type likewise suggest, with the exception of the AmE-1 data, an instance of (continuing) drift.

CanE exhibits more formal behaviour for CAN and MAY for both Permission and Root possibility meanings. This is seen in letters, but not in diaries, with newspapers showing a less clear scenario, which indicates a stylistic shift in CanE, with personal writing being less formal, and correspondence more formal than in BrE.

We also said that epistemic uses of CANNOT are already attested in the LModE period and were to expand their functions. Epistemic CAN, however, was, little surprisingly, not found in the LModE data. MAY appears to expand its epistemic readings in LModE, which is not substantiated by the CanE data, which was related to a bias in the CanE data, as 20th-century data strongly suggests and expansion of this function.

We will next see to which extent the parallel forms of COULD and MIGHT may fit into this interpretation.

7.4 Functions of COULD and MIGHT

In this section the parallel forms of CAN and MAY, COULD and MIGHT, are analyzed. While COULD and MIGHT are often treated as the historical past tense forms of CAN and MAY, they developed a considerable degree of semantic independence early on in their history.

The basic functions of COULD and MIGHT can be arranged along two dichotomies: on the one hand, functions in past contexts and non-past contexts, and on the other hand, in epistemic and non-epistemic (root) functions. Table (7.4) illustrates these uses.

An analysis of the data yields the results shown in figures (7.14) and (7.17). While none of the differences between the varieties (for each period) is statistically significant (95% level), it is worthwhile to compare the non-epistemic and epistemic functions across the varieties. Different kinds of information have been condensed into these figures, which should be read as follows: All percentages are given for COULD and are calculated in relation to MIGHT.

Prototype From	Function	Example
MIGHT and COULD	Non-Epistemic possibility	and if this be the truth – as I am assured it is – *could* almost wish myself A Grand Vizier (BrE-1), **non-past**
		A member moved, that all these pieces *might* be referred to the Diplomatic Committee [...]. THURO supported this motion, and requested that ... (BrE-2&3), **past**
	Epistemic possibility	Your stance can conceive how painfull my situation has grown, ere I *could* be anywise unfortunate (CanE-1), **non-past**
		yet there were no immediate funds applicable to that purpose, yet he considered the object *might* be obtained by exchange of property (CanE-3), **past**

Table 7.4: COULD and MIGHT – semantic categories and examples

This means that the percentages of COULD and MIGHT added yield 100%. In addition, absolute frequencies are provided in parentheses to help interpret the reliability of particular findings. The first figure in parentheses is the absolute frequency for COULD, followed by the one for MIGHT, e.g. in figure (7.14) the information "(43 vs. 5)" in period 1 in AmE should be read as "43 occurrences of COULD (89.6%), as opposed to 5 of MIGHT, in non-epistemic uses (equals 100% - 89.6% = 10.4%)".

The uses of COULD and MIGHT will be discussed separately for both past and non-past contexts. For past contexts, figure (7.14) shows the distribution. We can see that the major function of COULD in past contexts is to code for non-epistemic readings across all varieties. In period 1, more than 64% of all BrE functions of COULD are non-epistemic, a percentage that is even higher in CanE (87.5) and AmE (89.6), while in period 2+3, no variety is below 79%.

Epistemic functions are, in terms of absolute frequencies, represented less. In relation to MIGHT, COULD plays a marginal role in coding for epistemic modality. This result is what was to be expected. As Coates (1983: 165) points out, epistemic COULD only codes for one aspect of epistemic meanings, i.e. "tentative possibility". For Coates (1983: 166) the "pressing question" is why epistemic COULD exists at all in the light of epistemic MIGHT. From the LModE perspective, epistemic MIGHT is used predominantly in the data –

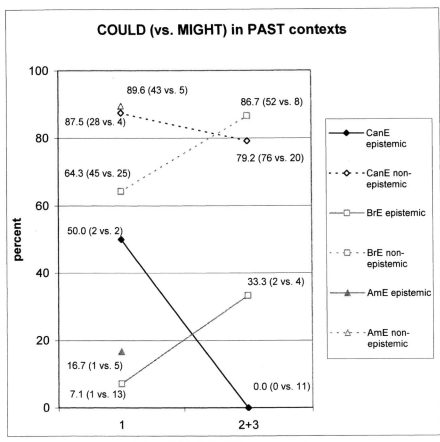

Figure 7.14: COULD in past contexts
Percentages calculated in relation to MIGHT (COULD and MIGHT = 100%),
(n vs. n), with the first number showing n for COULD

except in CanE, for which the absolute frequencies are very low (2 vs. 2) –,
and BrE shows a similar preference for MIGHT in past contexts, as it did in
EModE (Kytö 1991a: 216).

The data in non-past contexts may provide a lead into the origin of epistemic COULD. Epistemic COULD is not only facing strong competition from
MIGHT, but also from MAY, which makes the results for non-past contexts
even more interesting. For non-past uses, as shown in figure (7.15), we not

only see a similar low frequency occurrence of epistemic COULD, but a frequency and developmental pattern that is almost parallel for CanE and BrE:

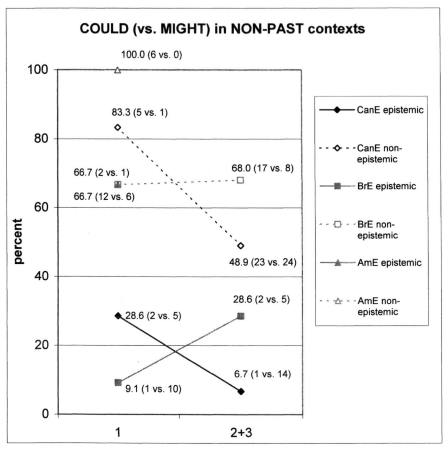

Figure 7.15: COULD in non-past contexts
Percentages calculated in relation to MIGHT (COULD and MIGHT = 100%),
(n vs. n), with the first number for COULD

Here, we see the same decrease of epistemic COULD in CanE and likewise an increase in BrE compared to past contexts. Would this be an indicator for the origin of epistemic COULD, which Coates (1983: 164) suggests to have arisen "by analogy with MIGHT"? We have an indicator for this hypothesis in the occurrences of epistemic COULD and MIGHT in AmE in period 1. In figure

(7.15), two thirds of the AmE epistemic meanings are coded by COULD, and only one third by MIGHT (while the occurrence in past contexts of COULD is much lower at 16.7%). This suggests that epistemic COULD was first developed in AmE, followed either by later parallel development in BrE or a contact scenario with AmE[81] or CanE. Statistical testing shows a significant difference between the AmE and BrE figures, while the AmE and CanE frequencies do not (cf. appendix 7.10). This would suggest the placement of AmE and BrE on opposite ends of a spectrum, where AmE is most innovative in its use of epistemic COULD, BrE most conservative and CanE in between. Epistemic COULD shows a marked difference in non-past and past contexts (cf. appendix 7.10), which suggests a spread from non-past to past contexts.

This scenario of origin might explain the opposed trajectories for CanE and BrE. While CanE started out with relatively high percentages for epistemic COULD, BrE underwent a time lag of some 25-50 years, i.e. one or two generations. By the time BrE had followed suit – be it by import of the feature from AmE or by parallel development – CanE appears to have taken the reverse development towards the BrE percentages from one or two generations earlier.

7.4.1 Negative contexts
We have seen in figures (7.1) and (7.2) a strong tendency of COULD to appear in negative contexts, and a modest preference for MIGHT in positive sentences in the data. Here, we shall inquire into this distribution in a four-grid pattern of dichotomies, based on past/non-past and epistemic/non-epistemic meanings.

Table (7.5) shows the data for negatives in past and non-past contexts. In negative sentences, epistemic uses play no important role (grey shadings). Neither of the varieties uses COULD or MIGHT in negative past epistemic contexts, while in negative non-past contexts only three occurrences are shown in periods 2+3 in CanE. Likewise interesting is the pattern of distribution for past non-epistemic contexts: in all three varieties, out of 123 occurrences, only one is coded by MIGHT, and again in CanE. For CanE in period 2+3 we can see that these uses occur in unconventional contexts, which fits with the notion of extreme variability in period 2. The uses in non-past, non-epistemic contexts show very low frequencies. However, MIGHT seems to have some currency in negative contexts in BrE, with, in total, 3 occurrences of negative MIGHT.

---

[81] This would not be the only time when AmE would lead developments in the modal complex. Mair and Leech (2006), for instance, show in their survey of recent changes that AmE appears to lead changes in the semi-modals in the late 20th century in what they call a "follow-my-leader scenario".

Negative contexts, PAST					
Past Non-epistemic			**Past Epistemic**		
BrE1	COULD 16	MIGHT 0	BrE1	COULD 0	MIGHT 0
BrE2+3	COULD 29	MIGHT 0	BrE2+3	COULD 0	MIGHT 0
CanE1	COULD 6	MIGHT 0	CanE1	COULD 0	MIGHT 0
CanE2+3	COULD 47	MIGHT 1	CanE2+3	COULD 0	MIGHT 0
AmE1	COULD 24	MIGHT 0	AmE1	COULD 0	MIGHT 0
Negative contexts, NON-PAST					
Non-past Non-epistemic			**Non-past Epistemic**		
BrE1	COULD 3	MIGHT 2	BrE1	COULD 0	MIGHT 0
BrE2+3	COULD 3	MIGHT 1	BrE2+3	COULD 0	MIGHT 0
CanE1	COULD 2	MIGHT 0	CanE1	COULD 0	MIGHT 0
CanE2+3	COULD 2	MIGHT 0	CanE2+3	COULD 0	MIGHT 3
AmE1	COULD 1	MIGHT 0	AmE1	COULD 0	MIGHT 0

Table 7.5: COULD and MIGHT in negative contexts, past and non-past

Given the data in table (7.5), it seems clear that COULD displays a clear preference in negative contexts. This preference means, however, that COULD and MIGHT are competing on a level playing field only in affirmative contexts, to which we shall turn now.

7.4.2 Affirmative contexts
Figure (7.16) shows the distribution in past context. Epistemic uses, i.e. the solid lines, remain unchanged in affirmative contexts when compared to the overall data in figure (7.14). In other words, the lower halves of both charts are identical, as all tokens in this area come exclusively from affirmative sentences.

For non-epistemic uses, changes can be seen between the two figures, however. The differences between CanE and BrE become even more pronounced in affirmative contexts when compared to the overall data in figure (7.14), as the differences in both periods are greater than before. This can be seen in the dotted lines in the upper halves of both figures. The most pronounced difference, in period 1, reaches significance (cf. appendix 7.11). The 30.9 percent points of difference in period 1 between BrE (53.7) and CanE (84.6) is the second biggest difference in the entire variable complex (and up from 23.2 in fig. 7.14). In period 2+3, the difference is almost 20% in period 2+3, between 60.4% and 79.5% (up from 7.5% in figure 7.14). This again yields opposite trajectories in CanE and BrE, with AmE (79.2) patterning with CanE (84.6) in period 1, indicating the existence of a North-American feature of modal usage of COULD and MIGHT by 1800, which gave preference to non-epistemic COULD.

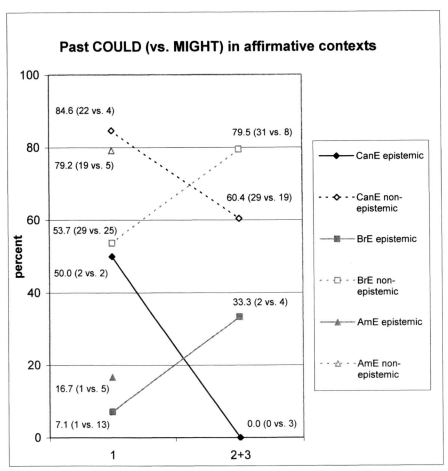

Figure 7.16: COULD (vs. MIGHT) in past contexts in affirmative clauses

Moving on to the second category, figure (7.17) on the next page provides the data for the uses in affirmative non-past contexts. For epistemic uses, a decrease can be seen in CanE, with an increase in BrE, with is roughly parallel to the overall changes in figure (7.15). In BrE, moreover, non-epistemic uses change from the overall data (figure 7.15) only marginally and within the overall trend. In CanE, however, a different picture emerges, as CanE decreases its use of non-epistemic COULD in affirmative contexts by almost 30 percent (75

to 46.7%) from period 1 to 2+3. One could say while COULD holds its territory in BrE, CanE changes towards a preference for MIGHT in CanE, with
COULD falling under the 50% mark.

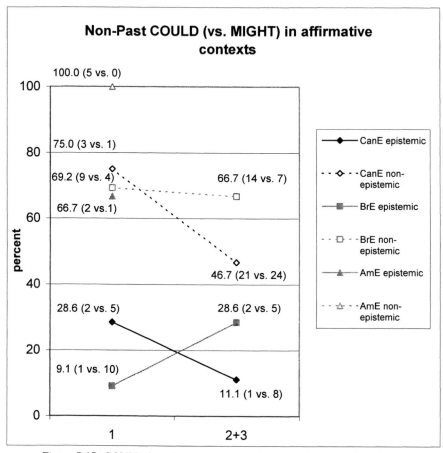

Figure 7.17: COULD (vs. MIGHT) in non-past contexts in affirmative clauses

One may conclude from this that a divergence between CanE and BrE in non-
epistemic uses can be seen in the period. This divergence is shown almost
identically in the overall data and in affirmative contexts, with more pronounced changes in affirmative contexts in CanE, which allows us to take a
closer look at the three periods in CanE on the basis of the overall data.

7.4.3 COULD and MIGHT and the three stages of new-dialect formation

Based on the data in figures (7.14) and (7.15), it was suggested that epistemic COULD is a feature that was first developed in AmE in non-past contexts and transferred into CanE and BrE. The data from CONTE-pC for CanE provide a window into the three stages of dialect development as outlined in chapter (5). Table (7.6) shows the data for three periods in CanE:

CanE - epistemic	period 1	period 2	period 3
COULD non-past	28.6 (2)	12.5 (1)	0 (0)
MIGHT non-past	71.4 (7)	87.5 (7)	100 (8)
COULD past	50 (2)	0 (0)	0 (0)
MIGHT past	50 (2)	100 (2)	100 (9)

Table 7.6: Epistemic COULD and MIGHT in CanE in percent (n)

While the absolute numbers of the data in table (7.6) are too low to produce significance, we may nevertheless gauge the extent of influence. The outcome is in both data sets, in period 3, remarkably homogeneous with no occurrences of epistemic COULD in period (3). In this period, MIGHT is used as the only epistemic marker, which fits well with Coates' statement of the prevalence and aptitude of MIGHT in these contexts (1983: 146). It seems that the dialect formation process would have favoured the suppression of COULD in those contexts. In BrE, on the other hand (cf. figures 7.14 and 7.15), epistemic COULD is used in both past and non-past contexts, as summarized in table (7.7):

BrE - epistemic	period 1	period 2+3
COULD non-past	9.1 (1)	28.6 (2)
MIGHT non-past	90.9 (10)	71.4 (5)
COULD past	7.1 (1)	33.3 (2)
MIGHT past	92.9 (13)	66.6 (4)

Table 7.7: Epistemic COULD and MIGHT in BrE in percent (n)

Comparing the last two tables, we see that epistemic COULD is gaining ground in BrE in period 2+3, which is not the case in CanE, where it decreases instead over periods 2 and 3. AmE input, which favours epistemic COULD in two thirds of all contexts in period 1 (12 vs. 6 in figure 7.15), is reversed in CanE in period 2+3 to the detriment of COULD. CanE does not follow AmE patterns and it does not seem to follow BrE either, which shows increases in epistemic COULD. We could, therefore, conclude that the dialect-formation process caused the choice of one variant to code for epistemic uses in CanE: MIGHT.

How would this account fit into Trudgill's three stage model? While the three-period data is not as solid as one would hope for, it still allows some hypotheses about new-dialect formation. It is obvious that period 2 in CanE does not exhibit the variation projected by stage II. Instead, period 1 shows the highest degree of variability, with a reduction already starting in period 2. This confirms the suggestion made earlier that stage I could be comprised of three phases: rudimentary levelling, interdialect development *and* extreme variability, as shown in table (7.3), before the levelling process is started in stage II. The data on COULD and MIGHT supports the suggestion which was derived from data on CAN and MAY.

7.5 COULD and MIGHT: epistemic developments

It has been suggested, as pointed out above, that epistemic COULD emerged in analogy to MIGHT (Coates 1983: 167). In PDE varieties, MIGHT is apparently becoming more and more synonymous with epistemic MAY, and is abandoning its semantic function as a marker of tentative epistemic possibility, which is taken over by COULD (ibid; cf. Gresset 2003 for an opposing view). Diachronically, COULD and MIGHT have been largely limited to root uses until the EModE period (see Kytö 1991a: 203). Epistemic MIGHT, which was first emerging in ME, was still used in "predominantly non-epistemic contexts in 17th century American English" (ibid: 152), while epistemic COULD entered the epistemic path later than MIGHT (ibid: 156). The development of COULD was probably "more dynamic" (ibid: 148) in expanding its functions, including epistemic readings, than was the case for MIGHT. Today, we have strong evidence that epistemic meanings[82] are the most common ones in a corpus of present-day AmE and BrE (Biber *et al.* 1999: figure 6.12), both in the written and speech genres.

The developmental scenario with MIGHT starting the grammaticalization process earlier than COULD is reverberated in Gresset's assessment of the present-day situation, which suggests that MIGHT has moved further along the cline towards epistemic meanings:

> *might* is purely epistemic [...], *could* may take an apparent epistemic interpretation in the relevant contexts, i.e. in epistemically oriented ones. *Could*, then, is not purely epistemic and *might* and *could* are not strictly synonymous. (Gresset 2003: 95f).

---

[82] Referred to as 'extrinsic-possibility' meanings in Biber *et al.* (1999)

Nevertheless, in present-day BrE, Facchinetti (2000: 239) quantifies epistemic readings as the majority function of COULD with 37% (ICE-GB) of all instances. Our LModE data show an interesting pattern in the apparent conservatism of CanE, which prefers epistemic MIGHT over COULD (see table 7.6), and behaves more conservatively than BrE (see table 7.7). While the evidence is too slim to allow for any firm statement, AmE data from period 1 employs epistemic COULD most consistently (see figures 7.15, 7.17) in non-past contexts, but not in past contexts. Table (7.8) presents the overall uses of COULD and MIGHT in their epistemic and non-epistemic functions.

COULD & MIGHT	CanE-1	CanE-2+3	BrE-1	BrE-2+3	AmE-1
epistemic	11% (4)	10% (11)	17% (14)	9% (6)	11% (6)
non-epistemic	89% (32)	90% (96)	83% (70)	91% (60)	89% (48)

Table 7.8: Epistemic and non-epistemic COULD and MIGHT in three varieties

Taken together, epistemic uses represent between 9-17% in the data and no sizeable extension of epistemic readings can yet be seen in the LModE data. The predominant attestation of MIGHT in epistemic readings and the vast majority of uses of COULD in non-epistemic uses as seen in figures (7.14) – (7.17), accounting for more than double the frequency of the other functions combined, suggests that the loss of root meanings had not yet started by the mid-19th century. Abraham's (2002: 20) finding, which exclusively attests MIGHT in epistemic readings in present-day spoken AmE is not matched in the LModE data, and neither are the 37% of epistemic readings for COULD in Facchinetti's BrE data. In (7.9) some examples of the predominant non-epistemic uses of COULD and MIGHT are provided:

(7.9) a.   I have written three times to the Surveyor General for Instructions and **could** never get even an acknowledgement.
(CanE, letters-3)
   b.   Upon application to Monsieur De Longueil at Montreal, to know which of the people wished to settle on the River Chateangaye in order that I **might** fill up the plan, - he said he **could** not inform me.
(CanE, letters-1)
   c.   We met Mrs Gordon & followed her up Dundas Street that Mary **might** see her.
(CanE, letters-1)

The two most prominent contexts in the LModE data COULD and MIGHT are when used as past-tense forms of CAN and MAY (7.9b & c) and in Root possibility readings (7a). These functions represent uses other than the most frequent ones in present-day Englishes, and this findings suggests that the developments leading to the present-day state had not yet started.

7.6 Conclusion

We have seen in this section that the distributional differences between CAN and MAY are, despite considerable differences in terms of percentages, in some cases not borne out by a chi-square test at the 95% level or Fisher's Exact Test. CAN/COULD is clearly preferred in negative contexts, and MAY/MIGHT show a modest preference for affirmative contexts. These tendencies were already found in EModE, and their continuation in all three varieties are best explained as an instance of (continuing) drift.

We could also show considerable variation of CAN and MAY across the three genres. CAN and MAY overlap in their uses of Root possibility and Permission. While changes in frequency in Root possibility are best accounted for as instances of drift, showing generally an increase of CAN, uses of Permission readings are better interpreted as part of long-term trend from MAY towards CAN. While the figures seem to corroborate the trend, statistical testing does not always produce significance for our data sets, which opens room for debate whether the 95% significance level criteria may be too strict a criterion for some slow-moving changes and low token samples.

COULD and MIGHT were shown to produce very similar distributions in both past and non-past contexts with one important exception: the use of epistemic COULD in non-past contexts in AmE. AmE was shown to use epistemic COULD significantly differently than in BrE (period 1). This change was shown to proceed differently in BrE and CanE (and with different percentages for AmE-1), which suggests some independent development in all three varieties. In early CanE, only one form, MIGHT, was used to code for epistemic readings, while BrE tended to use COULD more often. COULD and MIGHT in epistemic readings together, however, do not yet show an increase in discourse frequency in both CanE and BrE, with comparable levels in AmE-1.

A close-up on the CanE data led to a review of Trudgill's three stages for CAN and MAY and suggested and expansion of the phenomena of stage I, rudimentary levelling and interdialect development, to include 'extreme variation'. This is corroborated by the data sets for epistemic COULD and MIGHT, which show more variation in stage I than in stage II. The inverse V-curve, which was found in four – including the MC data in five different data sets – was interpreted as a result of normative influence in period 1.

Epistemic readings of CAN were not attested in the LModE data, while epistemic CAN'T appears to have served as a foothold for the recent, 20th-century innovation epistemic CAN. CanE prefers rather epistemic MIGHT than COULD, but generally, the expansion of epistemic uses had not yet taken off in the LModE period.

8 MUST vs. HAVE TO

The variable complex around MUST and its younger competitor HAVE TO is part of the "obligation/necessity cluster" of the English modals (Coates 1983: 31). This cluster comprises two groups, which are semantically differentiated. There are, on the one hand, those modal expressions that are markers of weak obligation/necessity (centering around SHOULD, OUGHT, and BE OBLIGED), and on the other hand, those which represent the strong obligation/necessity cluster, with the variables MUST and HAVE (GOT) TO and GOT TO at its core in PDE.

In this chapter we shall focus on the strong obligation cluster, which has recently received considerable attention in present-day varieties of English (PDE) (e.g. Krug 1998, 2000, Tagliamonte 2004).[83] Krug (2000) takes a detailed look at the development of HAVE TO and includes some LModE data from ARCHER, which may serve as a point of reference here. This chapter aims to complement the developmental picture of HAVE TO and MUST from a Canadian real-time perspective. First, the competing variants in our varieties and the variable context is established. After this, second, the rise of modal HAVE TO in LModE will be illustrated, which is, third, followed by a look into the semantic functions before, fourth, the epistemic development will be reviewed and, fifth, the data is related to the theory of new-dialect formation.

The central modal MUST and the semi-modal HAVE TO are good candidates for a corpus-based diachronic study, since both occur at higher frequencies than other markers of obligation. BE SUPPOSED TO, OUGHT TO and SHOULD are usually considered weak obligation markers (Myhill 1995: 174, Palmer 1990: 123), and tend to be, with the exception of the latter, relatively low in frequency for grammatical items (cf. Krug 2000: fig. 2.1; app. 1). NEED (TO) has been researched as a strong obligation marker (Biber, Conrad and Reppen 1998: 204) but occurs only once in the data (in the BrE section). Therefore, MUST and HAVE TO, with its younger variants (HAVE) GOT TO, are the variables chosen in the present study, which leaves us with the same focus as Myhill (1995: 165). For historical reasons that are outlined below in section (8.1), the present study cannot draw on exactly the same set of strong obligation markers as Myhill's.

---

[83] An earlier version of this study appeared as Dollinger (2006b).

A number of studies survey aspects of the emergence of HAVE TO as a modal auxiliary. Biber, Conrad and Reppen (1998: 205-210) and Biber (2004) provide a general outline of the development of HAVE TO and MUST since 1650, while Krug (2000: ch. 3) outlines the development in greater detail for the same period, both for AmE and BrE. Myhill's (1995) paper draws mainly from American drama data since the first quarter of the 19th century. While his study contains highly interesting results, it was not designed along strictly quantitative lines, which limits its use for comparisons. For 20th-century British and American English, a real-time study has recently been made available (Jankowski 2004).

8.1 The variables MUST and competing semi-modals

A number of variants have been found to compete with MUST. Krug (2000) lists HAVE TO, HAVE GOT TO, GOT TO, and the more recent, phonologically reduced form, GOTTA. In the LModE data, however, (HAVE) GOT TO does not appear as a modal in any of our corpora.

This is in fact little surprising if we consider the history of the form. Visser (1969-73: 2411) considers modal GOT TO as having come into general use in the third decade of the 19th century. It is attested in Dickens's *Oliver Twist* from the 1830s (Krug 2000: 61), and first occurrences in ARCHER are found in the drama and fiction sections in the first half of the 19th century for BrE (Krug 2000: 79) and the second half of the 19th century for AmE (Krug 2000: 77). Considering this chronology, our written data, although including less formal letter writing from CONTE-pC, do not yet include the new variant. We are left, consequently, with HAVE TO and MUST as the forms expressing strong obligation.

8.1.1 HAVE TO

In the light of modest corpora sizes, we will be confronted with low token frequencies of HAVE TO in the LModE data. This becomes even more apparent in relation to Krug's assessment that the critical stage of grammaticalization of HAVE TO occurred only around 1850, which coincides with our cut-off point. Considering that we are operating at a period prior to the "notable frequentative development" (Krug 2000: 81) of HAVE TO, the raw data do not seem too discouraging (see table 8.2, figures in parentheses). In total, 699 tokens of MUST and HAVE TO were found in four corpora. This includes 149 instances of HAVE TO, which shows clearly that MUST was the more prominent form.

Some formal considerations are necessary at this stage. There are two types of constructions of HAVE TO, contiguous HAVE TO, where HAVE is adjacent to TO, and discontinuous HAVE TO. The contiguous construction follows the pattern HAVE TO + verb + object, as in the canonical example *I have to write a letter* (Visser 1969-73: 1482). Discontinuous HAVE TO follows the pattern HAVE + object + TO + VERB, as in *I have a letter to write*. Both constructions have been discussed quite extensively (e.g. Fischer 1994, Brinton 1991, Visser 1969-73; van der Gaaf 1931). Brinton (1991: 43 [web: 27]) shows that the two constructions split off in EModE and started down the road of grammaticalization at different points in time; as a result, only the construction HAVE TO + verb + object is "now [in PDE] almost fully grammaticalized".

It will be interesting to see how the discontinuous construction figures in our four corpora. For the present purpose, we will not only look at objects that are placed between HAVE and TO, but distinguish between contiguous HAVE TO and discontinuous HAVE + X + TO, where X is *any* constituent. The results are shown in table (8.1), examples in (8.1):

Corpus and periods	HAVE + X + TO + verb	
	n	per 10,000 words
CanE 1-3	13	1.04
AmE-1	1	0.19
BrE 1-3	9	0.75
NW-BrE-1	48	1.60

Table 8.1: Occurrences of discontinuous HAVE TO (HAVE + X + TO + verb)

Discontinuous constructions of any type are somewhat more difficult to categorize. (8.1a) has a possessive element and is therefore still relatively straightforward; it may be paraphrased with minor changes of meaning, but diachronically important ones, as in *I have to pay Bills* (see Visser 1969-73: 1482f and Brinton 1991: 40f [web: 25f] for semantic nuances, Fischer 1994 for the importance of 'movable' objects).

(8.1) a. I have **Bills** to pay & my own remittances   NW-BrE1
      b. Four companies of the 20th have **orders** to hold   CanE-3
         themselves
      c. but have **nothing** to do with snow or ice   BrE-1
      d. when you have **occasion** to write to me   AmE-1

To a lesser degree some possessive element is also discernible in (8.1b) and (8.1d), but the contiguous variant is, if not impossible for those examples, at least stylistically awkward. Negative constructions like (8.1c), however, present a special problem for categorization. Syntactic units like *nothing, nothing else, not much* have been put "as a rule" between HAVE and the TO infinitive since OE (Visser 1969-73: 1484), which complicates the proper classification of negative constructions. To circumvent the semantic fuzziness of examples like these, we will not consider discontinuous constructions here and make word order our prime criterion for HAVE TO instead, that is, we will focus on contiguous HAVE TO.

There is, however, a special type of discontinuous construction of the HAVE + X + TO type that nevertheless has an immediate bearing on our case study. This construction is discontinuous HAVE and TO when separated by an *adverb*, a construction usually referred to as adverb interpolation. In PDE, there seems to be little evidence for adverb interpolation between HAVE and TO. Krug does not find any tokens in the spoken component in the BNC, which leads him, among other data, to state that HAVE and TO "resist adverb interpolation most strongly and perhaps do not permit it at all" (2000: 58).

In earlier periods, adverb interpolation was not always so rare, as it occurs with modest frequency in our LModE data, as shown in (8.2):

(8.2) a. I have only to add that if it is your wish   (CanE-l2)
       b. I have only to add that I beg you'll please offer   (CanE-l1)
       c. I have only to observe that Marentile will never   (CanE-l2)
       d. I have now to request   (CanE-l1)
       e. he has only to direct his brother in law   (BrE-n3)
       f. I have also to tell you from M={r}s= Ann Legh   (NW-BrE-l1)

This construction is likely to act an intermediate step towards the grammaticalization of HAVE TO. In the context of contiguous HAVE TO, adverb interpolation points to the emerging nature of a structure that had not yet been syntacticized (Givón, in Hopper 1991: 18), i.e. had not yet had a fixed word order. Fischer (1994: 146) argues that the juxtaposition of HAVE and TO is the crucial factor for grammaticalization, which would still have been in its early stages in the late 18th century. While this intermediate stage will also need to be excluded from the analysis as it appears to be categorically too ambivalent to be left in our data (cf. Visser 1969-73: 1474, Brinton 1991: 19 [web: 12]), it is interesting to point out that Canadian data figures prominently here. This points towards some variation in periods 1 and 2 and would fit our suggested new stage I, which includes extreme variability, as suggested in the previous chapter.

8.1.2 Controlling the variable contexts

For the variables MUST and HAVE TO, a number of variable contexts will need to be excluded from the case study. First, all suppletive forms for MUST are discarded. Since we are looking for forms where HAVE TO competes with MUST, all forms in which the incomplete paradigm of MUST would prompt the use of HAVE TO are ruled out. This is the case in past tense contexts and after modals. Environments where MUST cannot be used are called syntactic (Myhill 1995), as in (8.3a):

(8.3) a. Wednesday 22nd Gas **had to** go to the Mill   (CanE- 12)
         (syntactic)
      b. for the Township of Tyendinaga I **have to** state   (CanE-13)
         (non-syntactic)
      c. Dear Mama says I **must not** use it   (CanE-13)
         (non-syntactic)
      d. The Indians then disappeared but left the loaf of (CanE-d1)
         bread in the road where the travellers **must** pass
         and were seen no more
         (past tense MUST)

In (8.3b), HAVE TO could be substituted with MUST without a significant change of meaning, therefore, it is included in the data. In contrast, all instances of MUST NOT are discarded on semantic grounds, as in (8.3c), because they cannot be paraphrased with HAVE NOT TO. There is one form, as illustrated in (8.3d) that is excluded from the variable context: past tense MUST. As has been pointed out before (Denison 1998: 176), MUST in the past tense was on its way out by the end of the 18th century and would unnecessarily distort the picture of emerging HAVE TO. One occurrence in CONTE-pC, none in AmE-1 and 18 occurrences in NW-BrE-1 testify to its decline and justify the approach to control the context.

Second, the existence of formulaic phrases would also need to be considered. In studies on a PDE variety (Tagliamonte 2004: 38), invariant collocations with MUST are ruled out; Jankowski's (2004: 92) diachronic study of 20th century AmE and BrE drama excludes the phrase *I must say* for both BrE and AmE. A search in CONTE-pC revealed no single instance of *I must say*, and the collocation is found neither in the AmE or BrE data; it occurs three times in NW-BrE-1. Instead, MUST and HAVE TO were found as showing variation in combination with verbs of expression in the 1st person singular across all periods, as can be seen in (8.4):

(8.4) a. I <u>Must Inform</u> You of the Measurement of   (CanE-l2)
       b. I <u>have to inform</u> you that Every Crown Lo   (CanE-l3)
       c. I **must request** You to inform H. Exc.y te   (CanE-l1)
       d. I **have to request**, you will be pleased   (CanE-l1)

On account of this variation, no instances are classified and ruled out as formulaic phrases.

Third, all forms of discontinuous HAVE TO are excluded for the reasons outlined above (which also rules out clear cases of possessive HAVE TO, cf. Visser 1969-73: 1474f). The corrected instances are only slightly smaller than the raw data from table (8.1) and are shown in table (8.2):

Corpus	HAVE TO		MUST	
	n	per 10,000	n	per 10,000
CanE 1-3	(29) 17	1.36	(74) 73	5.84
AmE-1	(7) 4	0.78	(27) 26	5.06
BrE 1-3	(11) 2	0.17	(92) 87	7.29
NW-BrE-1	(31) 22	0.73	(357) 334	11.13

Table 8.2: Frequencies in corrected variable contexts, (n) and raw data in parentheses

8.2 The rise of HAVE TO

If we compare the normalized word counts in table (8.2) with each other, it is surprising that CanE appears to be more progressive than both AmE and BrE in its use of almost double the number of HAVE TO (1.36) than found in AmE (.78). We need to keep in mind, however, that table (8.2) does not include AmE data from the early 19th century, which would likely increase the overall count. The compatibility of AmE (.78) and NW-BrE (.73) suggests the importance of regional BrE varieties for AmE. Note also that all instances of HAVE TO found in the corpora are root uses (cf. section 8.3).

Figure (8.1) provides a cross-section for period 1 in the letter genre alone. We see that AmE is most innovative in its use of HAVE TO, followed, with some gap, by CanE.

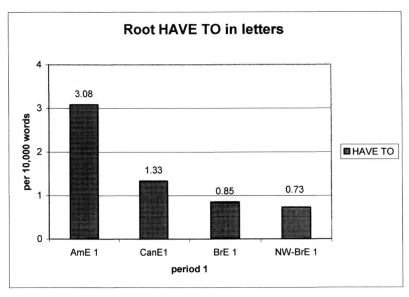

Figure 8.1: Root HAVE TO in letters in four varieties (period 1)
Normalized per 10,000 words

What is interesting in table (8.2), and is less obvious in figure (8.1), is that CanE seems to pattern with AmE rather than BrE. This impression is confirmed by statistical testing, indicting that HAVE TO is preferred over MUST in comparable contexts in CanE and AmE but *not* in BrE at this point of development (cf. appendix 8.1). This patterning would be even clearer with additional AmE data, which is likely to increase the AmE normalized word count, and would therefore bring it closer to the overall CanE average of 1.78 per 10,000 words. This result lends linguistic support to the direct import of loyalist speech patterns with the first wave of immigration that peopled Ontario and set, in accordance with the founder principle (Mufwene 1996), the tone for future developments.

Concerning these two modal expressions, however, CanE and BrE were already distinct, which would mean that we may extend claims of the American base of CanE that have hitherto been based on the external language history and lexis (e.g. Avis 1978a: 37) to the strong obligation markers. On the other hand, however, CanE and AmE show quantifiable, albeit statistically non-significant, differences, which suggests the existence of embryonic syntactic features of CanE. Both CanE and AmE had departed from the forms of BrE that were its foundations. In its use of HAVE TO, however, CanE may have even overtaken the older North-American variety, although this remains a hypothesis in need of further study.

Corpus linguistic research over the past two decades has yielded important insights into the spread of features in different genres (e.g. Rissanen *et al.* 1992, Nevalainen and Raumolin-Brunberg 2003). An analysis by genre in CONTE-pC tracks the rise of HAVE TO more closely and shows its spread between genres. Figure (8.2) charts the distribution of HAVE TO by genre for the late 18th and early 19th centuries in CanE:

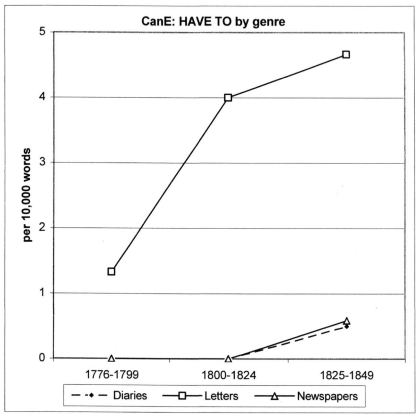

Figure 8.2: HAVE TO by genre in CanE
Normalized per 10,000 words

It is evident that HAVE TO is first attested in the letter genre, with diaries and newspapers picking up some 50 years later. The early occurrence of HAVE TO in a genre that tends to employ informal written language styles is clearly shown and testifies to a spread of modal HAVE TO from informal to more formal contexts. We might even surmise that this distribution is indirect evidence that HAVE TO entered the language not only via informal *written* styles, but ultimately, via informal *spoken* styles. This line of thought, however reasonable it may seem, is ultimately not substantiated by the data and must therefore remain a hypothesis.

As was shown in table (8.2), Canadians tended to employ HAVE TO to a greater extent than their contemporaries in Britain, and possibly the USA. By taking a closer look at the earliest period in our data,[84] however, we may qualify this result, which will reveal a slightly different picture for the frequency counts across all periods in table (8.2). Here, the letter genre is of particular interest, as it is to be expected to exhibit less prescriptive influence than newspapers. Figures (8.3) and (8.4) show the diachronic development of root uses of HAVE TO and MUST in the letter genre:

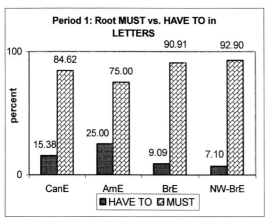

Figure 8.3: *HAVE TO and MUST in period 1*

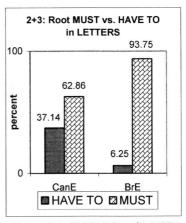

Figure 8.4: *HAVE TO and MUST in period 2+3*

---

[84] Diaries would be another good – indirect – indicator of the vernacular. However, the nature of the syntactic variables would make the exclusion of some source texts necessary. This would leave us in at least two cases with only one diary per period, making the results prone to idiosyncratic stylistic influences. This is not the case in the letter sections, as letters by at least six informants (AmE-1, up to 64 in the case of CanE-3) are included per period.

It will be noticed for period 1 that HAVE TO in letters patterns into a group which shows the lowest incidences and includes BrE and NW-BrE. This group contrasts with AmE as the most advanced variety and CanE in the middle. Statistical testing, however, does not produce significance for the differences, with the exception of AmE and NW-BrE, the biggest differences, reaching significance at the 90% level (cf. appendix 8.2). In Period 2+3, however, CanE witnesses a marked increase of HAVE TO (figure 8.4). This increase is also responsible for CanE appearing to lead the change towards HAVE TO in comparison to AmE over all periods in table (8.2) and is significant (appendix 8.3; Fisher's Exact Test).

While figures (8.3) and (8.4) suggest continuing American influence on CanE in the first half of the 19th century, the external settlement history renders this unlikely. As we have seen in chapter (3), Americans were unwanted in Canada and American immigration was even prohibited for a short period after the War of 1812 (a policy, which was given up later on). While there always continued to be "a considerable American element" of newcomers (Landon 1967: 47), by far the most profound demographic impact came from the British Isles, and here mostly from non-southeastern English speakers. However, this link to the British Isles is not shown in the data in figure (8.4), with CanE increasing its percentage of HAVE TO and BrE decreasing it in comparison to the preceding period (figure 8.3). This, again, confirms the loyalist hypothesis and would also suggest an instance of (directional) drift, inheriting the propensities for the further development of HAVE TO from the 1st wave immigrants. Within this general drift towards HAVE TO, however, there may be room for (possibly short-lived) CanE independent development.

If we interpret the data in figure (8.3) further, it seems that in period 1 CanE was more conservative than AmE, but already more progressive than British varieties, both in the ARCHER-1 data (BrE), as well as the data from the English North-West (NW-BrE). This indirectly corroborates the loyalist base theory of CanE. The demographics of the early days show that a great majority of settlers had come from the newly-founded USA; we have seen that by 1812 four fifths of all immigrants to Ontario were reported to have come from the United States. The increase of frequency in CanE from figure (8.3) to figure (8.4), however, is – for external reasons – very unlikely to be a result of AmE influence. Moreover, since BrE decreases its uses over the same period, it can hardly have been a result of the hundreds of thousand of British immigrants over the period. The distribution of HAVE TO therefore allows the possibility of an early independent Canadian development of this variable.[85]

The diverging development of CanE and BrE between pre-1800 and 1800-1849 data may indicate yet another development. By comparing the percentages in figures (8.3) and (8.4), it can be seen that CanE increases its uses of HAVE TO from 15.38 to 37.14 percent, while BrE decreases its uses from 9.09 to 6.25 percent. It seems that MUST was on its way to become a marker of BrE. Notwithstanding heavy BrE influence in Canada (Chambers 2004: 226), we witness the emergence of something like a distinct CanE pattern in the uses of HAVE TO for the period 2+3, *despite* the fact that there seems to have been "no awareness of Canadian English in the early period" (Avis 1978a: 36). HAVE TO vs. MUST are therefore prime candidates for an early focussing in early OntE, which would have been an unconscious process.

This line of thought must be put into perspective, however: while all varieties of English were headed towards more uses of HAVE TO at the expense of MUST, i.e. undergoing drift, CanE already went at its own pace, which was quite different to the path in BrE. By subdividing the period 1776-1849 for CanE, it can be shown that the normalized occurrences per 10,000 words corroborate this interpretation (see also table 8.6). In period 1: 1.33 HAVE TO per 10,000 words; in 2: 4.00 and in 3: 4.67; these figures show – unlike BrE – no decrease of HAVE TO and therefore no inclination towards more BrE frequencies during and after the War of 1812. This is surprising for a time of armed conflict between the British colony and US-America, especially as Anti-Americanism reached an unprecedented high during the war and immediately after (Landon 1967: 41), which would be expected to have its linguistic effects. Chambers (2004: 229-33), for example, documents pro-British linguistic attitudes that prevailed until the mid-1900s in Canada, which are to some degree a result of the War of 1812. Since the move away from BrE characteristics did not even stop in times of war, change towards HAVE TO in CanE must have occurred as a change from *below* and was criss-crossing political allegiances. Ontarians did not yet know, but they already spoke something that we may call early Canadian English in relation to HAVE TO, just as they preserved the more formal, more conservative use of MAY in more public genres, which was shown in the previous chapter.

Contrary to the preservation of MAY, which we have seen in chapter (7) in CanE, the change from MUST to HAVE TO must have occurred *without* social awareness (Labov 2001: 196), however, which left Canadians unaware of their

---

[85] It will need to be substantiated with 19th-century AmE data to what extent this change was indeed a Canadian independent development.

patterning with American usage. This is expected to stand in contrast with more overt, i.e. stereotypical, changes such as for spelling variables, for which we have seen a different scenario in section (5.1.2), figure (5.3).

What are the likely causes for the LModE spread of HAVE TO, which we have shown to be subject to diatopic variation? A view often expressed in the literature for the long-term rise of HAVE TO and other semi-modals links their increases in discourse frequency to the defective paradigm of central modals (e.g. Fischer 2003: 29). This means in our case that MUST could not provide for all functions: most notably, MUST NOT could not be used as a negation of MUST and there was no viable past tense form of MUST, apart from residual uses. The data in Krug (2000: 89), based on the ARCHER-1 drama and fiction sections, suggests a complex scenario: while there was a *connection* between the failure of the central modals to appear in certain contexts and the rise of semi-modals "evidence against a causal link between the genesis [of HAVE TO] and the defective paradigm of the central modal verb" (p. 96) is abundant. In other words, defective paradigms may have increased the rise of semi-modals, but were not the prime cause for their development. This reasoning is based on the observation that HAVE TO first occurred in non-syntactic contexts, i.e. in the present tense, which were contexts where MUST showed no formal shortcomings. Table (8.3) shows that the Canadian data lends further support to this line of argument:

Corpus	Root HAVE TO	
	present tense (non-syntactic)	other (syntactic)
CanE-1	3	0
CanE-2	6	5
CanE-3	10	5
AmE-1	4	3
BrE-1	2	4
BrE-2+3	2	3
NW-BrE-1	27	4

Table 8.3: HAVE TO in syntactic and non-syntactic contexts (n)

In the Canadian data, HAVE TO first occurs in non-syntactic contexts (CanE-1), which corroborates the idea that its rise was at least not exclusively conditioned by the defective paradigm of the central modal MUST. While the data for the AmE and BrE sections in ARCHER-1 are less clear, the difference in frequency in NW-BrE-1, with 27 occurrences in non-syntactic, and only four in syntactic contexts, nicely complements the scenario that HAVE TO got its first foothold in precisely the area where MUST was doing fine. Internal reasons seem, therefore, to be of less importance for this change. This suggests the type of externally-triggered change that Myhill (1995: 200) suggests for early AmE in the decline of "universal and absolute" undertones in the modal auxiliaries in exchange for more subjective ones.

So far we have dealt with HAVE TO on the formal level, without considering shades of modality. In the next section, we are mainly concerned with the distribution of epistemic readings across the corpora.

8.3 The modalities of MUST and HAVE TO

The basic distinction in terms of modality is between root and epistemic uses. Example (8.5) illustrates two epistemic cases, (8.5a) with MUST, (8.5b) with HAVE TO:

(8.5) a.   Your perfidious and under hand conduct   (CanE-l2)[86]
           towards me is such that nothing short of
           ruin of myself and family **must** be the
           consequence of it
       b. He **has to** be crazy to keep flying com-   (Joseph Heller,
           bat missions after all the close calls he's   *Catch-22* [1955: 45])
           had.

A search of all four corpora yielded no instances of epistemic HAVE TO, which further attests to its late development (cf. Krug 2000: 92). The epistemic uses of MUST, which managed to hold the territory of epistemic necessity almost exclusively until fairly recently in 20th-century English (e.g. Tagliamonte 2004 on PDE in York, England), are confronted with competition from other modal expressions, as we shall see later. The behaviour of MUST points to heavy layering of its functions, with epistemic meanings expanding in the period under investigation. This is truly remarkable for MUST, which is a form that has, allegedly, "been dying for centuries" (Krug 2000: 256).

8.3.1 Development of LModE epistemic MUST
The history of epistemic MUST shows that its progress towards more subjective readings has taken rather longer in comparison to other modals. While first

---

[86] This reading is epistemic while referring to a future state. Please note that Coates (1983: 42) regards epistemic MUST as usually *not* referring to the future.

epistemic uses of MOT, the older form of MUST, are well attested by the 14th century (Warner 1993: 174), they usually occurred in combination with epistemic adverbs such as *nedes* 'needs'. First unambiguous examples of epistemic MUST/MOT are already found by the middle of the ME period (Traugott 1999: 4), but MUST occurs in strong epistemic meanings not until the 17th century on its own (Traugott 1989: 42). Molencki (2003: 82) corroborates this date but adds that the collocations MUST NEEDS and MUST NECESSARILY were still quite common in some 18th and 19th century genres, before they became obsolete in the mid-19th century (p. 85). In the four corpora, four instances of MUST NECESSARILY are found in BrE-1, which suggests that this form did not survive long in pre-1776 AmE and was, if exported to Ontario in the first place, a victim of rudimentary levelling (a process from stage I) in period 1.

Collocations with MUST were not the only competitors for epistemic MUST, however. Considering the slow development of MUST from a weak to a strong epistemic marker over half a millennium, which other forms coded for its PDE functions in LModE? As the "focussing of the semantics of the modals continues throughout the modern period" (Warner 1993: 182), there are a number of likely competitors for epistemic MUST, which will be illustrated next.

8.3.2 Coding for epistemic necessity: LModE competition

The obvious choice for a competitor of epistemic MUST, HAVE TO, does not apply to our period as epistemic uses are not yet documented in the data. For this reason, the variable control outlined in section (8.1.2), which served to level the ground for HAVE TO, can be abandoned for the following study on root and epistemic MUST. In PDE, epistemic MUST typically encodes epistemic *necessity* (Palmer 1990: 55-8). Coates (1983: 170), for instance, notes a certain fuzziness between PDE epistemic WILL and epistemic MUST, which are mostly discriminated by the presence of a habitual aspect in WILL (p. 177). Interchangeable cases of epistemic MUST and WILL are also documented in Hopper and Traugott (1993: 80, with reference to Sweetser). In LModE, when the modal system underwent its fine-tuning, it seems that fuzzy borders were still more pronounced. The field of epistemic necessity was likely occupied by a number of variables: epistemic WILL (Coates 1983: 177), SHOULD (ibid: 69), possibly even OUGHT TO (ibid: 73-5) and BE BOUND TO (cf. Palmer 1990: 55f). The examples in (8.6) illustrate some of these likely competitors:

(8.6) a. Often, perhaps too often, we have lately, felt   (BrE-n2&3)
           called upon to state our impressions with regard
           to the vote by ballot, and once more we **are**
           bound to declare the continued bias of our
           judgment against that plausible, but inefficient
           and disgraceful, and if not inefficient, most
           dangerous and immoral measure.

       b. For Mr. McDonell I also received the Plans of   (CanE-l1)
           Sydney, Thurlo & Richmond, the others you
           will please send as soon as you may find it con-
           venient as they are much wanted many of the
           new camps wishing to settle near the Little and
           West Lakes & you **will** also be pleased to send
           a list of the lots […]

       c. Toronto 12th Office & the post Mastr. Affidavit   (CanE-l2)
           of Van Kleek's Hill to prove that my [xxx]
           Seller came into the Land Office. I **should** have
           left them there before I left the Citty <nw: city>
           but they escaped my memo-ry <le: memory> - I
           humbly hope Sir that you will have the good-
           ness to […]

       d. If he is to go, he **ought to** know it seasonably: - (AmE-l1)
           his time is up at Christmas; and nothing betwn
           us has past either as to his going, or staying

These may appear as a mixed bag from different semantic areas. We see that
(8.6a) does not qualify, as an important difference between epistemic MUST
and epistemic BE BOUND TO helps us in our assessment: while MUST marks
mostly present uses, BE BOUND TO is employed for futuritive epistemic uses
(Palmer 1990: 55). BE BOUND TO therefore does not seem to directly compete with epistemic MUST. While futuritive readings are possible for (8.6b),
there also seems to be an epistemic dimension present and, as Palmer (1990:
57) points out, sometimes these two functions are difficult to disentangle. Substitution with MUST seems possible in the second instance of WILL. (8.6c) is
an example of a hypothetical context that expresses the belief of the speaker.
However, substitution with MUST changes the meaning and does not work
here, although Palmer (1990: 59) states if SHOULD "marks epistemic necessity, it is related semantically not to *shall*, but to *must*". (8.6d) is an example

with OUGHT TO, which may be paraphrased with MUST with little change of meaning, if any. However, in (8.6d) root (deontic) readings are also possible.

In hindsight we know that, despite this competition, epistemic MUST was to gain ground. The modalities for MUST across three genres for CanE, AmE and BrE are shown in figure (8.5) for period 1. We see that MUST is still predominantly used in root senses in all varieties, while AmE is most advanced in its epistemic uses and CanE is lagging behind, with BrE in between:

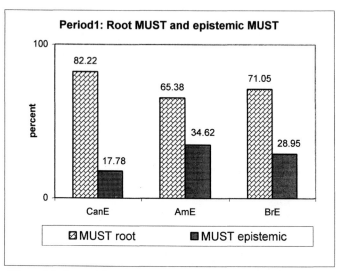

Figure 8.5: Root and epistemic MUST in CanE, BrE, AmE (period 1)

Although these differences appear to be sizeable, none is statistically significant between the varieties (appendix 8.4). This puts possible interpretations in between two extremes: random variation on the one hand and, on the other hand, parallel development in all three varieties of epistemic MUST without clear indicators for any cross-influence. We have little reason to assume that BrE, here lagging behind AmE, should have been much delayed in developing epistemic functions of MUST (cf. Mencken in Visser 1969-73: 1478), given its preferred usage of root MUST that we could see in figure (8.4). It is most likely that instances of continuing drift account for most of the observed changes relating to the strong obligation markers.

But what about HAVE TO? While MUST was expanding its frequencies in the epistemic realm, HAVE TO was still trying to gain a foothold in root functions. In PDE, epistemic HAVE TO is often found to correlate with inanimate subjects, as they rule out possessive readings. Krug (2000: 91 and fn 46) finds a correlation between epistemic HAVE TO and *in*animate clause subjects, a finding that matches with Tagliamonte's (2004: 44) result that deontic constructions, the largest subset of root uses, are "overwhelmingly animate". This finding is also expressed in our corpora. Table (8.3) exclusively features animate subject referents for (root) HAVE TO, which lends support to Krug's reasoning that *in*animate subjects are vital environments for the spread of epistemic meanings. By 1850, neither the shift towards epistemic readings of HAVE TO nor the pairing of root HAVE TO with inanimate subjects had occurred in our data, showing as yet no signs of the epistemic developments to come.

8.3.3 Epistemic and root uses: longterm perspective

If we attempt to link the LModE findings with studies of present-day varieties of English, we can relate to Abraham (2002), Leech (2003), and, above all, Smith (2003) to put the LModE data in perspective. Abraham (2002: 20) presents corpus-based data from spoken American English and finds no attestations of root MUST, but a substantial number of semi-modal HAVE TO (see table 6.2).

When compared to more detailed studies on English MUST, we see that MUST has been losing some ground in its root readings. Smith (2003: 263), in a comparison of BrE data from the 1960s and 1990s (LOB and FLOB written data; SEU and ICE-GB spoken data), concludes that MUST is "thriving only in its epistemic sense" and that the decline of MUST in its root sense "is pronounced in written and spoken modes and across all genres". But even in the epistemic realm, MUST has been losing ground since the 1960s, albeit much less so when compared to the decline in its root readings (Smith 2003: 257, tables 9 and 10). Leech (2003: 233), using the same data in his own analysis, shows increases for epistemic necessity for MUST and, congruent with Smith, decreases in root meanings.

From a LModE perspective, however, we can see that MUST was still expanding its uses in the epistemic realm. Figure (8.6), together with figure (8.5) from above, show the development until 1850. In both CanE and BrE, MUST was gaining ground as an epistemic modal – at the expense of its root meanings (see appendix 8.4 on the absolute figures for figures 8.5 and 8.6 and statistical tests).

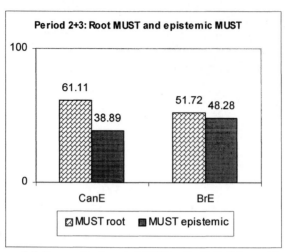

Figure 8.6: Root and epistemic MUST in CanE, BrE (period 2+3)

Interestingly, BrE shows the biggest increase, an increase of epistemic MUST that is significant. These data would suggest that a) MUST was expanding its use as a marker of epistemic readings in LModE, and b) MUST was doing so faster in BrE than in CanE, although AmE may be a good candidate as a leader (cf. figure 8.5), which might be shown once 19th-century AmE data will be available. There are strong signs in present-day BrE that MUST may be more generally losing ground to HAVE TO and other competitors (see Smith 2003) in both epistemic and root functions, but more predominantly in root functions (see Leech 2003) with semi-modal HAVE TO being on the rise. These developments occur in a 'prototypical modal' in both root and epistemic functions (Coates 1995: 57) and appear to be very gradual.

It is interesting to see that the increases of epistemic HAVE TO in present-day BrE, while still small in absolute numbers, far outnumber the increase of root HAVE TO by a relative comparison, as shown in table (8.4):

HAVE TO	LOB (1961)	FLOB (1991)	% change
Root	696 (91.9%)	742 (89.9%)	+ 6.6%
Epistemic	8 (1.1%)	26 (3.2%)	+ 225%

Table 8.4: HAVE TO in late 20th century written BrE (Smith 2003: 257)

The biggest percentile increases in table (8.4) by far are seen in epistemic readings of HAVE TO. When compared to the AmE data from Myhill (1996), which is summarized below in table (8.5), we can see that HAVE TO underwent a rather quick development. Myhill's data needs to be interpreted with caution, as his classificational system differs from the more traditional categories. However, an approximation of 'obligation' with 'root/deontic' allows us to use Myhill's data. The percentages refer to the proportion of the variable in relation to all other modal expressions surveyed by Myhill:

Period	Obligation MUST	Epistemic MUST	Obligation HAVE TO	Obligation GOT TO
1824-1855	100 (5.55%)	15 (0.83%)	0 (0%)	0 (0%)
1889-1936	210 (4.01%)	83 (1.59%)	38 (0.73%)	120 (2.29%)
1947-1987	15 (0.41%)[87]	70 (1.90%)	73 (1.98%)	98 (2.66%)

Table 8.5: American English drama data 1824-1987 (Myhill 1996: 374-377)
(n and percentage in relation to all modal auxiliaries in corpus); 'obligation' functions are roughly corresponding to root functions

The AmE data in period 1824-55 do not show root HAVE TO, in contrast to the CanE letter data from the period (e.g. table 8.2). For obligation MUST, roughly equated with root MUST for the present purposes, an increase until about WWII can be seen (1936) and then a sharp drop, which corroborates Leech's (2003), Smith's (2003) and Mair and Leech's (2006: 327) studies on late 20th-century BrE. Epistemic MUST, on the other hand, is still increasing and has outnumbered root MUST in the post-WWII period (1.90% overall in comparison to 0.41%). HAVE TO and GOT TO, in a root function, are also on the increase, which is in line with other studies (Krug 2000).

The evidence for MUST and HAVE TO is, taken together, overwhelming. HAVE TO, first attested in the letter genres in all varieties in our data, has apparently undergone a very quick development from a root modal to an epistemic modal and shows very high increases in this function (see the 1955 quote in example 8.5a from a Joseph Heller novel with epistemic reading). The evidence suggests that HAVE TO was still expanding its frequency in root uses in LModE, while MUST was expanding its functions as an epistemic marker. For the present-day situation, we have good indicators that MUST has already passed its climax as an epistemic marker, with epistemic HAVE TO showing high growth rates in Smith (2003). While Myhill (1996: 378) apparently does not survey epistemic HAVE TO, it would be highly unusual if it did not occur in AmE data from the period.

---

[87] Ehrman's (1966) descriptive study, based on one third of the 1961 Brown Corpus (AmE), focusses on the root functions of MUST, and does not explicitly discuss epistemic functions (cf. 1966: 68f).

Mair and Leech (2006: 327) suggest "at least some link between the fall of the modals and the rise of the semi modals", as spoken language data usually show a steeper decline of the core modals and a corresponding rise of the semi-modals. Their finding "places the encroachment of semi-modals on the territory of the modals in AmE speech, in frequency terms, beyond doubt" (ibid: 328). This 'encroachment' is further manifested in the 1990 Longman Corpus of Spoken American English, which shows that HAVE (GOT) TO is "more than 10 times as frequent as *must*" and is echoed in Biber *et al.* (1999: 488) for BrE and AmE conversation, where HAVE TO occurs more than twice as often as MUST in BrE and almost 10 times as often in AmE.

To summarize, we can say that all scenarios discussed for HAVE TO and MUST, both for LModE and PDE, comply fully with Abraham's thesis of root loss in the central modals in relation to MUST. We have good data for CanE and BrE for the extension of epistemic MUST (significance for Late Modern BrE is reached, see appendix 8.4), and the scenario tallies well with studies of present-day BrE and AmE, and, as far as the different classificational systems allow, diachronic AmE.

8.4 Three stages of new-dialect formation and the rise of HAVE TO

The variable HAVE TO was beginning to get increasingly employed as a modal auxiliary during our period, and we have produced CanE evidence that this functional expansion was not triggered by the incomplete paradigm of MUST. In this restructuring process of the strong obligation markers, a characteristic of early CanE emerged in its use of HAVE TO. The absolute figures for HAVE TO in CanE and BrE (for which we have diachronic data) are shown in table (8.6):

	Period 1	Period 2	Period 3
CanE	1.33 (2)	4.00 (6)	4.67 (7)
BrE	0.85 (1)	0.70 (1)	

Table 8.6: HAVE TO in CanE and BrE
(normalized per 10,000 words & n)

The development of HAVE TO occurs radically faster in CanE than in BrE, with BrE even slightly decreasing its percentage. Together with the AmE-1 data, and its normalized incidence of 3.08, 19th-century AmE would likely exhibit an even higher frequency. While the development of HAVE TO is likely the result, yet again, of drift, its progress appears to be much faster in colonial settings. The data in table (8.2) provides us with the a ratio of HAVE TO vs. MUST in BrE and NW-BrE, which is 2 vs. 87 for BrE and 22 vs. 334 for NW-BrE. Both of these figures lie below the 10% threshold suggested by Trudgill and would not have been carried into the speech of the next generation, had it not been for the AmE input, which figures 15.4% for HAVE TO as a strong obligation marker in our sample data and accounted for the major demographic input in period 1.

With HAVE TO as an ongoing change, however, table (8.6) shows no evidence of a stage of extreme variability and apparent levelling (stage II). Instead, HAVE TO increases steadily its frequency in CanE. Even the post-1815 immigrants did not stop the rise of HAVE TO. While NW-BrE was most conservative in its use of HAVE TO in period 1 (cf. figure 8.3), its input, at best, only slowed down the increase of HAVE TO in CanE. HAVE TO was bound to further increase, which suggests another alteration to Trudgill's scenario for newcomers like HAVE TO: changes which are part of an instance of long-term drift, such as the rise of HAVE TO, seem not to proceed through Trudgill's three stages. In dialect formation contexts these changes tend to be implemented more quickly than in the motherland context, but they do not seem to follow the new-dialect formation three-stage pattern.

8.5 Summary

Overall, we have found strong evidence that HAVE TO entered the language via informal styles. We have seen also that early CanE is not merely a conservative variety, as it is advanced in its frequency of modal HAVE TO in comparison to BrE. We produced evidence that CanE is in between (progressive) American usage and (most conservative) BrE usage. For the epistemic uses of MUST, CanE is, statistically non-significant, most conservative (fig. 8.5). These results seem to corroborate general statements about CanE, characterizing it as "more conservative linguistically than the United States and Australia [and other ex-colonies]" (Chambers 1998a: 253), but must allow for progressive behaviour of colonial varieties in comparison to BrE, as can be seen in the development of HAVE TO in the letter genre (fig. 8.3 & 8.4).

The accumulated evidence indicates that both colonial lag as well as linguistic progressivism occurred in the LModE modal system. The case of epistemic MUST tentatively suggests parallel developments towards epistemic uses *in all three* varieties, some of which moving faster (AmE) along the cline than others (BrE), while CanE seems to exhibit some colonial lag. In colonial settings, however, progressive features of modality prevail, relegating colonial lag to a myth, as suggested by Görlach.

While it may be safe to say that linguistic attitudes are typically subject to a colonial lag (Görlach's notion), the linguistic data for HAVE TO and MUST (Trudgill's approach) are more difficult to interpret and do not necessarily point in a given direction such as the 'preservation of conservative features in (ex-)colonial Englishes', even for a confined set of linguistic variables like the present one. The types of gradient changes witnessed in the modal system run counter to a broader, more permanent notion of a general lag of a certain variety and concepts of language drift play a pivotal role in those scenarios. If there is a lag, it is confined to certain variables, functions and contexts in any given period; moreover, it is not always the colonial variety that is lagging behind, quite to the contrary. For modal HAVE TO, AmE and CanE are the leaders.

For some time in the first half of the 19th century, however, we could show that CanE was markedly different than BrE in its use of HAVE TO. Whether Canadians would have noticed their linguistic distinctiveness remains to be seen, especially in the light of AmE data from the early 19th century. The difference in CanE and BrE is remarkable, but fails short of producing significance (appendix 8.2). Epistemic uses are steadily expanding for CanE and BrE MUST, making MUST a picture-book case for a highly regular trajectory towards more epistemic uses, which is in line with Abraham's general thesis of root loos.

Concerning new-dialect formation, we may propose another adaptation to Trudgill's model. In the case of HAVE TO, Trudgill's three stages do not seem to apply, as there is no phase of extreme variability in periods 2 or 3, and the majority form, MUST, could not oust the newcomer HAVE TO. Quite to the contrary, MUST managed to hold some ground, as can be in seen in present-day CanE and other varieties. We may say that new-dialect formation theory would need to be adapted for forms undergoing drift, i.e. parallel developments across the varieties, such as is the case with modal HAVE TO. The findings in chapter (7) on CAN/COULD and MAY/MIGHT, suggested that in Trudgill's theory stage I would need to be extended to allow for extreme variability. Now, the data suggest that a scenario for changes occurring as part of a large-scale drift, such as HAVE TO, is another exception.

Other phenomena can be interpreted by the theory without adaptations, however. The lack of MUST NECESSARILY collocations in AmE and CanE suggests that, for the latter variety, MUST NECESSARILY was a victim of early accommodation through rudimentary levelling. With these insights, we shall move on to chapter (9), the survey on SHALL and WILL.

9 SHALL vs. WILL

In this chapter we will deal with two sets of variables. SHALL and WILL, denoting prediction and/or volition, have been subject to a host of contemporary commentary since EModE times. In total, 391 instances of SHALL and 1017 instances of WILL are found in the four corpora. It is interesting, however, that more than 50 percent of tokens of WILL occur in CanE. The overall ratio of SHALL vs. WILL is 1 : 4.81 in CanE (118 vs. 568), but only 1 : 2.87 in BrE (127 vs. 336), which significantly prefers SHALL.[88]

First, the prescriptive rule governing SHALL and WILL and a review of previous research will be given. Second, SHALL and WILL in the first person will be focussed on in relation to three independent variables, which is followed by a treatment of select aspects in the second and third persons. This is completed with an account of SHALL and WILL in the three-stage model. The prescriptive rule will be a point of departure into the behaviour of SHALL and WILL.

9.1 The prescriptive rule and previous research

SHALL and WILL have served as variables to illustrate infractions against English grammar since EModE times. The background for this kind of criticism is found in a basic set of rules, which was first established by Wallis in 1653 (Gotti 2003a: 115f) and is shown here in table (9.1):

Person	Prediction = "Future Tense"	Volition[89] < OE *willan* 'to want'
I; we	shall	will
you; you	will	shall
he/she/it; they	will	shall

Table 9.1: The basic prescriptive rule governing SHALL and WILL (based on Wallis 1653, after Gotti 2003)

---

[88] Chi-square = 13.56 > 3.84 (95%) > 6.64 (99%), reaching significance at the 99% level.

[89] Volition in a very broad sense includes obligation and other meanings.

Once the basic rule got established in literary circles, it became perceived of as the prestigious usage that any social upstart would need to master. One of the reasons for the appeal of the rule lies in its apparent logic: prediction, i.e. future tense, and volition, can only be applied in the first person "insofar as we can regard ourselves as objects for speculation", respectively "the true subject of intention" (Boyd & Boyd 1980: 45).

The rule soon found its way into the prescriptive grammars of the 18th century (see Sundby *et al.* 1991: 190-192) and beyond. Tieken (1985: 127) places emphasis on the importance of the rule in Johnson's dictionary from 1755 and its subsequent propagation and elaboration in prescriptive grammars, most importantly Robert Lowth's grammar. Lowth adapted the rule to interrogative sentences (Boyd & Boyd 1980: 45), exactly inversing the paradigm in table (9.1) in those contexts and further refined the issue. But not only in Britain was the rule used as a device to tell proper from improper language, in North America Noah Webster castigated the "Scots and Irish, even of the first rank" (quoted in Tieken 1985: 129) for their ignorance concerning SHALL and WILL.

Once this canonical pattern became established and the social barriers were getting more permeable, a link between a person's usage and his or her intelligence was soon established. The logical consequence for early educators was to help social movers to acquire 'correct' grammar and overcome their linguistic burden, which included the proper use of SHALL and WILL (amongst other variables). Beal (2004: 97) points out that by the early 1700s the use of SHALL and WILL had become a "shibboleth of Scots speech" and was to remain one throughout the 19th century. It is clear, however, that also most other SIN-speakers (Scottish, Irish, Northern English) would have been subject to this kind of prescriptive criticism. Görlach (1999: 84) mentions the Irish in this context, Leonard (1929: 179) includes the Scottish and Irish, Wales (2002: 53) includes the Northern English. In other words, everyone that was not a speaker of southeastern English was deemed prone to show the 'wrong' distribution of SHALL and WILL. Two 20th century spin-offs of the obsession with these variables are found in Fowler and Fowler (1973 [^{3}1931]: 142-163), who elaborate the most refined system of rules governing the use of SHALL and WILL on 20 pages and in the 1st edition of the *Oxford English Dictionary* (1933), which attributes the infraction against the proper rule to "almost exclusively Scottish, Irish, provincial, or extra-British use" (OED-1, s.v. *will*, 16) since the 1600s.

In this respect, it is interesting to note that probably the most widely used grammar in Ontario during our period, Lindley Murray's *English Grammar*

(1795) (cf. section 3.3.3.1), did, in contrast to Lowth, not provide any rule governing the use of SHALL and WILL. For Murray's "first future tense", we merely find the following paradigm, and no further guidance of usage:

FIRST FUTURE TENSE.	
SINGULAR.	PLURAL.
1. I shall *or* will have.	1. We shall *or* will have.
2. Thou shalt *or* wilt have.	2. Ye *or* you shall *or* will have.
3. He shall *or* will have.	3. They shall *or* will have.

Table 9.2: Murray's (1795) paradigm for SHALL and WILL ([1968]: 46)

In table (9.2), we can see the conservatism shown in most grammars of the day in terms of the pronouns *ye* and *thou*, and the 2nd person forms *shalt* and *wilt*, which, with the exception of Quaker use of *thou*, are not attested in the four corpora. However, in terms of the modal verb, Murray's paradigms are surprisingly liberal, which is quite in contrast to the absolute rules found elsewhere in Murray's grammar. As Boyd & Boyd (1980: 47f) show, liberalism was met with contempt by the American educated elite in the late 19th century, which makes Murray's stance surprising for the most influential school grammar of its day. American elitist sentiments can be seen in the following excerpt:

> [I]n New England it is noteworthy that even the boys and girls use *shall* and *will* correctly; and in New York, New Jersey, and Ohio, in Virginia, Maryland, and South Carolina, fairly educated people of English stock do the same; while Scotchmen and Irishmen, even when they are professionally men of letters, and by the great mass of the people of the Western and South-western United States, the words are used without discrimination, or, if discrimination is attempted, *will* is given the place of *shall*, and *vice versa*... . Why, indeed, do we suffer a smart little verbal shock when the Irish servant says, "Will I put some more coal on the fire?" ... But those who have genuine, well-trained English tongues and ears are shocked and do laugh. (Richard G. White (1870), qtd. in Boyd & Boyd 1980: 47f)

New England is regarded to have been the exception in the American context, while New York and New Jersey, which both are important in the Ontarian settlement context, are listed among the prime perpetrators. Pennsylvania, which was the single-most important input area to Ontario in period 1, is not mentioned. We will see whether Murray's neglect to prescribe the use of modals may be in any way indicative of the usage in North America, Murray's place of origin.

Given the apparent prominence of regulations governing SHALL and WILL in early grammars and even some of today's usage guides, it is little surprising that SHALL and WILL, and to a lesser extent also SHOULD and WOULD, are among the most widely studied modal auxiliaries in EModE and LModE. Concerning the research history, a host of studies on the tradition of the prescriptive rules is available: e.g. Fries 1925, parts in Leonard 1929, Taglicht 1970, Moody 1974, Taubitz 1975, Boyd & Boyd 1980[90], Tieken 1985, Arnovick 1997. Earlier studies mainly focus on the genesis of an independent category for the English future tense.[91]

In comparison to this host of studies, corpus-based enquiries, both in the older and newer sense of the word, are comparatively few, but have recently attracted considerable interest. Apart from early studies by Fries (1925) and parts in Taglicht (1970), the studies by Kytö (1991a), Myhill (1995), Rissanen (2000), Gotti et al. (2002), Gotti (2002, 2003) and Nurmi (2003) are recent additions.

9.2 SHALL and WILL

Ever since the publication of John Wallis' grammar in 1653, some argue even a generation earlier (Gotti 2003: 115), the most important independent variable governing the 'proper' use of SHALL and WILL was considered to be grammatical person. The semantic contents of SHALL and WILL – and, as we shall see in the next chapter, SHOULD and WOULD – are, however, notoriously polysemous, which is bound to pose serious limitations to any empirical study. This is especially true in historical studies, as the researcher often has no reliable means to decide on the semantic function of a given variable other than stretches of co-text.

9.2.1 Semantic notions and the variable context

SHALL and WILL occur in both root meanings and epistemic meanings, as well as in indeterminate, mixed meanings. As has been pointed out in Kytö (1991a: 285), " 'pure future' uses of the verbs often convey tinges of uncertainty, likelihood and other probabilities", i.e. have an epistemic dimension. As a result, the semantic analysis has been usually left aside in much of the previ-

---

[90] I am indebted to Laurel Brinton for drawing my attention to the writings of Julian Boyd.
[91] Kytö (1991a: 288, fn 14) provides a list of these studies.

ous research and has focussed on grammatical person and syntactic context instead.[92]

For PDE, Coates (1983: 168) identifies the meanings of WILL as follows (table 9.3):

WILL	Meaning	Example
root uses	willingness	I mean I don't think the bibliography should suffer because we can't find a publisher who *will* do the whole thing.
	intention	I *'ll* put them in the post today.
epistemic uses	predictability	Your Lordship *will* know what her age was.
	prediction	I think the bulk of this years students *will* go into industry.

Table 9.3: Functions of WILL in PDE
(based on Coates 1983: 169-185, stress marks omitted)

The meanings of 'willingness' and 'intention' are hard to discriminate semantically, which is further complicated by WILL's function as a marker of futurity. The two epistemic uses are somewhat more fuzzy. While predictability focusses more on the confidence level of the speaker, prediction is rather a future tense marker that may or may not include some aspects of (epistemic) uncertainty. It is clear that a fairly unambiguous discrimination of the two root uses as well as the two epistemic uses is a delicate matter. For SHALL, we are faced with similar problems (table 9.4):

SHALL	Meaning	Example
root uses	intention	A: I don't want one, you have it! B: I *shall* save it up, we'll share it.
	obligation	Before passing a sentence, the court *shall* consider any report made in respect of him by the Prison Commissioners.
epistemic uses	addressee's volition	*Shall* I ring you at 11 p.m. after you get back?

Table 9.4: Functions of SHALL in PDE
(based on Coates 1983: 185-203)

Discriminating between the subclasses is no easy task. For instance, the obligation meaning seems to be determined primarily by the presence of a second or third person grammatical subject, *the court* in table (9.4), and is reinforced by

---

[92] An exception is Gotti (2002, 2003a), who classifies all instances of SHALL (and WILL) by 'pragmatic function', i.e. the perceived semantic content of the modal in context, for one section of the Helsinki Corpus (1640-1710).

the legal context. However, the interpretation is very close to the meaning of 'intention', which, in this example, is construed from the dialogue context. More critically, the 'addressee's volition' meaning could also be perceived as asking for permission, which would be a root meaning. From the examples shown in tables (9.3) and (9.4), the problem of categorization becomes clear. For instance, the prime criterion that distinguishes 'willingness' WILL from 'intention' uses seems to be the grammatical person of the subject: *I* vs. *a publisher* makes all the difference.

It is clear from these examples that the semantic undertones of SHALL and WILL are harder to discriminate than was the case for CAN and MAY. In the light of these classification problems, semantic notions will largely be disregarded for SHALL and WILL in the present study, which will focus on other independent variables.[93] For this reason, we will not survey the epistemic development of SHALL and WILL, which does not affect the testability of the any of the research questions, since in Abraham (2002) both functions are considered a temporal modals and are ruled out. This procedure is based on the hypothesis that in comparable genres the distributions between the semantic notions will be roughly equivalent.

9.2.2 Data selection

For the selection of the data, all instances of SHALL (including SHAN'T) and WILL (including WON'T and other forms) were extracted. Contractions, *'ll,* are not frequent in our corpora. Apart from NW-BrE, short form *'ll* occurs four times (twice in CanE and twice in BrE). In NW-BrE, however, or *'l* contractions occur 234 times. If counted as WILL, these contractions would comprise 8.2% of all WILL uses in NW-BrE, a substantial number. While these kinds of contractions are traditionally considered as a form of WILL, I follow Kytö's example and exclude these forms on account of their ambiguous etymologies.

Other contractions include *won't,* or *wont, shan't* or *shant. Shan't* occurs only once in NW-BrE in all corpora, while forms of WON'T are slightly better represented: 3 *won(')t* in CanE, one in BrE, 12 in NW-BrE and no token in AmE. In general, we can conclude that contractions are not very popular in our type of data before 1850, with the exception of *'(l)l* contractions in the regional NW British data.

---

[93] This procedure has a long tradition in philological research, e.g. Fries (1925). But note that some researchers, e.g. Gotti (2003a, 2003b) have recently carried out diachronic corpus analyses of the semantics of SHALL and WILL. Gotti (2003b: 290f) sees an increase of epistemic WILL from late ME to late EModE, increasing from 0.1 to one occurrence per 10,000 words, a rise that is expected to continue in later ModE.

9.2.3 SHALL and WILL and the choice of independent variables
Previous studies have shown that a very large number of independent variables can be investigated: medium (speech-based, non-speech based texts), grammatical subject, type of subject (animate/inanimate) semantic meaning, sentence type, clause type, pragmatic function, type of verb (static/dynamic), voice (active/passive), author's sex, participant relationship (in letters), level of formality, to name just the most important ones, and any combination of these. We can benefit from previous research as it draws our attention to two independent variables that should help us establish a focus for our study in conjunction with grammatical person: genre and sentence type.

9.2.3.1 Genre (text type)
While genre is included in most empirical studies on SHALL and WILL, there is no conclusive cumulative evidence as to the effect of genre for the choice of SHALL and WILL. Kytö (1991a) and Gotti (2003a) are two benchmarks in corpus linguistics for SHALL and WILL. Kytö's (1991a: 294f) study on EModE reveals a preponderance of WILL in "colloquial language (private letters) and speech-based texts (sermons and trial proceedings)" and treats the rise of WILL (in the first person) as a change from below. In contrast Gotti (2003a: 162), using a subset of Kytö's data, reaches the conclusion that "the correlation between the choice of either auxiliary [SHALL or WILL] and a specific genre does not seem to be relevant", apart from a preponderance of SHALL in legal texts.

The CanE data in figure (9.1) show that WILL is used differently across the genres, which seems to corroborate Kytö's point of view. Absolute frequencies (n) are provided for each column both figures shown on the next page. Figure (9.1) shows that the letter genre is practically the only genre where WILL is used in the 1st and 2nd persons. The data for SHALL, figure (9.2), shows a strong, although decreasing, number of instances of 1st person SHALL in the letter genre. Given this genre-dependent variation, it seems advisable to limit our study to the letter section. While an occasional glance to the other genres, may be provided, the letter genre shows greater potential to unravel significant distribution patterns in CanE and the other varieties.

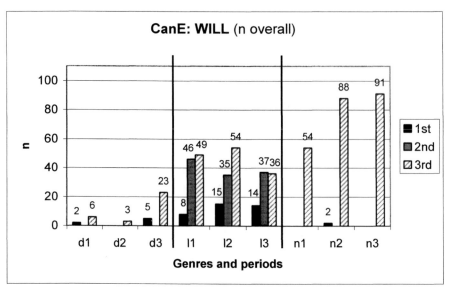

Figure 9.1: WILL by genre in CanE
(absolute frequencies)

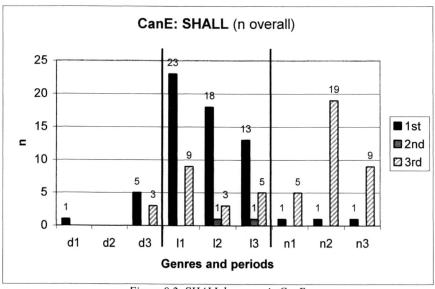

Figure 9.2: SHALL by genre in CanE
(absolute frequencies)

9.2.3.2 Sentence type

The variable sentence type is used to distinguish between three basic structures: declarative affirmative, declarative negative and interrogative (both affirmative and negative) sentences. Both Gotti (2003a) and Kytö (1991a) do not distinguish between declaratives and interrogatives throughout their studies. SHALL and WILL occur in the following distribution in the three basic sentence types in CanE and BrE (figure 9.3):

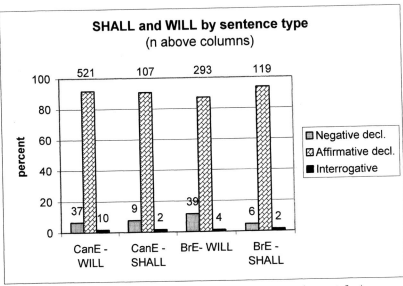

Figure 9.3: CanE and BrE (overall) by sentence type (percent & n)

It can be seen that the vast majority, around 90%, of all instances of SHALL and WILL occur in affirmative declarative sentences in the data. While some distributions may still be gleaned from negative declarative sentences, the data for interrogatives will not allow, with absolute figures between 2 and 10 across three periods and genres, for meaningful comparisons and focus will be given to the letter genre.

9.2.4 SHALL and WILL in the first person

In this section, the distribution of SHALL and WILL is restricted to the letter components of the corpora. In contrast to the type of change we have seen for MUST and HAVE TO, the wrong use of SHALL and WILL was highly stigmatized, which makes them prime candidates for change from above. As such, they are expected to display the characteristics of changes from above even more clearly than we have seen for CAN and MAY. In the first person in period 1, we find the distribution in four data sets as shown in figure (9.4):

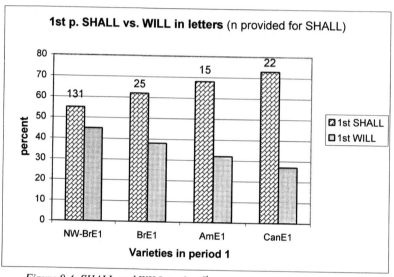

Figure 9.4: SHALL and WILL in the 1ˢᵗ person, letter sections (period 1)

While none of these differences in distributional frequency is statistically significant (cf. appendix 9.1), we can identify trends: AmE patterns with CanE on the one hand and the two British varieties pattern on the other hand. This is, in essence, the same overall ranking as was found for root HAVE TO in figure (8.1), although this time CanE, and not AmE, is on one extreme of the spectrum. In contrast to HAVE TO, where the North American varieties were most advanced, here they are the most conservative ones. The distribution is figure (9.4) also means that there is no indicator in the data that would explain why Murray's grammar does not provide guidance for 1ˢᵗ person SHALL and WILL.

Based on the hypothesis that within genres we can assume an equal representation of all meanings and functions we can say something about WILL's primary function of a marker of futurity. The prescriptive rule states that SHALL is to be used in the 1ˢᵗ person, while WILL is used in the 2ⁿᵈ person to denote future. In figure (9.4) we see that Canadians adhere to the prescriptivist rule more strictly, albeit only slightly more so than the Americans. Compared to American data from a century earlier (Kytö 1991a: 294, table 4), we see an increase of WILL in AmE-1, which fits well with the general trend towards WILL that can also be inferred from PDE evidence.

In which sense may this distribution be an indicator of conservatism and co-lonial lag? CanE in period 1 appears to be most conservative in its use of 1st person SHALL from a PDE perspective, followed by AmE and BrE, with regional NW-BrE being most advanced. After all, CanE and AmE use 1st person SHALL more frequently than the British varieties. In order to single out what is more conservative, we need to be certain about the actual usage and distribution of the feature until this point of the development. Contemporary grammars and studies on the genesis of rules do not necessarily help us here, but a number of descriptivist studies are available.

9.2.4.1 Diachronic development
Taglicht's study (1970: 206) corroborates the prescriptivist rule as complying with actual usage in 17th-century letters. For other genres, we see that WILL has *always* been the predominant usage for the first person in BrE drama throughout the Modern English period, and therefore probably also in spoken language. Fries' (1925) study illustrates the prevalence of WILL in drama data for BrE:

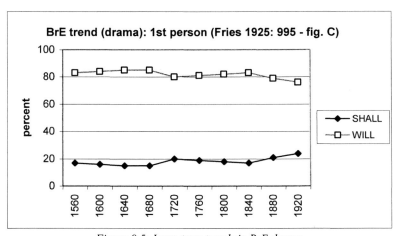

Figure 9.5: Long-term trends in BrE drama
(from Fries 1925: 995. figure C)

If we accept the data from Fries (1925), which forms the input for figure (9.5), as a base for comparison with our letter data, we may say that CanE may be considered more conservative than the other two varieties, by adhering more closely to conventional rules, and that it uses SHALL more often.

This conservatism in CanE was not to last long, however. Figure (9.6) shows a remarkable departure of CanE from BrE usage, and perhaps also from AmE. The diachronic development of CanE and BrE up to 1850 shows diametrical trends for CanE and BrE. While statements concerning AmE are based on a mere linear interpolation of AmE data from 1750-1799 and 1850-1799, with no actual data for period 2+3 (see table 6.3), BrE and CanE usage did in fact divert in the first half of the 19th century in respect to 1st person SHALL and WILL:

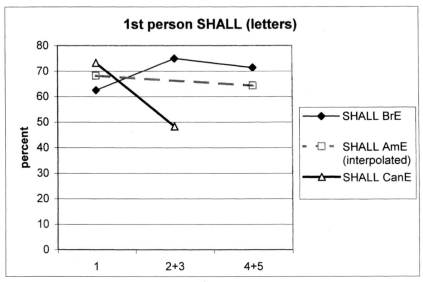

Figure 9.6: Diachronic variation of 1st person SHALL in CanE, BrE and AmE

In CanE the uses of first person SHALL drop below the 50% mark during the first half of the 19th century (period 2+3), while the uses increase notably, yet not significantly, during that period in BrE letters. What is most important, however, is that the corresponding increase of WILL in CanE is statistically significant (appendix 9.2). CanE and BrE in period 2+3 also show significant differences at the 90% level. If we compare this to the interpolated AmE data from periods 1 and 4+5, a greater departure from the rule can be seen in CanE than could be expected if AmE were the major influence. Canadian usage embarked on a different path, parting with its AmE roots and not adopting the prevailing BrE features, but going a third way instead.

While prescriptivists on both sides of the Atlantic favoured the traditional prescriptive rule, Canadians use it in less than 50% of all contexts and do not seem to have followed it very strictly at all in period 2+3. This development is a reversal of the conservatism shown in figure (9.4), where CanE used SHALL most often.

How can this behaviour be explained? The answer to this question is highly interesting, especially in relation to Trudgill's theory. By taking a more micro-linguistic perspective, we will be able to unearth a highly influential factor for this change. As we have seen, the use of WILL in the 1st person is frequently attributed to Scottish, Irish, and Northern English influence in contemporary sources.

9.2.4.2 SIN-speakers

We have seen that SIN speakers have been blamed for their ignorance of 'proper' usage pertaining to SHALL and WILL. How do SIN-speakers figure in the CONTE-pC letter section? Figure (9.7) provides the data and makes it clear that the 'usual SIN suspects' may indeed be responsible for this rapid change in CanE:

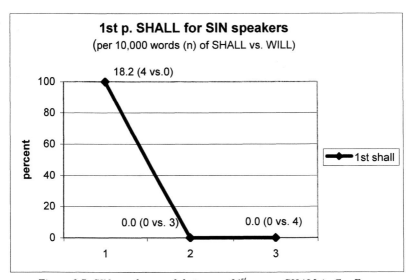

Figure 9.7: SIN-speakers and their use of 1st person SHALL in CanE

While the absolute numbers are relatively low due to only small numbers of clearly identified SIN-speakers (cf. appendix 1), the normalized frequencies of 18.2 occurrences of 1st person SHALL per 10,000 words, with no occurrences of 1st person WILL, allows us to draw some conclusions in relation to periods 2 and 3. There is a radical change between periods 1 and 2, i.e. during the time of the War of 1812. We have seen that at that time, after 1815, SIN-speakers arrived in Ontario, but not in significant numbers from south of the border. The SIN-speakers, coming with the second wave of immigrants, seem to have triggered – or at least drastically accelerated – the change towards 1st person WILL, since not a single occurrence of 1st person SHALL is found in their data.

Trudgill's theory of dialect mixing places special emphasis on the ratio of immigrants from different dialect areas. We know from chapter (3) that the vast majority of second wave immigrants did not come from southern England, but from the north, Scotland and Ireland, i.e. the SIN-speakers, a fact which is, partly due to the high number of unidentified letter writers, not directly matched in the data.

It seems that we have gathered evidence that concerns one key area of modal usage, and is evidenced in a markedly different distribution of SHALL and WILL in the first person in CanE. The reasoning behind the relatively confined linguistic influence of the second wave immigrants is based on the founder principle, i.e. the notion that the British immigrants came too late to influence Canadian speechways in more profound ways – with the exception of linguistic enclaves such as Peterborough or the Ottawa Valley, where they founded new settlements. The distribution of SHALL and WILL in the first person is evidence for a kind of more profound linguistic change, however. The SIN data show that WILL was used predominantly in the 1st person, which influenced the emerging variety by accelerating the decline of 1st person SHALL.

Let us again review the population density of Ontario around the time when the second wave immigrants left for Canada. Map (3.3) showed the population densities in Ontario in 1808 and 1840, respectively. There can be little doubt that SIN speakers were the majority in periods 2 and 3. In section (3.3), the post-1815 immigration was detailed, which covers periods 2 and 3 in the corpus data. Map (3.1) showed that large stretches of land were still unsettled, which were usually taken up by the newcomers. This scenario would entail the settlement of the newcomers in relatively self-contained units in order to override the founder principle.

Considering the sparse population density in period 1, we would expect CanE to be influenced by more than mere attitudes in periods 2+3, and this influence is found in the significant increase of 1st person WILL. Stratification of this change by social class provides yet another layer of description.

9.2.4.3 Social class
Social class stratification, which correlates with SIN-speakers in that they were largely lower class members, provides another view on this change. A closer look at the social stratification in CONTE-pC's letter section is presented in figure (9.8) below:

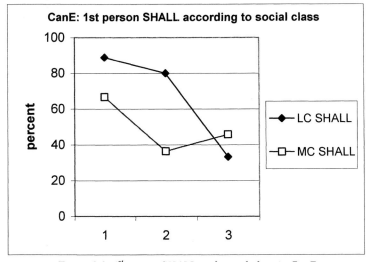

Figure 9.8: 1st person SHALL and social class in CanE

We can see in figure (9.8) that the change away from 1st person SHALL and towards WILL was led predominantly by lower class (LC) speakers. Until 1825, period 2, the lower class uses SHALL more consistently than the middle class. This is what we would expect for a change from above, only that in this case the LC undergoes hypercorrection, as predicted by Trudgill for stage I. This scenario points to the linguistic accommodation of social climbers, which would also make this a change from *above*. Usually change from above is associated with overt prestige (Labov 2001: 273f), which is effective until 1824. In period 3, when prestige loses its force, the majority form is selected.

The sharp decline in the uses of SHALL among the LC accounts for a good part of the difference between the BrE and CanE data shown in figure (9.6). A sharp fall occurs from period 2 to 3, i.e. 1825-1849, when the host of second-wave immigrants from Britain came to Canada. As we have seen in chapter (3), the vast majority of immigrants were not only SIN speakers but also members of the lower class. While hypercorrection was effective in periods 1 and 2, one generation later extreme variability can be seen, with WILL already in the majority.

In the CanE letter data, on the whole, we may say that for 1st person SHALL and WILL, CanE is more progressive after 1800 on account of second-wave immigrants. Since 90% of them were speakers of a non-southeastern variety, and the vast majority were members of the lower class, there is little surprise that CanE is leading this change in the data. While the opposite direction of the change, usage towards SHALL, would be a clear case of change from *above*, towards overt prestige, the change in the reverse direction, towards WILL, seems to comply better with change from *below*, as it shows little effect on social awareness: large numbers of immigrants were beginning to write the way they had been talking for quite some time, as indicated by Fries' BrE drama data (figure 9.5).

9.2.4.4 SHALL and WILL and the three stages

The data suggest a prominent role for SIN-speakers in the new-dialect formation process. To what extent does this scenario fit Trudgill's three stages? Extreme variability and the choice of the majority form are the two aspects we can test with our data.

Firstly, table (9.5) shows the occurrence of SHALL and WILL per 25-year period in CanE and 50-year period in BrE in letters, the best represented genre. The CanE periods 2 and 3 may be interpreted as exhibiting 'extreme' variation, with their more level percentages for SHALL and WILL, which are close to the 50% mark. In BrE, however, which did not undergo the same contact phenomena, this variability cannot be seen.

CanE-letters	period 1	period 2	period 3
SHALL	73.3 (22)	60.0 (18)	40.0 (10)
WILL	26.7 (8)	40.0 (15)	60.0 (15)
BrE-letters	period 1	period 2+3	
SHALL	62.5 (25)	75.0 (24)	
WILL	37.5 (15)	25.0 (8)	

Table 9.5: SHALL and WILL diachronically in CanE and BrE (letters)

We said earlier in chapter (7) that the development of CAN and MAY would be delayed in rural contexts, where the SIN-speakers settled, by one generation, and that period 2 corresponds to stage I and period 3 to stage II. The data fit this delayed development again better: it is in period 3 that WILL takes over, which one would ascribe to apparent levelling (original stage II), when children were selecting the majority form WILL.

Secondly, we know that in present-day CanE SHALL is confined to formulaic phrases, as in the rest of North America. Given the majority input of non-southeastern English populations and their purported preference for WILL, it seems safe to say that the majority variant won out in the long run. Our data show that the 2nd wave immigrants did have an effect on the CanE modal system. Of all things, CanE was more advanced in its use of 1st person WILL in comparison to BrE. With these findings, a brief look at the variables in the 2nd and 3rd persons may be in order.

9.2.5 SHALL and WILL in the second and third persons
The distribution of SHALL and WILL in the second and third persons in relation to two variables is discussed in this section. Figure (9.9) on the next pages presents a summary view of the second and third persons. As can be seen there are no drastic changes in the distribution of SHALL and WILL. The most pronounced diachronic change appears to be in CanE concerning the 3rd person, but even this change is statistically not significant overall. However, CanE and BrE overall show significant differences overall (cf. appendix 9.3).

This section focusses on third person uses as the context where the variation between the modal forms is greatest. If the context is distinguished in terms of type of subject and voice, we see that the picture begins to show a more variable pattern.

9.2.5.1 Type of subject
The type of subject has been considered as influencing the choice of SHALL and WILL not only in terms of grammatical person, but also in other respects. Similar to what we have seen for the spread of HAVE TO, inanimate third person subjects have been considered to play a special role also for WILL. Since inanimate subjects cannot express volition, they serve as a clear indicator of the expanding use of WILL as a marker of futurity. Kytö (1991a: 310) finds empirical evidence for this reasoning in the early 1500s, a change which was largely completed by the end of the 18th century. For the two best represented varieties, CanE and BrE, figure (9.10) shows the animate and inanimate subject referents:

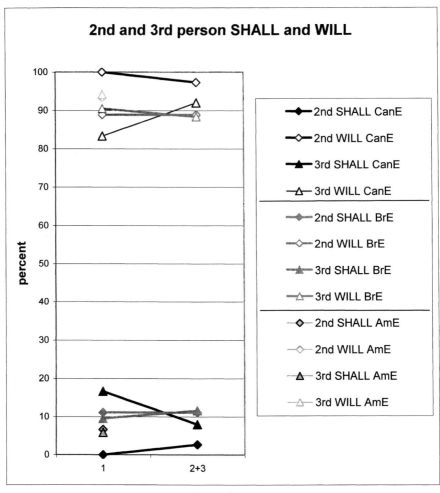

Figure 9.9: Diachronic changes for 2ⁿᵈ and 3ʳᵈ person SHALL and WILL in three varieties

The most important finding in figure (9.10) is that between periods 1 and 2+3 no significant changes can be found. This shows that by the beginning of period 1, WILL has become the prime marker in the third person, including uses in the future, as can be seen in its use in non-animate subjects in both BrE and CanE.

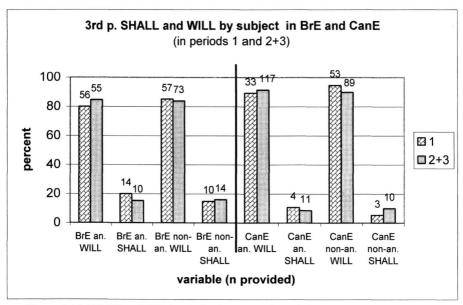

Figure 9.10: SHALL and WILL with third person subject referents in BrE and CanE
(subject types: animate vs. non-animate)

While CanE shows slightly higher percentages for 3rd person WILL than BrE in figure (9.10), none of the fluctuations are significant, neither diatopically nor diachronically, which suggests a phenomenon of continuing drift, of a change that had been well under way by the time immigration to North America happened. Kytö (1991a: 310) shows that the percentages of WILL in non-animate subject referents increased from 19.3 via 59.4 to 84.2% between the beginning and the end of the EModE period. The latter percentage is roughly the same in our period, which suggests that the change from SHALL to WILL as a marker of futurity had been completed by the beginning of the LModE period.

9.2.5.2 Voice
Another independent variable in connection with SHALL and WILL is voice. The type of subject, whether animate or non-animate, has been suggested to govern these variables in combination with voice, i.e. active or passive sentence structures. Kytö (1991a: 308-311), again, investigates this set of independent variables for EModE BrE and AmE. She reasons that SHALL (just as SHOULD, which is surveyed in a different context, see below) is to be expected to occur more frequently in passive constructions because of its more

formal character. Figure (9.11) shows the data for third person grammatical subjects, and their occurrences in active and passive clauses:

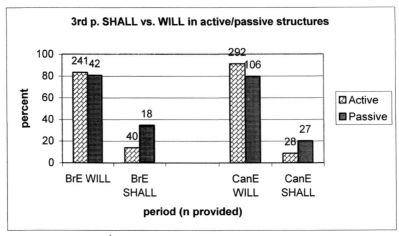

Figure 9.11: 3ʳᵈ person SHALL vs. WILL in active and passive clauses
(in BrE and CanE , overall, with n provided)

Kytö's (1991a: 308) prediction that passive constructions "should offer a context favouring the generally receding forms SHALL [...]" is borne out, as SHALL is used more often than in active sentences in both varieties.

We see that CanE tends to employ more WILL in active sentences (over 90% of all cases), while BrE uses SHALL in more than 15% of all active sentences. This difference does not appear to be very strong in figure (9.11), but BrE uses SHALL significantly more often than CanE in active sentences (cf. appendix 9.3). This indicates a preference of BrE in comparison to CanE for SHALL as opposed to WILL and would suggest that CanE is more progressive than BrE also for 3ʳᵈ person usage. This partly accounts for the slightly higher use of WILL in CanE in figure (9.10), which is in the 5% range, when compared to BrE.

9.2.5.3 The three stages

The general change can be summarized with SHALL managing to hold on in active clauses, while its use with inanimate subjects has almost completely given way to WILL by the mid-19ᵗʰ century. While this change towards WILL in the 3ʳᵈ person had already been completed, making it inadequate to trace new-dialect developments (cf. again figure 9.10 and the low incidence of

SHALL), the use of passives serves us well for this purpose. We have said that passive constructions favour SHALL and table (9.6) shows the frequencies in passive contexts.

CanE - passive	period 1	period 2	period 3
SHALL	25.0 (7)	20.0 (10)	18.1 (10)
WILL	75.0 (21)	80.0 (40)	81.9 (45)
BrE - passive	period 1	period 2+3	
SHALL	31.3 (10)	28.9 (8)	
WILL	68.7 (22)	71.1 (20)	

Table 9.6: 3rd person SHALL and WILL in passive constructions
(in CanE and BrE, percent and n; overall)

In contrast to previous cases, in table (9.6) we have a scenario that does not show a phase of extreme variability in period 2 (or period 3, for that matter). While we can again say that the majority form WILL was constantly gaining ground in passive contexts, where SHALL held on longer, the decline of SHALL happened only in small increments, which are not statistically significant in CanE from one period to another (cf. appendix 9.3). Again, as we have already seen for CAN and MAY in Permission readings, for long-term trends CONTE's 25-year data do not reach statistical significance. In like manner as the decline of permissive MAY, 3rd person SHALL recedes from passive contexts over longer periods of time, in a roughly linear recession that seems to be largely unaffected by processes of new-dialect formation.

9.2.6 Summary

We have seen that SHALL and WILL are different types of variables than both CAN and MAY and MUST and HAVE TO. The major reason seems to be that SHALL and WILL were subject to high levels of awareness. We could gain insights for three types of independent variables: grammatical person (mostly the 1st person), type of subject and voice (both of which mostly for 3rd person uses).

The most dramatic change is seen in 1st person SHALL: CanE starts off most conservative, but becomes most progressive in period 2+3. While the data do not directly contradict the loyalist base theory on account of the missing AmE data, data interpolation (between AmE-1 and AmE4+5) casts some doubt on the pervasiveness of the loyalist base theory on all linguistic levels. Taken together with the Canadian SIN-data and social class data from the period, a relatively reliable indicator for an overriding of the loyalist base, perhaps some numerical swamping as suggested by Scargill, of 1st person SHALL could be found. It is important to stress, however, that this finding does not falsify the loyalist base theory as a whole, but suggests the introduction of a different process for variables that operate above the level of consciousness. The interpretation is linked to demographic findings that suggest that the second-wave immigrants were the first settlers in more than just those areas that are known today as 'linguistic pockets' or relic areas, such as Peterborough or the Ottawa Valley. One type of their influence manifests itself in the changing distribution of SHALL/WILL in the 1st person.

Voice was shown to have an influence on SHALL and WILL, as the former tends to recede more slowly in passive clauses (3rd person) and CanE and BrE show significant differences, with BrE adhering more to SHALL than CanE. By the beginning of period 1, WILL had become firmly associated with the third person for both animate and inanimate subject referents.

Concerning Trudgill's three stages, the prediction of extreme variability was not met for SHALL and WILL. In passive contexts SHALL was seen to recede steadily, which allows no such interpretation, but matches the interpretation for CAN and MAY from section (7.3.4.2): neither change shows statistical significance at 95%, as both changes are part of long-term trends. It seems that long-term changes are largely unaffected by the new-dialect formation process.

10   SHOULD, WOULD and OUGHT TO

The variables SHOULD and WOULD have usually been treated within studies on SHALL and WILL (Kytö 1991a, Nurmi 2003), but have not quite gained the attention of the latter set, while OUGHT TO has been relegated to the sidelines. More recently, SHOULD in relation to OUGHT TO has gained some attention (Myhill 1997, Nordlinger and Traugott 1997), which has opened up a new avenue of inquiry. But also in relation to SHOULD and WOULD, recent findings (Nurmi 2003: 106) suggest that their treatment in the context of SHALL and WILL may be misleading as the "sociolinguistics of SHOULD and WOULD do not follow those of WILL and SHALL". In one aspect, however, the two sets behave similarly, which is of importance for the present study. In like manner as SHALL and WILL, SHOULD and WOULD were also identified as 'problem areas' for certain groups of speakers, such as the Scottish (Beal 2004: 97), which can be extended, as was the case for SHALL and WILL, to SIN speakers more generally.

Nurmi's reasoning is largely based on external criteria such as author's sex[94] and text type, and her findings are interesting as they are based on 20-year period divisions in the CEES (a letter corpus)[95], which are comparable to CONTE's 25-year periods. Backed up by Nurmi's findings, it seems justified to carry out the analyses of SHOULD and WOULD independently of SHALL and WILL. Additionally, an attempt will be made to go in a new direction for SHOULD and WOULD by considering basic functional distinctions of their use in hypothetical and non-hypothetical contexts. The data are then compared to Trudgill's three stages of development in new-dialect formation theory. All three variants will then be surveyed in their development of epistemic meanings.

---

[94] The term sex is consciously used here to distinguish it from the social construct gender. This is done to distinguish studies that are based entirely on the dichotomy of biological sex from those which implicitly consider the social dimension, i.e. gender. Some readers may wish to use the labels 'biological gender' and 'social gender' instead.

[95] *Corpus of Early English Correspondence* (cf. Nevalainen and Raumolin-Brunberg 2003: 43-52 for a brief introduction of its design features).

10.1 The variable context

In total, 836 tokens were analyzed in CanE and BrE and their diachronic development is traced over the periods (290 instances of SHOULD, 502 of WOULD and 44 of OUGHT TO). Additionally, the NW-BrE and AmE corpora were searched to illustrate variant forms.

10.1.1 LModE variants

A word on variant and short forms may be in order, before we proceed with the semantic analyses. In LModE texts, a number of interesting variants of SHOULD and WOULD occur. Not only do we have spelling variants such as *woud* (9 times in BrE1, BrE2+3; twice in CanE), *wou'd* (3 times BrE1), and *shoud* (twice in BrE1), but also the forms *shd* and *wd*, which only occur in BrE letters (BrE2+3: 4). This is even more interesting, as in NW-BrE-1, we have 89 occurrences of sh^d and 200 of w^d, while *shd* and *wd* occur 3, respectively 8 times. It seems, however, that these short forms might be conventions of LModE BrE correspondence.

The contractions *shou(l)dn't, wou(l)dn't* or any of its variants, which are ubiquitous today in all but the most formal styles, do not occur in any corpus. It seems that these short forms are post-1850 conventions, or at least, gained greater currency after that date.

10.1.2 Semantic notions

As Coates points out (1983: 58), SHOULD, which is a marker of weak obligation, has four functions in Modern English: it has a root meaning, accounting for c. 40% of uses in PDE (10.1a), and an epistemic meaning, c. 20% (10.1b), it functions as a quasi-subjunctive, c. 10% (10.1c), and is used in hypotheticals, 20% (10.1d):

(10.1) a. we should immediately send an army
b. as soon as the festival of Beriam […] should be over
c. From ancient times the town had the privilege that no [foreigner] should reside there.
d. I should be very glad if the old House was made habitable again.

(all examples taken from BrE2+3)

The functional load of WOULD is, in contrast, much smaller. WOULD is, on the one hand, past tense form of WILL (17%). As such, it shares all the functions of WILL (intention, willingness, predictability and prediction) in the past tense. Because of the same problems of the semantic categorization of WILL, no detailed semantic analysis of WOULD is attempted here. The main function of WOULD in PDE, however, is as a hypothetical marker (10.2a & b), which accounts for 83% of its uses in written texts (Coates 1983: 205):

(10.2) a. it would be better to give it to som [sic] person   (3)
        b. it would be difficult to ascertain the quantity made upon   (3)
            the Crown & Clergy lands, except by reckoning it our
            Seventh
        c. I know […] he would not come with a worthless person   (1)
                                (all examples taken from CanE letters)

While some hypotheticals may still carry some shades of volitional meanings, as in (10.2c), on the whole, the function of denoting hypothetical situations is clearly distinguishable from other uses. As SHOULD and WOULD compete in this area, hypothetical meanings are a prime candidate for a fresh look at these variables.

10.2 Hypothetical SHOULD and WOULD

Hypotheticals are most often found in conditional sentences, either with or without the condition expressed. Coates (1983: 213) notes that most cases of WOULD are instances of WILL in the sense of making a prediction (*if p, then q*) and considers these functions as instances of epistemic WILL. The results for hypothetical functions are shown in figures (10.1) and (10.2) for CanE and BrE. The data is arranged along grammatical person subject.

We can see that in both scenarios, in CanE as well as in BrE, the distribution is surprisingly similar in both varieties and for each person subject. It should also be noted that hypothetical SHOULD is not limited to first person subjects, as Coates (1983: 221) found for present-day BrE. In our period, SHOULD is slightly favoured only in BrE in the 1st person. Statistical testing yields neither of the differences by grammatical subject as significant between the varieties (appendix 10.1), which supports the argument that in the case of hypothetical SHOULD and WOULD can be explained as an incidence of parallel development in BrE and CanE. This interpretation is supported by the diachronic development in the 3rd person, as shown in figure (10.3).

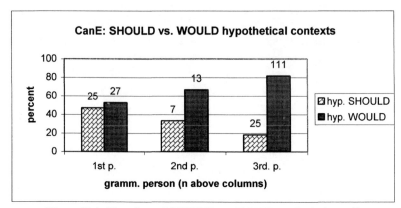

Figure 10.1: Hypothetical SHOULD vs. WOULD in CanE (overall)

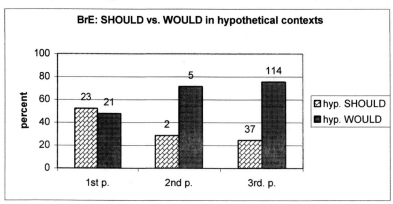

Figure 10.2: Hypothetical SHOULD vs. WOULD in BrE (overall)

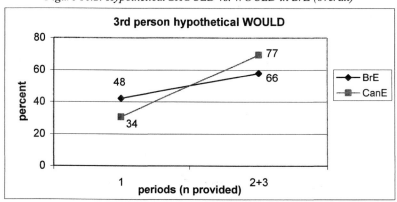

Figure 10.3: Hypothetical WOULD in 3rd person contexts in BrE and CanE

While CanE increases from a lower level and surpasses BrE in its use of WOULD, figure (10.3) suggests that these changes are relatively similar and are better interpreted as a general increase of WOULD in hypothetical contexts at the expense of SHOULD. In the case of these hypotheticals, we are likely to see an effect of drift, however. However, we cannot say without more data, whether this is continuing drift, i.e. reflecting changes that had been underway when the developmental split happened, in our case with the AmE varieties that formed the OntE input, or directional drift, i.e. by way of shared propensities of the language that would lead to parallel changes. For now, it is important to point out that BrE second wave immigrants did not trigger or reinforce this change.

10.3 Non-hypothetical OUGHT TO, SHOULD and WOULD

In this section we will take a brief look at the two main competitors of non-hypothetical SHOULD, which is non-hypothetical WOULD and, historically interesting, OUGHT (TO).[96] OUGHT TO is considered, just a SHOULD, a weak obligation marker. In contrast to SHOULD, however, OUGHT TO has barely managed to successfully remain part of the English modal auxiliary system.

OUGHT TO has a long history, however. Formally OUGHT TO meets all NICE criteria plus the additional three criteria shown in example (6.1b), despite taking TO and no bare infinitive as the other core modals. Historically OUGHT TO derives from a preterit-present verb, OE *āgan* 'to owe', i.e. OUGHT with infinitive TO (cf. table 6.1).

Most importantly, OUGHT (TO) has been in a state of flux concerning its modal status for some time. Mencken is reported as having stated that OUGHT TO was replacing SHOULD in AmE in the 1930s (Denison 1998: 170). While some commentators, e .g. Coates (1983: 70), think of it as being on its way out today, some counter evidence is found by Quirk *et al.* (1985) in its spread *without* TO among British youth (Denison 1998: 170).

10.3.1 LModE diachronic development in non-hypotheticals

OUGHT TO has been competing in two functions of SHOULD, probably since EModE times. Denison (1998: 170) says about the LModE usage that its "meaning is close to, but not identical with *should*". On the basis of the four

---

[96] Other competitors are HAD BETTER and possibly HAD/WOULD RATHER (Denison 1998: 173), which occur very sparingly in CONTE-pC and only in period 3 (cf. appendix 6).

functions of SHOULD outlined in example (10.1), Coates (1983: 69) identifies the root and epistemic meanings of SHOULD as the area of competition with OUGHT TO (cf. examples 10.1a & b). Globally, we can compare the uses of non-hypothetical SHOULD to OUGHT TO, which is their functional overlap, both for root and epistemic uses. They share these functions with non-hypothetical WOULD. Figures (10.4) and (10.5) show the distribution of SHOULD, WOULD and OUGHT TO in BrE and CanE from a diachronic perspective.

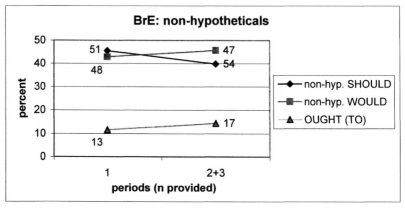

Figure 10.4: SHOULD vs. OUGHT TO vs. WOULD in non-hypotheticals in BrE

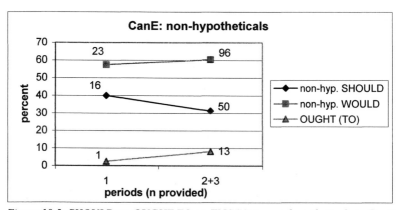

Figure 10.5: SHOULD vs. OUGHT TO vs. WOULD in non-hypotheticals in CanE

The parallel patterns in figure (10.4) for BrE and figure (10.5) in CanE indicate that both varieties change in the same direction, possibly due to continuing drift. However, CanE and BrE start off at rather different levels for WOULD in period 1, with CanE disfavouring SHOULD, while OUGHT TO is playing only a very marginal role. BrE favours SHOULD in period 1 and uses OUGHT TO more often than in CanE. Most importantly, the use of non-hypothetical SHOULD is significantly disfavoured in CanE (cf. appendix 10.2). OUGHT TO, on the other hand, is barely present in CanE, and does not surpass the 10% threshold. It would be interesting to see, if, and in what contexts, OUGHT TO occurs in late-19th-century data.

Concerning the developmental changes from periods 1 to 2+3, however, all changes may be coincidental as none reaches statistical significance (cf. appendix 10.2). What is nevertheless striking, however, is that all changes, as subtle as they may be, seem to proceed almost exactly parallel, as all trajectories not only point in the same direction, but proceed at almost exactly the same rate (as a comparison of the two figures reveals). Could this be coincidental? While this is a possibility, a better scenario might be to account for the changes as caused by a drift of SHOULD and OUGHT (TO) in non-hypothetical contexts. What is interesting is that CanE diverges farther from BrE usage between periods 1 and 2+3. While SHOULD and WOULD are used at roughly equal percentages in BrE 1 and 2+3, the gap widens in CanE, which prefers WOULD even more in period 2+3 than in 1. This is another indicator for a possible characteristic feature of CanE in the 19th century that can only be fully investigated with adequate AmE data. The difference between CanE and BrE is either caused by AmE input in CanE, by independent Canadian development, or a combination of both.

10.3.2 Hypotheticals and non-hypotheticals in the three stages
We again need to checking the data for signs of extreme variability and majority forms in CanE, for which table (9.6) shows the results in 25-year intervals for hypothetical SHOULD and WOULD:

CanE – hypotheticals	period 1 = stage I	period 2 = stage II	period 3 = stage III
hyp. SHOULD	23.3 (14)	33.3 (23)	25.0 (20)
hyp. WOULD	76.7 (46)	66.7 (45)	75.0 (60)

Table 10.1: Hypothetical SHOULD and WOULD in CanE

We see that period 2 shows the highest degree of variability, which corresponds to Trudgill's prediction for stage II and fits the scenario for the first wave of settlement. In this scenario, Trudgill's stages are equated with CONTE-pC's first three periods. The change between periods 2 and 3 is significant (cf. appendix 10.3), which could be a result of second wave immigration that would need to be confirmed with post-1800 SIN-data.

Figure (10.6) shows the results for non-hypotheticals. We see that OUGHT TO does not influence the scenario very much, as it never reaches percentages close enough to seriously contend with SHOULD and WOULD. In period 2, however, it manages to stay above the 10% threshold and occurs again in period 3, again below the threshold.

In CanE, OUGHT TO must be considered a low frequency item that managed to increase its frequency in periods 2 and 3, which could be the result of post-1815 BrE input, if the higher percentages in figure (10.4) for BrE can serve as an indicator. Figure (10.6) also shows that period 2 can again be perceived of as showing the largest degree of variability, which is predicted in stage II for the 1st wave of settlement. Before and after, WOULD dominates the functions, and uses of its competitors are lower.

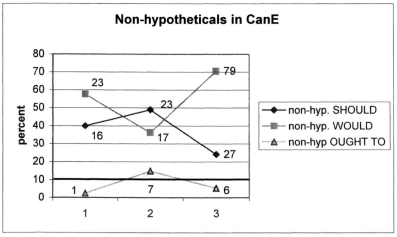

Figure 10.6: Non-hypotheticals in CanE

This impression is corroborated by statistical testing (cf. appendix 10.4). The changes in SHOULD and WOULD in periods 2 and 3 are highly significant. In period 2, WOULD was not the majority variant, as SHOULD reached almost 50% . Trudgill argues that close runners-up which are, for one reason or other, linguistically unmarked, may have a better chance of being selected. For WOULD, we have a case in point, as it was the majority variant in hypotheticals in periods 2 and 3 (cf. figure 10.1), and this majority use in hypotheticals made WOULD more likely to be a linguistically unmarked variant in the sense that its use in hypothetical contexts would provide a foothold in non-hypotheticals. This scenario within new-dialect formation theory offer some explanation for the increase of WOULD in figure (10.6).

10.4 Epistemic modality in early CanE

SHOULD and WOULD have been surveyed in hypothetical and non-hypothetical contexts above, but these categories cut across the epistemic non-epistemic distinction an are not directly comparable in our comparison outlined in chapter (6.1.3). OUGHT TO is also going to take a role more centre stage in the treatment of the expansion of epistemic meanings. In figure (10.6), the increase of OUGHT TO is significant in period 2 (appendix 10.4), which results in its reaching the threshold level of 10%. This implies that OUGHT TO occurred at a discourse frequency that was high enough to be taken up by a new generation. The case of OUGHT TO will be reviewed in detail in the following section.

10.4.1 OUGHT TO

OUGHT TO has generally escaped the attention given to the more 'central' modals, which have a higher discourse frequency than OUGHT TO. Concerning the syntactic development of OUGHT TO, Harris (1986: 349) argues that OUGHT TO, which was found in ME with and without a bare infinitive (the TO being considered optional), ousted OUGHT without TO, leaving a syntactically ambiguous structure with TO, which is responsible for its demise in PDE.

More recently, descriptive corpus studies have been made available. Myhill (1997) describes the relationship of OUGHT TO with select functions of SHOULD, and Nordlinger and Traugott (1997) provide a theoretical scenario of its development as an epistemic modal via a cline of deontic readings. Myhill shows that in AmE, obligatory SHOULD is used for suggestions "which represent individual opinions" since the late 1920s in his data, whereas deontic OUGHT TO implies "a general agreement about a suggestion" (1997: 20). He classifies OUGHT TO in relation to SHOULD by discourse function, and explicitly excludes a number of contexts in which he sees "a very strong tendency to use either *should* or *ought [to]*" (p. 7), which includes epistemic OUGHT TO, i.e. the variable we are most interested in this section.

Nordlinger and Traugott (1997) specifically investigate the development of epistemic readings and suggest, based on data from OE to PDE, a developmental scenario starting with possessive meanings in OE ('to own, to have'), via deontic meanings (first of narrow scope, confined to the subject, then of wide scope, embracing the entire clause) and more subjective readings to finally epistemic readings, first of a weak kind, starting in EModE, and since ModE times of a strong, more subjective kind (p. 315). Provided their dating is precise, the last step in the development of OUGHT TO falls within the period of the present study, and we should find some CanE evidence for it.

While epistemic OUGHT TO developed, as Nordlinger and Traugott show, in late ME, their earliest unambiguous example of epistemic OUGHT TO is from 1675-76. At the same time, they argue that the EModE examples "are all weakly subjective, and it is not until the twentieth century that we find more strongly subjective examples" (p. 314), with weakly subjective modals appealing to societal norms and strongly subjective ones solely to the speaker's beliefs (see Lyons' 1977: 797 distinction between subjective and objective epistemicity). The first use of epistemic OUGHT TO in the OED is from 1849 and must be considered weakly subjective (Nordlinger and Traugott 1997: 313). The CanE data have, among 12 occurrences of modal OUGHT TO, one epistemic use, as shown in (10.3):

(10.3)   If Upper Canada were merely a young, healthy Pro-vince <le: Province>, with no protection on the Continent of America but its character, its industry, and the agricultural diffi-culties <le: difficulties> it has to contend with - its filial attachment to its Government - the bravery it has shewn in its defence - and the mercy it has extended to its captured assailants, **ought to** be sufficient to make its aggressors ashamed of their late attempt to force upon their neighbours, institutions which they conscientiously and unequivocally reject.

(CanE, newspapers-3, 1838)

The passage appeared in a newspaper special edition, in a kind of political pamphlet, and while the writer's opinion and assessment is made clear, it also appeals to some sort of 'moral norm' and to the expectations of decent citizens and is therefore not as strongly subjective as (10.4), a 20th-century example from Visser (1969), quoted in Nordlinger and Traugott (1997: 314):

(10.4)   There *ought to* be some high bidding at Mssrs. Sotheby's on Dec. 18th.

However, in (10.3) we still see enough subjectivity by the reference to the speaker's belief that it is best classified as an epistemic. Table (10.2) shows the semantics of OUGHT TO for the Canadian data.

OUGHT TO	CanE-1	CanE-2	CanE-3
deontic – narrow		3 (letters), 1 news	2 (diaries)
deontic – wide	1 (letters)	2 (letters)	2 (newspaper)
epistemic (weak)			1 (newspaper)

Table 10.2: OUGHT TO in CanE

The differentiation between narrow and wide scope in this context was introduced by Nordlinger and Traugott (1997: 303) and is used to distinguish a modal that "is part of the propositional content of the clause", imposing the action only on the subject (narrow scope) from a modal affecting the "truth of the proposition as a whole" that is external to the proposition (wide scope). Example (10.5) shows two instances:

(10.5) a.   Mr Neave sent a note to Mamma saying he had a   (CanE,
             headache & "that I **ought to** think myself lucky   diaries-3)
             that for to night I had escaped my iniquities [sic]
             (all imaginery) towards him unpunished."
                                            (narrow scope)
                                    [I, OUGHT TO (think ...)]
        b.   I think it very necessary that all Land business   (CanE,
             Possible [sic] **ought to** be Imediately Done owing   letters-2)
             in Particular to the Troublesom times – and
             Should Suppose the council and commission
             would willingly attend to all they Posibly can
                                            (wide scope)
             OUGHT TO [Land business, (immediately done)]

Nordlinger & Traugott (1997) claim that wide-scope deontics are an important step in the development of epistemic readings of OUGHT TO. The one instance in the CanE data, from period 1, is shown in (10.6). Interestingly, it is of a narrow scope:

(10.6) Traders are the last Men in this very remote part of   (CanE,
        the province, that **ought to** be appointed to such   letters-1)
        public offices, or to the adminstration of Public
        Justice as Majestrates;

                                        (narrow scope)
              [traders, OUGHT TO (be appointed – last)]

We see from table (10.2) that Nordlinger and Traugott's scenario holds in
CanE, with epistemics following narrow and wide-scope deontic readings and
wide-scope deontics occurring after narrow-scope deontic uses.

But what can we say about the development of epistemic OUGHT TO?
Does it expand at the expense of its root readings, as predicted by Abraham
(2001)? Unfortunately, no study of the phenomenon does yet seem to exist in
present-day English, and Myhill (1997) explicitly excludes epistemic readings.
However, in his AmE data, ranging from 1889 to 1987 in three periods, Myhill
shows a clear, consistent decline over the 20th century in the percentage of
OUGHT TO in relation to select functions where OUGHT TO competes with
SHOULD (1997: 8). Likewise, Leech (2003: 228) reports a sharp decline of
OUGHT TO in the period between the early 1960s and 1990s for AmE and
BrE. He, moreover, notices a tendency for infrequent modals, such as OUGHT
TO, to "become even more marginal" (p. 235). Biber *et al.* (1999: 487) omit
OUGHT TO from their discussion of the modals on the grounds of its low fre-
quency and see its use in interrogatives and negation, as "extremely rare and
largely confined to BrE" (p. 484). Biber *et al.* (1999: 489), however, also report a couple of hundred tokens of OUGHT TO in their corpus of BrE and
AmE, while Kennedy (2002: 77), in his survey of the British National Corpus,
finds almost 6,000 tokens of OUGHT TO, which is roughly a tenth of the incidence of the mid-frequency modal MIGHT. These figures show that OUGHT
TO, while considered rare, is in use and not as rare as it is sometimes characterized.

Coates (1983: 70) classifies 89% of OUGHT TO as root uses and 11% as
epistemic readings in her two corpora of mid-20th-century BrE. The percentage
for epistemics would compare with our one instance of epistemic readings in
the Canadian data, which is equivalent to 8%. Given the lack of more recent
semantic analyses of OUGHT TO (based on ICE-GB or the BNC[97]), we cannot
say whether OUGHT TO has expanded its epistemic functions. When we compare the present-day frequencies to the low occurrences in figure (10.6), we
might say that OUGHT TO has been dying for a couple of centuries now. The

---

[97] Krug (2000: 204-206) offers a brief syntactic analysis of BNC data.

expansion of OUGHT TO into the epistemic realm, which was shown to start in period 3 in the CanE data, fits with theories of root loss in core modals. This extension might be one stone in the puzzle of low-frequency OUGHT TO, which has been dying for centuries, but which still manages to hold on to some functions in PDE.

Form OUGHT TO we move on to WOULD, the most frequent modal in hypotheticals and in non-hypotheticals by the end of the period under investigation.

10.4.2 WOULD

WOULD has been studied in various ways, usually in reference to its hypothetical or irrealis functions (Larreya 2003, Ward *et al*. 2003, Ziegeler 2000 for a diachronic development until EModE), but few attempts have been made to match the multiple functions of WOULD with the basic epistemic/non-epistemic distinction. While Coates (1983: 213) defines epistemicity as including hypothetical uses, as a kind of cover term, more recently Ward, Birner and Kaplan (2003) define epistemic WOULD very narrowly as requiring a 'salient open proposition', which allows only one type of construction as in (10.7):

(10.7) B: Are you the Meredith that was listed in the Graduate Student News?
M: Yes, that would be me [out of the class of all Merediths who are graduate students].

Using Coates' broader concept of epistemic WOULD we can say that in 1960s BrE epistemic functions were "more frequent than Root in all categories" (1983: 220), but most uses are documented in non-hypothetical contexts (between 40 and 80 percent).

The functions of WOULD include all those of WILL, as shown in table (9.3): 'willingness' and 'intention' as root uses and 'predictability' and 'prediction' as epistemic uses. Coates (1983: 213) also includes the function of a 'general hypothetical marker' as in (10.8), which can be interpreted as a prediction:

(10.8) God knows what would happen to me if I ever got caught.

In order to assess the expansion of epistemic uses in the LModE Canadian corpus, we would ideally rule out uses of WOULD in conditionals because of the uncertainty to ascribe the hypothetical function to any single part of a conditional sentence (Dancygier 1998). We apply Coates' categories of predictability (referring to the present) and prediction (referring to the past) in (10.9a & b):

(10.9) a. Who's at the doorstep? That **would** be the milkman.
            ['I confidently "predict" that around this time of the day, the milkman is likely on our doorstep'; it's the milkman out of the possible classes of visitors at this time of the day]
        b. The judge said today that it was unlikely that the jury **would** be able to reconsider their verdict.

In both examples, (10.9a) and (10.9b), however, we will use 'prediction' in all temporal contexts. We can also see that Ward *et al.*'s (2003) subclass of epistemic WOULD seems to be included in example (10.9a). This type of epistemic uses of WOULD, is subsumed under the function of a pragmatic marker of politeness (see 10.10b) The following categories are applied to the Canadian data and include two epistemic types with two root uses (and one intermediate root function), as shown in example (10.10):

(10.10) a. **Epistemic** (belief of speaker)   (CanE,
             We dined at six. I thought the day **would**   diaries-3)
             never end, & went to my room at half past
             nine
         b. **Epistemic** (tentative politeness)   (CanE,
             I wish to know if the present time **would** be a   letters-3)
             suitable one for my partner & self to call on
             the Governor & you, ...
         c. **Root** (volition)   (CanE,
             Kingston had made Father some offer, yester-   diaries-3)
             day for the House & Lot in town. and [sic!]
             thinking more of it since him & me went to
             town to see Anderson, after waiting and hunt-
             ing some time we   found him but he **would**
             not come out to Allow us more then <nw:
             than> 200 hundred Dollars, which we could
             not think of taking and so we parted.

   d. **Root** (intention)   (CanE,
      Mr Ball gave notice that he **would** on Satur-   newspapers-3)
      day move for leave to bring in a Bill to repest
      [sic] the second By-law past [sic] in the first
      session ...
   e. **Root** (volition/intention)   (CanE,
      Mamma now got much better ... Mr McDon-   diaries-3)
      ald came ... she took some Oysters for her
      dinner, which she relished very much and then
      went to sleep. Aunt Maria said she **would** sit
      in her room until she awoke.

The results from the CanE data are highly genre specific and are shown in table (10.3).

WOULD	d1	d2	d3	l1	l2	l3	n1	n2	n3
epistemic	65%	50%	41%	35%	62%	60%	67%	46%	50%
	(13)	(4)	(24)	(16)	(28)	(26)	(2)	(6)	(13)
non-epistemic	35%	50%	59%	65%	38%	40%	33%	54%	50%
	(7)	(4)	(34)	(30)	(17)	(17)	(1)	(7)	(13)

Table 10.3: Epistemic and non-epistemic WOULD in CanE

While the newspaper genre shows an almost constant 50-50 split between epistemic and non-epistemic functions, the diaries see a decline of epistemic uses. The second highest percentage of epistemic uses is found in the diary data from period-1, which we can attribute to the educated middle-class usage of Anne Powell, whose diary is the sole source for modals in diary-1[98]. This shows that epistemic uses were available at the beginning of our period. Looking at the letter data, however, we see a reversal of epistemic and non-epistemic uses between period 1 and 2 that would comply with societal developments as suggested by Myhill (1995) and the increasing use of WOULD as a marker of politeness.

Dossena (2003: 216) finds that already in EModE "WOULD in epistemic contexts clearly increase" in certain genres, signalling a change in politeness strategies. The early 19th-century data suggest that in Canada another such increase can be seen. Likewise, Coates (1983: 210) notes that for 1960s BrE the effect of WOULD, when referring to the present "is one of politeness", as

---

[98] Benjamin Smith's diary is kept in keyword style, including no modals.

shown in our data in *I would beg the favour* (letters-2). This reversal[99] of the ratio of epistemic and non-epistemic uses in the letter section complies with a trend towards a more central role of epistemicity in the functions of WOULD. In 1960s BrE, epistemic WOULD is already by far the most prevalent function of WOULD, hovering around the 80% mark across the genres (Coates 1983: 220). Examples such as in (10.9b) above, a request, albeit hedged by epistemic WOULD, do not figure prominently in period 1, however. The Canadian letter data, with its lower-class writers, suggest that a pragmatically triggered change was in progress in the early 19th century.

While WOULD in the letter genre is expanding its frequencies for epistemic functions, we have a somewhat steady distribution, with some fluctuation in the other genres. A general root loss for WOULD can only partially be confirmed for the letter genre.

10.4.3 SHOULD

How does the main competitor for WOULD fare in the epistemic realm? In 1960s BrE, epistemic SHOULD represents a minority function when compared to root uses. However, in written manuscript sources, epistemic SHOULD accounts for c. 60% of all uses, since "in private letters and diaries we tend to communicate probabilities, rather than give advice", while for other genres the percentages are less than 15% (Coates 1983: 67). The LModE CanE data from all contexts are shown in table (10.4):

SHOULD	CanE-1	CanE-2	CanE-3
epistemic	50% (16)	56% (24)	50% (24)
non-epistemic	50% (16)	44% (20)	50% (24)

Table 10.4: SHOULD, including conditional contexts

The percentages for Coates' study on 1960s BrE are almost matched in the Canadian LModE data for SHOULD, which comprise mostly manuscript sources. This result comes as a surprise, as previous studies suggest sizeable increases of SHOULD since LModE times. For AmE, Myhill (1997: 8), reports drastic decreases of OUGHT TO and increases of SHOULD, which, for the latter, are not borne out in CanE data versus the BrE data from the 1960s. When we eliminate the conditional sentences, which are hypothetical, however, we get a glimpse of what is actually going on:

---

[99] Pearson's chi-square = 6.85 and significant at p = 0.01; all other changes in table (9.8) are non-significant, the second-biggest change (d1-d2) at Fisher's Exact: p = 0.38.

SHOULD	CanE-1	CanE-2	CanE-3
epistemic	0% (0)	9% (2)	15% (4)
non-epistemic	100% (16)	91% (20)	85% (24)

Table 10.5: SHOULD, conditional contexts ruled out

Two examples of the use of epistemic SHOULD in non-conditional sentences are shown in (10.11a & b):

(10.11) a. I herewith transmit to Your Honor Copy of the order of 10th April respecting their removal out of the Town, and also Copy of the American General Dearborns order of 20th April last by which he declared the said Records **should** be safe from danger from the Troops under his command. (CanE, letters-2, 1813)

b. Therefore by my paying keeping for the use of the Land, I considered, I **should** have a claim prior to Mr. Wilson. (CanE, letters-3, 1836)

c. One bushel of the shells of peas, will make several dozen bottles of beer. - The beer **should** be put into strong bottles, kept into a cool cellar, and the corks **should** be secured with wire. (CanE, news-papers-1)

When compared with the use in (10.11c), which has a root meaning of 'offering advice' (to ensure that the process of home-brewing is to be successful), the epistemic element in the other two examples becomes clear. After eliminating the conditional examples in the CanE data, there is, in fact, a modest, but steady increase in epistemic uses of SHOULD over time, from 0% to 9% and, finally, 15% in period 3.

The long-term perspective of changes since LModE times is more complex. For post-WWII BrE, Leech (2003: 233) does not note a significant increase of epistemic SHOULD, with levels remaining around the 10% mark of all uses of SHOULD. Leech points out that the root use of SHOULD, in the sense of a weak obligation, is on the increase, at the expense of, above all, its epistemic sense (p. 234). This change is apparently linked to societal influences in the late 20th century and its "tendency to suppress or avoid overt claims to power or authority by the writer" (Myhill 1995: 237). These tendencies result in a decline of root MUST and an increase of root SHOULD.

These trends are certainly not yet evidenced in the LModE CanE data, where SHOULD is expanding in its epistemic uses, which fits with Abraham's (2001) general prediction for the immediate period under investigation.

10.5 Summary

The auxiliaries were shown to specialize in particular functions. WOULD was, at the expense of SHOULD, increasingly used as the modal auxiliary in hypothetical contexts (figures 10.1-10.3), with some evidence for parallel developments in the varieties. In non-hypothetical contexts, changes also seem driven by parallel developments, but show CanE as significantly disfavouring SHOULD in contrast to BrE (figures 10.4 and 10.5).

We have seen that SHOULD and WOULD, when distinguished by their hypothetical and non-hypothetical uses, meet Trudgill's requirement of extreme variability in period 2 (see table 10.1 for hypotheticals and figure 10.6 for non-hypotheticals). OUGHT TO does not play a major role, with BrE showing slightly higher frequencies than in CanE. These results seem to corroborate Trudgill's scenario of a threshold for minority forms; the frequencies of OUGHT TO are around the 10% cut-off value in the period, and in period 2 slightly higher, which would ensure their transmission into the next generation of speakers.

As for the epistemic uses of these three modals, OUGHT TO seems to expand its functions, and its life expectancy, with an expansion into the epistemic area. WOULD is already used at frequencies that are similar to those found in mid-20th-century BrE. WOULD expands its epistemic functions also with the help of pragmatic functions such as a politeness marker. SHOULD, while roughly appearing in equal parts in root and epistemic uses, manages to expand its epistemic readings in non-conditional contexts. On the whole, the thesis of root loss can be indirectly corroborated with the expansion of epistemic readings for OUGHT TO, SHOULD, and partially so for WOULD.

This completes the empirical part of the eleven modal expressions in LModE. After detailing various aspects of ten core modals and one semi-modal in a diachronic dimension in Late Modern CanE and BrE, which was at times supported by evidence from AmE and NW-BrE varieties from period 1, we shall now move on to the final chapter. In chapter (11), the results will be amalgamated to allow for generalizations of the LModE modal system in Canada, to assess Trudgill's new-dialect formation theory and its three stages and to answer statements on the status of CanE, including its alleged conservatism.

11 CONCLUSION

This study of eleven modal expressions – ten core modals and one semi-modal – was aimed to assess changes in CanE in relation to BrE over time and to AmE and a regional variety of BrE, NW-BrE, in pre-1800 data. This chapter sets out to provide answers based on the cumulative evidence for the five basic sets of questions laid out in the introduction. These questions were:

1) How can the use of modal auxiliaries be characterized in early CanE and how does this development comply with the known semantic trajectories for modals (Traugott 1989) and the theory of root loss (Abraham 2001)?
2) How conservative is early CanE modal usage? Does it undergo a colonial lag (Marckwardt 1958, Trudgill 2004)? How far does the founder principle apply (Mufwene 1996)?
3) Which of the existing theories on the origin of CanE (Bloomfield 1948 or Scargill 1957) fits the data better?
4) To what extent do the modals in CanE provide evidence for existing models of new-dialect formation (Trudgill 2004)?
5) When did CanE focus (Le Page and Tabouret-Keller 1985), i.e. become a distinct variety that began to be perceived as distinct by some of its speakers?

Issue (1) is the prerequisite to answer the remaining four questions and is necessarily explored first. The theory of root loss in central modals will be reviewed in light of the cumulative evidence as a first application of the data. This is followed by an assessment of three core questions in the present study. In a first step, information on question (2) provides the background for an assessment of the two dominant theories on the origin of CanE in relation to the Ontarian context (3). As data from a number of input varieties is lacking, however, for issues (2) and (3), a method of heuristic reasoning will be applied. In a second step, a summary of the cumulative results also provides the baseline for an assessment of the three-stage model of new-dialect formation and some adaptations to the existing model will be suggested, before, finally, an attempt will be made to tackle the question of focussing in early OntE, for which different levels of speaker awareness involved in the various changes will be considered. The chapter is completed by an assessment and prospects of research avenues in diachronic CanE in particular and LModE in general.

11.1 The modals in early Canadian English

This section reviews the distributional patterns of the modal auxiliaries as well as their formal characteristics in early CanE in contrast to up to three varieties.

The survey of CAN and MAY looked at uses denoting Permission on the one hand and Root possibility on the other hand, which are the variables' two areas of functional/notional overlap. Because of their genre-specific distributions each text type was looked at individually. Results showed that permission uses of MAY figure generally more prominently in CanE than in BrE. This finding revealed that letter writers in early Ontario employed MAY, i.e. the conservative – more formal way – of asking for permission, more often than their BrE peers.

CAN showed a strong tendency in both CanE and BrE to become the prime form to code for Permission. By the end of the period in 1850, CAN had reached this status in all genres, except in CanE letters. Since we interpreted this change as an instance of drift, CanE letter conventions can be seen as lagging behind the BrE norm of the day.

An instance of drift is also suggested by the data for CAN and MAY in Root possibility uses. Here, CanE and BrE show largely parallel diachronic behaviours, as both increase their percentages of CAN in diaries and letters (with the exception of the newspaper genre in CanE). The emergence of an inverse V-curve in CanE, which surfaced for CAN/MAY and COULD/MIGHT in various contexts in the shorter 25-year intervals, was attributed to the influence of prescriptive norms in period 1, which kept informal CAN in check until the next generation of CanE speakers made their selections in favour of CAN.

COULD and MIGHT were investigated in a four-field grid as both variables were studied in epistemic and non-epistemic uses and in past and non-past contexts. Generally, CAN and COULD were shown to occur almost uncontested by MIGHT in negative sentences and MAY figuring as the majority variant in affirmative contexts. We could see that CanE and BrE change in opposite directions. While most changes did not reach statistical significance at 95%, the recurring pattern still suggests a slow-moving change in one direction: CanE decreasing epistemic uses and non-epistemic uses of COULD (and a corresponding increase of MIGHT), with BrE changing in the reverse direction. As the changes proceed very slowly, it is difficult to gather samples that produce statistical significance for the given 25-year periods.

Epistemic COULD figured most prominently in AmE-1, which produced statistical significance in comparison to BrE, and with CanE in between. What is important here is that CanE developed in a different direction than BrE, which might indicate an independent development. However, if AmE was the innovator here and BrE followed suit, CanE went down a more conservative path, as for COULD and MIGHT in general, a criss-cross pattern between CanE and BrE resurfaced in every diachronic development chart.

The analysis of COULD and MIGHT in affirmative contexts alone produced very similar percentages than the overall figures for CanE and BrE, but not for AmE-1. The pattern for COULD and MIGHT showed a North American prevalence of COULD, in contrast to BrE, which used MIGHT in almost half the cases in period 1.

In this study of the modal auxiliaries, one semi-modal played a significant role in LModE. Semi-modal HAVE TO shows a highly interesting developmental scenario, as the results gleaned from the case study of MUST vs. HAVE TO are very different from both CAN/MAY and COULD/MIGHT.

HAVE TO is most frequently attested in CanE, and its incidence increases in letters half a century before diaries and newspapers show the first instances of modal HAVE TO. All instances are, however, root uses. It is interesting that NW-BrE is most conservative in its use of HAVE TO. As non-southeastern varieties of English figure more prominently in the Ontario settlement input than southeastern ones, HAVE TO is unlikely to have been influenced by SIN varieties.

HAVE TO is, moreover, first attested in non-syntactic contexts, i.e. those contexts where MUST was not limited by its incomplete paradigm, which lends further support to the argument that the causes for the origin of HAVE TO lie elsewhere, possibly in the more profound social changes of the period, as suggested for early AmE by Myhill (1995). In the epistemic realm, MUST was still the major form across the board. Epistemic uses appear rarely in CanE when compared to AmE and BrE.

Both SHALL and WILL, and to some extent SHOULD and WOULD were subject to the most overt criticisms in comparison to the other modal auxiliaries. Prescriptivists usually targeted non-southeastern English speakers as violating the prescriptive rule governing SHALL and WILL, and early Ontarians were no exception. However, CanE was shown to be most conservative in period 1 for 1st person SHALL and adhered to the prescriptive rule most consistently. However, in the following periods CanE changes from the most conservative to the most progressive variety (period 2+3), for which significance levels are reached. This change indicates, just as we said for epistemic COULD, an independent CanE development. In this case we were able to pinpoint a likely cause for the change with the distribution of both variables in the SIN data: while early immigrants adhered to SHALL in the first person, displaying colonial lag and hypercorrection in period 1 as suggested by Trudgill, in periods 2 and 3, when the bulk of SIN-speakers came to Canada, no occurrences are found in the SIN data from CONTE-pC. It is likely, of course, that a bigger sample would reveal some instances of 1st person SHALL, the overall pattern would hold, at least for period 3. In this period, lower class speakers used 1st person WILL in the majority of all instances.

The independent variable 'type of subject' (animate vs. inanimate) showed that WILL had taken a firm hold with inanimate subjects in the period. This continuation of a drift from EModE provided evidence for further semantic bleaching of WILL and a reinforcement of its use as a marker of the future tense. Concerning voice, passive sentences revealed higher percentages of 3rd person SHALL, especially so in BrE (statistically significant in relation to CanE).

Finally, SHOULD and WOULD were looked at in hypothetical and in non-hypothetical contexts. For the latter, OUGHT TO was included as a core modal auxiliary that competed with the other two forms in the area of weak obligation. Hypothetical SHOULD was preferred in the 1st person in both CanE and BrE and the patterns are strikingly similar in both varieties. This was interpreted as an instance of drift and parallel development in both varieties.

In non-hypotheticals, three variables were surveyed, as SHOULD and WOULD competed with OUGHT TO. While OUGHT TO only played a minor role in frequency, it showed interesting behaviour in relation to its functional expansion, as will be summarized in section (11.2). Most importantly, non-hypothetical SHOULD was significantly disfavoured in CanE when compared to BrE, which also used OUGHT TO more often than the former. As the changes appear to be another instance of drift, which is suggested by a parallel diachronic pattern at different frequency levels in CanE and BrE, the use of non-hypothetical WOULD in CanE may be considered more progressive. A higher incidence of WOULD in CanE at the expense of SHOULD was not matched in the BrE data, which is evidence for the loyalist base theory.

The formal characteristics of modal auxiliaries in the period are quickly summarized. Variation was mostly confined to the aspect of contractions, which were shown to be generally very scarce in all four corpora, which allows the generalization that pre-1850 LModE did not employ them to any greater degree. In the case of *shouldn't* or *wouldn't*, no instances of short forms were found at all. When short forms do occur, it is usually in BrE or NW-BrE, which suggests a later spread from BrE to other varieties world-wide.

With this descriptive background, we can proceed to the interpretation of these distributions and frequencies. The first such task is the interpretation of the data in the theory of root loss in central modals (Abraham 2001).

11.2 Epistemicity and late-modern CanE

The development of epistemic functions in Late Modern Canadian English can be used to gauge the theory of a general root loss in the central modals. We said in chapter (6), in section (6.1.3), that the rise of epistemic uses at the expense of root uses is one of two major conditions for Abraham's thesis (2001, 2002) that seeks to explain why English modals behave very differently in relation to the modals in other Germanic languages. There are a number of differences, the most important being that the English modals lost their status of full verbs and were more fully grammaticalized. As a result, they interact differently with features of aspect than modal verbs in other Germanic languages.

While these relationships are complex and not yet fully understood, Abraham (2001) is a comprehensive attempt to account for these differences. In the present study we have not considered at all the interdependency of modality and aspect (see Ziegeler 2006, 2003, Coates 1983: 99f). The second of Abraham's central theses, besides the loss of root meaning ('Rootschwund'), is the breakdown of a system of lexical aspect, aktionsart, sometime after the Old English period, i.e. the "radical deaspectualization of the English lexicals" (Abraham 2001: 8). The development of a new system of aspect from Middle English onwards is exemplified in the formation of a present perfect and progressive aspect (ibid: 28), the latter of which expanded its use in the 19th century (Smitterberg 2005). There remains some uncertainty as to this scenario of aspect. Brinton's assessment (1988: 58), for instance, that post-verbal particles "constitute a rich and productive system of aktionsart marking in Modern English", would at least in part run counter to the notion of a complete abandonment of lexical aktionsart in the English verbal system. Clearly, more work needs to be dedicated to this aspect of the English aspect.

The present study can only provide insights to the development of epistemicity and the connected loss of the root meanings in central modals. Do the Canadian data, then, confirm the assessment that the core modals appear to be losing their root meanings, as asserted in the following quotation:

> MVs [modal verbs] in American Modern [present-day] English have lost
> the root readings (with the exception of *must* and, to a certain extent,
> *may*). While the full range of MVs still exists, they are either used only
> epistemically (*may, must, can*) or exclusively as temporal auxiliaries
> ((*shall*), *will*). As to their root meanings, fully lexical paraphrases have
> replaced the modals (*be permitted* instead of root *may*, *have to* instead of
> root *must* with a personal object, as well as their negations). (Abraham
> 2002: 22)

American English has frequently been put forward as the leader of the development in 20th-century English (e.g. Mair and Leech 2006, Mair 2006), and we
have seen some instances, e.g. for HAVE TO, where AmE appears to be most
advanced as well, with Canadian English following at its heels, and well before
BrE varieties. However, as it will become clear in the next section, no simple
statement as to the conservatism or progressivism of the modal auxiliaries
seems possible.

Table (11.1) condenses the results concerning epistemic use in a schematic
format. It focusses on CanE and PDE distributions, but refers to the other
LModE varieties (AmE, BrE, NW-BrE) by period where findings are available. Starting at the top of table, we found that CAN'T, in comparison to CAN,
acquired epistemic readings some 200 years before CAN, for the latter of
which this development appears to be a very recent phenomenon. Problem
cases are MAY, with its decrease of epistemic uses in CanE2+3, which was,
however, claimed as an exception in Abraham (2002) due to the existence of
lexicalized formulae including MAY. This issue would need to be followed up
to see whether this is another possible reason for MAY diverting from the
trend (we argued above that the CanE data may show a bias in this respect).
Epistemic COULD and MIGHT fit the overall hypothesis of epistemic expansion. MIGHT seems to have lost its root readings in some genres of AmE today (Abraham 2002) and has also expanded further its epistemic uses, which
were already majority uses in LModE.

MUST, even more so than COULD and MIGHT, shows a clear and steady
expansion in a picture-book case, so to speak, of epistemic readings. Semi-
modal HAVE TO, however, has begun, perhaps most likely in the early 20th-
century, to acquire epistemic readings, and OUGHT TO acquired strong epistemic readings in the 19th century, but appears to be generally on its way out in
present-day varieties, but has likely prolonged its life span by way of an expansion of its epistemic readings.

EPISTEMIC modals	LModE data			PDE
	CanE-1	CanE-2	CanE-3	
epistemic CAN'T	-- (emerging AmE-1, BrE-1)	emerging	emerging	epistemic as negation of MUST (Coates 1983: 166)
epistemic CAN	--	--	--	epistemic uses are attested in late 20th century and emerging (Coates 1995)
epistemic MAY*	c. 40%	slump (decrease) (BrE: increase, AmE majority use, Myhill 1995)		higher frequencies in PDE, sharp cline today (Leech 2003)
epistemic COULD	between 10 and 17% (BrE decrease, AmE 11%) minority use, stagnating			majority uses in BrE (Facchinetti 2002), AmE (Biber et al. 1999)
epistemic MIGHT	majority use (also in BrE)			exclusively used as epistemic (Biber et al. 1999: 491), becoming synonymous with MAY (Coates 1983)
epistemic MUST*	expansion (also BrE)	expansion (also BrE)	expansion (also BrE)	only thriving use today; MUST is losing ground (Smith 2003, Leech 2003)
		matched in AmE (Myhill 1996)		
epistemic HAVE TO	--	--	--	attestations from mid-20th century BrE, (Smith 2003, Krug 2000: 89), AmE (see example 8.5b), expanding today
epistemic OUGHT TO (strong sense)	--	--	emerging (BrE, Nordlinger & Traugott 1997)	becoming more marginal, in all readings (Leech 2003, Myhill 1997)
epistemic WOULD genre sensitive; use as politeness marker (Dossena 2003)	35-67% of all forms	expansion (letters) decrease (diaries) fluctuation (news)		BrE majority function (Coates 1983)
epistemic SHOULD	0% of all forms	expansion in non-conditionals		BrE minority function (Coates 1983); stagnant in late 20th-centjury BrE (Leech 2003)

Table 11.1: Changes in epistemic modals in CanE, with reference to BrE and AmE (* = modals excluded from root loss theory in Abraham 2002)

SHOULD expanded in non-typical contexts, i.e. outside of the conditional clause, while WOULD has a more complex distribution, being highly genre specific and with its multiple functions, one of which as a politeness marker since at least EModE (Dossena 2003), has expanded its epistemic readings in this way.

It appears to be the case that the theory of root loss, *Rootschwund*, can at least be supported for its effect on the expansion of epistemic uses since LModE times, in some cases since EModE and ME times. As for the temporal modals SHALL and WILL, which we did not survey in this respect, even WILL, when surveyed along semantic lines, has been shown to demonstrate a tendency from ME to EModE (Gotti 2003b: 290f) to increase its epistemic frequency. In summary, we may say that there can be little doubt as to the expansion of epistemic readings in core modals.

These results, however, can be but one piece in the puzzle of the development of the English modals, but in some respects the LModE data even strengthen aspects of Abraham's thesis beyond its original scope. When we read that in

> Modern English *must* is evenly divided between deontic [i.e. root, SD] and epistemic uses and that *can* and *may* are still quite normal as DMVs [deontic, i.e. root modal verbs] (Abraham 2001: 32),

we can add that MUST is, in our data, heavily leaning towards the epistemic side. At the end of the period in 1850, epistemic readings are the majority use of MUST, which is still the case in present-day conversation data (Biber *et al.* 1999: 494), while present-day written data show a rather even distribution along the lines of a 50-50 split. This means that in some genres, such as the ones surveyed in CanE, epistemic readings were already dominant 150 years ago.

While CAN is indeed usually used as a root modal today, MAY is used almost exclusively as an epistemic (Biber *et al.* 1999: 491), so we might say that MAY has already come to the end of its 'modality cycle', as it were. It is, however, precisely the development of MAY in the Canadian data that does not match with the root loss prediction. On the whole, however, there seems to be little doubt that the central modals as a group (including OUGHT TO) are becoming epistemic markers and the tendencies can already be seen in Late Modern Canadian English, with no sign of semi-modal HAVE TO taking on epistemic readings. This stage was apparently to follow in 20th-century English, or perhaps in late 19th-century English, but certainly not before then.

11.3 Colonial lag and the founder principle

The descriptive account above provides the basis for the reasoning concerning colonial lag and the founder principle. Table (11.2) is an attempt of a summary of the results for that purpose, which was arrived at by a means of heuristic reasoning. In the table, CanE is compared to BrE for conservative vs. progressive behaviour in the surveyed modals on a five-step scale. AmE and NW-BrE data are provided where available, so that table (11.2) may serve as a visual overview.

The assessment is necessarily heuristic, however, as neither all input varieties – which consist of at least eight groups in period 1, and at least nine groups in period 2 (cf. chapter 3) – nor AmE diachronic data were available. Besides the BrE data from ARCHER-1 – which were taken, due to the characteristics of ARCHER-1, to represent the southeastern standard –, NW-BrE and AmE from period 1 serve as reference points. These are enough data for some generalizations, if the findings are compared with trends in the English language that have occurred since, but too little data to gauge all influences to their precise extent, which is why this approach is best referred to as heuristic reasoning

The reasoning behind the heuristics applied here is easily illustrated for the collocation of MUST NECESSARILY, which, as was shown earlier, was used for epistemic uses until the beginning of 19th century. BrE is used as a benchmark for all comparisons. The fact that MUST NECESSARILY does not occur in CanE and AmE, but in BrE and NW-BrE is taken as an indicator, in hindsight of the present-day situation, of a progressive development in North American English. This reasoning is heuristic not only because of unavailable input data, but also in terms of the limited size of the corpora: for instance, MUST NECESSARILY could have been used in some AmE or CanE writing of the period. The data, however, is treated as indicative that MUST NECESSARILY was used *less frequently* in North America to denote epistemic meaning than in BrE varieties. This kind of reasoning, applied to all variables, produces table (11.2), which shows the results for the 19 surveyed contexts in a visual format (see Dollinger forthc. for a detailed methodological presentation of this approach).

Grey shading indicates the assessment of OntE in relation to BrE, with AmE and NW-BrE serving as further reference points. The results are necessarily a simplification, as some variables change their behaviour across the periods. For instance, in CanE 1st person SHALL is more conservatively used in period 1, but shows the lowest incidence in period 2+3 (figure 9.6), with 1st person WILL becoming the majority variant.

VARIABLES		Function and/or context	Conservative	Towards cons.	Neutral	Towards progr.	Progressive
changes from **above**	CAN & MAY	1) permission			■		
		2) root poss.		■			
		3) affirmative contexts			(AmE-1)		
		4) negative contexts			(AmE-1)		
	OUGHT TO	5) overall				■	
	SHALL & WILL	6) 1st person	(NW-BrE)		(AmE-1)	■	
		7) 2nd person			■		
		8) 3rd person				■	
		9) inanimate subjects			■		
		10) passive structures				■	
changes from **below**	SHOULD & WOULD	11) hypotheticals			■		
		12) non-hypotheticals				■	
	MUST & HAVE TO	13) root uses				■	(AmE-1)
		14) epistemic uses		(AmE-1)			
		15) ep. MUST NECESS.		(NW-BrE)			(AmE-1)
	COULD & MIGHT	16) affirmative contexts			(AmE-1)		
		17) negative contexts			(AmE-1)		
		18) epistemic uses	■				(AmE-1)
		19) non-epistemic uses		■			

Table 11.2: Conservative and progressive behaviour of LModE modal auxiliaries (for CanE compared to BrE, with data from AmE-1 and NW-BrE- where applicable)

In cases of diachronic changes within the period, greater importance was given to the direction of changes, so that 1st person SHALL and WILL uses were placed in the 'toward conservative' usage category, considering features of both periods.

All changes have also been classified according to their level of awareness among speakers. This assessment is based on contemporary commentary, as reflected in the previous sections. As we can see in table (11.2), there is no general tendency for either changes from above or from below to proceed either in a conservative or progressive direction. Table (11.3) regroups each change according to its suggested level of awareness.

change from	conservative	neutral	progressive
above	1	5	4
below	3	3	3
TOTAL	4	8	7

Table 11.3: Changes classified by level of awareness in CanE

We see in table (11.3) that both conservative and progressive behaviour, as well as neutral instances of drift, are found in the CanE data. However, progressive behaviour is more prevalent in CanE (7 variables) than conservative patterns (4 variables), with neutral behaviour found also in eight cases.

In chapter (5), two notions of colonial lag were introduced: Görlach's notion, which limits the phenomenon to language attitudes, suggested that colonial lag operates exclusively on changes from above, and Trudgill's notion, which merely confines a lag to roughly the first generation of settlers regardless of the type of change.

The data suggest that Görlach's notion is too restrictive, as we have more conservative uses classified as changes from *below*, i.e. undergoing some time lag, in table (11.3). The results also show that conservative uses in the modals affected the first generation of settlers, which reflects the rather progressive use of modals in early Canada (Permission MAY, epistemic MUST, 1st person SHALL), when compared to BrE. As a number of progressive uses were also shown, Trudgill's notion of colonial lag could be fully corroborated, with the exception of epistemic COULD, which changed from a more progressive to a more conservative use in CanE2+3. On the whole, however, while Trudgill's notion of a lag applies better to the data, the modal auxiliary complex, for the eleven modals surveyed is, generally speaking, slightly more progressive in CanE than in BrE.

11.4 M. Bloomfield (1948) or Scargill (1957, 1985)

The results from the previous section provide the basis for an assessment of the two major scenarios of the origin of CanE. Bloomfield's (1948) paper rests on the founder principle and early AmE input, while Scargill (1957) stresses numerical swamping with British forms in the post-1815 period. In Scargill (1985) this notion was extended to a discussion of CanE as an offshoot of BrE, without any reference to AmE, which must be considered as a highly biased point of view.

Table (11.4) summarizes the results from chapters (7) to (10) in light of four possible scenarios of influences in CanE. Each distribution is assigned the category that is supported most clearly from the distributions shown for each variable. Loyalist base (or AmE input), parallel development (or drift), independent CanE development, and BrE influence are the four categories:

Loyalist base (American influence)	Parallel development, drift	Independent CanE development	British influence
hypothetical WOULD (sign. diff. from BrE)	hypothetical WOULD	1st person SHALL and WILL	1st person SHALL and WILL
HAVE TO (most likely when compared to AmE-1)	hypothetical SHOULD	epistemic COULD	OUGHT TO
non-epistemic COULD	2nd and 3rd person SHALL and WILL overall	SHALL/WILL in passives (possibly also AmE)	
root possibility CAN	SHALL and WILL in negative and positive contexts		
	epistemic MUST		

Table 11.4: Influences on early CanE
(grey shadings emphasize mixed influence)

Two changes in table (11.4), 1st person SHALL and hypothetical WOULD, allow two interpretations and are therefore listed twice (grey shadings). Table (11.4) provides a rough overview of the influences on the modals in early

OntE. The classification suggests that the following factors were affecting the modal system in early CanE in decreasing order of importance:

1) Drift / Parallel development
2) Loyalist base input
3) Independent Canadian development
4) British influence

Table 11.5: Heuristic ranking of influences on early OntE modals

The most pervasive factor operating on the modal auxiliaries are parallel changes in all varieties as a result of drift. This, however, is followed by the AmE loyalist input in second place, and by independent CanE developments as the third most important factor. British influence ranks in last position as the fourth factor.

It needs to be stressed that the ranking in table (11.5) does not show importance of each of these factors for individual changes, but only an overall assessment based on table (11.4), and, ultimately, table (11.2). We have seen that the BrE influence was decisive for the rise of 1st person WILL – one of the most spectacular changes throughout the period. The dialect mixing in period 2, with massive British lower class input, is significant as it turned the tide towards 1st person WILL, and possibly also caused a short comeback of OUGHT TO. These changes indicates that BrE influence was important in the development of CanE and an essential "ingredient" in the formation of CanE despite ranking last in the above scale.

The ranking in table (11.5) shows that both Bloomfield and Scargill focussed only on a selection of these four factors. While Bloomfield identified AmE as a major influence, which is largely borne out in our scenario (ranking in second place after drift), Scargill went surely too far in his criticism of the AmE input for early Canada and exaggerated the numerically least prevalent British influence. For the modals surveyed, table (11.5) puts these influences in relation to each other offers are more balanced developmental scenario than both M. Bloomfield's and Scargill's.

These general findings enable us to gauge, moreover, the role of dialect contact in early Ontario. AmE and BrE influence, as a result of contact situations, are the second and fourth most important scenarios. In table (11.4), dialect contact is directly linked with up to six out of 14 changes (two changes are represented twice in the table) and therefore figures quite prominently as an active force in early Ontario.

The role of language contact for the groups identified in chapter (3), however, remains to be examined.

11.5 The modal auxiliaries and the three stages of new-dialect formation

To what extend do these findings comply with Trudgill's (2004) theory of new-dialect formation? We suggested earlier that the *semi-tabula rasa* situation in early Ontario may necessitate adaptations, but also that the type of the variables, being grammatical rather than phonological, might require changes.

The data were applied to Trudgill's original three stages of development, as was shown in table (5.1). In order to accommodate some findings, three modifications were made to the original proposal in the course of the present study.

First, based on the results for CAN and MAY in the middle and lower class sections, Trudgill's stage I was extended to *include* extreme variability, which was originally projected for stage II. This provided a slightly restructured developmental sequence, as is summarized in table (11.5):

STAGE I NEW	rudimentary levelling	interdialect development	extreme variability
STAGE II	apparent levelling		extreme variability
STAGE III	choice of majority forms		reallocation

Table 11.6: Trudgill's three stages of new-dialect formation adapted (modification shaded grey)

Stage I was modified to include 'extreme variability' (stage I new). This, slightly revised sequence, allows us to accommodate the changes in the modal auxiliaries and may provide a starting point for grammatical changes in general.

Second, it was suggested that in a comprehensive theory of new-dialect formation one would need to allow for different levels of development in different settings, depending on the settlement patterns in a given location. In Ontario, recent sociohistorical research showed that SIN, i.e. non-Southern English English, speakers settled largely in rural areas and were less likely to be exposed to the norms of the cities (section 3.3.3 details the external reasoning behind this line of thought). We would therefore work, as seen in data on CAN/MAY and for 1st person SHALL, with an urban and a rural layer in the new-dialect formation process, so to speak. The urban layer was settled in period 1, and the periods in CONTE-pC would match the stages in table (11.6).

For the rural layer, which was settled a generation after the urban layer in Ontario, the development would start one stage later. This reasoning yields the rural and urban scenarios shown in table (11.7):

periods in CONTE	urban settings	rural settings
1 (1776-99)	STAGE I NEW	N/A
2 (1800-24)	STAGE II	STAGE I NEW
3 (1825-49)	STAGE III	STAGE II
4 (1850-74)		STAGE III

Table 11.7: Urban and rural developmental scenarios in early Ontario

These two scenarios would eventually merge, possibly in period 5 (1875-99), and influences expanding from the already settled urban centres would be expected. Scenarios of the geographical spread of changes, such as cascade diffusion (from an urban centre spreading outwards) and contagious diffusion (between neighbouring areas) (Wolfram and Schilling-Estes 1998: 142-148) or other diffusion models (cf. Chambers and Trudgill 1998: 172-185) would account for the blend of two standards into a more uniform dialect, which would be expected to have started by 1875.

A third adaptation to Trudgill's model concerns very slowly proceeding instances of drift. We have seen for passive SHALL, permission CAN, epistemic COULD, HAVE TO and 3rd person SHALL/WILL that long-term changes in the language do not proceed in steps that fit the three-stage model. We have seen for these variables, which represent changes that occur in most varieties, a steady progression in a given direction, *without* a phase of extreme variability. For this reason, it is proposed that slowly-moving long-term changes are largely unaffected by contact situations.

Apart from these three adaptations, the data allow interpretations in Trudgill's model. Rudimentary levelling was found in the loss of MUST NECESSARILY in stage 1 in CanE and AmE, as opposed to BrE, and the original model accounts for changes in 1st person SHALL in terms of variability, for SHOULD and WOULD in both hypothetical as well as non-hypothetical contexts, and for variability of MIGHT in negative contexts in CanE, which is not evidenced in AmE or BrE. Majority forms, a key factor in Trudgill (2004), were selected in period 3 for 1st and 3rd person WILL, and possibly also for WOULD in both hypothetical as well as non-hypothetical contexts. The idea of a threshold was applied to HAVE TO, whose input from AmE was above the 10% mark and was carried over into CanE, as well as for OUGHT TO in non-hypotheticals, where the BrE input in period 2 increased the frequency in CanE beyond the 10% mark, and therefore OUGHT TO remained in CanE in period 3.

The use of lower class data enabled us to approximate post-1815 regional BrE input. Since lower class speakers were in the majority in early Ontario, Trudgill's emphasis on input demography was not contradicted. Overall, the available data met basic requirements for a test against Trudgill's theory, and it was shown that the theory is a step towards unravelling the processes that are unravelled when dialects meet in a new location. The data presented extends Trudgill's model in three respects, and these changes will need to be tested against other variables and settings. It would be interesting to see, whether a re-analysis of the ONZE tape recordings would also fit the revised stage I new, and whether the New Zealand data may possibly be divided into an urban and a rural layer.

11.6 Dating Canadian English: focussing

One question remains to be asked, i.e. when did CanE, in the sense of a focussed variety, come into existence? We said in chapter (6) that LModE changes in the modal complex are unlikely to be categorical changes, but more characteristic of stylistic changes. How are varieties defined regarding to internal criteria? In a recent cross-comparison of around 60 varieties of world Englishes, Kortmann and Schneider (2004: 5) find that "only very few of the formal variants" are confined to some varieties, or possibly even unique to a single variety. In most cases, then, particular distributions of *shared* features are used to distinguish varieties on an internal basis. In this respect, defining early CanE internally on the basis of the distributions of features that are shared with other varieties, e.g. AmE or BrE, is nothing from the ordinary.

I suggested tentatively elsewhere (Dollinger 2006a: 13) that a focussed variety could have existed in Ontario as early as 1825. In the light of the more complete modal data in the present study, this date would match with some changes, e.g. 1st person SHALL and WILL, but not with others, e.g. hypothetical WOULD. We said in section (11.5) that a unique dialect would be expected to have come into existence in the period 1875-1900. Before that date, the new-dialect formation process would have been completed in period 3, 1825-49, only in urban centres.

If we venture farther and try to gauge the "birthday" of Canadian English as a focussed variety, we would probably view focussing as an unconscious process. For the urban layer, the 3-period progression for the suggested Canadian developments, such as the rapid rise of 1st person WILL, epistemic COULD and WILL in passive constructions all show some changes between period 2 and 3, which would suggest 1850 as a start date. This almost coincides with Reverend Geikie's infamous remarks on "Canadian English" as an abhorrent dialect, that named the variety for the first time in his speech from 1857. One could conceive, given this dating, that the beginning focussing process of the new variety might have triggered the infamous speech and that it was no coincidence it was delivered at that point in time. The rural layer, however, was lagging one stage behind. By the end of period 3, we might speak of Canadian English as such in urban areas, which still had to undergo further unification in rural areas. These focussing processes after 1850, I suggest, were partly conscious processes that were powered by political developments such as Confederation. By 1900, both urban and rural layers would have largely merged. The oldest data from apparent-time studies picks up this focussing development in the 1920s, which was by then further reinforced by the political events during World War I and ensuing Canadian national pride (Chambers 1995a: 165).

11.7 Further research avenues

This completes the descriptive summary and interpretation of modal usage in early Ontario in light of the theory of new-dialect formation. A few strands of inquiry will need to be left for future studies. While we reviewed the external history in detail and found a number of immigrant groups that are of importance, the present study used a maximum of three benchmark varieties for comparison with CanE, and in some cases only one. While historical corpora of the Irish, Scots, Gaelic speakers, German, Dutch, First Nations would be highly desirable, the fact that there is no machine-readable corpus of early 19th AmE available at present, is the most obvious desideratum. Once this gap is filled by either ARCHER-II (Meyer 2002: 142) or the *Corpus of Early American English* (Kytö 2004: 132f), a more complete diachronic picture of these forms in North American English can emerge. Before then, however, no developmental scenario of CanE will be complete.

In this respect, data from some immigrant groups promise to show contact phenomena in early Ontario. In terms of language contact, this would be, among others, the German, Scots Gaelic and Dutch loyalists in period 1. The role of French influence in the areas bordering Quebec or in the Detroit-Windsor region would also promise an interesting contact study. Concerning dialect contact, input corpora of early 19th-century Scotland, Ireland, Ulster and Northern England are the most urgent desiderata in relation to early OntE.

While the present study has taken first steps in this direction, it is self-evident that better data might qualify some of its findings.

The notion of a colonial lag was shown not to apply to all modal auxiliaries, and it would probably be best to discard it, much along the lines of Görlach (1987), and replace it with empirical cross-comparisons for particular variables in various varieties, as shown in figures (11.1) and (11.2), which are reproduced from the empirical part.

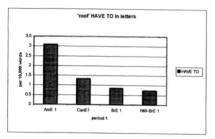

Figure 11.1: Reproduction of figure (8.1)   *Figure 11.2: Reproduction of figure (9.4)*

With data from LModE input varieties, rankings for conservative and progressive behaviours could be established for particular variables, as shown in figures (11.1) and (11.2) for HAVE TO and 1st person SHALL. When accumulated, this method of comparison would finally provide assessments of the status of a given variety for a given area of inquiry (phonology, morphology, syntax, possibly overall) at a given point in time.

To further test new-dialect formation theory, it would seem worthwhile to break down the data more closely than could be done in the present study and to link it with corpora from the input areas referred to above. With data of this kind, we should be able to put the theory of dialect mixing under greater scrutiny. With the three modifications offered, however, Trudgill's theory was not falsified in the present study. On the contrary, it provided a good scenario for approaches to new-dialect formation in early Ontario.

As can be seen from appendix (6), the present study did not include semi-modal auxiliaries that played a minor role in the period under investigation, but are of great importance in more recent changes in the English modal complex today. However, to trace their early development back into LModE is left for further enquiry.

I hope to have shown that the diachronic study of Canadian English reveals insights that are needed to tell the story of a given LModE variable, such as the modal auxiliaries, in full. These more complete stories would challenge and relativize, in some cases even refute, popular concepts like 'colonial lag'. Trudgill's (2004) theory of new-dialect formation provides a good framework for such enterprises, and, as was shown in the present case study, has great potential, with minor adaptations, to increase our understanding of the developmental processes of colonial Englishes and other varieties.

12 APPENDICES

Appendix 1: Corpus of Early Ontario English

	period	newspapers	diaries	(semi-)official letters
1	1776 - 1799	Upper Canada Gazette, ca. 2,800 Canada Constellation, ca. 1,700	Benjamin Smith, ca. 1,800 Anne Powell, ca. 6,200	various authors, ca. 100 letters
		sum: 4,500 words	**sum: 8,000 words**	**sum: 15,000 words**
2	1800 - 1824	Upper Canada Guardian, ca. 8,200 Upper Canada Gazette, ca. 5,000 Kingston Gazette, ca. 1,400	Benjamin Smith, ca. 8,500 Ely Playter, ca. 8,500 *Eleanora Hallen, ca. 3,700 (not incl. in pC)*	various authors, ca. 100 letters
		sum: 14,600 words	**sum: 20,700 words**	**sum: 15,000 words**
3	1825 - 1849	Upper Canada Gazette, ca. 8,500 Niagara Argus, ca. 4,500 Gore Gazette, ca. 3,000	Sophia MacNab, ca. 11,400 *Charlotte Harris, ca. 9,200*	various authors, ca. 100 letters
		sum: 16,000 words	**sum: 20,600 words**	**sum: 15,000 words**
4	1850 - 1874	Hamilton Gazette, ca. 6,000 Perth Courier, ca. 7,500	*Charlotte Harris, ca. 8,200* Sophia Harris, ca. 12,500	various authors, ca. 100 letters
		sum: 13,500 words	**sum: 20,700 words**	**sum: 15,000 words**
5	1875 - 1899	London Free Press, ca. 8,500 Wingham Times, ca. 2,500	Fanny Chadwick, ca. 10,000 Lucy Harris, ca. 10,000 Amelia Harris, ca. 1,000	various authors, ca. 100 letters
		sum: 11,000 words	**sum: 21,000 words**	**sum: 15,000 words**
		sum total: ca. 59,600 words	**sum total: ca. 91,000 words**	**sum total: ca. 75,000 words**

Textual sources of the Corpus of Early Ontario English. *CONTE-pC (grey shaded), and CONTE (provisional design): periods, texts and sample sizes (number of words). CONTE-pC size: ca. 125,000 words; CONTE size: ca. 225,000 words.*

Period	SIN-speakers	Lower Class	Middle Class
1	2,200	3,200	11,700
2	1,700	1,000	14,000
3	1,000	3,100	12,000

Sample sizes for SIN-speakers and social class subsections.

Appendix 2: Ontario names

Names for the geographical area officially known as Ontario since the Canadian Confederation in 1867 (sources Francis, Jones and Smith 2000; Bothwell 1986, Lower 1970)

Year	Legislation	Name of present-day Ontario	Remarks
1763	Treaty of Paris	Part of Rupert's Land	Claimed by the Hudson's Bay Company
1774	Quebec Act	Part of Province of Quebec	Incorporated (annexed) into the enlarged (old) Province of Quebec in an attempt to prevent American land taking west of Montreal, including present-day Ohio, Indiana, Michigan, Illinois and Wisconsin (White 1985: 51).
1791	Constitutional Act	*Upper Canada*	Founded as response to loyalist American immigration
1841	Act of Union	*Canada West*	Part of the United Province of Canada, with Ontario being referred to as Canada West, Quebec as Canada East
1867	British North America Act	*Ontario*	Ontario, as a result of the Confederation of the "Dominion of Canada", consisting at first of Ontario, Quebec, New Brunswick and Nova Scotia

Appendix 3: Immigration data

Appendix 3.1: British Isles immigration
Emigration from British Isels to major non-European destinations. Based on Akenson (1999: 11, table 1, and 12, table 2; unrevised data; the BNA and USA are data identical with Cowan 1961: 288)

Year	to British North America (BNA) = Canada	% from Irish ports to BNA	to the USA	to Australia
1815	680		1,209	N/A
1816	3,370		9,022	N/A
1817	9,797		10,280	N/A
1818	15,136		12,429	N/A
1819	23,534		10,674	N/A
1820	17,921		6,745	N/A
1821	12,955		4,958	320
1822	16,013		4,137	875
1823	11,355		5,032	543
1824	8,774		5,152	780
1825	8,741	78.3	5,551	485
1826	12,818	81.8	7,063	903
1827	12,648	72.2	14,526	713
1828	12,084	55.4	12,817	1,056
1829	13,307	57.9	15,678	2,016
1830	30,574	63.3	24,887	1,242
1831	58,067	70.6	23,418	1,561
1832	66,339	55.9	32,782	3,733
1833	28,808	60.5	29,109	4,093
1834	40,060	71.4	33,074	2,800
1835	15,573	60.7	26,720	1,860
1836	34,226	56.6	37,774	3,124
1837	29,884	75.2	36,770	5,054
1838	4,577	49.9	14,332	14,021
1839	12,658	71.0	33,536	15,786
1840	32,293	74.1	40,642	15,850
1841	38,164	63.1	45,017	32,625
1842	54,123	61.7	64,852	8,534
1843	23,518	46.3	28,335	3,478
1844	22,924	54.1	43,660	2,229
1845	31,803	62.7	58,538	830
TOTAL	702,724	N/A (63.9 avg.)	698,719	124,511
Average per annum	22,688.5		22,539.3	4,980.4

Appendix 3.2: Arrivals at Quebec

Arrivals at the port of Quebec from the British Isles, Continental Europe and the Maritimes Colonies, 1829-1855 (source: Cowan 1961: 289)

Year	England	Ireland	Scotl.	Cont. Europe	Mari-times	TOTAL	Engl. %	Irel. %	Scotl. %	Eur. %	Marit. %	TOT. %
1829	3565	9614	2643	0	123	15945	22.36	60.29	16.58	0.00	0.77	100
1830	6799	18300	2450	0	451	28000	24.28	65.36	8.75	0.00	1.61	100
1831	10343	34133	5354	0	424	50254	20.58	67.92	10.65	0.00	0.84	100
1832	17481	28204	5500	15	546	51746	33.78	54.50	10.63	0.03	1.06	100
1833	5198	12013	4196	0	345	21752	23.90	55.23	19.29	0.00	1.59	100
1834	6799	19206	4591	0	339	30935	21.98	62.09	14.84	0.00	1.10	100
1835	3067	7108	2127	0	225	12527	24.48	56.74	16.98	0.00	1.80	100
1836	12188	12590	2224	485	235	27722	43.97	45.42	8.02	1.75	0.85	100
1837	5580	14538	1509	0	274	21901	25.48	66.38	6.89	0.00	1.25	100
1838	990	1456	547	0	273	3266	30.31	44.58	16.75	0.00	8.36	100
1839	1586	5113	485	0	255	7439	21.32	68.73	6.52	0.00	3.43	100
1840	4567	16291	1144	0	232	22234	20.54	73.27	5.15	0.00	1.04	100
1841	5970	18317	3559	0	240	28086	21.26	65.22	12.67	0.00	0.85	100
1842	12191	25532	6095	0	556	44374	27.47	57.54	13.74	0.00	1.25	100
1843	6499	9728	5006	0	494	21727	29.91	44.77	23.04	0.00	2.27	100
1844	7698	9993	2234	0	217	20142	38.22	49.61	11.09	0.00	1.08	100
1845	8833	14208	2174	0	160	25375	34.81	55.99	8.57	0.00	0.63	100
1846	9163	21049	1645	896	0	32753	27.98	64.27	5.02	2.74	0.00	100
1847	31505	54310	3747	0	0	89562	35.18	60.64	4.18	0.00	0.00	100
1848	6034	16582	3086	1395	842	27939	21.60	59.35	11.05	4.99	3.01	100
1849	8980	23126	4984	436	968	38494	23.33	60.08	12.95	1.13	2.51	100
1850	9887	17976	2879	849	701	32292	30.62	55.67	8.92	2.63	2.17	100
1851	9677	22381	7042	870	1106	41076	23.56	54.49	17.14	2.12	2.69	100
1852	9276	15983	5477	7256	1184	39176	23.68	40.80	13.98	18.52	3.02	100
1853	9585	14417	4745	7456	496	36699	26.12	39.28	12.93	20.32	1.35	100
1854	18175	16165	6446	11537	857	53180	34.18	30.40	12.12	21.69	1.61	100
1855	6754	4106	4859	4864	691	21274	31.75	19.30	22.84	22.86	3.25	100
1856	10353	1688	2794	7343	261	22439	46.14	7.52	12.45	32.72	1.16	100
1857	15471	2016	3218	11368	24	32097	48.20	6.28	10.03	35.42	0.07	100
1858	6441	1153	1424	3578	241	12837	50.18	8.98	11.09	27.87	1.88	100
1859	4846	417	793	2722	0	8778	55.21	4.75	9.03	31.01	0.00	100

Appendix 3.3: First land surveys

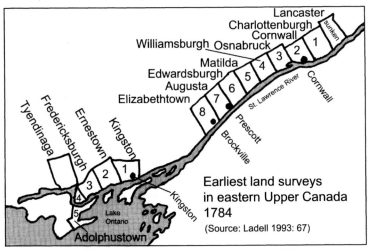

First land surveys in eastern Upper Canada 1784
The surveyed townships were first referred to by numbers, then by names
(source Ladell 1993: 67, fig. 5.3)

Appendix 3.4: Ontario districts

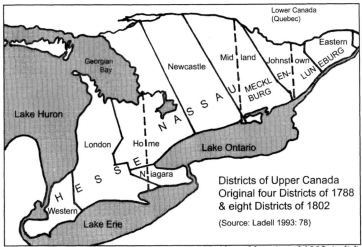

Administrative districts in Ontario in 1788 (dotted lines) and 1802 (solid)
(source Ladell 1993: 78, fig. 6.2)

Appendix 4: Demographic studies around 1812

District	Main town(s)	Gourlay's data	Smith's data
Western District	Sandwich (Windsor), Detroit	*no relevant information*	Sandwich: principally French
London District	London, Ont.	Norwich: 10 families from NY 1 from Nova Scotia (Quakers)	Woodhouse: NJ, NY, PA; Charlotteville: NJ, NY, PA Walsingham: majority Dutch Windham: US Oxford: NY, VT & other US Norwich: mostly NY (Quakers) Talbot settlement: almost all US
Niagara District	Niagara, Niagara-on-the-Lake	*no relevant information*	*no relevant information*
Gore District	Hamilton	*no relevant information*	*not mentioned*
Home District	Toronto	no feedback received	*no relevant information*
Newcastle District	Peterbor-ough	*no relevant information*	*no relevant information*
Midland District	Belleville, Kingston, Picton, Wellington	*no relevant information*	*no relevant information*
Johnstown District	Perth, Prescott	Perth: 3 families, 1 man from Perth (Scot) 5 fam., 1 man (Lanark, Scot.), 1 fam. (Murray ?) 2 fam. (Ayrshire, Scot) 3 single men (Forfar, Scot) 1 man fr. (Dumfries, Wales) 1 widow, 6 kids, (Yorksh., N-Engl) 1 man (Berwicksh., N-Engl/Scot) 3 fam. (Edinburgh, Scot)	*no relevant information*
Ottawa District	Ottawa	(upper) Lancaster: Scottish (open-ing roads in 1816); an Irish mill owner is mentioned Longeuil: from US	*not mentioned*
Eastern District	Cornwall	*no relevant information*	*no relevant information*

Demographic information on origins of settlers in Gourlay (1822) and Smith (1813) around the War of 1812.

Appendix 5: Social networks in early Ontario

Two schematic depictions of a typical network of letter writers in early Ontario, based on CONTE-pC:

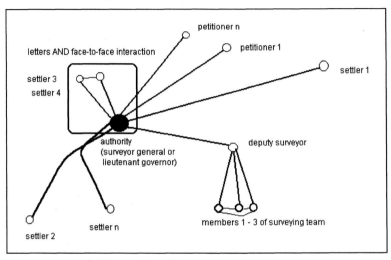

(a) Network based on writer-recipient structure

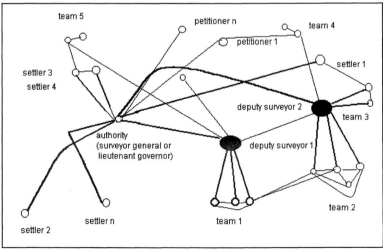

(b) Network based on face-to-face communication

While scenario (a) is a reflection of the sender-receiver relationship of the letters in CONTE (all of which are addressed to an authority), scenario (b) rearranges the network on the basis of face-to-face interaction. Deputy surveyors, i.e. the land surveyors in the field, were among the most mobile people in early Ontario, and would be likely agents for the transmission of linguistic changes between surveying teams, settlers and governmental employees. This is why scenario (b) is the more appropriate reconstruction.

Appendix 6: Semi-Modals in early CanE

Some LModE semi-modal expression in CanE. HAVE TO is discussed in the present study and provides a benchmark for comparison.

per 10,000 words	CanE1	CanE2	CanE3
ABLE TO	1.81	1.55	1.92
ABOUT TO	0.00	0.44	0.58
APT TO	0.00	0.22	0.19
BE TO	5.78	5.09	5.58
GOING TO	0.36	0.22	1.73
HAD BETTER	0.00	0.00	0.58
HAD RATHER	0.00	0.00	0.19
HAVE GOT	0.00	0.00	0.00
HAVE TO	1.08	2.43	3.46
LIKELY TO	0.72	0.44	0.00
NEED (TO)	0.00	0.00	0.00
OBLIGED TO	3.61	0.44	3.65
SHOULD/WOULD RATHER	0.00	0.00	0.38
SUPPOSED TO	0.00	0.00	1.15
WANT TO	0.36	0.00	0.58

BE TO figures most prominently and is employed to express arrangements of some sort. Note also that GOING TO is gaining ground, while ABLE TO seems to have reached a stable incidence already by period 1.

Appendix 7: Statistics for CAN (COULD) / MAY (MIGHT)

Chi–square levels are significant when greater than 3.84 (95% level) and follow the model laid out in Nelson, Wallis and Arts (2002). Following Woods *et al.* (1986: 144) and as shown elsewhere (Dollinger forthc.), chi-square testing will be provided for tables which include cells of less than five occurrences. They will be compared with Fisher Exact Test results (calculated at http://home.clara.net/sisa/fisher.htm), which are given preference in cases where they disagree (e.g. see AmE at the bottom of this page. In Fisher's Exact Test, significance is reached when p-values are lower than 0.05.

Appendix 7.1

Negative contexts

	CAN	MAY
CanE	49	5
BrE	63	5

Chi-square = 0.02 < 3.84 i.e. <u>not</u> significant.

Affirmative contexts

	CAN	MAY
CanE	112	180
BrE	89	168

Chi-square = 0.52 < 3.84 i.e. <u>not</u> significant.

Negative contexts

	CAN	MAY
CanE	49	5
AmE	7	2

Chi-square = 0.15 < 3.84 i.e. <u>not</u> significant.
Fischer = 0.26 > 0.05, i.e. <u>not</u> significant.

Affirmative contexts

	CAN	MAY
CanE	112	180
AmE	20	50

Chi-square = 1.48 < 3.84 i.e. <u>not</u> significant.

CanE exhibits no significant variation in comparison to AmE and BrE for variables CAN and MAY.

CanE

	MAY	CAN
Aff.	180	112
Neg.	5	49

Chi-square = 23.38 > 3.84 i.e. <u>significant</u>.

BrE

	MAY	CAN
Aff.	168	89
Neg.	5	63

Chi-square = 34.00 > 3.84 i.e. <u>significant</u>.

AmE

	MAY	CAN
Aff.	50	20
Neg.	2	7

Chi-square = 2.93 < 3.84 i.e. <u>not</u> significant.
Fisher = 0.006 < 0.05, i.e. <u>significant</u>

The choice of CAN and MAY is affected by affirmative and negative contexts in CanE and BrE, as well as in AmE (Fisher Exact).

Appendix 7.2

CanE

	MIGHT	COULD
Aff.	53	74
Neg.	4	57

Chi-square = 16.81 > 3.84 i.e. <u>significant</u>.

COULD

	Aff.	Neg.
CanE	74	57
AmE	73	57

Chi-square = 0.001 < 3.84 i.e. <u>not</u> significant.

BrE

	MIGHT	COULD
Aff.	74	73
Neg.	5	57

Chi-square = 20.62 > 3.84 i.e. <u>significant</u>.

MIGHT

	Aff.	Neg.
CanE	53	4
BrE	74	5

Chi-square = 0.002 < 3.84 i.e. <u>not</u> significant.

Appendix 7.3

MAY and MIGHT in affirmative contexts in LModE:

	MAY	MIGHT
CanE	180	53
BrE	168	74

Chi-square = 0.99 < 3.84 i.e. <u>not</u> significant.

	MAY	MIGHT
CanE	180	53
AmE	50	11

Chi-square = 0.14 < 3.84 i.e. <u>not</u> significant.

	MAY	MIGHT
BrE	168	74
AmE	50	11

Chi-square = 1.07 < 3.84 i.e. <u>not</u> significant.

Appendix 7.4

Absolute numbers for CAN and MAY in three varieties. The data is presented by genre, d = diary, l = letters, and n = newspapers, and period, 1 = 1776[100]-1799, 2 = 1800-1824, 3 = 1825-1849.

		d1	d2	d3	l1	l2	l3	n1	n2	n3
CanE	CAN	2	0	4	18	25	14	2	14	11
	MAY	2	0	1	16	10	15	8	24	25
BrE	CAN	5		5	24		19	16		15
	MAY	12		4	16		8	15		23
AmE	CAN	4			9			5		
	MAY	4			12			17		

'Root possibility' uses in three varieties

---

[100] 1750 for the ARCHER data.

Appendix 7.5

Absolute numbers for CAN and MAY in three varieties. The data is presented by genre, d = diary, l = letters, and n = newspapers, and period, 1 = 1776[101]-1799, 2 = 1800-1824, 3 = 1825-1849.

		d1	d2	d3	l1	l2	l3	n1	n2	n3
CanE	CAN	1	0	2	2	5	3	0	2	3
	MAY	1	0	0	11	5	11	0	0	0
BrE	CAN	2	4		1	3		4	6	
	MAY	2	1		6	2		4	2	
AmE	CAN	0			0			4		
	MAY	1			3			0		

'Permission' uses in three varieties

Appendix 7.6

Root possibility uses of CAN

BrE-d	CAN	MAY
1	5	12
2+3	5	4

Chi-square = 1.04 < 3.84, i.e. not significant.

CanE-l	CAN	MAY
1	18	16
2+3	39	25

Chi-square = 0.24 < 3.84, i.e. not significant.

BrE-n	CAN	MAY
1	16	15
2+3	15	23

Chi-square = 0.56 < 3.84, i.e. not significant.

CanE-d	CAN	MAY
1	2	8
2+3	25	49

Chi-square = 0.52 < 3.84, i.e. not significant.
Fisher = 0.49 > 0.05, i.e. not significant.

n-1	CAN	MAY
CanE	2	8
BrE	16	15

Chi-square = 1.72 < 3.84, i.e. not significant.
Fisher = 0.14 > 0.05, i.e. not significant.

CanE-n	CAN	MAY
1	2	2
2+3	4	1

Chi-square = 0.3 < 3.84, i.e. not significant.
Fisher = 0.52 > 0.05, i.e. not significant.

BrE-l	CAN	MAY
1	24	16
2+3	19	8

Chi-square = 0.27 < 3.84, i.e. not significant.

n-2+3	CAN	MAY
CanE	25	49
BrE	15	23

Chi-square = 0.2 < 3.84, i.e. not significant.

---

[101] 1750 for the ARCHER data.

Appendix 7.7

Permission uses of CAN

CanE-d	CAN	MAY
1	1	1
2+3	1	0

Chi-square = 0.25 < 3.84;
Fisher = 1.0 > 0.05, i.e. not
significant.

BrE-d	CAN	MAY
1	2	2
2+3	4	2

Chi-square = 0.3 < 3.84;
Fisher = 1.0 > 0.05, i.e. not
significant.

1-1	CAN	MAY
CanE	2	11
BrE	1	6

Chi-square = 0.37 < 3.84;
Fisher = 1.0 > 0.05, i.e. not
significant.

CanE-1	CAN	MAY
1	2	11
2+3	8	16

Chi-square = 1.01 < 3.84;
Fisher = 0.44 > 0.05, i.e. not
significant.

BrE-1	CAN	MAY
1	1	6
2+3	3	2

Chi-square = 1.83 < 3.84;
Fisher = 0.22 > 0.05, i.e. not
significant.

1-2+3	CAN	MAY
CanE	8	16
BrE	3	2

Chi-square = 0.78 < 3.84;
Fisher = 0.34 > 0.05, i.e. not
significant.

CanE-n	CAN	MAY
1	0	0
2+3	5	0

Chi-square cannot be calculated; Fisher = 1.0 > 0.05; i.e.
not significant.

BrE-n	CAN	MAY
1	4	4
2+3	6	2

Chi-square = 0.4 < 3.84;
Fisher = 0.61 > 0.05, i.e. not
significant.

Appendix 7.8

Root possibility	CAN	MAY	Permission	CAN	MAY
CanE-1	18	16	CanE-1	2	11
BrE-1	24	16	BrE-1	1	3
CanE 2+3	39	25	CanE 2+3	9	16
BrE 2+3	19	8	BrE 2+3	6	2

Contingency table for letters in CanE and BrE

Appendix 7.9

Incidences of CAN and MAY in section of clearly identified SIN-speakers:

CanE-SIN	CAN	MAY
11	3	0
12	2	1
13	1	2

Appendix 7.10

Select contingency tables in figures (7.14) and (7.15) on COULD and MIGHT

non-past	epistemic COULD	epistemic MIGHT
AmE	12	6
CanE	2	5

Chi-square = 1.31 < 3.84;
Fisher = 0.18 > 0.05, i.e. not significant.

non-past	epistemic COULD	epistemic MIGHT
AmE	12	6
BrE	1	10

Chi-square = 5.05 > 3.84;
Fisher = 0.006 < 0.05, i.e. significant.

AmE	epistemic COULD	epistemic MIGHT
past	1	5
non-past	12	6

Chi-square = 2.08 < 3.84;
Fisher = 0.06 > 0.05 i.e. not significant at 95%, but significant at 80% level (> 1.64).

Appendix 7.11

past	COULD	MIGHT
CanE	22	4
BrE	29	25

Fisher = 0.01 < 0.05, i.e. significant; Fisher is given preference.
Chi-square = 2.63 < 3.84, i.e. not significant, but significant at 80% level (> 1.64).

Appendix 8: Statistics for MUST / HAVE TO

Appendix 8.1

The significance levels indicate that CanE and AmE are similar, whereas CanE and AmE are dissimilar to BrE.

	HAVE TO	MUST
CanE	17	73
AmE	4	26

Chi-square = 0.40 < 3.84;
Fisher = 0.59, i.e. not significant.

	HAVE TO	MUST
CanE	17	73
BrE	2	87

Chi-square = 11.68 > 3.84;
Fisher = 0.0004, i.e. significant.

	HAVE TO	MUST
BrE	2	87
AmE	4	26

Chi-square = 5.47 > 3.84;
Fisher = 0.035, i.e. significant.

Appendix 8.2

Statistical testing relating to figures (8.3) and (8.4):

1	HAVE TO	MUST
CanE	2	11
AmE	2	6

Chi-square = 0.24 < 3.84; Fisher = 0.62, i.e. not significant.

1	HAVE TO	MUST
AmE	2	6
BrE	1	10

Chi-square = 0.74 < 3.84; Fisher = 0.55, i.e. not significant.

1	HAVE TO	MUST
CanE	2	11
BrE	1	10

Chi-square = 0.19 < 3.84; Fisher = 0.99, i.e. not significant.

1	HAVE TO	MUST
BrE	1	10
NW-BrE	22	288

Chi-square = 0.06 < 3.84; Fisher = 0.56, i.e. not significant.

1	HAVE TO	MUST
AmE	2	6
NW-BrE	22	288

Chi-square = 3.32 < 3.84; Fisher = 0.12, i.e. not significant at 95%, but significant at 90% level (> 2.71).

Appendix 8.3

2+3	HAVE TO	MUST
CanE	13	22
BrE	1	15

Chi-square = 3.82 < 3.84, i.e. not significant at 95%, but significant at 90% (> 2.71). Fisher = 0.039 < 0.05 and significant; Fisher is given preference

Appendix 8.4

	CanE-1	CanE 2+3	BrE-1	BrE 2+3	AmE-1
root MUST	17	22	29	15	18
ep. MUST	3	14	10	22	8

CanE-1 to AmE-1: Chi-square = 0.87; Fisher = 0.30, not significant.
CanE-1 to BrE-1: Chi-square = 0.58; Fisher = 0.51, not significant.
BrE-1 to AmE-1: Chi-square = 0.08; Fisher = 0.78, not signficiant.
CanE-1 to CanE2+3: Pearson = 2.23, Fisher = 0.057, not significant.
BrE-1 to BrE 2+3: Pearson = 4.34 significant increase at 95% and 99% levels.

Appendix 9: Statistics for SHALL / WILL

Appendix 9.1

1st person SHALL and WILL in the period 1:

period 1	SHALL	WILL
CanE	22	8
NW-BrE	131	106

Chi-square = 1.52 < 3.84 i.e. not significant at the 95% level.

period 1	SHALL	WILL
AmE	15	7
BrE	25	15

Chi-square = 0.07 < 3.84 i.e. not significant at the 95% level.

period 1	SHALL	WILL
NW-BrE	131	106
BrE	25	15

Chi-square = 0.32 < 3.84 i.e. not significant at the 95% level.

period 1	SHALL	WILL
CanE	22	8
AmE	15	7

Chi-square = 0.05 < 3.84 i.e. not significant at the 95% level.

Appendix 9.2

Increase of WILL in CanE from period 1 to 2+3:

CanE	WILL	SHALL
period 1	8	22
period 2+3	30	28

Chi-square = 3.95 > 3.84 i.e. significant at the 95% level.

CanE and BrE by period

period 1	WILL	SHALL
CanE	8	22
BrE	15	25

Chi-square = 0.61 < 3.84 i.e. not significant at the 95% level.

BrE increase of SHALL

CanE	SHALL	WILL
period 1	25	15
period 2+3	24	8

Chi-square = 0.41 < 3.84 i.e. not significant at the 95% level.

CanE and BrE by period

period 2+3	WILL	SHALL
CanE	30	28
BrE	8	24

Chi-square = 3.49 < 3.81 i.e. not significant at the 95% level, but significant the 90% level (> 2.71).

Appendix 9.3

Contingency tables for chi-square testing of 3rd person SHALL and WILL in syntactic contexts.

overall 3rd p.	SHALL	WILL
CanE-1	9	45
CanE-2+3	8	92

Chi-square = 2.39 < 3.84 i.e. not significant at the 95% level.

active 3rd p.	SHALL	WILL
CanE 1-3	28	292
BrE 1-3	40	241

Chi-square = 3.98 > 3.84 i.e. significant at the 95% level.

passive 3rd p.	SHALL	WILL
CanE-1	7	21
CanE-2	10	40

Chi-square = 0.21 < 3.84 i.e. not significant at the 95% level.

passive 3rd p.	SHALL	WILL
CanE-2	10	40
CanE-3	10	45

Chi-square = 0.05 < 3.84 i.e. not significant at the 95% level.

Appendix 10: Statistics for SHOULD / WOULD / OUGHT TO

Appendix 10.1

	hyp. SHOULD	hyp. WOULD
CanE-1	25	27
BrE-1	23	21

Chi-square = 0.08 < 3.84, i.e. not significant.

	hyp. SHOULD	hyp. WOULD
CanE-2	7	13
BrE-2	2	5

Chi-square = 0.06 < 3.84, Fisher = 0.99 > 0.05, i.e. not significant.

	hyp. SHOULD	hyp. WOULD
CanE-3	25	111
BrE-3	37	114

Chi-square = 1.24 < 3.84, i.e. not significant.

Appendix 10.2

Non-hypotheticals in BrE and CanE

non-hyp.	SHOULD	OUGHT TO
BrE-1	51	13
BrE-2+3	54	17

Chi-square = 0.06 < 3.84 i.e. not significant at the 95% level.

non-hyp.	SHOULD	WOULD
CanE-1	16	23
CanE-2+3	50	96

Chi-square = 0.40 < 3.84 i.e. not significant at the 95% level.

non-hyp.	SHOULD	WOULD
BrE-1	51	48
BrE-2+3	54	47

Chi-square = 0.04 < 3.84 i.e. not significant at the 95% level.

non-hyp.	SHOULD	WOULD
CanE-2+3	50	96
BrE-2+3	54	47

Chi-square = 5.23 > 3.84 i.e. significant at the 95% level.

Appendix 10.3

Hypotheticals in CanE

hyp.	WOULD	SHOULD
period 1	46	14
period 2	45	23

Chi-square = 0.49 < 3.84 i.e. not significant at the 95% level.

hyp.	WOULD	SHOULD
period 2	45	23
period 3	60	20

Chi-square = 6.43 > 3.84 i.e. significant at the 95% level.

Appendix 10.4

Non-hypotheticals in CanE

non-hyp.	WOULD	SHOULD
period 1	23	16
period 2	17	23

Chi-square = 1.06 < 3.84 i.e. not significant at the 95% level.

non-hyp.	WOULD	SHOULD
period 2	17	79
period 3	23	27

Chi-square = 9.61 > 3.84 i.e. significant at the 95% level and > 6.64 significant at 99% level.

non-hyp.	WOULD	OUGHT TO
period 1	23	1
period 2	17	7

Chi-square = 0.90 < 3.84 i.e. not significant at the 95% level. Fisher = 0.048 < 0.05 and significant; Fisher's Exact is given preference.

non-hyp.	WOULD	OUGHT TO
period 2	17	7
period 3	79	6

Chi-square = 1.03 < 3.84 i.e. not significant at the 95% level.

BIBLIOGRAPHY

NB: The addition [CIHM] after the title of reprint historical sources, followed by a number, is the unique microfiche ID of the *Canadian Institute for Reproduction of Historical Manuscripts.*

Aarts, Bas and April McMahon (eds). 2006. *The handbook of English linguistics* [Blackwell Handbooks in Linguistics]. Oxford: Blackwell.

Abraham, Werner. 2002. Modal verbs: epistemics in German and English. In *Modality and its interaction with the verbal system* [Linguistik Aktuell 47], Sjef Barbiers, Frits Beukema and Wim van der Wurff (eds), 19-50. Amsterdam: Benjamins.

Abraham, Werner. 2001. Modals: toward explaining the 'epistemic non-finiteness gap'. In R. Müller and M. Reis (eds), 7-36.

Ahrend, Evelyn R. 1934. Ontario speech. *American Speech* 9: 136-139.

Ade, George. 1961 [1900]. The fable of the Michigan counterfeit who wasn't one thing or the other. In *The ordeal of American English,* C. Merton Babcock (ed.), 11-13. Boston: Houghton Mifflin.

Akenson, Donald H. 1999. *The Irish in Ontario. A study in rural history.* 2nd ed. Montreal: McGill-Queen's University Press.

Alexander, Henry. 1940. *The story of our language.* Toronto: Nelson.

Algeo, John (ed.). 2001a. *The Cambridge history of the English language. Vol. VI: English in North America.* Cambridge: Cambridge University Press.

Algeo, John. 2001b. Volume editor's preface. In J. Algeo (ed.), xv-xxvii.

Allen, Harold B. 1989. Canadian Raising in the Upper Midwest. *American Speech* 64(1): 74-75.

Allen, Harold B. 1980. Review of "Avis, Walter S. and A. M. Kinloch. 1979 [sic!]. Writings on Canadian English. 1972-1975. Toronto" *Journal of English Linguistics* 14(March): 36-39.

Allen, Harold B. (ed.). 1973-76. *Linguistic atlas of the Upper-Midwest.* Minneapolis: University of Minnesota Press.

Allen, Harold B. 1975 [1959]. Canadian-American differences along the middle border. In J. K. Chambers (ed.), 102-108.

Al-Wer, Enam. 2003. New dialect formation: focussing of –kum in Amman. In D. Britain and J. Cheshire (eds), 59-67.

Ammon, Ulrich. 1995. *Die deutsche Sprache in Deutschland, Österreich und der Schweiz. Das Problem der nationalen Varietäten.* Berlin: de Gruyter.

Anon. 1955. Editorial. *Journal of the Canadian Linguistic Association* 1(2 Oct.): 2.

Arnovick, Leslie K. 1997. Proscribed collocations with *shall* and *will*: the eighteenth century (non-)standard reassessed. In D. Stein and J. Cheshire (eds), 135-151.

Arnovick, Leslie K. 1990. *The development of future constructions in English. The pragmatics of modal and temporal* will *and* shall *in Middle English* [Berkeley Insights in Linguistics and Semiotics 2]. New York: Lang.

Arthurs, James. 1988. Terminology vs jargon: Canadian hockey talk. In A. R. Thomas (ed.), 155-163.

Ash, Sharon. 2003. A national survey of North American dialects. In *Needed research in American dialects.* [Publication of the American Dialect Society 88], Dennis Preston (ed.), 57-73. American Dialect Society: Duke University Press.

Avery, Peter, Alexandra D'Arcy and Keren Rice. 2006. Introduction. *Canadian Journal of Linguistics* 51(2&3): 99-104.

Avis, Walter S. 1978a. Canadian English in its North American context. In T. Vincent, G. Parker and S. Bonnycastle (eds), 35-49.

Avis, Walter S. 1978b [1975]. Some French-Canadian loan-words in Canadian English In T. Vincent, G. Parker and S. Bonnycastle (eds), 157-171.

Avis, Walter S. 1978c [1973]. Eskimo words in Canadian English. In T. Vincent, G. Parker and S. Bonnycastle (eds), 142-156.

Avis, Walter S. 1978d [1965]. Problems in the study of Canadian English. In T. Vincent, G. Parker and S. Bonnycastle (eds), 3-12.

Avis, Walter S. 1975 [1954 & 1955]. Speech differences along the Ontario-United States border. In J. K. Chambers (ed.), 67-77.

Avis, Walter S. 1973a. The English language in Canada In *Current trends in linguistics. Vol. 10/1,* Thomas Sebeok (ed.), 40-74. The Hague: Mouton.

Avis, Walter S. 1972a. So Eh? is Canadian, Eh? *Canadian Journal of Linguistics* 17(2): 89-104.

Avis, Walter S. 1972b. The phonemic segments of an Edmonton idiolect. In *Studies in linguistics in honor of Raven I. McDavid, Jr.,* Lawrence M. Davis (ed.), 239-250. Alabama: University of Alabama Press.

Avis, Walter S. 1969a. A note on the speech of Sam Slick In *The Sam Slick anthology,* Reginald E. Watters and Walter S. Avis (eds), xix-xxix. Toronto: Clarke, Irwin & Co.

Avis, Walter S. 1969b. Canadian English [bibliography]. *Canadian Journal of Linguistics* 15(1): 70-73.

Avis, Walter S. 1967. Introduction. In *A dictionary of Canadianisms on historical principles,* Walter S. Avis, Charles Crate, Patrick Drysdale, Douglas Leechman, Matthew H. Scharill and Charles L. Lovell (eds), xii-xv. Toronto: Gage.

Avis, Walter S. (ed.). [1965]. *A bibliography of writings on Canadian English, 1857-1965.* Toronto: Gage.

Avis, Walter S. 1964. Canadian English [bibliography]. *Canadian Journal of Linguistics* 9(2): 120-123.

Avis, Walter. S. 1960. Canadian English / Anglo-Canadien [bibliography]. *Journal of the Canadian Linguistic Association* 6(1, Spring): 87f.

Avis, Walter S. 1958. Canadian English / Anglo-Canadien [bibliography]. *Journal of the Canadian Linguistic Association* 4(1, Spring): 107f.

Avis, Walter S. 1957. Canadian English / Anglo-Canadien [bibliography]. *Journal of the Canadian Linguistic Association* 3(2, Oct.): 97.

Avis, Walter S. 1956a. Speech differences along the Ontario-United States border. III: Pronunciation. *Journal of the Canadian Linguistic Association* 2(1, Mar.): 41-59.

Avis, Walter S. 1956b. Canadian English [bibliography]. *Journal of the Canadian Linguistic Association* 2(2, Oct.): 82.

Avis, Walter S. 1955. Speech differences along the Ontario-United States border. II: Grammar and syntax. *Journal of the Canadian Linguistic Association* 1(1, Mar.): 14-19.

Avis, Walter S. 1954. Speech differences along the Ontario-United States border. I: Vocabulary. *Journal of the Canadian Linguistic Association* 1(1, Oct.): 13-18.

Avis, Walter S. 1950. *The speech of Sam Slick.* MA Thesis, Queen's University, Kingston, Ontario.

Avis, Walter S., Patrick D. Drysdale, Robert J. Gregg, Victoria E. Neufeldt and Matthew H. Scargill (eds). 1983. *Gage Canadian dictionary.* Toronto: Gage.

Avis, Walter S. and A. M. Kinloch (eds). [1978]. *Writings on Canadian English, 1792-1975. An annotated bibliography.* Toronto: Fitzhenry & Whiteside.

Avis, Walter S., Charles Crate, Patrick Drysdale, Douglas Leechman, Matthew
    H. Scharill and Charles L. Lovell (eds). 1967. *A dictionary of Canadianisms
    on historical principles.* Toronto: Gage.
Ayearst, Morley. 1939. A note on Canadian speech. *American Speech* 14: 231-
    233.
Babitch, Rose M. 1988. Diachronic interlinguistic contact as reflected in the
    typological structure of today's Acadian fishermen's terminology. In A. R.
    Thomas (ed.), 121-137.
Babitch, Rose M. 1979. The English of Acadians in the seventeenth century. In
    *Papers from the Third Annual Meeting of the Atlantic Provinces Linguistic
    Association,* Moshe Starets (ed.), 96-115. Church Point, PEI: Université de
    St. Anne.
Baeyer, C. V. [1977]. *The ancestry of Canadian English* (pre-publication
    draft). [no place/publisher]. Located at UBC Libraries.
Bähr, Dieter. 1981. *Die englische Sprache in Kanada. Eine Analyse des* Survey
    of Canadian English [Tübinger Beiträge zur Linguistik 165]. Tübingen:
    Narr.
Bähr, Dieter. 1977. *A bibliography on writings on the English language in
    Canada from 1857-1976.* Heidelberg: Winter.
Bailey, Richard W. 1996. *Nineteenth-century English.* Ann Arbor: University
    of Michigan Press.
Bailey, Richard W. 1991. Dialects of Canadian English. *English Today* 27: 20-
    25.
Bailey, Richard W. 1982. The English language in Canada. In *English as a
    world language,* Richard W. Bailey and Manfred Görlach (eds), 134-176.
    Ann Arbor: University of Michigan Press.
Bailey, Richard W. 1981. Haliburton's eye and ear. *Canadian Journal of
    Linguistics* 26: 90-101.
Barber, Katherine (ed.). ^{2}2004 [^{1}1998]. *Canadian Oxford dictionary.* 2nd ed.
    Toronto: Oxford University Press.
Barbiers, Sjef. 2002. Modality and polarity. In *Modality and its interaction
    with the verbal system* [Linguistik Aktuell 47], Sjef Barbiers, Frits Beukema
    and Wim van der Wurff (eds), 51-73. Amsterdam: Benjamins.
Barron, Anne and Klaus P. Schneider (eds). 2005. *The pragmatics of Irish
    English* [Trends in Linguistics. Studies and Monographs 164]. Berlin:
    Mouton de Gruyter.
Bateman, Stanley C. 1975. *Survey of Canadian English. A comparison of the
    language patterns of English-speaking New Brunswickers at two different
    levels of education.* M.Ed. Thesis, University of New Brunswick.

Bausenhart, Werner. 1989. *German immigration and assimilation in Ontario, 1793-1918*. New York: Legas.

Beal, Joan C. 2004. *English in modern times 1700-1945*. London: Arnold Hodder.

Bengtsson, Elna. 1956. *The language and vocabulary of Sam Slick*. Part 1. [Uppsala Canadian Studies 5]. Copenhagen: Munksgaard.

Berger, Christine M. 2005. *The dialect topography of Canada: method, coverage, interface and analyses*. MA Thesis, University of Vienna.

Bergs, Alexander. 2005. *Social networks and historical sociolinguistics. Studies in morphosyntactic variation in the Paston Letters (1421-1503)* [Topics in English Linguistics 51]. Berlin: Mouton de Gruyter.

Biber, Douglas. 2004. Modal use across registers and time. In *Studies in the history of the English language II. Unfolding conversations* [Topics in English Linguistics 45], Anne Curzan and Kimberly Emmonds (eds), 189-216. Berlin: Mouton de Gruyter.

Biber, Douglas, Stig Johansson, Geoffrey Leech, Susan Conrad and Edward Finegan. 1999. *Longman grammar of spoken and written English*. Harlow: Pearson.

Biber, Douglas, Susan Conrad and Randi Reppen. 1998. *Corpus linguistics. Investigating language structure and use*. Cambridge: Cambridge University Press.

Biber, Douglas, Edward Finegan and Dwight Atkinson. 1994. ARCHER and its challenges: compiling and exploring a representative corpus of historical English registers. In *Creating and using English language corpora* [Language and Computers 13], Udo Fries, Gunnel Tottie and Peter Schneider (eds), 1-13. Amsterdam: Rodopi.

Biber, Douglas and Edward Finegan. 1995. The ARCHER Corpus. *ICAME Journal* 19: 148.

Blain, Eleanor M. 1989. *The Bungee dialect of the Red River settlement*. MA Thesis, University of Manitoba.

Bloomfield, Morton W. 1948. Canadian English and its relation to eighteenth century American speech. *Journal of English and Germanic Philology* 47: 59-66 [reprinted in Chambers (1975a), 3-11].

Boberg, Charles. 2005a. The Canadian Shift in Montreal. *Language Variation and Change* 17(2): 133-154.

Boberg, Charles. 2005b. The North American Regional Vocabulary Survey: new variables and methods in the study of North American English. *American Speech* 80(1): 22-60.

Boberg, Charles. 2004a. Ethnic patterns in the phonetics of Montreal English. *Journal of Sociolinguistics* 8(4): 538-568.

Boberg, Charles. 2004b. English in Canada: phonology. In E. Schneider *et al.* (eds), 351-365.

Boberg, Charles. 2000. Geolinguistic diffusion and the U.S.-Canada border. *Language Variation and Change* 12: 1-24.

Bondesen, Sheila. 2004. *English spelling variation in Canadian newspapers.* MA Thesis, University of Laval, Quebec.

Bothwell, Robert. 1986. *A short history of Ontario.* Edmonton: Hurtig.

Boyd, Julian and Zelda Boyd. 1980. Shall and will. In *The state of language,* Leonard Michaels and Christopher Ricks (eds), 43-53. Berkeley: University of California Press.

Brinton, Laurel J. 1991. The origin and development of quasimodal *HAVE TO* in English. Ms., University of British Columbia; online: http://www.english.ubc.ca/~lbrinton/haveto.pdf (27 May 2005).

Brinton, Laurel J. 1988. *The development of English aspectual systems. Aspectualizers and post-verbal particles* [Cambridge Studies in Linguistics 49]. Cambridge: Cambridge University Press.

Brinton, Laurel J. and Leslie K. Arnovick. 2006. *The English language. A linguistic introduction.* Oxford: Oxford University Press.

Brinton, Laurel J. and Margery Fee. 2001. Canadian English. In *The Cambridge History of the English Language. Vol. VI. English in North America,* John Algeo (ed.), 422-440. Cambridge: Cambridge University Press.

Britain, David and Jenny Cheshire (eds). 2003. *Social dialectology. In honour of Peter Trudgill* [Impact 16]. Amsterdam: Benjamins.

Britton, Derek (ed.). 1996. *English historical linguistics 1994* [Current Issues in Linguistic Theory 135]. Amsterdam: Benjamins.

Brown, Roger and Albert Gilman. 1989. Politeness theory and Shakespeare's four major tragedies. *Language in Society* 18: 159-212.

Brunger, Alan G. 1990. The distribution of Scots and Irish in Upper Canada, 1851-1871. *Canadian Geographer* 34: 252.

Burant, Jim. 1985. s.v. 'Print industry'. In: *The Canadian encyclopedia,* James H. Marsh (ed.), 1482-1483. Edmonton: Hurtig.

Burnett, Wendy. 2006. Linguistic resistance on the Maine-New Brunswick border. *Canadian Journal of Linguistics* 51(2&3): 161-176.

Burnett, Wendy. 1992-2003. *Linguistic atlas of the Atlantic Provinces. Volumes 1-6,* Ms., Mount Allison University.

Burnett, Wendy. 2001. New Brunswick English and the American standard: evidence of convergence. *Proceedings of the Twenty-fifth Annual Meeting of the Atlantic Provinces Linguistic Association* 25: 60-70.

Buss, Helen M. 1991. *Canadian women's autobiography in English: an introductory guide for researchers and teachers* [RIAW Papers 24]. Ottawa: CRIAW.

Butler, Gary R. and Ruth King. 1984. Conversational strategies in a bilingual context: code-switching in L'Anse-à-Canards, Newfoundland. In *Papers from the Eighth Annual Meeting of the Atlantic Provinces Linguistic Association*, J. Barnstead, B. E. Gesner, W. T. Gordon and M. Holder (eds), 11-18. Halifax: Dalhousie University.

Butters, Ronald B. 2001. Grammatical structure. In *The Cambridge history of the English language. Vol. IV: 1776-1997*, Suzanne Romaine (ed.), 325-339. Cambridge: Cambridge University Press.

Bybee, Joan and Suzanne Fleischman (eds). 1995. *Modality in grammar and discourse.* Amsterdam: Benjamins.

Cameron, Wendy, Sheila Haines and Mary McDougall Maude. 2000. *English immigrant voices. Labourer's letters from Upper Canada in the 1830s.* Montreal: McGill-Queen's University Press.

Campbell, Art. 1986. *Words and expressions of the Gaspé.* Grand Cascadia, Que.: Privately published.

Campbell, Patrick. 1937 [1792]. *Travels in the interior inhabited parts of North America in the years 1791 and 1792* [Champlain Society Publication 23], H. H. Langton (ed.). Toronto: Champlain Society.

Campey, Lucille H. 2005. *The Scottish pioneers of Upper Canada, 1784-1855: Glengarry and beyond.* Toronto: Natural Heritage/Natural History.

Canniff, William. 1869 [1971]. *The settlement of Upper Canada.* Toronto: Dudley and Burns.

Canniff, William. 1872. *History of the Province of Ontario (Upper Canada)* [CIHM 26811]. Toronto: A. H. Hovey.

Carroll, Susanne. 1983. Remarks on FOR-TO infintives. *Linguistic Analysis* 12(4): 415-451.

Carter, Kathryn. 1997. *Diaries in English by women in Canada, 1753-1995: an annotated bibliography.* [Feminist Voices 4]. Ottawa: CRIAW.

Casselman, Bill. 1995. *Casselman's Canadian words. A comic browse through words and folk saying invented by Canadians.* Toronto: Copp, Clark.

Chamberlain, A. F. 1890. Dialect research in Canada. *Dialect Notes.* 2: 43-56.

Chambers, J. K. forthc.b. English in Canada. In *Varieties of World English*, Tometro Hopkins (ed.). London: Cassell Academic.

Chambers, J. K. forthc.a. A linguistic fossil: positive *any more* in the Golden Horseshoe. In *LACUS Forum 33: Variation*, Peter Reich, William J. Sullivan, Arle R. Lommel (eds), Houston, TX: LACUS.

Chambers, J. K. 2006. Canadian Raising retrospect and prospect. *Canadian Journal of Linguistics* 51(2&3): 105-118.

Chambers, J. K. 2005. Sociolinguistics and the language faculty. Canadian Journal of Linguistics 50(1&2&3&4): 215-39.

Chambers, J. K. 2004. 'Canadian Dainty': the rise and decline of Briticisms in Canada. In R. Hickey (ed.), 224-241.

Chambers, J. K. 2002. Dynamics of dialect convergence. *Journal of Sociolinguistics* 6(1): 117-130.

Chambers, J. K. 2000. Region and language variation. *English World-Wide* 21(2): 169-199.

Chambers, J. K. 1998a. English: Canadian varieties. In *Language in Canada*, John Edwards (ed.), 252-272. Cambridge: Cambridge University Press.

Chambers, J. K. 1998b. Social embedding of changes in progress. *Journal of English Linguistics* 26(1): 5-36.

Chambers, J. K. 1995a. The Canada-U.S. border as a vanishing isogloss: the evidence of *chesterfield. Journal of English Linguistics* 23: 155-166.

Chambers, J. K. 1995b. *Sociolinguistic theory.* Oxford: Blackwell.

Chambers, J. K. 1994. An introduction to dialect topography. *English World-Wide* 15: 35-53.

Chambers, J. K. 1993. 'Lawless and vulgar innovations': Victorian views on Canadian English. In S. Clarke (ed.), 1-26.

Chambers, J. K. 1991. Canada. In *English around the world. Social perspectives*, Jenny Cheshire (ed.), 89-107. Cambridge: Cambridge University Press.

Chambers, J. K. 1989. Canadian Raising: blocking, fronting, etc. *American Speech* 64(1): 75-88.

Chambers, J. K. 1988. Acquisition of phonological variants. In A. R. Thomas (ed.), 650-665.

Chambers, J. K. 1987a. Introduction: comparative sociolinguistics of (aw) fronting. *Toronto Working Papers in Linguistics* 7: 104-108.

Chambers, J. K. 1987b. The complementizer 'cep'fer. *American Speech* 62: 378-379.

Chambers, J. K. 1986. Three kinds of standard in Canadian English. In W. C. Lougheed (ed.), 1-19.

Chambers, J. K. 1985. Group and individual participation in a sound change in progress. In *Methods/Méthodes V. 1984. Papers from the Fifth International Conference on Methods in Dialectology*, Henry J. Warkentyne (ed.), 119-136. Victoria, B.C.: University of Victoria.

Chambers, J. K. 1981a. The Americanization of Canadian Raising. In *Papers from the Parasession on Language and Behavior. Chicago Linguistic Society. May 1-2, 1981*, Carrie S. Masek, Roberta A. Hendrick and Mary F. Miller (eds), 20-35. Chicago: University of Chicago.

Chambers, J. K. 1981b. 'Lawless and vulgar innovations': Victorian views of Canadian English. *Toronto Working Papers in Linguistics* 2: 13-44.

Chambers, J. K. 1980. Linguistic variation and Chomsky's 'homogeneous speech community'. In *Papers from the Fourth Annual Meeting of the Atlantic Provinces Linguistic Association. Univeristy of New Brunswick, Frederickton, N.B., 12-13 December 1980*, A. Murray Kinloch and A. B. House (eds), 1-31. Fredericton: University of New Brunswick.

Chambers, J. K. (ed.). 1979a. *The languages of Canada* [Série 3L Series 3]. Montréal: Didier.

Chambers, J. K. 1979b. Introduction. In J. K. Chambers (ed.), 1-11.

Chambers, J. K. 1979c. Canadian English. In J. K. Chambers (ed.), 168-204.

Chambers, J. K. (ed.). 1975a. *Canadian English. Origins and structures.* Toronto: Methuen.

Chambers, J. K. 1975b. [1974]. The Ottawa Valley twang. In J. K. Chambers (ed.), 55-60.

Chambers, J. K. 1975c. Introduction. In J. K. Chambers (ed.), vii-ix.

Chambers, J. K. 1973. Canadian Raising. *Canadian Journal of Linguistics* 18(2): 113-135.

Chambers, J. K. and Troy Heisler. 1999. Dialect Topography of Québec City English. *Canadian Journal of Linguistics* 44(1): 23-48.

Chambers, J. K. and Peter Trudgill. 1998. *Dialectology.* 2nd ed. Cambridge: Cambridge University Press.

Chambers, J. K. and Margaret F. Hardwick. 1986. Comparative sociolinguistics of a sound change in Canadian English. *English World-Wide* 7: 124-146.

Chambers, J. K., Peter Trudgill and Natalie Schilling-Estes (eds). *The handbook of language variation and change.* Oxford: Blackwell.

Cichocki, Wladyslav. 1997. Canadian English. [Review of S. Clarke (ed.). 1993]. *American Speech* 72(3): 314-318.

Cichocki, Wladyslaw. 1988. Uses of dual scaling in social dialectology: multidimensional analysis of vowel variation. In A. R. Thomas, 187-199.

Cichocki, Wladyslaw. 1986. *Linguistic applications of dual scaling in variation studies.* PhD Thesis, Univeristy of Toronto.

Clarke, George E. 1999. The career of Black English: a literary sketch. In L. Falk and M. Harry (eds), 122-145.

Clarke, John. 2001. *Land, power and economics on the frontier of Upper Canada.* Montreal: McGill-Queen's University Press.

Clarke, Sandra. 2006. *Nooz or nyooz?*: the complex construction of Canadian identity. *Canadian Journal of Linguistics* 51(2&3): 225-246.

Clarke, Sandra. 2004a. Newfoundland English: phonology, In E. Schneider *et al.* (eds), 366-382.

Clarke, Sandra. 2004b. Newfoundland English: morphology and syntax. In B. Kortmann *et al.* (eds), 303-318.

Clarke, Sandra. 1997a. English verbal –*s* revisited: the evidence from Newfoundland. *American Speech* 72: 227-259.

Clarke, Sandra. 1997b. Language in Newfoundland and Labrador: past, present and future. *Journal of the CAAL (Canadian Association of Applied Linguistics)* 19(1-2): 11-34.

Clarke, Sandra. 1993a. Introduction. In S. Clarke (ed.), vii-xi.

Clarke, Sandra. 1993b. The Americanization of Canadian pronunciation: a survey of palatal glide usage. In S. Clarke (ed.), 85-108.

Clarke, Sandra (ed.). 1993c. *Focus on Canada* [Varieties of English around the World G11]. Amsterdam: Benjamins.

Clarke, Sandra. 1991. Phonological variation and recent language change in St. John's English. In *English around the world. Sociolinguistic perspectives*, Jenny Cheshire (ed.), 108-122. Cambridge: Cambridge University Press.

Clarke, Sandra. 1985. Sociolinguistic variation in a small urban context: The St. John's Survey. In H. J. Warkentyne (ed.), 143-153.

Clarke, Sandra. 1982. Sampling attitudes to dialect varieties in St. John's. In *Languages in Newfoundland and Labrador.* 2nd ed., Harold J. Paddock (ed.), 90-105. St. John's, Nfld: Memorial University of Newfoundland.

Clarke, Sandra. 1981. Dialect stereotyping in rural Newfoundland. In *Proceedings of the Fifth Annual Meeting of the Atlantic Linguisitc Association*, Terrence K. Pratt (ed.), 39-57. Charlottetown, P.E.I.: University of Prince Edward Island.

Clarke, Sandra and Marguerite MacKenzie. 2001. A bibliography of writings on Newfoundland English. arts-srv.arts.mun.ca/linguistics/resources/nfengbib.pdf (9 Aug. 2005).

Clarke, Sandra, Ford Elms and Amani Youssef. 1995. The third dialect of English: some Canadian evidence. *Language Variation and Change* 7: 209-228.

Clyne, Michael (ed.). 1992. *Pluricentric languages. Differing norms in different nations.* Berlin: Mouton de Gruyter.

Coates, Jennifer. 1995. The expression of root and epistemic possibility in English. In *Modality in grammar and discourse* [Typological Studies in Language 32], J. Bybee and S. Fleischmann (eds), 55-66. Amsterdam: Benjamins.

Coates, Jennifer. 1983. *The semantics of the modal auxiliaries*. London: Croom Helm.

Cobden, M. 1986. Editors panel. The standard in Canadian journalism. In: *In search of the standard in Canadian English* [Strathy Language Unit Occasional Papers 1], W. C. Lougheed (ed.), 120-125. Kingston: Queen's University.

Colbourne, B. W. 1982. *A sociolinguistic study of Long Island, Notre Dame, Newfoundland.* MA Thesis, Memorial University Newfoundland.

Cooley, Marianne. 1992. Emerging standard and subdialectal variation in Early American English. *Diachronica* 9(2): 167-187.

Corrigan, Karen P. 2000. 'What bees to be maun be': aspects of deontic and epistemic modality in a northern dialect of Irish English". *English World-Wide* 21(1): 25-62.

Cowan, Helen. 1978. *British immigration before Confederation.* Ottawa: Canadian Historical Association.

Cowan, Helen. 1961. *British immigration to British North America. The first hundred years.* Rev. and enl. ed. Toronto: University of Toronto Press.

Craig, Gerald M. 1963. *Upper Canada. The formative years 1784-1841* [Canadian Centenary Series]. Toronto: McClelland and Stewart.

Creswell, Thomas J. 1994. Dictionary recognition of developing forms: the case of *snuck.* In *Centennial usage studies* [Publications of the American Dialect Society 78], Greta D. Little and Michael Montgomery (eds), 144-154. Tuscaloosa: University of Alabama Press.

Cruikshank, E. A. 1900. Immigration from the United States in Upper Canada, 1784-1812 – its effects and results. *Proceedings of the Thirty-Ninth Annual Convention of the Ontario Educational Association* [CHIM 01329], 262-283.

Cullen, Constance. 1971. Dialect reserch on Prince Edward Island. *The English Quarterly. A publication of the Canadian Council of Teachers of English* 4(3, Fall): 51-53.

Curzan, Anne and Kimberly Emmonds (eds). 2004. *Studies in the history of the English language II. Unfolding conversations* [Topics in English Linguistics 45]. Berlin: Mouton de Gruyter.

DAI-A = Dissertation Abstracts International, Series A.

D'Arcy, Alexandra F. 2005b. The development of linguistic constraints: phonological innovations in St. John's English. *Language Variation and
Change* 17(3): 327-355.

D'Arcy, Alexandra F. 2005a. *Like: syntax and development.* PhD Thesis, University of Toronto.

Dancygier, Barbara. 1998. *Conditionals and prediction. Time, knowledge, and
causation in conditional constructions.* Cambridge: Cambridge University
Press.

Darnell, Regna. 2005. Linguistic anthropology in Canada: some personal re-
flections. Canadian Journal of Linguistic 50(1/2/3/4): 151-172.

Davey, William. 1985. The stressed vowel phonemes of a New Brunswick
idiolect and Central/Prairie Canadian English. In *Papers from the Ninth Annual Meeting of the Atlantic Provinces Linguistic Association November 8-9
1985*, Lilian Falk, K. Flikeid and Margaret Harry (eds), 25-32. Halifax: St.
Mary's University.

Davey, William and Richard MacKinnon. 2002. Atlantic lexicon. In *Papers
from the 26th Annual Meeting of the Atlantic Provinces Linguistic Association,* Sandra Clarke (ed.), 157-170. St. John's, Nfld: Memorial University.

Davey, William and Richard MacKinnon. 1995. A report on the Dictionary of
Cape Breton English. In *Papers from the Nineteenth Annual Meeting of the
Atlantic Provinces Linguistic Association, Charlottetown, Prince Edward
Island, November 10-11, 1995*, Donna L. Lillian (ed.), 21-34. Charlotte-
town: University of Prince Edward Island.

Davey, William and Richard MacKinnon. 1999 [1996]. The use of nicknames
in Cape Breton. In L. Falk and M. Harry (eds), 63-77.

Davidson, Alexander. 1845. *The Canada spelling book. Intended as an
introduction to the English language.* 42nd thousand. Niagara: George
Hodgkinson.

Davies, Peter (ed.). *Reader's Digest Success with words. A North American
guide to the English language.* Pleasantville, NY: Reader's Digest Association.

Davis, David L. (ed.). 1967. *Glossary and handbook of Canadian – British
words.* Vancouver: Price Printing and Pauline's Books.

Davison, John. 1987. On saying /aw/ in Victoria. *Toronto Working Papers in
Linguistics* 7: 109-122.

Dawkins, Richard. 1989. *The selfish gene.* New edition. Oxford: Oxford University Press.

DCHP-1 = Avis, Walter S., Charles Crate, Patrick Drysdale, Douglas Leechman, Matthew H. Scharill, and Charles L. Lovell (eds). 1967. *A dictionary of Canadianisms on historical principles.* Toronto: Gage.

DCHP-2 = *A dictionary of Canadianisms on historical principles.* 2nd ed. In prep. Ed. by Stefan Dollinger, Laurel J. Brinton and Margery Fee. Department of English, Unversity of British Columbia. www.dchp.ca (25 Dec. 2006).

De Cillia, Rudolf. 1998. *Burenwurscht bleibt Burenwurscht. Sprache und gesellschaftliche Mehrsprachigkeit in Österreich.* Klagenfurt: Drava.

Denison, David. 1998. Syntax. In *The Cambridge history of the English language. Vol. IV: 1776-1997,* Suzanne Romaine (ed.), 92-329. Cambridge: Cambridge University Press.

Denison, David. 1993. *English historical syntax: verbal constructions* [Longman Linguistics Library]. London: Longman.

De Decker, Paul M. 2002. *Beyond the city limits: a study of the Canadian Vowel Shift in an Ontario small town.* MA Thesis, University of York, Ont.

De Haan, Ferdinand. 2005. Typological approaches to modality. In W. Frawley (ed.), 27-69.

Depraetere, Ilse and Susan Reed. 2006. Mood and modality in English. In B. Aarts and A. McMahon (eds), 269-290.

Dept. of State. 1979. = Anon. *The Canadian family tree.* 1979. Department of the Secretary of State. Multiculturalism Directorate. Don Mills, Ont.: Corpus.

De Wolf, Gaelan Dodds. 1995. The accent of teachers in Vancouver English. *American Speech* 70(3): 329-336.

De Wolf, Gaelan Dodds. 1993. Local patterns and markers of speech in Vancouver English. In. S. Clarke (ed.), 269-293.

De Wolf, Gaelan Dodds. 1992. *Social and regional factors in Canadian English: a study of phonological variables and grammatical items in Ottawa and Vancouver* [Studies in Phonetics 2]. Toronto: Canadian Scholar's Press.

De Wolf, Gaelan Dodds. 1990a. Analytical tools in a Labovian framework: a mainframe comparison of Canadian urban sociodialect data. *Journal of English Linguistics* 22(1): 119-128.

De Wolf, Gaelan Dodds. 1990b. Patterns of usage in urban Canadian English. *English World-Wide* 11(1): 1-31.

De Wolf, Gaelan Dodds. 1990c. Social and regional differences in grammatical usage in Canadian English: Ottawa and Vancouver. *American Speech* 65(1): 3-32.

De Wolf, Gaelan Dodds. 1988a. *A study of selected social and regional factors in Canadian English: a comparison of phonological variables and gram-*

matical items in Ottawa and Vancouver. PhD Thesis, University of Victoria, B.C.

De Wolf, Gaelan Dodds. 1988b. On phonological variability in Canadian English in Ottawa and Vancouver. *Journal of the International Phonetic Association* 18(2): 110-124.

De Wolf, Gaelan Dodds. 1985. Methods in statistical analysis of compatible data from two major Canadian urban sociolinguistic surveys. In: H. J. Warkentyne (ed.), 191-196.

De Wolf, Gaelan Dodds. 1983. A comparison of phonetically-ordered phonological variables in two major Canadian urban surveys. *Journal of the International Phonetic Association* 13: 90-96.

De Wolf, Gaelan Dodds. 1981. Transcription, coding, and data analysis of the SVEN survey. In *Methods/Méthodes IV. Papers from the fourth International Conference on Methods in Dialectology*, Henry J. Warkentyne (ed.), 62-65. Victoria, B.C.: University of Victoria.

De Wolf, Gaelan Dodds, Robert J. Gregg, Barbara P. Harris, and Matthew H. Scargill (eds). [5]1997. *Gage Canadian Dictionary.* 5th ed. Toronto: Gage.

De Wolf, Gaelan Dodds and Erika Hasebe-Ludt. 1988. Canadian urban survey methodology: a summary of research techniques and results. In A. R. Thomas, 55-66.

Dictionary of Canadian biography. Gen. ed. by Francess G. Halpenny. Toronto: University of Toronto Press.

Dillard, J. L. 1985. *Toward a social history of American English* [Contributions to the Sociology of Language 39]. Berlin: Mouton de Gruyter.

Dillon, Virginia M. 1968. *The Anglo-Irish element in the speech of the southern shore of Newfoundland.* MA Thesis, Memorial University of Newfoundland.

Dollinger, Stefan. forthc. Taking permissible shortcuts? Limited evidence, heuristic reasoning and the modal auxiliaries in early Canadian English. In *Empirical and analytical advances in the study of English language change*, Susan M. Fitzmaurice and Donka Minkova (eds). Berlin: Mouton de Gruyter.

Dollinger, Stefan. 2007a. English-German bilingualism in British Columbia past to present: data, evidence, challenges. In *Tracing English through time: explorations in language variation. A festschrift for Herbert Schendl on the occasion of his 65th birthday* [Austrian Studies in English 85], Ute Smit, Stefan Dollinger, Julia Hüttner, Gunther Kaltenböck, Ursula Lutzky (eds), 51-77. Wien: Braumüller.

Dollinger, Stefan. 2007b. The importance of demography for the study of historical Canadian English: three examples from the Corpus of Early Ontario English. In '*Of Varying Language and Opposing Creed': New Insights into Late Modern English* [Linguistic Insights 28], Javier Pérez Guerra, Dolores González Álvarez, Jorge L. Bueno Alonso, and Esperanza Rama Martínez (eds), 105-136. Bern: Peter Lang.

Dollinger, Stefan. 2006a. Oh Canada! Towards the Corpus of Early Ontario English. In A. Renouf and A. Kehoe (eds), 7-25.

Dollinger, Stefan. 2006b. The modal auxiliaries *have to* and *must* in the Corpus of Early Ontario English: gradient change and colonial lag. *Canadian Journal of Linguistics* 51(2/3): 287-308.

Dollinger, Stefan. 2006c. Towards a fully revised and extended edition of the *Dictionary of Canadianisms on Historical Principles* (DCHP-2): background, challenges, prospects. *Historical Sociolinguistics/Sociohistorical Linguistics* 6. http://www.let.leidenuniv.nl/hsl_shl/DCHP-2/DCHP-2/DCHP-2.htm (18 Aug. 2007).

Dollinger, Stefan. 2005. Review of 'Raymond Hickey (ed.). 2004. *Legacies of colonial English. Studies in transported dialects.* Cambridge: CUP (= Studies in English Language)'. *LinguistList* 16. http://linguistlist.org/pubs/reviews/get-review.cfm?SubID=57158 (25 Dec. 2006).

Dollinger, Stefan. 2004. Historical corpus compilation and 'philological computing' vs. 'philological outsourcing': a LModE test case. *VIEWS* 13(2): 3-23. Online version at: http://www.univie.ac.at/Anglistik/ang_new/online_papers/views.html (16 April 2005).

Dollinger, Stefan. 2003. What the capitalization of nouns in Early Canadian English may tell us about 'colonial lag' theory: methods and problems. *VIEWS* 12(1): 24-44. Online version at: http://www.univie.ac.at/Anglistik/ang_new/online_papers/views/03_1/DOL_SGLE.PDF (16 August 2005).

Dollinger, Stefan and Laurel J. Brinton. forthc. Canadian English lexis: past, present and future In Special volume of *Anglistik, Focus on Canadian English*, Matthias Meyer (ed.). Heidelberg: Winter.

Dorland, Arthur G. 1968. *The Quakers in Canada, a history*. New ed. Toronto: Ryerson Press.

Dossena, Marina. 2003. Hedging in Late Middle English, Older Scots and Early Modern English: the case of SHOULD and WOULD. In D. Hart (ed.), 197-221.

Douglas, R. Alan. 2001. *Uppermost Canada: the Western District and the Detroit frontier 1800-1850*. Detroit: Wayne State University Press.

Drew, S. S. 1979. *The phonology of St. John county, New Brunswick*. MA Thesis, University of New Brunswick, Fredericton.

Editing Canadian English. 2000. 2nd ed., Catherine Cragg, Barbara Czarnecki, Iris Hossé Phillips, Katherine Vanderlinden and Sheila Protti (eds). Prepared for the Editor's Associaton of Canada. [1st ed. 1987]. Toronto: McFarlane Walter & Ross.

Edwards, John. 1999. Reactions to three types of speech sample from rural black and white children. In L. Falk and M. Harry (eds), 107-121.

Edwards, John (ed.). 1998. *Language in Canada.* Cambridge: Cambridge University Press.

Ehrman, Madeline E. 1966. *The meanings of the modals in present-day American English.* The Hague: Mouton.

Eliason, Norman E. 1956. *Tarheel Talk: an historical study of the English language in North Carolina to 1860.* Chapel Hill: University of North Carolina Press.

Emeneau, M. B. 1935. The dialect of Lunenburg, Nova Scotia. *Language* 11: 140-147. [reprinted in J. K. Chambers (ed.). 1975a, 34-39].

Emery, George. 1971. Negro English in Amber Valley, Alberta. In *Linguistic diversity in Canadian society,* Regna Darnell (ed.), 45-59. Edmonton: Linguistic Research.

England, G. A. 1925. Newfoundland dialect items. *Dialect Notes* 5: 322-346.

English, John and Kenneth McLaughlin. 1983. *Kitchener. An illustrated history.* Waterloo, Ont.: Wilfried Laurier University Press.

Esling, John H. 1991. Sociophonetic variation in Vancouver. In *English around the world. Sociolinguistic perspectives,* Jenny Cheshire (ed.), 123-133. Cambridge: Cambridge University Press.

Esling, John H. 1986. Some analyses of vowels by social group in the survey of Vancouver English. *Working Papers of the Linguistic Circle of the University of Victoria* 5(1): 21-32.

Esling, John H. and Henry J. Warkentyne. 1993. Retracting of /æ/ in Vancouver English. In S. Clarke, 229-246.

Evans, Mary S. 1930. Terms from the Labrador Coast. *American Speech* 6: 56-58.

Facchinetti, Roberta, Manfred Krug and Frank Palmer (eds). 2003. *Modality in contemporary English* [Topics in English Linguistics 44]. Berlin: Mouton de Gruyter.

Facchinetti, Roberta. 2003. Pragmatic and sociological constraints on the functions of *may* in contemporary British English. In Facchinetti, Krug and Palmer (eds), 301-327.

Facchinetti, Roberta. 2002. Can. In *Variation in central modals. A repertoire of forms and types of usage in Middle English and Early Modern English*, Maurizio Gotti, Marina Dossena, Richard Drury, Roberta Facchinetti and Maria Lima (eds), 45-65. Bern: Lang.

Facchinetti, Roberta. 2000. *Can* and *could* in contemporary British English: a study of the ICE-GB corpus. In *New frontiers of corpus research* [Language and Computers. Studies in Practical Linguistics 36], Pam Peters, Peter Collins and Adam Smith (eds), 229-246. Amsterdam: Rodopi.

Fairman, Tony. 2006. Word in English Record Office Documents of the early 1800s. In M. Kytö, M. Rydén and E. Smitterberg (eds), 56-88.

Fairman, Tony. 2003. Letters of the English labouring classes and the English language, 1800-34. In *Insights into Late Modern English* [Linguistic Insights 7], Marina Dossena and Charles Jones (eds), 265-82. Bern: Lang.

Falk, Lilian. 1999a [1990]. Between emphasis and exaggeration: verbal emphasis in the English of Cape Breton. In L. Falk and M. Harry (eds), 51-62.

Falk, Lilian. 1999b. Three nineteenth-century literary representations of Nova Scotia dialect. In L. Falk and M. Harry (eds), 198-214.

Falk, Lilian. 1990. Between emphasis and exaggeration: verbal emphasis in the English of Cape Breton Island. In *Papers from the Fourteenth Annual Meeting of the Atlantic Provinces Linguistic Association, Memorial University of Newfoundland, St. John's, Newfoundland, November 9-10, 1990*, Jim Black (ed.), 39-49. St. John's: Memorial University.

Falk, Lilian. 1989. Regional usage in the English of Cape Breton Island. In *Papers from the Thirteenth Annual Meeting of the Atlantic Provinces Linguistic Association, University of New Brunswick, Saint John, New Brunswick, November 3-5, 1989*, D. H. Jory (ed.), 114-128. St. John: University of New Brunswick.

Falk, Lilian. 1985. The use of Nova Scotia idiom in books for young readers. In *Papers from the Ninth Annual Meeting of the Atlantic Provinces Linguistic Association November 8-9*, 1985, Lilian Falk, K. Flikeid and Margaret Harry (eds), 42-51. Halifax: St. Mary's University.

Falk, Lilian, 1984. Regional varieties in English in Nova Scotia. In *Papers from the Eighth Annual Meeting of the Atlantic Provinces Linguistic Association*, J. Barnsted, B. E. Gesner, W. T. Gordon and M. Holder (eds), 33-41. Halifax: Dalhousie University.

Falk, Lilian. 1980. On the attitudes of dialect differences in Canada. *Sift* (St. Mary's University, Halifax, N.S.) Vol. 6.

Falk, Lilian. 1979. The use of *they* with indefinite singular antecedent. In *Papers from the Third Annual Meeting of the Atlantic Provinces Linguistic Association*, Moshe Starets (ed.), 82-92. Church Point, P.E.I.: Université de St. Anne.

Falk, Lilian and Margaret Harry (eds). 1999. *The English language in Nova Scotia. Essays on past and present developments in English across the province*. Lockeport. N.S.: Roseway Publishing.

Fee, Margery and Janice McAlpine. ^{2}2007 [^{1}1997]. *Guide to Canadian English usage*. 2nd ed. Toronto: Oxford University Press.

Fee, Margery. 1992a. Canadian English. In *The Oxford companion to the English language,* Tom McArthur (ed.), 179-183. Oxford: Oxford University Press.

Fee, Margery. 1992b. Canadian dictionaries in English. In *The Oxford companion to the English language,* Tom McArthur (ed.), 178-179. Oxford: Oxford University Press.

Fee, Margery. 1991. Frenglish in Quebec English newspapers. In *Papers from the Fifteenth Annual Meeting of the Atlantic Provinces Linguistic Association November 8-9, 1991, University College of Cape Breton, Sydney, Nova Scotia*, William J. Davey and Bernard LeVert (eds), 12-23. Sydney, N.S.: University College of Cape Breton.

Fischer, Olga. 2003. The development of the modals in English. In D. Hart (ed.), 17-32.

Fischer, Olga. 1994. The development of quasi-auxiliaries in English and changes in word order. *Neophilologus* 78: 137-164.

Flikeid, Karin. 1999. Incorporations from English in Nova Scotia Acadian French. In L. Falk and M. Harry (eds), 158-182.

Fowler, H. W. and F. G. Fowler. 1973 [^{3}1931]. *The King's English*. 3rd ed. Oxford: Oxford University Press.

Francis, R. Douglas, Richard Jones and Donald B. Smith. 2000. *Origins. Canadian history of Confederation*. 4th ed. Toronto: Harcourt Brace.

Frawley, William (ed.). 2005. *The expression of modality*. [The Expression of Cognitive Categories 1]. Berlin: Mouton de Gruyter.

Friend, David, Julia Keeler, Dan Liebman, and Fraser Sutherland *et al.* (eds). 1997. *ITP Nelson Canadian Dictionary of the English Language. An Encyclopedic Reference*. Toronto: ITP Nelson.

Fries, Charles C. 1925. The periphrastic future with *shall* and *will* in Modern English. *PMLA* 40: 963-1024.

Garzone, Giuliana. 2001. Deontic modality and performativity in English legal texts. In M. Gotti and M. Dossena (eds), 153-173.

Geikie, Rev. A. Constable. 1857. Canadian English. Read before the Canadian Institute, 28 March, 1857. *Canadian Journal of Science, Literature and History* 2: 344-355. [reprinted in: R. H. Southerland (ed.) 1977. *Readings on language in Canada*, 4-16. Calgary: Department of Linguistics.

Gell-Mann, Murray. 1994. *The quark and the jaguar. Adventures in the simple and the complex.* New York: Freeman.

Gentilcore, R. Louis (Gen. ed.). 1993. *Historical atlas of Canada.* Vol. II: The land transformed. 1800-1891. Toronto: University of Toronto Press.

Gerson, Carole. 1994. *Canada's early women writers: texts in English to 1859.* [CRIAW Papers 33]. Ottawa: CRIAW.

Gibson, Deborah J. 1976. *A thesis on eh.* MA Thesis, University of British Columbia.

Gleason, H. A. Jr. 1982. Canadian English. Unpublished Ms. University of Toronto, Department of Linguistics.

Gold, Elaine. 2007. Aspect in Bungi: expanded progressives and be perfects. Paper presented at the 2007 Conference of the Canadian Linguistic Association, Saskatoon, Sask. May 2007.

Gold, Elaine. 2004a. Teachers, texts and Early Canadian English: Upper Canada 1791-1841. In *Proceedings of the 2003 Annual Conference of the Canadian Linguistic Association.* CD-ROM. Sophie Burelle and Stana Somesfalean (eds), 85-96. Montreal: Université du Québec à Montréal.

Gold, Elaine. 2004b. Yiddish words in Canadian English: spread and change. In *Yiddish after the Holocaust*, Joseph Sherman (ed.). Oxford: Boulevard; Centre for Hebrew and Jewish Studies.

Gold, Elaine. 2003. English Shmenglish: Yiddish borrowings into Canadian English. In *Proceedings of the 2002 Annual Conference of the Canadian Linguistic Association.* Sophie Burelle and Stana Somesfalean (eds), 108-120. Montréal: Université de Montréal.

Gold, Elaine and Mireille Tremblay. 2006. *Eh?* and *Hein?*: Discourse particles or national icons? *Canadian Journal of Linguistics* 51(2&3): 247-264.

Goosens, Louis. 1987. The auxiliarization of the English modals: a functional grammar view. In *Historical development of auxiliaries* [Trends in Linguistics. Studies and Monographs 35]. Martin Harris and Paolo Ramat (eds), 111-143. Berlin: Mouton de Gruyter.

Gordon, Elizabeth, Lyle Campbell, Jennifer Hay, Margaret Maclagan, Andrea Sudbury and Peter Trudgill. 2004. *New Zealand English. Its origins and evolution.* Cambridge: Cambridge University Press.

Gordon, Elizabeth and Gillian Lewis. 1998. New-dialect formation and Southern Hemisphere English: the New Zealand short front vowels. *Journal of Sociolinguistics* 2(1): 35-51.

Gordon, Matthew J. 2005. Review of Trudgill (2004). *Journal of Sociolinguistics* 9(1): 146-150.

Gotti, Maurizio. 2006. Prediction with SHALL and WILL: a diachronic perspective. In A. Renouf and A. Kehoe (eds), 99-116.

Gotti, Maurizio. 2003a. Pragmatic uses of *shall* and *will* for future time reference in Early Modern English. In D. Hart (ed.), 108-170.

Gotti, Maurizio. 2003b. *Shall* and *will* in contemporary English: a comparison with past uses. In R. Facchinetti, M. Krug and F. Palmer (eds), 267-300.

Gotti, Maurizio. 2002. Pragmatic uses of SHALL future constructions in Early Modern English. In D. Minkova and R. Stockwell, 301-324.

Gotti, Maurizio. 2001. Semantic and pragmatic values of *shall* and *will* in Early Modern English statutes. In M. Gotti and M. Dossena (eds), 89-111.

Gotti, Maurizio, Marina Dossena, Richard Dury, Roberta Facchinetti and Marina Lima. 2002. *Variation in central modals. A repertoire of forms and types of usage in Middle English and early modern English.* Bern: Lang.

Gotti, Maurizio and Marina Dossena (eds). 2001. *Modality in specialized texts. Selected papers of the 1st CERLIS Conference* [Linguistic Insights 1]. Bern: Lang.

Gourlay, Robert. 1822. *Statistical account of Upper Canada. Compiled with a view to a grand system of emigration* [CIHM 35937]. London: Simkin & Marshall.

Görlach, Manfred. 2003. An annotated bibliography of writings of English in North America. *Arbeiten aus Anglistik und Amerikanistik* 28(1): 107-166.

Görlach, Manfred. 1999. *English in nineteenth-century England. An introduction.* Cambridge: Cambridge University Press.

Görlach, Manfred. 1991a [1987]. The identity of Canadian English. In M. Görlach (ed.), 108-121.

Görlach, Manfred. 1991b [1987]. English as a world language – the state of the art. In M. Görlach (ed.), 10-35.

Görlach, Manfred. 1987. Colonial lag? The alleged conservative character of American English and other 'colonial' varieties. *English World-Wide* 8(1): 41-60.

Görlach, Manfred (ed.). 1991c. *Englishes. Studies in varieties of English 1984-1988* [Varieties of English Around the World G9]. Amsterdam: Benjamins.

Graham, Robert S. 1957. The transition from German to English in the German settlements of Saskatchewan. *Journal of the Canadian Linguistic Association* 3(1, March): 9-13.

Grant-Russell, Pamela. 1999. The influence of French on Quebec English: motivation for lexical borrowing and integration of loanwords. *LACUS Forum* 25: 473-86.

Greenleaf, Elizabeth B. 1931. Newfoundland words. *American Speech* 6: 306.

Gregg, Robert J. 2004 [1984]. *The Survey of Vancouver English. A sociolinguistic study of urban Canadian English* [Strathy Language Unit Occasional Papers 5], Gaelan Dodds de Wolf, Margery Fee and Janice McAlpine (eds). Kingston: Queen's University.

Gregg, Robert J. 1993. Canadian English lexicography. In S. Clarke (ed.), 27-44.

Gregg, Robert J. 1992. The Survey of Vancouver English. *American Speech* 67(3): 250-267.

Gregg, Robert J. 1988. The study of linguistic change in the Survey of Vancouver English. In A. R. Thomas (ed.), 434-441.

Gregg, Robert J. 1985. The Vancouver Survey: analysis and measurement – grammatical usage. In H. J. Warkentyne (ed.), 179-184.

Gregg, Robert J. 1984. *Final report to the Social Sciences and Humanities Research Council of Canada on an urban dialect survey of the English spoken in Vancouver*. Ms. Vancouver: Linguistics Department, University of British Columbia, 140 pp.

Gregg, Robert J. 1983. Local lexical items in the sociodialectal Survey of Vancouver English. *Canadian Journal of Linguistics* 28(1): 17-23.

Gregg, Robert J. 1981. General background to the Survey of Vancouver English (SVEN). In H. J. Warkentyne (ed.), 41-47.

Gregg, Robert J. 1973a. The diphthongs əi and ai in Scottish, Scotch-Irish and Canadian English. *Canadian Journal of Linguistics* 18(2): 136-145.

Gregg, Robert J. 1973b. The linguistic survey of British Columbia: the Kootenay region. In *Canadian languages and their social context*, Regna Darnell (ed.), 105-116. Edmonton: Linguistic Research.

Gregg, Robert J. 1957a. Notes on the pronunciation of Canadian English as spoken in Vancouver, B.C. *Journal of the Canadian Linguistic Association* 3(1, March): 20-26.

Gregg, Robert J. 1957b. Neutralisation and fusion of vocalic phonemes in Canadian English as spoken in the Vancouver area. *Journal of the Canadian Linguistic Association* 3(2, Oct.): 78-83.

Gresset, Stéphane. 2003. Towards a contextual micro-analysis of the non-equivalence of might and could. In R. Facchinetti, M. Krug and F. Palmer (eds), 81-99.

Haggo, Douglas and Koenraad Kuiper. 1985. Stock auction speech in Canada and New Zealand. In *Regionalism and national identity. Multi-disciplinary essays on Canada, Australia and New Zealand*, Reginald Berry and James Acheson (eds), 189-197. Christchurch: Association for Canadian Studies in Australia and New Zealand.

Hagiwara, Robert. 2006 Vowel production in Winnipeg. *Canadian Journal of Linguistics* 51(2&3): 127-142.

Halford, Brigitte K. 1998. Canadian English: linguistic identity in the Pacific North West. In H. Lindquist *et al*. (eds), 125-136.

Halford, Brigitte K. 1996. *Talk units. The structure of spoken Canadian English* [ScriptOralia 87]. Tübingen: Narr.

Haliburton, Thomas Chandler. 1836. *The clock-maker, or the sayings and doings of Samuel Slick of Slickville*. Halifax: Howe.

Hamilton, Donald E. 1964. Standard Canadian English: pronunciation. In *Proceedings of the Ninth International Congress of Linguists. Cambridge, Mass., August 27-31, 1962*, Horace G. Lunt (ed.), 456-459. The Hague: Mouton.

Hamilton, Donald E. 1958a. *The English spoken in Montreal: a pilot study*. MA Thesis, Université de Montréal.

Hamilton, Donald E. 1958b. Notes on Montreal English. *Journal of the Canadian Linguistic Association* 4(1, Spring): 70-79.

Hamilton, Sandra A. 1997. *Canadianisms and their treatment in dictionaries*. MA Thesis, University of Ottawa, Ont.

Hampson, Eloise L. 1982. Age as a factor in language attitude differences. In *Papers from the Sixth Annual Meeting of the Atlantic Provinces Linguistic Association*, Sandra Clarke and Ruth King (eds), 51-62. St. John's, Nfld: Memorial University.

Hansen, Marcus L. and J. B. Brebner. 1940. *The mingling of the Canadian and American peoples. Vol. 1 Historical*. New Haven: Yale University Press.

Harris, Barbara P. 1983. Handsaw or harlot? Some problem etymologies in the lexicon of Chinook Jargon. *Canadian Journal of Linguistics* 28(1): 25-32.

Harris, Barbara P. 1981. Etymological problems in the lexicon of Chinook Jargon: some proposed solutions. Part I: words of French and Canadian French origina. *Working Papers of the Linguistic Circle of the University of Victoria* 1(2): 218-232.

Harris, Barbara P. 1975. *Slected political, cultural, and socio-economic areas of Canadian history as contributors to the vocabulary of Canadian English*. PhD Thesis, University of Victoria, B.C.

Harris, R. Cole (ed.). 1987. *Historical atlas of Canada. Vol. I: From the beginning to 1800.* Toronto: University of Toronto Press.

Harris, Martin. 1986. English *ought (to).* In D. Kastovsky and A. Szwedek, 347-358.

Harris, Martin and Paolo Ramat (eds). 1987. *Historical development of auxiliaries* [Trends in Linguistics. Studies and Monographs 35]. Berlin: Mouton de Gruyter.

Harry, Margaret. 1999. The place names of Nova Scotia. In: L. Falk and M. Harry (eds), 78-103.

Hart, David (ed.). 2003. *English modality in context. Diachronic perspectives* [Lingusitic Insights 11]. Bern: Lang.

Hasebe-Ludt, Erika. 1985. Methodology of spontaneous speech analysis. In H. J. Warkentyne (ed.), 197-200.

Hasebe-Ludt, Erika. 1981. Aspects of spontaneous speech in the urban dialect study of Vancouver English. In H. J. Warkentyne (ed.), 57-61.

Heller, Joseph. 1994 [1955]. *Catch-22.* New York: Simon and Schuster.

Hickey, Raymond (ed.). 2004a. *Legacies of colonial English. Studies in transported dialects* [Studies in English Language]. Cambridge: Cambridge University Press.

Hickey, Raymond. 2004b. Introduction. In R. Hickey (ed.), 1-30.

Hickey, Raymond. 2004c. Dialects of English and their transportation. In R. Hickey (ed.), 33-58.

Hickey, Raymond. 2004d. Development and diffusion of Irish English. In R. Hickey, 82-117.

Hickey, Raymond. 2004e. *A sound atlas of Irish English* [Topics in English Linguistics 48]. Berlin: Mouton de Gruyter.

Hodgins, J. George (ed.). 1895. *Documentary history of education in Upper Canada. [in 28 vols.] Vol. III: 1836-1840* [CIHM 4975]. Toronto: Warwick Brothers & Rutter.

Hofmann, Peter J. 2003. *Language and politeness. Directive speech acts in Brazilian Portuguese, Costa Rican Spanish and Canadian English.* PhD Thesis: New York State University at Stony Brook.

Holder, Maurice A. 1979. The [s] pronunciaton of /z/ in Maritimes English. In *Papers from the Third Annual Meeting of the Atlantic Provinces Linguistic Association,* Moshe Starets (ed.), 28-32. Church Point, PEI: Université de St. Anne.

Hollett, Pauline. 2006. Investigating St. John's English: real- and apparent-time perspectives. *Canadian Journal of Linguistics* 51(2&3): 143-160.

Hopper, Paul J. 1991. On some principles of grammaticization. In *Approaches to grammaticalization. Vol. I*, Elizabeth Closs Traugott and Bernd Heine (eds), 18-35. Amsterdam: Benjamins.

Hopper, Paul J. and Elizabeth Closs Traugott. 1993. *Grammaticalization.* Cambridge: Cambridge University Press.

House, Anthony B. 1985. English language in Francophone New Brunswick. In *A literary and linguistic history of New Brunswick*, Reavley Gair (ed.), 75-81. Frederickton, N.B.: Fiddlehead Poetry Books & Goose Lane Editions.

Hultin, Neil C. 1967. Canadian views of American English. *American Speech* 42: 243-260.

Hung, Henrietta. 1987. Canadian Raising à la Montréalaise. *Toronto Working Papers in Linguistics* 7: 123-139.

Hung, Henrietta, John Davison and J. K. Chambers. 1993. Comparative sociolinguistics of (aw)-fronting. In S. Clarke, 247-268.

Idsardi, William J. 2006. Canadian Raising, opacity, and rephonemicization. *Canadian Journal of Linguistics* 51(2&3): 119-126.

Inglis, Stephanie. 1999. Written Mi'kmaq-Engish as used by the Mi'kmaw communities in Cape Breton. In L. Falk and M. Harry (eds), 146-157.

Ireland, R. J. 1979. *Canadian spelling. An empirical and historical survey of selected words.* PhD Thesis: York University, Ont.

Jacobsson, Bengt. 1994. Recessive and emergent uses of modal auxiliaries in English. *English Studies* 2: 166-182.

Jankowski, Bridget. 2004. A transatlantic perspective of variation and change in English deontic modality. *Toronto Working Papers in Linguistics* 23(2): 85-113.

Jolly, Grace. 1983. La codification de l'anglais canadien. In *La norme linguistique,* E. Bédard and J. Maurais (eds), 731-762. Québec: Conseil de la language français.

Joos, Martin. 1942. A phonological dilemma in Canadian English. *Language* 18: 141-144. [reprinted in J. K. Chambers (ed.). 1975a, 79-82].

Joy, Richard J. 1972. *Languages in conflict: the Canadian experience* [Carleton Library 61]. Toronto: McClelland and Stewart.

Kastovsky, Dieter and Aleksander Szwedek (eds). 1986. *Linguistics across historical and geographical boundaries. In honour of Jacek Fisiak on the occasion of his fiftieth birthday.* Berlin: Mouton de Gruyter.

Kennedy, Graeme. 2002. Variation in the distribution of modal verbs in the British National Corpus. In *Using corpora to explore linguistics variation* [Studies in Corpus Linguistics 9], Randi Reppen, Susan M. Fitzmaurice and Douglas Biber (eds), 73-90. Amsterdam: Benjamins.

Kerswill, Paul. 2002. Koineization and accommodation. In J. K. Chambers, P. Trudgill and N. Schilling-Estes (eds), 669-702.

Kiesling, Scott F. 2004. English input to Australia. In R. Hickey (ed.), 418-439.

King, Ruth. 1998. Language in Ontario. In J. Edwards (ed.), 400-413.

King, Ruth and Sandra Clarke. 2002. Contesting meaning: Newfie and the politics of ethnic labelling. *Journal of Sociolinguistics* 6(4): 537-556.

Kinloch, A. Murray. 1999 [1980]. The vowel phonemes of Halifax and General Canadian English [with an introduction by the editors of the 1999 reprint]. In L. Falk and M. Harry (eds), 17-26.

Kinloch, A. Murray. 1995. [1990-1995]. The significance for the study of Canadian English of the work of Harold B. Allen. *Journal of English Linguistics* 23(1-2): 167-183.

Kinloch, A. Murray. 1985. The English language in New Brunswick 1784-1984. In *A literary and linguistic history of New Brunswick*, Reavley Gair (ed.), 59-74. Fredericton, N.B.: Fiddlehead Poetry Books & Goose Lane Editions.

Kinloch, A. Murray. 1983a. The phonology of Central/Prairie Canadian English. *American Speech* 58: 31-35.

Kinloch, A. Murray. 1983b. English in Newfoundland [Review of Paddock (1981)]. *American Speech* 58: 186-188.

Kinloch, A. Murray. 1983c. Canadian English. In P. Davies (ed.), 114-118.

Kinloch, A. Murray. 1983d. Central and Prairie Canadian. In P. Davies (ed.), 131-133.

Kinloch, A. Murray. 1983e. Maritime dialects. In P. Davies, 425-427.

Kinloch, A. Murray. 1972/73. Survey of Canadian English: a first look at New Brunswick results. *The English Quarterly. A publication of the* Canadian Council of Teachers of English 5(4, winter): 41-51.

Kinloch, A. Murray and Walter S. Avis. 1989. Central Canadian English and Received Standard English. A comparison of pronunciation. In *English across cultures, cultures across English. A reader in cross-cultural communication,* Ofelia García and Ricardo Otheguy (eds), 403-420. Berlin: Mouton de Gruyter.

Kinloch, Murray A. and Ismail M. Fazilah. 1993. Canadian Raising: /au/ in Frederickton, New Brunswick. *Linguistica Atlantica* 15: 105-114.

Kinloch, Murray A. and Anthony B. House. 1978. The English language in New Brunswick and Prince Edward Island: research published, in progress, and required. *Journal of the Atlantic Provinces Linguistic Association* 1: 34-45.

Kirwin, William J. 1993. The planting of Anglo-Irish in Newfoundland. In S. Clarke (ed.), 65-84.

Kirwin, William J. 1968. Bibliography of writings on Newfoundland English. *Regional Language Studies* (St. John's Nfld.) 1: 4-7.

Klinck, Carl F. (gen. ed.). 1976. *Literary history of Canada. Canadian literature in English.* Toronto: University of Toronto Press.

Klinge, A. and H. H. Müller (eds). 2005. *Modality: studies in form and function.* London: Equinox.

Kortmann, Bernd, Kate Burridge, Rajend Mesthrie, Edgar W. Schneider and Clive Upton (eds). 2004. *A handbook of varieties of English. Vol. II: Morphology and syntax.* Berlin: Mouton de Gruyter.

Kortmann, Bernd and Edgar W. Schneider. 2004. General introduction. In E. W. Schneider, *et al.* (eds), 1-9.

Krug, Manfred G. 2000. *Emerging English modals. A corpus-based study of grammaticalization* [Topics in English Linguistics 32]. Berlin: Mouton de Gruyter.

Krug, Manfred G. 1998. *Gotta* – the tenth central modal in English? Social, stylistic and regional variation in the British National Corpus as evidence of ongoing grammaticalization. In H. Lindquist *et al.* (eds), 177-91.

Kuiper, Koenraad and Douglas Haggo. 1985. On the nature of ice hockey commentaries. In *Regionalism and national identity. Multi-disciplinary essays on Canada, Australia, and New Zealand,* Reginald Berry and James Acheson (eds), 167-175. Christchurch: Association for Canadian Studies in Australia and New Zealand.

Kurath, Hans. 1972. Relics of English folk speech in American English. In *Studies in linguistics in honor of Raven I. McDavid, Jr.,* Lawrence M. Davis, (ed.), 367-375. Alabama: University of Alabama Press.

Kurath, Hans. 1972. [1939]. *Linguistic atlas of New England.* New York: AMS Press.

Kytö, Merja. 2004. The emergence of American English: evidence from seventeenth-century records in New England. R. Hickey (ed.), 121-57.

Kytö, Merja. 1996. *Manual to the Diachronic Part of the Helsinki Corpus of English Texts.* 3rd ed. University of Helsinki.

Kytö, Merja. 1991a. *Variation in diachrony, with early American English in focus. Studies on CAN/MAY and SHALL/WILL.* Bern: Lang.

Kytö, Merja. 1991b. *Can (could)* vs. *may (might)*: regional variation in Early Modern English. In *Historical English syntax* [Topics in English Linguistics 2], Dieter Kastovsky (ed.), 233-289. Berlin: Mouton de Gruyter.

Kytö, Merja. 1987. On the use of modal auxiliaries indicating 'possibility' in Early American English. In M. Harris and P. Ramat, 145-170.

Kytö, Merja, Mats Rydén and Erik Smitterberg (eds). 2006. *Nineteenth-century English: stability and change.* Cambridge: Cambridge University Press.

Kytö, Merja, Juhani Rudanko and Erik Smitterberg. 2000. Building a bridge between the present and the past: a corpus of 19th-century English. *ICAME Journal* 24: 85-97.

Kytö, Merja and Matti Rissanen. 1983. The syntactic study of Early American English. The variationist at the mercy of his corpus? *Neuphilologische Mitteilungen* 84: 470-490.

Labov, William. 2001. *Principles of linguistic change. Vol. 2: Social factors* [Language in Society 29]. Oxford: Blackwell.

Labov, William. 1991. The three dialects of English. In *New ways of analyzing sound change* [Quantitative Analysis of Linguistic Structure 5], Penelope Eckert (ed.), 1-44. San Diego: Academic Press.

Labov, William. 1981. What can be inferred about change in progress from synchronic descriptions? In *Variation omnibus* [NWAVE VIII], David Sankoff and H. Cedergren (eds), 177-200. Edmonton: Linguistic Research.

Labov, William, Sharon Ash and Charles Boberg. 2006. *The Atlas of North American English. Phonetics, phonology and sound change.* Berlin: Mouton de Gruyter.

Ladell, John L. 1993. *They left their mark. Surveyors and their role in the settlement of Ontario* [Association of Ontario Land Surveyors. 1892-1992 Centenary Volume]. Toronto: Dundurn Press.

Lambert, W. E., R. C. Hodgeson, R. C. Gardner and J. Fillebaum. 1960. Evaluation reactions to spoken language. *Journal of Abnormal and Social Psychology* 60: 44-51.

Lanari, C. E. 1994. *A sociolinguistic study of the Burin region of Newfoundland.* M.A. Thesis, Memorial Univeristy of Newfoundland, Department of Linguistics.

Landon, Fred. 1967 [1941]. *Western Ontario and the American frontier.* Toronto: McClelland & Stewart.

Langton, H. H. (ed.). 1950. *A gentlewoman in Upper Canada. The journals of Anne Langton.* Toronto: Clarke, Irwin and Co.

Larreya, Raul. 2003. Irrealis, past time reference and modality. In R. Facchinetti, M. Krug and F. Palmer (eds), 21-45.

Lass, Roger. 2004. South African English. In R. Hickey (ed.), 363-386.

Lass, Roger. 1990. Where do extraterritorial Englishes come from? Dialect input and recodification in transported Englishes. In *Papers from the 5ᵗʰ International Conference on English Historical Linguistics 1987*, Sylvia Adamson, Vivien Law, Nigel Vincent and Susan Wright [Fitzmaurice] (eds), 245-280. Amsterdam: Benjamins.

Lee, Robert C. 2004. *The Canada Company and the Huron Tract, 1826-1853. Personalities, profits and politics.* Toronto: Natural Heritage / Natural History Inc.

Leech, Geoffrey. 2003. Modality on the move: the English modal auxiliaries 1961-1992. In R. Facchinetti, M. Krug and F. Palmer (eds), 223-240.

Lehn, Walter. 1959. Vowel contrasts in a Saskatchewan English dialect. *Journal of the Canadian Linguistic Association* 5(2, Fall): 90-98.

Leitner, Gerhard. 1992. English as a pluricentric language. In *Pluricentric languages. Differing norms in different nations,* Michael Clyne (ed.), 179-237. Berlin: Mouton de Gruyter.

Léon, Pierre R. and Philippe Martin (eds). 1979. *Toronto English. Studies in phonetics to honour C. D. Rouillard* [Studia Phonetica 14]. Montréal: Didier.

Leonard, Sterling A. 1929 [1962]. *The doctrine of correctness in English usage 1700-1800.* New York: Russell & Russell.

Le Page, Robert and Andrée Tabouret-Keller. 1985. *Acts of identity. Creole-based approaches to language and ethnicity.* Cambridge: Cambridge University Press.

Lightfoot, David W. 1979. *Principles of diachronic syntax.* Cambridge: Cambridge University Press.

Lighthall, W. Douw. 1889. Canadian English. *The Week* (Toronto), 16 August 1889, 581-583.

Lilles, Jaan. 2000. The myth of Canadian English. *English Today* 62(16/2): 3-9; 17.

Lindquist, Hans, Staffan Klintborg, Magnus Levin and Maria Estling (eds). 1998. *The major varieties of English. Papers from MAVEN 97, Växjö 20-22 November 1997* [Acta Wexionensia Humaniora Humanities 1.1998]. Växjö: Växjö University.

Lougheed, William C. (ed.). 1988. *Writings on Canadian English 1976-1987. A selective, annotated bibliography* [Strathy Language Unit, Occasional Papers 2]. Kingston, Ont.: Queen's University.

Lougheed, William C. (ed.). 1986. *In search of the standard in Canadian English* [Strathy Language Unit Occasional Papers 1]. Kingston, Ont.: Queen's University.

Lovell, Charles J. 1956. Whys and hows of collecting for the Dictionary of Canadian English: Part II: Excerption and quotation. *Journal of the Canadian Linguistic Association* 2(1, March): 23-32.

Lovell, Charles J. 1955b. Whys and hows of collecting for the Dictionary of Canadian English: Part I: Scope and source material. *Journal of the Canadian Linguistic Association* 1(2, Oct.): 3-8.

Lovell, Charles J. 1955a. Lexicographic challenges of Canadian English. *Journal of the Canadian Linguistic Association* 1(1, March): 2-5.

Lowell, James R. 1859. *The Biglow papers.* 1st series. London: Trübner.

Lower, J. A. 1970. *A nation developing. A brief history of Canada.* Toronto: Ryerson.

Lyons, John. 1977. *Semantics.* Cambridge: Cambridge University Press.

M., J. B. 1936. Do we speak American? *Winnipeg Free Press.* 20 June 1936: 29.

Macafee, Caroline. 2004. Scots and Scottish English. In R. Hickey (ed.), 59-81.

MacDonald, Norman. 1939. *Canada, 1763-1841. Immigration and settlement. The administration of the imperial land regulations.* London: Longmans, Green and Co.

Mackey, William F. 1998. The foundations. In J. Edwards (ed.), 13-35.

MacMahon, Michael K. C. 1998. Phonology. In S. Romaine (ed.), 373-535.

Magee, Joan. 1985. *A Scandinaivan heritage. 200 years of Scandinavian presence in the Windsor-Detroit border region* [Dundurn Local History Series 3]. Toronto: Dundurn Press.

Mair, Christian. 2006. *Twentieth-century English: history, variation and standardization.* Cambridge: Cambridge University Press.

Mair, Christian. 2002. Three changing patterns of verb complementation in Late Modern English: a real-time study based on matching text corpora. *English Language and Linguistics* 6: 105-131.

Mair, Christian and Geoffrey Leech. 2006. Current changes in English syntax. In B. Aarts and A. McMahon (eds), 318-342.

Manning, Alan and Robert Eatock. 1983. The influence of French on English in Quebec. *LACUS Forum* 9: 496-502.

Marckwardt, Albert H. 1958. *American English.* New York: Oxford University Press.

Matsuno, Keiko. 1999. *The English vowel system of the Ojibwe First Nation community in Garden River.* M.A. Thesis, Michigan State University.

Mazerolle, David. 1993. *Avant tu také off, please close the lights. Moncton dictionary.* Edited by Herb Curtis. Fredericton, N.B.: Non-Entity Press.

Mazurkewich, Irene, Frances Fister-Stoga, David Mawle, Marcelle Somers and Sandra Thibaudeau. 1984. A new look at language attitudes in Montreal. *McGill Working Papers in Linguistics* 2(1): 145-163.

McArthur, Tom. 1989. *The English language as used in Quebec. A survey* [Strathy Language Unit Occasional Papers 3]. Kingston, Ont.: Queen's University.

McCafferty, Kevin. 2004. Innovation in language contact. *Be after V-ing* as a future gram in Irish English, 1670 to the present. *Diachronica* 21(1): 113-160.

McConnell, Ruth E. 1978. *Our own voice. Canadian English and how it came to be*. [1979 reprint with new subtitle *Canadian English and how it is studied*]. Toronto: Gage.

McCrum, Robert, William Cran and Robert MacNeil. 1986. *The story of English*. New and rev. ed. London: Faber and Faber.

McDavid, Raven I. 1981. Webster, Mencken, and Avis: spokesmen for linguistic autonomy. *Canadian Journal of Linguistics* 26(1): 118-125.

McDavid, Raven I. 1980a. [Reviews of] Scargill, M. H. 1977. A short history of Canadian English. Victoria, B.C. and McConnell, Ruth E. 1979 [sic! 1978] Our own voice: Canadian English and how it is studied. Toronto. *Journal of English Linguistics* 14(March): 45-58.

McDavid, Raven I. (ed.-in-chief) *et al.* 1980b. *Linguistic atlas of the Middle and South Atlantic States*. Chicago: University of Chicago Press.

McDavid, Raven I. 1971. Canadian English [Review of Orkin (1970)]. *American Speech* 46(3-4): 287-289.

McDavid, Raven I. 1963. *See* Mencken (1963)

McDavid, Raven I. 1954. Linguistic geography in Canada: an introduction. *Journal of the Canadian Linguistic Association* 1(1, Oct.): 3-8.

McDavid, Raven I. 1951. Midland and Canadian words in upstate New York. *American Speech* 26(4): 248-256.

McDavid, Raven I. and Virginia Glenn McDavid. 1952. *h* before semivowels in the Eastern United States. *American Speech* 28: 41-62.

McLay, W. S. W. 1930. A note on Canadian English. *American Speech* 5: 328f.

Mein Smith, Philippa. 2005. *A concise history of New Zealand*. Cambridge: Cambridge University Press.

Meechan, M. 1999. *The Mormon drawl: religion, ethnicity and phonological variation in Southern Alberta*. PhD Thesis, University of Ottawa.

Mencken, Henry L. 1963. *The American language.* One volume abridged edition. Ed. by Raven I. McDavid, with David W. Maurer. New York: Knopf.

Mencken, Henry L. 1936. *The American language.* 4th ed. New York: Knopf.

Meseck, Birgit. 1995. Kanadisches Englisch. In *Handbuch Englisch als Fremdsprache,* Rüdiger Ahrens, Wolf-Dietrich Bald and Werner Hüllen (eds), 37-39. Berlin: Schmidt.

Meyer, Charles F. 2002. *English corpus linguistics. An introduction.* Cambridge: Cambridge University Press.

Milroy, James. 1992. *Linguistic variation and change. On the historical sociolinguistics of English.* Oxford: Blackwell.

Milroy, Lesley. 1987. *Language and social networks.* 2nd ed. [Language in Society 2]. Oxford: Blackwell.

Minkova, Donka and Robert Stockwell (eds). *Studies in the history of the English language. A millennial perspective* [Topics in English Linguistics 39]. Berlin: Mouton de Gruyter.

Molencki, Rafal. 2003. What must needs be explained about *must needs.* In D. Hart (ed.), 71-87.

Montgomery, Michael. 2003. The history of American English. In D. Preston (ed.), 1-23.

Montgomery, Michael. 1995. The linguistic value of Ulser emigrant letters. *Ulster Folklife* 41: 26-41.

Moodie, Susanna. 1989 [1852]. *Roughing it in the bush; or, life in Canada* [Reprint of 2nd ed.] [New Canadian Library]. Toronto: McClelland & Stewart.

Moody, Patricia A. 1974. *Shall* and *will*: the grammatical tradition and dialectology. *American Speech* 49: 67-78.

Mufwene, Salikoko S. 2001. *The ecology of language evolution.* Cambridge: Cambridge University Press.

Mufwene, Salikoko S. 1996. The founder principle in creole genesis. *Diachronica* 13: 83-134.

Mufwene, Salikoko S., John R. Rickford, Guy Bailey and John Baugh (eds). 1998. *African-American English. Structure, history and use.* London: Routledge.

Murdoch, Margaret. 1985. A proposal for standardization of computer coding systems in linguistic surveys. In H. J. Warkentyne (ed.), 185-190.

Murdoch, Margaret. 1981. Visual-aural prompting in the Vancouver Survey questionnaire. In H. J. Warkentyne (ed.), 48-56.

Murray, Lindley. 1795 [1968]. *English grammar* [English Linguistics 1500-1800, 106. A Collection of Facsimile Reprints], R. C. Alston (ed.). Menston: Scholar Press.

Murray, Thomas E. 1998. More on *drug/dragged* and *snuck/sneaked*. Evidence from the American Midwest. *Journal of English Linguistics* 26(3): 209-221.

Müller, Reimar and Marga Reis (eds). 2001. *Modalität und Modalverben im Deutschen* [Linguistische Berichte: Sonderheft 9]. Hamburg: Buske.

Myhill, John. 1997. *Should* and *ought*: the rise of individually oriented modality in American English. *English Language and Linguistics* 1(1): 3-23.

Myhill, John. 1996. The development of the strong obligation system in American English. *American Speech* 71(4): 339-388.

Myhill, John. 1995. Change and continuity in the functions of American English modals. *Linguistics* 33: 157-211.

Nelson, William H. 1961. *The American Tory*. Oxford: Clarendon.

Nelson, Gerald, Sean Wallis and Bas Aarts. 2002. *Exploring natural language. Working with the British component of the International Corpus of English.* Amsterdam: Benjamins.

Nevalainen, Terttu. 2000. Mobility, social networks and language change in Early Modern England. *European Journal of English Studies* 4/3: 253-264.

Nevalainen, Terttu and Helena Raumolin-Brunberg. 2003. *Historical sociolinguistics: language change in Tudor and Stuart England* [Longman Linguistics Library]. London: Pearson Education.

Nevalainen, Terttu and Helena Raumolin-Brunberg (eds). 1996a. *Sociolinguistics and language history. Studies based on the Corpus of Early English Correspondence* [Language and Computers: Studies in Practical Linguistics 15]. Amsterdam: Rodopi.

Nevalainen, Terttu and Helena Raumolin-Brunberg. 1996b. The Corpus of Early English Correspondence. In T. Nevalainen and H. Raumolin-Brunberg (eds), 39-54.

Nordlinger, Rachel and Elizabeth Closs Traugott. 1997. Scope and the development of epistemic modality: evidence from ought to. *English Language and Linguistics* 1(2): 295-317.

Norris, Darrell A. 1989. Migration, pioneer settlement, and the life course: the first families of an Ontario township. In *Historial essays on Upper Canada. New Perspectives* [Carleton Library Series 146], J. K. Johnson and G. Bruce (eds), 175-201. Ottawa: Carleton University Press.

Noseworthy, Ronald G. 1971. *A dialect survey of Grand Bank, Newfoundland.* MA Thesis, Memorial University, Nfld.

Nurmi, Arja. 2003. *Youe shall see I will conclude in it:* sociolinguistic variation of WILL/WOULD and SHALL/SHOULD in the sixteenth century. In
D. Hart (ed.), 89-107.

Nuyts, Jan. 2005. The modal confusion: on terminology and the concepts
behind it. In A. Klinge and H. H. Müller (eds), 5-38.

Nuyts, Jan. 2001. *Epistemic modality, language, and conceptualization. A cog-
nitive-pragmatic perspective* [Human Cognitive Processing 5]. Amsterdam:
Benjamins.

Nylvek, Judith A. 1993a. *Canadian English in Saskatchewan. A sociolingistic
survey of four selected regions.* PhD Thesis, University of Victoria, B.C.

Nylvek, Judith A. 1993b. A sociolinguistic analysis of Canadian English in
Saskatchewan: a look at urban versus rural speakers. In S. Clarke (ed.), 201-
228.

Nylvek, Judith A. 1992. Is Canadian English in Saskatchewan becoming more
American? *American Speech* 67(3): 268-278.

Nylvek, Judith A. 1984. *A regional and sociolinguistic survey of Saskatchewan
English.* M.A. Thesis, University of Victoria, B.C.

OED. 2002. = *Oxford English Dictionary. CD-ROM version 3.00.* Oxford:
Oxford University Press.

Oldireva, Larisa. 2002. *Preterite and past participle form in English 1680-
1790. Standardisation processes in public and private writing* [Studia
Anglistica Upsaliensia 120]. PhD Thesis, Uppsala University.

Orkin, Mark M. 1973. *Canajan, eh?* Don Mills, Ont.: General Publishing.

Orkin, Mark M. 1970 [1971]. *Speaking Canadian English. An informal
account of the English language in Canada.* Reprint. New York: McKay
Company.

Orkin, Mark M. 1971. *Speaking Canadian French. An informal account of the
French language in Canada.* Revised ed. Toronto: General Publishing.

Owens, Thompson W. and Paul M. Baker. 1984. Linguistic insecurity in
Winnipeg: validation of a Canadian index of linguistic insecurity. *Language
in Society* 13: 337-350.

Paddock, Harold J. 1982. Newfoundland dialects of English. In *Languages in
Newfoundland and Labrador.* 2nd ed., Harold J. Paddock (ed.), 71-89. St.
John's, Nfld: Memorial University of Newfoundland.

Paddock, Harold J. 1981. *A dialect survey of Carbonear, Newfoundland*
[Publications of the American Dialect Society 68]. Alabama: University of
Alabama Press.

Paddock, Harold J. 1966. *A dialect survey of Carbonear, Newfoundland.* M.A.
Thesis, Memorial University of Newfoundland.

Padolsky, Enoch and Ian Pringle. 1984. Demographic analysis and regional dielect surveys in Canada: data collection and use. In *Canadian papers in rural history. Vol. IV.* Donald H. Akenson (ed.), 240-275. Gananoque, Ont.: Langdale Press.

Padolsky, Enoch and Ian Pringle. 1981. *A historical source book for the Ottawa Valley. A linguistic Survey of the Ottawa Valley.* Ottawa: Carleton University, Linguistic Survey of the Ottawa Valley.

Palmer, Frank R. 2003. Modality in English: theoretical, descriptive and typological issues. In R. Facchinetti, M. Krug and F. Palmer (eds), 1-17.

Palmer, Frank R. 2001. *Mood and modality.* 2nd ed. Cambridge: Cambridge University Press.

Palmer, Frank R. 1990. *Modality and the English modals.* 2nd ed. London: Longman.

Palmer, Joe D. and Brigitte Harris. 1990. Prestige differential and language change. *Bulletin of the Canadian Association of Applied Linguistics* 12(1): 77-86.

Paradis, Carole. 1980. La règle de Canadian Raising et l'analyse en structure syllabique. *Canadian Journal of Linguistics* 25(1): 35-44.

Parry, Caroline (ed.). 1994. *Eleanora's diary. The journals of a Canadian pioneer girl.* Richmond Hill: Scholastic Canada.

Partridge, Eric. 1968 [1951]. Australian English. In E. Partridge and J. W. Clark (eds), 85-89.

Partridge, Eric and John W. Clark (eds). 1968 [1951]. *British and American English since 1900. With contributions on English in Canada, South Africa, Australia, New Zealand and India.* New York: Greenwood Press.

Parvin, Viola E. 1965. *Authorization of textbooks for the schools of Ontario. 1846-1950.* Toronto: University of Toronto Press.

Patterson, G. 1895, 1896, 1897. Notes on the dialect of the people of Newfoundland. *Journal of American Folklore* 8: 27-40; 9: 19-37; 10: 203-213.

Pi, Chia-Yi Tony. 2006. Beyond the isogloss: isographs in dialect topography. *Canadian Journal of Linguistics* 51(2&3): 177-184.

Picard, Marc. 1977. Canadian Raising: the case against re-ordering. *Canadian Journal of Linguistics* 22(2): 144-155.

Plank, Frans. 1984. The modals story retold. *Studies in Language* 8(3): 305-364.

Poff, Deborah and Lindsey Arnold. 1999. Women and language. In L. Falk and M. Harry (eds), 183-197.

Polson, James. 1969. *A linguistic questionnaire for British Columbia: a plan for a postal survey of dialectal variation in B.C., with an account of recent research*. M.A. Thesis, University of British Columbia.

Poplack, Shana. 1985. Contrasting patterns of code-switching in two communities. In H. J. Warkentyne (ed.), 363-385.

Poplack, Shana and Sali Tagliamonte. 2004. Back to the present: verbal –*s* in the (African American) English diaspora. In R. Hickey (ed.), 203-223.

Poplack, Shana and Sali Tagliamonte. 2001. *African American English in the diaspora* [Language in Society 30]. Oxford: Blackwell.

Poplack, Shana and Sali Tagliamonte. 2000. The grammaticalization of *going to* in (African American) English. *Language Variation and Change* 11: 315-342.

Poplack, Shana and Sali Tagliamonte. 1994. -*s* or nothing: marking the plural in the African-American diaspora. *American Speech* 69: 227-259.

Poplack, Shana and Sali Tagliamonte. 1993. African American English in the diaspora: evidence from old-line Nova Scotians. In S. Clarke (ed.), 109-150.

Poplack, Shana and Sali Tagliamonte. 1991. African American English in the diaspora: evidence from old-line Nova Scotians. *Language Variation and Change* 3: 301-339.

Poplack, Shana and Sali Tagliamonte. 1989. There's no tense like the present: verbal –*s* inflection in Early Black English. *Language Variation and Change* 1: 47-84.

Poplack, Shana, James A. Walker and Rebecca Malcolmson. 2006. An English "like no other"?: language contact and change in Quebec. *Canadian Journal of Linguistics* 51(2&3): 185-214.

Poteet, Lewis J. 1999. Some observations on the South Shore lexicon. In L. Falk and M. Harry (eds), 17-38.

Poteet, Lewis, J. 1988. *The South Shore phrase book. A new, revised and expanded Nova Scotia dictionary, complete with two appendices.* Hanstsport, N.S.: Lancelot Press.

Potter-MacKinnon, Janice. 1993. *While the women only wept. Loyalist refugee women*. Montreal: McGill-Queen's University Press.

Pratt, Terrence K. 1993. The hobglobin of Canadian English spelling. In S. Clarke (ed.), 45-64.

Pratt, Terrence K. (ed.). 1988. *Dictionary of Prince Edward Island English*. Toronto: University of Toronto Press.

Pratt, Terrence K. 1982. I dwell in possibility: variable /ay/ in Prince Edward Island. *Journal of the Atlantic Linguistic Association* 4: 27-35.

Pratt, Terrence K. and Scott Burke (eds). 1998. *Prince Edward Island sayings*. Toronto: University of Toronto Press.

Preston, Dennis R. (ed.). 2003. *Needed research in American dialects* [Publication of the American Dialect Society 88]. American Dialect Society: Duke University Press.

Priestley, F. E. L. 1968 [1951]. Canadian English. In E. Partridge and J. W. Clark (eds), 72-84.

Pringle, Ian. 1986. The complexity of the concept of standard. In W. C. Lougheed (ed.), 20-38.

Pringle, Ian. 1985. Attitudes to Canadian English. In *The English language today,* Sidney Greenbaum (ed.), 183-205. Oxford: Pergamon.

Pringle, Ian. 1983. The concept of dialect and the study of Canadian English. *Queen's Quarterly* 90(1): 100-121.

Pringle, Ian. 1981. The Gaelic substratum in the English of Glengarry County and its reflection in the novels of Ralph Connor. *Canadian Journal of Linguistics* 26: 126-140.

Pringle, Ian and Enoch Padolsky. 1983. The linguistic survey of the Ottawa Valley. *American Speech* 58(4): 327-344.

Pringle, Ian, Ian R. H. Dale and Enoch Padolsky. 1985. Procedures to solve a methodological problem in the Ottawa Valley. In H. J. Warkentyne (ed.), 477-494.

Pyles, Thomas and John Algeo. 1993. *The origins and development of the English language.* 4th ed. Fort Worth: Harcourt Brace Jovanovich.

Quirk, Randolph, Sidney Greenbaum, Geoffrey Leech and Jan Svartvik. 1985. *A comprehensive grammar of the English language.* London: Longman.

Quinn, Heidi. 1999. Variation in New Zealand English syntax and morphology. In New Zealand English [Varieties of English Around the World, G25], Allan Bell and Koenraad Kuiper (eds), 173-197. Amsterdam: Benjamins.

Rayburn, Alan. 1997. *Place names of Ontario.* Toronto: University of Toronto Press.

Read, Colin and Ronald J. Stagg (eds). 1985. *The Rebellion of 1837 in Upper Canada. A collection of documents.* Ottawa: Champlain Society and Ontario Heritage Foundation with Carleton University Press.

Reaman, G. Elmore. 1957. *The trail of the black walnut.* Toronto: McClelland & Stewart.

Reid, Richard M. 1990. *The Upper Ottawa Valley to 1855* [Carleton Library Series 157]. Ottawa: Carleton University Press.

Renouf, Antoinette and Andrew Kehoe (eds). 2006. *The changing face of corpus linguistics.* [Language and Computers: Studies in Practical Linguistics 55]. Amsterdam: Rodopi.

Richards, Donna. 1988. *Prestige and standard in Canadian English: evidence from the Survey of Vancouver English.* PhD Thesis, University of British Columbia.

Rickford, John R. 1999. *African American vernacular English. Features, evolution, educational implications* [Language in Society, 26]. Malden: Blackwell.

Rissanen, Matti. 2000. Standardization and the language of early statutes. In L. Wright, 117-130.

Rissanen, Matti, Ossi Ihalainen, Terttu Nevalainen and Irma Taavitsainen (eds). 1992. *History of Englishes. New methods and interpretations in historical linguistics.* Berlin: Mouton de Gruyter.

Ritt, Nikolaus. 2004. *Selfish sounds and linguistic evolution. A Darwinian approach to language change.* Cambridge: Cambridge University Press.

Ritt, Nikolaus. 1995. Language change as evolution: looking for linguistic 'genes'. *VIEWS.* 4(1): 43-56, online version: http://www.univie.ac.at/Anglistik/views/archive.htm (2 Jan. 2006).

Rodman, Lilita. 1993. Student-designed projects on Canadian English. In *Language variation in North American English: research and teaching*, A. Wayne Glowka and Donald M. Lance (eds), 144-150. New York: Modern Language Association of America.

Romaine, Suzanne (ed.). 1998. *The Cambridge history of the English language. Volume IV 1776-1997.* Cambridge: Cambridge University Press.

Rosenfelder, Ingrid. 2005. *Canadian Raising in Victoria, B.C.: an acoustic analysis. M.A. Thesis.* Department of English, University of Heidelberg, Germany. http://www.rzuser.uni-heidelberg.de/~irosenfe/CanadianRaising/Zula_IRosenfelder.pdf (2 Sep. 2005).

Sandilands, John. 1977 [1913]. *Western Canadian dictionary and phrasebook. Facsimile edition of the 1913 [2nd] edition, with an introduction by John Orrell.* Edmonton: University of Alberta Press.

Sapir, Edward. 1949 [1921]. *Language. An introduction to the study of speech.* New York: Harcourt, Brace and World.

Sautter, Udo. 2000. *Geschichte Kanadas* [Beck Wissen 2137]. München: Beck.

Scargill, Matthew H. 1985 [reprinted 1988, 2000]. English language. In *The Canadian encyclopedia.* Vol. I., James H. Marsh (ed.), s.v. "English language". Edmonton: Hurtig.

Scargill, Matthew H. 1977. *A short history of Canadian English.* Victoria, B.C.: Sono Nis.

Scargill, Matthew H. 1974. *Modern Canadian English usage. Linguistic change and reconstruction.* Toronto: McClelland and Stewart in Cooperation with the Canadian Council of Teachers of English.

Scargill, Matthew H. 1957. Sources of Canadian English. *Journal of English and Germanic Philology* 56: 611-614 [reprinted in Chambers (ed.). 1975a, 12-15].

Scargill, Matthew H. 1956. Eighteenth-century English in Nova Scotia. *Journal of the Canadian Linguistic Association* 2(1): 3.

Scargill, Matthew H. 1955. Canadian English and Canadian culture in Alberta. *Journal of the Canadian Linguistic Association* 1(1, Mar.): 26-29.

Scargill, Matthew H. 1954. A pilot study of Alberta speech: vocabulary. *Journal of the Canadian Linguistic Association* 1(1, Oct.): 21f.

Scargill, Matthew H. and Henry J. Warkentyne. 1972. The survey of Canadian English: a report. *The English Quarterly. A publication of the* Canadian Council of Teachers of English 5(3, Fall): 47-104.

Schendl, Herbert. 2002. Mixed language texts as data and evidence in English historical linguistics. In D. Minkova and R. Stockwell (eds), 51-78.

Schneider, Edgar W., Kate Burridge, Bernd Kortmann, Rajend Mesthrie and Clive Upton (eds). 2004. *A handbook of varieties of English. A mulitmedia reference tool. Vol. I: Phonology.* Berlin: Mouton de Gruyter.

Schneider, Edgar W. 2004. The English dialect heritage of the southern United States. In R. Hickey (ed.), 262-309.

Schneider, Edgar W. 2002. Investigating variation and change in written documents. In J. K. Chambers, P. Trudgill and N. Schilling-Estes (eds), 67-96.

Schneider, Edgar W. 1984. A bibliography of writings on American and Canadian English (1965-1983). In *A bibliography of writings on varieties of English, 1965-1983,* Wolfgang Viereck, Edgar W. Schneider and Manfred Görlach (eds), 89-213; index: 215-223. Amsterdam: Benjamins.

Schryer, Frans J. 1998. *The Netherlandic presence in Ontario. Pillars, class and Dutch ethnicity.* Waterloo, Ont.: Wilfried Laurier University Press.

Scott, N. C. 1939. kəneidiən caught and cot. *Maître Phonétique* 66(3): 22.

Scott, S. Osborne and D. A. Mulligan. 1951. The Red River dialect. *The Beaver.* December: 42-45.

Scvr, Georgij S. and T. I. Kasatkina. 1977. Some notes on Canadian English. *Kwartalnik Neofilologiczny* 24: 403-408.

Seary, E. R. 1971. *Place names of the Avalon Peninsula of the island of Newfoundland.* Toronto: University of Toronto Press.

Seary, E. R. 1958. The French element in Newfoundland place names. *Journal of the Canadian Linguistic Association* 4(1, Spring): 63-69.

Seary, E. R., G. M. Story and W. J. Kirwin. 1968. *The Avalon Peninsula of Newfoundland: an ethno-linguistic study* [National Museum of Canada, Bulletin No. 219. Anthropological Series 81]. Ottawa: Queen's Printer.

Seguinot, Candace L. 1976. *Some aspects of the intonation of yes-no questions in Canadian English.* PhD Thesis, University of Toronto.

Simon-Vandenbergen, A. M. 1984. Deontic possibility: a diachronic view. *English Studies* 65(4): 362-365.

Sledd, James. 1978. What are we going to do about it now that we're number one? *American Speech* 53: 175-194.

Smith, Michael. 1813 [1985]. *A geographical view of the province of Upper Canada, and promiscuous remarks on the government. In two parts, with an appendix containing a complete description of the Niagara Falls and remarks relative to the situation of the immigrants respecting the war* [CIHM 49860]. Hartford: Hale and Hosner.

Smith, Nicholas. 2003. Changes in the modals and semi-modals of strong obligation and epistemic necessity in recent British English. In R. Facchinetti, M. Krug and F. Palmer (eds), 241-266.

Smitterberg, Eric. 2005. *The progressive in 19th-century English. A process of integration* [Language and Computers 54]. Amsterdam: Rodopi.

Stabile, Julia M. 2002. *Toronto newspapers, 1798-1845. A case study in print.* PhD Thesis, University of Toronto.

Stein, Dieter and Jenny Cheshire (eds). 1997. *Taming the vernacular. From dialect to standard language.* London: Longman.

Stevenson, Roberta C. 1977. *The pronunciation of English in B.C.* M.A. Thesis, University of British Columbia.

Stewart, Murray. 1999. *Cuffer Down. Expressions form The Nashwaak & Over North recalled by an old Taymite.* No place: No publisher.

Stobie, Margaret. 1967-68. Backgrounds of the dialect called Bungi. *Manitoba Historical Society Transactions.* Series 3, Number 24. http://www.mhs. mb.ca/docs/transactions/3/bungidialect.shtml (22 Aug. 2005).

Story, G. M. 1957. Research in the language and place-names of Newfoundland. *Journal of the Canadian Linguistic Association* [later renamed *Canadian Linguistic Journal*] 3/2 (Oct.): 47-55.

Story, G. M., W. J. Kirwin and J. D. A. Widdowson (eds). 1982 [2nd ed. 1990] *Dictionary of Newfoundland English.* Toronto: University of Toronto Press.

Sudbury, Andrea. 2004. English on the Falklands. In R. Hickey (ed.), 402-417.

Sutherland, Fraser. 2000. Sprightly muddles and errors. *English Today* 64(16/4):19f.

Sundby, Bertil, Anne Kari Bjørge and Kari E. Haugland. 1991. *A dictionary of English normative grammar 1700-1800.* Amsterdam: Benjamins.

Tagliamonte, Sali. 2006a. *"So cool, right?"*: Canadian English entering the 21ˢᵗ century. *Canadian Journal of Linguistics* 51(2&3): 309-332.

Tagliamonte, Sali. 2006b. Historical change in synchronic perspective: the legacy of British dialects. In A. van Kemenade and L. Bettelou (eds), 477-506.

Tagliamonte, Sali. 2005. 'So who? *Like* how? *Just* what?' Discourse markers in the conversations of young Canadians. *Journal of Pragmatics* 37(1): 1896-1915.

Tagliamonte, Sali. 2004. Have to, gotta, must: Grammaticalisation, variation and specialization in English deontic modality. In *Corpus approaches to grammaticalization in English*, Hans Lindquist and Christian Mair (eds), 33-55. Amsterdam: Benjamins.

Tagliamonte, Sali and Alexandra D'Arcy. 2005. "When people say, 'I was like': the quotative system in Canadian youth". *Pennsylvania Working Papers in Linguistics* 10(2): 257-272.

Tagliamonte, Sali and Alexandra D'Arcy. 2004. '*He's like*; *She's like*': the quotative system in Canadian youth. *Journal of Sociolinguistics* 8(4): 493-514.

Tagliamonte, Sali and Rachel Hudson. 1999. *Be like* et al. beyond America: the quotative system in British and Canadian youth. *Journal of Sociolinguistics* 3(2): 147-172.

Taglicht, J. 1970. The genesis of the conventional rules for the use of shall and will. *English Studies* 51: 193-213.

Talman, J. J. and R. Talman. 1977. The Canadas 1763-1812. In *Literary history of Canada. Canadian literature in English. Vol. I.*, C. F. Klinck (ed.), 97-105. Toronto: University of Toronto Press.

Taubitz, Ronald M. 1975. *A study of "shall" and "will" by various grammarians.* PhD Thesis, Arizona State University.

Thain, Chris. 2003 [1987]. *Cold as a Bay Street banker's heart. The ultimate Prairie phrase book.* Calgary: Fifth House Ltd.

Thay, Edrick. 2004. *Weird Canadian words. How to speak Canadian.* Edmonton: Folklore Publishing.

Thomas, A. 1979. The pronunciation of /h/. In P. R. Léon, and P. Martin (eds), 111-128.

Thomas, Alan R. (ed.). 1988. *Methods in dialectology. Proceedings of the Sixth International Conference held at the Univerity College of North Wales, 3rd-7th August 1987* [Multilingual Matters 48]. Clevedon: Multilingual Matters.

Thomas, Eric R. 1991. The origin of Canadian Raising in Ontario. *Canadian Journal of Linguistics* 36: 147-170.

Tieken-Boon van Ostade, Ingrid. 2000a. Social network analysis and the history of English. *European Journal of English Studies* 4(3): 211-216.

Tieken-Boon van Ostade, Ingrid. 2000b. Social network analysis and the language of Sarah Fielding. *European Journal of English Studies* 4(3): 291-302.

Tieken-Boon van Ostade, Ingrid. 1996. Social network theory and eighteenth-century English. The case of Boswell. In D. Britton (ed.), 327-337.

Tieken-Boon van Ostade, Ingrid. 1991. Samuel Richardson's role as a linguistic innovator: a sociolinguistic analysis. In *Language usage and description. Studies presented to N.E. Osselton on the occasion of his retirement*, Ingrid Tieken-Boon van Ostade and John Frankis (eds), 47-57. Amsterdam: Rodopi.

Tieken-Boon van Ostade, Ingrid. 1987. *The auxiliary do in eighteenth-century English. A sociohistorical-linguistic approach.* Leiden: ICG Printing.

Tieken-Boon van Ostade, Ingrid. 1985. 'I will be drowned and no man shall save me': the conventional rules for *shall* and *will* in eighteenth-century English grammars. *English Studies* 66(2): 123-142.

Tilly, George A. 1980. *Canadian English in the novels of the 1970's.* PhD Thesis, York University, Ont.

Toon, Thomas E. 1981. Making a North American dictionary after Avis. *Canadian Journal of Linguistics* 26: 142-149.

Traugott, Elizabeth Closs. 1999. Why *must* is not *moot*. Paper read at the 14th International Conference of Historical Linguistics, Vancouver.

Traugott, Elizabeth Closs. 1989. On the rise of epistemic meanings in English: an example of subjectification in semantic change. *Language* 65(1):31-55.

Traugott, Elizabeth Closs. 1972. *A history of English syntax. A transformational approach to the history of English sentence structure.* New York: Holt, Rinehart & Winston.

Trudgill, Peter. 2006. Dialect mixture versus monogenesis in colonial varieties: the inevitability of Canadian English? *Canadian Journal of Linguistics* 51(2&3): 265-286.

Trudgill, Peter. 2004. *New dialect formation. The inevitability of colonial Englishes.* Edinburgh: Edinburgh University Press.

Trudgill, Peter. 2001. Sociohistorical linguistics and dialect survival: a note on another Nova Scotian enclave. In *Language structure and variation*, Magnus Ljung (ed.), 195-201. Stockholm: Almqvist & Wiksell.

Trudgill, Peter. 1986. *Dialects in contact*. Oxford: Blackwell.

Trudgill, Peter. 1985. New-dialect formation and the analysis of colonial dialects: the case of Canadian Raising. In H. J. Warkentyne, 35-45.

Trudgill, Peter. 1981. Linguistic accomodation: sociolinguistic observations on a sociopsychological theory. In *Papers from the Parasession on Language and Behavior. Chicago Linguistic Society. May 1-2, 1981.* Carrie S. Masek, Roberta A. Hendrick and Mary F. Miller (eds), 218-237. Chicago: University of Chicago.

Trudgill, Peter. 1974. Linguistic change and diffusion: description and explanation in sociolinguistic dialect geography. *Language in Society* 3: 215-246.

Trudgill, Peter and Jean Hannah. 2002. *International English. A guide to varieties of Standard English.* 4th ed. London: Arnold.

Trudgill, Peter, Elizabeth Gordon, Gillian Lewis and Margaret Maclagan. 2000. Determinism in new-dialect formation and the genesis of New Zealand English. *Journal of Linguistics* 36: 299-318.

Trudgill, Peter, Elizabeth Gordon and Gillian Lewis. 1998. New-dialect formation and Southern Hemisphere Englishes: the New Zealand short front vowels. *Journal of Sociolinguistics* 2(1): 35-51.

Upward, Christopher. 2000. Canadian spelling choices. *English Today* 64(16/4): 20f.

Urion, Carl. 1971. Canadian English and Canadian French (a review) [of Orkin 1970 and 1971]. In *Linguistic diversity in Canadian society*, Regna Darnell (ed.), 33-44. Edmonton: Linguistic Research.

Vance, Timothy J. 1987. 'Canadian Raising' in some dialects of the northern United States. *American Speech* 62(3): 195-210.

Van Bergen, Linda and David Denison. 2007. A corpus of late eighteenth-century prose. In Beal, Joan C., Karen P. Corrigan and Hermann Moisl (eds). *Creating and digitizing language corpora. Vol. 2, Diachronic databases.* Basingstoke: Palgrave, 228-46.

Van der Auwera, Johan. 1986. The possibilities of *may* and *can*. In D. Kastovsky and A. Szwedek (eds), 1067-1076.

Van der Gaaf, W. 1931. *Beon* and *habban* connected with an inflected infinitive. *English Studies* 13: 176-188.

Van Herk, Gerard and James A. Walker. 2005. S marks the spot? Regional variation and early African American correspondence. *Language Variation and Change* 17: 113-131.

Van Kemenade, Ans and Bettelou Los (eds). 2006. *The handbook of the history of English.* Malden, MA: Blackwell.

Vincent, Thomas, George Parker and Stephen Bonnycastle (eds). 1978. *Walter S. Avis: essays and articles. Selected from a quarter century of scholarship at the Royal Military College of Canada, Kingston.* Kingston: Royal Military College of Canada.

Visser, F. Th. 1969-73. *An historical syntax of the English language.* Vol. III/1. Syntactical units with two verbs; Vol. III/2. Syntactical units with two and more verbs. Leiden: Brill.

Wales, Katie. 2002. 'North of Watford Gap'. A cultural history of Northern English (from 1700). In R. Watts and P. Trudgill (eds), 45-66.

Walker, Douglas C. 2006. Canadian English in a Francophone family. *Canadian Journal of Linguistics* 51(2&3): 215-224.

Walker, Douglas C. 1975. Another Edmonton idiolect: comments on an article by Professor Avis. In J. K. Chambers (ed.), 129-132.

Walker, James A. 2005. The *ain't* constraint: *not*-contraction in early African American English. *Language Variation and Change* 17: 1-17.

Wanamaker, Murray G. 1981. Walter S. Avis: gōd wīs secg. *Canadian Journal of Linguistics* 26(1): 87-89.

Wanamaker, Murray G. 1976/77. Who controls writing standards?. *The English Quarterly* 9: 45-52.

Wanamaker, Murray G. 1965. *The language of King's County, Nova Scotia.* PhD Thesis, University of Michigan.

Ward, Gregory, Betty J. Birner and Jeffrey P. Kaplan. 2003. A pragmatic analysis of the epistemic *would* contruction in English. In R. Facchinetti, M. Krug and F. Palmer (eds), 71-79.

Warkentyne, Henry J. (ed.). 1985. *Methods/Méthodes V. 1984. Papers from the Fifth International Conference on Methods in Dialectology.* Victoria, B.C.: University of Victoria.

Warkentyne, Henry J. 1983. Attitudes and language behavior. *Canadian Journal of Linguistics* 28: 71-76.

Warkentyne, Henry J. 1971. Contemporary Canadian English: a report of the Survey of Canadian English. *American Speech* 46(3-4): 193-199.

Warkentyne, Henry J. and A. C. Brett. 1981a. Changing norms in Canadian English usage. *Working Papers of the Linguistic Cirlce of the University of Victoria* 1(1): 197-217.

Warkentyne, Henry J. and A. C. Brett. 1981b. British and American influences on Canadian English. *Working Papers of the Linguistic Cirlce of the University of Victoria* 1(2): 294-310.

Warner, Anthony R. 1993. *English auxiliaries. Structure and history.* Cambridge: Cambridge University Press.

Watts, Richard and Peter Trudgill (eds). 2002. *Alternative histories of English.* London: Routledge.

Weld, Isaac. 1968. [1807]. *Travels through the States of North America, and the Provinces of Upper and Lower Canada during the Years 1795, 1796, and 1797.* 4th ed. illustrated and embellished with sixteen plates. With a new introduction by Martin Roth. 2 vols. [Series in American Studies]. New York: Johnson Reprint Cooperation.

Wells, John C. 1982. *Accents of English.* Cambridge: Cambridge University Press.

Whalen, A. C. 1978. *The effects in varying contexts on the adding and droppoing of (h) by grade IV and grade IX students on New World Island, Nfld.* M.Ed. Thesis, Memorial University, Nfld.

White, Randall. 1985. *Ontario 1610-1985. A political and economic history* [Ontario Heritage Foundation, Local History Series 1]. Toronto: Dundurn Press.

Wick, Neil. 2004. *Analyzing language variation and change as a complex adaptive system.* Unpublished Master of Arts Major Research Paper, York University, Toronto.

Wilson, H. Rex 1973. Dialect literature: a two-way street?. *Canadian Journal of Linguistics* 18(2): 157-160.

Wilson, H. Rex. 1958. *The dialect of Lunenburg County, Nova Scotia. A study of the English of the county, with reference to its sources, preservation of relics, and vestiges of bilingualism.* PhD Thesis, University of Michigan.

Wilson, J. Donald. 1978 [1970]. The pre-Ryerson years. In *Egerton Ryerson and his times,* Neil MacDonald and Alf Chaiton (eds), 9-42. Toronto: MacMillan.

Winks, Robin W. 1997. *The blacks in Canada. A history.* 2nd ed. Montreal: McGill-Queen's University Press.

Wolfram, Walt and Natalie Schilling-Estes. 2004. Remnant dialects in the coastal United States. In R. Hickey (ed.), 172-202.

Wolfram, Walt and Natalie Schilling-Estes. 1998. *American English. Dialects and Variation.* Oxford: Blackwell.

Wood, J. David. 2000. *Making Ontario. Agricultural colonization and landscape re-creation before the railway.* Montreal: McGill-Queen's University Press.

Woods, Howard B. 1999 [1979]. *The Ottawa Survey of Canadian English.* With a forword by Peter Trudgill [Strathy Language Unit Occasional Papers 4]. Kingston: Queen's University.

Woods, Howard B. 1993. A synchronic study of English spoken in Ottawa: is Canadian English becoming more American? In S. Clarke (ed.), 151-178.

Woods, Howard B. 1991. Social differentiation in Ottawa English. In *English around the world. Sociolinguistic perspectives*, Jenny Cheshire (ed.), 134-152. Cambridge: Cambridge University Press.

Woods, Natalie J. 1997. The formation and development of New Zealand English: interaction of gender-related variation and linguistic change. *Journal of Sociolinguistics* 1(1): 95-125.

Woods, Anthony, Paul Fletcher and Arthur Hughes. 1986. *Statistics in language studies.* Cambridge: Cambridge University Press.

WordSmith. 1998. Version 3.00.00, programmed by Mike Scott

Wright, Laura (ed.). 2000. *The development of standard English: theories, descriptions, conflicts.* Cambridge: Cambridge University Press.

Yuen, Adrienne L. 1994. *Gallicisms: an analysis leading towards a prototype Gallicisms checker.* M.A. Thesis, University of Ottawa, Ont.

Zeller, Christine. 1993. Linguistic symmetries, asymmetries, and border effects within a Canadian/American sample. In S. Clarke (ed.), 179-200.

Ziegeler, Debra. 2006. *Interfaces with English aspect: diachronic and empirical studies* [Studies in Language Companion 82]. Amsterdam: Benjamins.

Ziegeler, Debra. 2003. On the origins of modality in English. In D. Hart (ed.), 33-69.

Ziegeler, Debra. 2000. *Hypothetical modality. Grammaticalization in an L2 dialect* [Studies in Language Companion Series 51]. Amsterdam: Benjamins.

General Index

Atlantic crossings 290
mid-Atlantic **69**, 98
New England 47, 57, 67, **68**, 98
interdialect development 138, 140, **141**,
166, 186, 200, 202
intra-dialectal variation 143
Inuit 54
inverse V-curve 182, 183, 202, 268
Irish
Northern input 149
Southern input 88
Irish English 22, 47, 52, 79, 80, 84, 85,
88, 96, 124, 132, 283, 289
Irish immigration 73, 77, 79, **81**, **83**, 88,
141
pre-1812 97
Irish influence 47
Joos, Martin 21, 29, 328
koinéization 139, 144
Kortmann, Bernd 282
Kytö, Merja 4, 7, 102, 107, 134, 154, 163,
164, 171, 172, 173, 174, 175, 190, 193,
200, 230, 232, 233, 235, 236, 243, 245,
246, 249, 283
Labov, William 15, 19, 33, 102, 164, 215,
241
land surveyors 73, 114, 190, 294
language contact 38, 97, 121, 131, 137,
141, 280, 283
letters
semi-official 108, 114, 117, 167
levelling
apparent levelling 140, **143**, 144, 148,
166, 182, 186, 225, 243, 280
rudimentary levelling **140–41**, 142,
144, 186, 200, 202, 218, 226
lower class 85, 87, 93, 108, 111, 115, 117,
118, 168, 183, 184, 185, 186, 241, 242,
264, 270, 279, 280, 282
loyalist base theory 179, 214, 247, 270
See Bloomfield, Morton W.
Loyalists 19, 22, 66, 68, 122, **123**, **131**
African American 75
and dialect contact 141
French-speakers 74
German-speakers 71
late loyalists 66

Mair, Christian 102, 154, 161, 165, 195,
223, 224, 272
majority form 126, 140, 149, 150, 166,
184, 186, 226, 241, 242, 243, 247, 255,
280
Maritimes dialect survey 34
MAY
affirmative contexts **175**
epistemic 189–90
main functions 177–79
permission **181**, 277 *See CAN*
root possibility *See CAN*
McDavid, Raven I. 3, 4, 9, 10, 11, 21, 27,
34, 39, 56
medium
spoken 52, 57, 107, 108, 160, 161,
163, 188, 190, 200, 201, 208, 213,
221, 224, 237
written 49, 56, 60, 103, 107, 113, 187,
188, 200, 213, 221, 222, 251, 264,
274
Mencken, H. L. 2, 4, 12, 17, 21, 220, 253
merger
low-back vowel 32
middle class 13, 14, 31, 87, 91, 92, 93,
104, 105, 108, 116, 117, 130, 167, 184,
185, 186, 203, 241, 263
MIGHT
epistemic 192, 201, 203, 273, 299
negative contexts 174
non-past contexts *See COULD*
past contexts *See COULD*
modality
deontic **157**
dynamic 157, **159**
epistemic **157**
necessity 5, 162, 163, 164, 205, 217,
218, 219, 221
obligation 139, 158, 161, 162, 163,
164, 171, 205, 206, 211, 220, 223,
224, 225, 227, 231, 250, 253, 265,
270
permission 54, 59, 84, 157, 158, 162,
163, 164, 171, 172, 177, 179, 180,
181, 182, 183, 184, 188, 232, 268,
276, 281
possibility 163, 171, 172, 177, 179,
181, 184, 185, 187, 278

Studies in Language Companion Series

A complete list of titles in this series can be found on the publishers' website, *www.benjamins.com*

69 **TANAKA, Lidia:** Gender, Language and Culture. A study of Japanese television interview discourse. 2004. xvii, 233 pp.

68 **MODER, Carol Lynn and Aida MARTINOVIC-ZIC (eds.):** Discourse Across Languages and Cultures. 2004. vi, 366 pp.

67 **LURAGHI, Silvia:** On the Meaning of Prepositions and Cases. The expression of semantic roles in Ancient Greek. 2003. xii, 366 pp.

66 **NARIYAMA, Shigeko:** Ellipsis and Reference Tracking in Japanese. 2003. xvi, 400 pp.

65 **MATSUMOTO, Kazuko:** Intonation Units in Japanese Conversation. Syntactic, informational and functional structures. 2003. xviii, 215 pp.

64 **BUTLER, Christopher S.:** Structure and Function – A Guide to Three Major Structural-Functional Theories. Part 2: From clause to discourse and beyond. 2003. xiv, 579 pp.

63 **BUTLER, Christopher S.:** Structure and Function – A Guide to Three Major Structural-Functional Theories. Part 1: Approaches to the simplex clause. 2003. xx, 573 pp.

62 **FIELD, Fredric:** Linguistic Borrowing in Bilingual Contexts. With a foreword by Bernard Comrie. 2002. xviii, 255 pp.

61 **GODDARD, Cliff and Anna WIERZBICKA (eds.):** Meaning and Universal Grammar. Theory and empirical findings. Volume 2. 2002. xvi, 337 pp.

60 **GODDARD, Cliff and Anna WIERZBICKA (eds.):** Meaning and Universal Grammar. Theory and empirical findings. Volume 1. 2002. xvi, 337 pp.

59 **SHI, Yuzhi:** The Establishment of Modern Chinese Grammar. The formation of the resultative construction and its effects. 2002. xiv, 262 pp.

58 **MAYLOR, B. Roger:** Lexical Template Morphology. Change of state and the verbal prefixes in German. 2002. x, 273 pp.

57 **MEL'ČUK, Igor A.:** Communicative Organization in Natural Language. The semantic-communicative structure of sentences. 2001. xii, 393 pp.

56 **FAARLUND, Jan Terje (ed.):** Grammatical Relations in Change. 2001. viii, 326 pp.

55 **DAHL, Östen and Maria KOPTJEVSKAJA-TAMM (eds.):** Circum-Baltic Languages. Volume 2: Grammar and Typology. 2001. xx, 423 pp.

54 **DAHL, Östen and Maria KOPTJEVSKAJA-TAMM (eds.):** Circum-Baltic Languages. Volume 1: Past and Present. 2001. xx, 382 pp.

53 **FISCHER, Olga, Anette ROSENBACH and Dieter STEIN (eds.):** Pathways of Change. Grammaticalization in English. 2000. x, 391 pp.

52 **TORRES CACOULLOS, Rena:** Grammaticization, Synchronic Variation, and Language Contact. A study of Spanish progressive -ndo constructions. 2000. xvi, 255 pp.

51 **ZIEGELER, Debra:** Hypothetical Modality. Grammaticalisation in an L2 dialect. 2000. xx, 290 pp.

50 **ABRAHAM, Werner and Leonid KULIKOV (eds.):** Tense-Aspect, Transitivity and Causativity. Essays in honour of Vladimir Nedjalkov. 1999. xxxiv, 359 pp.

49 **BHAT, D.N.S.:** The Prominence of Tense, Aspect and Mood. 1999. xii, 198 pp.

48 **MANNEY, Linda Joyce:** Middle Voice in Modern Greek. Meaning and function of an inflectional category. 2000. xiii, 262 pp.

47 **BRINTON, Laurel J. and Minoji AKIMOTO (eds.):** Collocational and Idiomatic Aspects of Composite Predicates in the History of English. 1999. xiv, 283 pp.

46 **YAMAMOTO, Mutsumi:** Animacy and Reference. A cognitive approach to corpus linguistics. 1999. xviii, 278 pp.

45 **COLLINS, Peter C. and David LEE (eds.):** The Clause in English. In honour of Rodney Huddleston. 1999. xv, 342 pp.

44 **HANNAY, Mike and A. Machtelt BOLKESTEIN (eds.):** Functional Grammar and Verbal Interaction. 1998. xii, 304 pp.

43 **OLBERTZ, Hella, Kees HENGEVELD and Jesús SÁNCHEZ GARCÍA (eds.):** The Structure of the Lexicon in Functional Grammar. 1998. xii, 312 pp.

42 **DARNELL, Michael, Edith A. MORAVCSIK, Michael NOONAN, Frederick J. NEWMEYER and Kathleen M. WHEATLEY (eds.):** Functionalism and Formalism in Linguistics. Volume II: Case studies. 1999. vi, 407 pp.

41 DARNELL, Michael, Edith A. MORAVCSIK, Michael NOONAN, Frederick J. NEWMEYER and Kathleen M. WHEATLEY (eds.): Functionalism and Formalism in Linguistics. Volume I: General papers. 1999. vi, 486 pp.

40 BIRNER, Betty J. and Gregory WARD: Information Status and Noncanonical Word Order in English. 1998. xiv, 314 pp.

39 WANNER, Leo (ed.): Recent Trends in Meaning–Text Theory. 1997. xx, 202 pp.

38 HACKING, Jane F.: Coding the Hypothetical. A comparative typology of Russian and Macedonian conditionals. 1998. vi, 156 pp.

37 HARVEY, Mark and Nicholas REID (eds.): Nominal Classification in Aboriginal Australia. 1997. x, 296 pp.

36 KAMIO, Akio (ed.): Directions in Functional Linguistics. 1997. xiii, 259 pp.

35 MATSUMOTO, Yoshiko: Noun-Modifying Constructions in Japanese. A frame semantic approach. 1997. viii, 204 pp.

34 HATAV, Galia: The Semantics of Aspect and Modality. Evidence from English and Biblical Hebrew. 1997. x, 224 pp.

33 VELÁZQUEZ-CASTILLO, Maura: The Grammar of Possession. Inalienability, incorporation and possessor ascension in Guaraní. 1996. xvi, 274 pp.

32 FRAJZYNGIER, Zygmunt: Grammaticalization of the Complex Sentence. A case study in Chadic. 1996. xviii, 501 pp.

31 WANNER, Leo (ed.): Lexical Functions in Lexicography and Natural Language Processing. 1996. xx, 355 pp.

30 HUFFMAN, Alan: The Categories of Grammar. French lui and le. 1997. xiv, 379 pp.

29 ENGBERG-PEDERSEN, Elisabeth, Michael FORTESCUE, Peter HARDER, Lars HELTOFT and Lisbeth Falster JAKOBSEN (eds.): Content, Expression and Structure. Studies in Danish functional grammar. 1996. xvi, 510 pp.

28 HERMAN, József (ed.): Linguistic Studies on Latin. Selected papers from the 6th International Colloquium on Latin Linguistics (Budapest, 23–27 March 1991). 1994. ix, 421 pp.

27 ABRAHAM, Werner, T. GIVÓN and Sandra A. THOMPSON (eds.): Discourse, Grammar and Typology. Papers in honor of John W.M. Verhaar. 1995. xx, 352 pp.

26 LIMA, Susan D., Roberta L. CORRIGAN and Gregory K. IVERSON: The Reality of Linguistic Rules. 1994. xxiii, 480 pp.

25 GODDARD, Cliff and Anna WIERZBICKA (eds.): Semantic and Lexical Universals. Theory and empirical findings. 1994. viii, 510 pp.

24 BHAT, D.N.S.: The Adjectival Category. Criteria for differentiation and identification. 1994. xii, 295 pp.

23 COMRIE, Bernard and Maria POLINSKY (eds.): Causatives and Transitivity. 1993. x, 399 pp.

22 McGREGOR, William B.: A Functional Grammar of Gooniyandi. 1990. xx, 618 pp.

21 COLEMAN, Robert (ed.): New Studies in Latin Linguistics. Proceedings of the 4th International Colloquium on Latin Linguistics, Cambridge, April 1987. 1990. x, 480 pp.

20 VERHAAR, John W.M. S.J. (ed.): Melanesian Pidgin and Tok Pisin. Proceedings of the First International Conference on Pidgins and Creoles in Melanesia. 1990. xiv, 409 pp.

19 BLUST, Robert A.: Austronesian Root Theory. An essay on the limits of morphology. 1988. xi, 190 pp.

18 WIERZBICKA, Anna: The Semantics of Grammar. 1988. vii, 581 pp.

17 CALBOLI, Gualtiero (ed.): Subordination and Other Topics in Latin. Proceedings of the Third Colloquium on Latin Linguistics, Bologna, 1–5 April 1985. 1989. xxix, 691 pp.

16 CONTE, Maria-Elisabeth, János Sánder PETÖFI and Emel SÖZER (eds.): Text and Discourse Connectedness. Proceedings of the Conference on Connexity and Coherence, Urbino, July 16–21, 1984. 1989. xxiv, 584 pp.

15 JUSTICE, David: The Semantics of Form in Arabic. In the mirror of European languages. 1987. iv, 417 pp.

14 BENSON, Morton, Evelyn BENSON and Robert F. ILSON: Lexicographic Description of English. 1986. xiii, 275 pp.

13 REESINK, Ger P.: Structures and their Functions in Usan. 1987. xviii, 369 pp.

12 PINKSTER, Harm (ed.): Latin Linguistics and Linguistic Theory. Proceedings of the 1st International Colloquium on Latin Linguistics, Amsterdam, April 1981. 1983. xviii, 307 pp.

11 PANHUIS, Dirk G.J.: The Communicative Perspective in the Sentence. A study of Latin word order. 1982. viii, 172 pp.

10   **DRESSLER, Wolfgang U., Willi MAYERTHALER, Oswald PANAGL and Wolfgang Ullrich WURZEL:** Leitmotifs in Natural Morphology. 1988. ix, 168 pp.

9   **LANG, Ewald and John PHEBY:** The Semantics of Coordination. (English transl. by John Pheby from the German orig. ed. 'Semantik der koordinativen Verknüpfung', Berlin, 1977). 1984. 300 pp.

8   **BARTH, E.M. and J.L. MARTENS (eds.):** Argumentation: Approaches to Theory Formation. Containing the Contributions to the Groningen Conference on the Theory of Argumentation, October 1978. 1982. xviii, 333 pp.

7   **PARRET, Herman, Marina SBISÀ and Jef VERSCHUEREN (eds.):** Possibilities and Limitations of Pragmatics. Proceedings of the Conference on Pragmatics, Urbino, July 8–14, 1979. 1981. x, 854 pp.

6   **VAGO, Robert M. (ed.):** Issues in Vowel Harmony. Proceedings of the CUNY Linguistics Conference on Vowel Harmony, May 14, 1977. 1980. xx, 340 pp.

5   **HAIMAN, John:** Hua: A Papuan Language of the Eastern Highlands of New Guinea. 1980. iv, 550 pp.

4   **LLOYD, Albert L.:** Anatomy of the Verb. The Gothic Verb as a Model for a Unified Theory of Aspect, Actional Types, and Verbal Velocity. (Part I: Theory; Part II: Application). 1979. x, 351 pp.

3   **MALKIEL, Yakov:** From Particular to General Linguistics. Selected Essays 1965–1978. With an introduction by the author, an index rerum and an index nominum. 1983. xxii, 659 pp.

2   **ANWAR, Mohamed Sami:** BE and Equational Sentences in Egyptian Colloquial Arabic. 1979. vi, 128 pp.

1   **ABRAHAM, Werner (ed.):** Valence, Semantic Case, and Grammatical Relations. Workshop studies prepared for the 12th International Congress of Linguists, Vienna, August 29th to September 3rd, 1977. xiv, 729 pp. *Expected Out of print*